W9-BHB-288

Iron Range National Park, Qld.

WILD AUSTRALIA

SECOND EDITION
Published by Reader's Digest (Australia) Pty Limited (Inc. in NSW)
26-32 Waterloo Street, Surry Hills, NSW 2010

National Library of Australia cataloguing-in-publication data:
WILD AUSTRALIA. 2nd ed. Includes indexes. ISBN 0 86438 069 0
1. National parks and reserves – Australia – Guide-books
2. Australia – Description and travel – 1976 –
– Guide-books I. Reader's Digest Services
919.4'0463

All the material in this book appeared in the four Reader's Digest travel guides to the national parks of the states and territories, first published in paperback in 1987. These were based upon the first edition of Wild Australia.

Edited and designed by Reader's Digest (Australia) Pty Limited

Project Editor · David Underhill
Art Editor · Anita Sattler

Editor · Robert Campbell
Assistant Editor · Françoise Toman
Research Editor · Vere Dodds

All travelling photographic commissions were undertaken by Robin Morrison.

Wolf Creek Crater National Park, WA

WILD AUSTRALIA

READER'S DIGEST SYDNEY

CONTENTS

Introduction 7

PART ONE:

The nature of Australia 8

How the stage was set 10
Sun and rain: the great dictators 12
Grandeur in the high country 14
Fresh water: a precious bounty 16
Where the oceans hold sway 18
The eternal battle of the trees 20
Rainforests: a squandered heritage 22
The forests that welcome fire 24
Sentinels of the never-never 26

PART TWO:

Parks and people 28

Why we have national parks 30
Jacks and Jills of all trades 32
Staying alive in the bush 34
How the public can help 36
Making the most of your visit 37
WILDLIFE: Where animals find safety 38
RESTORATION: Nature gets another chance 40
HERITAGE LIST: An obligation to the world 42

PART THREE:

A guide to all national parks 44

MAP– Park regions of Wild Australia 47
ALICE SPRINGS REGION 48
Directory of parks 69
Reptiles of the inland 70
DARWIN REGION 72
Directory of parks 89
Wildlife in the Territory 90
VISITOR ACTIVITIES 92
DERBY & KUNUNURRA REGIONS ... 94
Directory of parks 103
Flowers as food 104
CARNARVON & PORT HEDLAND REGIONS 106
Directory of parks 115
PERTH REGION 116
Directory of parks 137
Mammals and reptiles of Western Australia 140
ESPERANCE & ALBANY REGIONS 142
Directory of parks 164
VISITOR ACTIVITIES 166

ADELAIDE REGION 168

Directory of parks 189

South Australian wildlife 192

Birdlife 194

VISITOR ACTIVITIES 196

MELBOURNE REGION 198

Directory of parks 232

Victoria's wildlife 236

Victoria's birds and flowers 238

VISITOR ACTIVITIES 240

LAUNCESTON & DEVONPORT REGIONS 242

Directory of parks 254

CONFRONTATION: How the west was won 256

HOBART REGION 258

Directory of parks 273

Plants in Tasmania's parks 274

Tasmanian birds and animals 276

VISITOR ACTIVITIES 278

CANBERRA REGION 280

Directory of parks 303

Wildflowers in the eastern parks 306

BROKEN HILL & MILDURA REGIONS 308

Directory of parks 315

SYDNEY REGION 316

Directory of parks 342

Birdlife in the eastern parks 346

LISMORE & GRAFTON REGIONS 348

Directory of parks 362

Wildlife in the eastern parks 364

VISITOR ACTIVITIES 366

BRISBANE REGION 368

Directory of parks 388

ROCKHAMPTON REGION 392

Directory of parks 408

Plants and wildlife in Queensland parks 412

TOWNSVILLE REGION 416

Directory of parks 441

GREAT BARRIER REEF: Guarding an underwater treasury 444

CAIRNS REGION 446

Directory of parks 471

Birds, butterflies and wildlife 476

VISITOR ACTIVITIES 478

General index 480

Useful addresses; Acknowledgments 488

Port Campbell National Park, Victoria

INTRODUCTION

What's in a name?

AUSTRALIA HAS more than 500 so-called national parks. Their status was proclaimed by state and territorial authorities under policies that used to differ widely. Many parks, especially among the 300-odd declared in Queensland, are mere islets or scraps of bush as small as one hectare. Some are huge, but so remote and inhospitable that their existence has little public relevance. And in a few parks, visitors have no place at all – the sites are really animal sanctuaries, or strictly for scientific research.

Nature reserves of that sort are important. But people expect direct benefits from something called a national park. The term should denote a significant area capable of accommodating the right of substantial numbers of visitors to enjoy its natural features and learn from them. Too many 'parks' do not meet this prescription. Bestowed indiscriminately, a proud title loses meaning. The effect, though surely not intended, is sometimes to mislead and disappoint the public.

In offering a frank comparison of park attractions, we aim not to dictate readers' tastes but to provide them with a fair basis for making choices of their own. This guide presents a revision and expansion of information first amassed in the 1984 edition of *Wild Australia*. It remains the only single publication to appraise the country's entire array of parks.

Simply identifying all of them demanded a trail-blazing effort. Because of the pace of acquisition and change since the 1950s, no complete list had existed. Even the names of some parks were difficult to establish. Legally gazetted titles conflicted with common usage, or hard-pressed administrators saved paperwork by lumping smaller sites anonymously into groups.

Financial strictures beset all parks services. Areas may be designated by the stroke of a pen, but funds for public facilities are a long time coming. Often as our researchers sought to define the merits of a park, they were told: 'We'd really rather you didn't mention that one'. A state information officer, confessing his ignorance of a newly acquired property, explained: 'We sent a fellow out there once to get material for a brochure. But he couldn't find the place...'

Not without qualms, a system of rating was instituted. Judgments behind all the ticks and crosses in the reference sections were made in consultation with park authorities, but they remain subjective and debatable. So are our assumptions of the broad areas of visitor interest. 'Scenic enjoyment' in one park derives from the intimate charm of a single waterfall; in another it may come from the sweeping grandeur of a whole mountain range or coastline. 'Day activities' indicates a good choice of things to do – but who can predict preferences? 'Family camping' supposes a desire to stay put for perhaps a week, in conditions not unduly primitive. 'Hard bushwalking' in most cases points to the challenge of backpack trekking and overnight camping.

Pictorially we have aimed for realism, not idealism. Rather than gathering in a selection of the prettiest and luckiest shots ever taken in national parks, we offer the results of one man's efforts. Robin Morrison, the touring photographer, was advised and guided by rangers in some parks. But for the most part he took his chances like any other member of the travelling public, limited in time and at the mercy of the weather.

After his year-long assignment for *Wild Australia*, covering more than 200 locations from Tasmania to North West Cape, Morrison had a suggestion. 'Tell your readers,' he said, 'that anything I did, they can do. With any luck they may see even more. And you can also tell them that most of the finest scenery in this country is not all that far away or hard to get to.'

He was right. In spite of the obvious modification of desirable countryside by two centuries of European settlement, unspoilt landscapes lie remarkably close to most major centres of population. Australians, nearly 90 per cent of whom lead their everyday lives in urban or suburban environments, need not go far to refresh themselves and recover their sense of community with more natural surroundings.

This book is published in the hope that readers will reach a fuller understanding of what remains of our physical heritage, that they will care for it, and above all that they will enjoy it.

THE EDITORS

PART ONE
The nature of Australia

Nothing in nature happens without a reason. Powerful influences shaped Australia's landscapes. Now they dictate where its unique plants grow. Knowing the meaning that lies behind scenery makes it all the more enjoyable.

Ancient but scarcely trodden, the Bungle Bungle Ranges stand in lonely dignity east of the Kimberleys, WA

How the stage was set

WEATHERING, given time enough, levels any land surface. Heights are worn down and basins are filled with the debris, to be compressed into fresh rock. With the ups and downs removed and gravity equalised, rock erosion stops. Only overlying soils or sands are subject to further attack.

But awesome pressures work tirelessly on the earth's crust. Sometimes they warp it, tilting an old land mass to a new angle of elevation. Sometimes the crust buckles, and another generation of mountains is thrust up. Molten material from below blasts or oozes through weak points in the crust. The height of the land is varied and erosion resumes. All these events have occurred time and again in Australia.

Eroded rock layers at Kings Canyon, NT, are tilted almost vertically. Once they formed towering domes

Rocks of the Australian land mass differ astonishingly in their age, their composition and their capacity to resist erosion. They include the world's oldest known formations as well as some of the youngest, and everything from the softest clays to the most impermeable granites. Climatic conditions vary widely. So do the surrounding oceans in their behaviour – some destroy the land, some help it to build. Most diverse of all are the soils produced by rock erosion, and the plant life they can sustain.

Flat landscapes, virtually featureless and usually parched, prevail across more than half of the continent. Weathering is all but complete, for much of this land has been undisturbed for eons. Ranges thrust up in the west, made from rocks that formed more than 3000 million years ago, are reduced to a smoothed shield, rarely outcropping from its sandy cover. Once-mighty rivers that drained the heights – and helped demolish them – can be traced only in chains of dismal salt pans. Seabeds to the east have become plains, at best marginally fertile.

Remnants of mountain systems in Central Australia and the far north and northwest are younger, though the age of their rocks still staggers the mind. Ranges such as the Musgraves and the Hamersleys, along with many in the Kimberleys and Arnhem Land, originated more than 1000 million years ago. Pushed up, they towered higher than Mt Kosciusko is now. All are in the late stages of destruction – but nature has not wasted them.

By the time the MacDonnell Ranges were forced up in Central Australia, perhaps 200-300 million years ago, material eroded from the Musgraves had re-formed as a bed of sedimentary rock. South of the MacDonnells, it was distorted and broken by their upheaval. Immense chunks of sandstone or cemented boulders were elevated at all angles, to be swamped later by a returning sea. New deposits of sediments buried all but the highest summits. Now, severely worn in their turn, the broad domes we call Ayers Rock and the Olgas jut incongruously from the central plain.

Nearby Mt Conner, similarly created, presents a surprising contrast. It is table-topped, and noticeably eroded only at the sides. When this mass was pushed up, its layers of sediments chanced to remain horizontal under their original capping of toughened material. To the north, on apparently similar country, are piled the huge boulders called the Devil's Marbles. Here a cracked block of granite has been eroded across and down all its joints. Such variations are essentially the products of chance – what types of rocks are exposed, and how their former bedding planes are tilted.

Ocean levels rose and fell – or the land fell and rose – repeatedly. Invading seas often divided ancestral Australia into islands. New rock material included increasing quantities of calcium from the remains of marine animals. Pavings of porous limestone formed widely. High and dry now, many are noted for their subterranean cave systems, eaten out by percolating rainwater.

Sometimes the seas were remarkably warm. Corals built reefs in the Gordon River district of Tasmania 350-400 million years ago. But 100 million years later an icecap reached to the Kimberleys, and Tasmania lay beside the South Pole. And after a further 100 million years, according to plant fossil evidence, Australia and Antarctica shared a subtropical climate. Like all continental land masses, they have been on the move.

At first all the continents were probably contained in a single cluster, which seems to have broken in two well over 200 million years ago. After that Australia, Antarctica, New Guinea, India, Africa, Arabia and South America were joined in a southern supercontinent which scientists call Gondwanaland. But the earth's rigid crust was fracturing. Rifts opened, and new molten matter welled up to force the modern continents apart.

Widening oceans filled the gaps. The crust

TRACING A VANISHED LANDSCAPE

ROCKS are of three types. Sedimentary rocks form from the debris of older rocks and the remains of aquatic animals. Sandstones, limestones and shales are commonest. Igneous rocks form from molten material. If it cools without reaching the air, it usually turns into granite. Lava cooling on the surface makes a basalt. Metamorphic rocks are the result of pressure and heat on sedimentary or igneous rocks. Sandstone becomes quartzite, shale becomes slate, granite becomes gneiss.

Sedimentary rocks form in flat layers, varying in hardness. Squeezed by earth movements, they bend into folds. Erosion removes the softer material in a fold, and only the stubs of tough ridges remain

Molten material pushing up into a fold forms granite. Erosion leaves a tough core (left). But if the material builds a volcano, the last of it may set as a hard-wearing plug of trachyte or rhyolite (right)

Beds of metamorphic rock are too rigid to fold. Instead they crack into blocks that are tilted and pushed up. Rates of erosion depend on the angle of tilt, as well as on the composition of the blocks

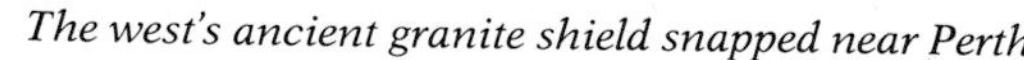

The west's ancient granite shield snapped near Perth

itself separated into mobile plates. Fifteen major plates and a few small ones now restlessly cover the globe. The section Australia rides on – along with India, New Guinea and part of New Zealand – is rafting very slowly northwestward because its eastern and southern neighbours are expanding.

Violent earth movements are inevitable at the edges of a plate. But Australia lies far from any collision zone. Since its isolation it has been the least disturbed of the continents. The last truly catastrophic event – the production of eastern and central Tasmania's dolerite columns and cappings by the intrusion of molten matter into old sandstones – was about 165 million years ago. Many geologists associate it with the start of the Gondwanaland breakup.

Early mountain ranges on the eastern mainland were well worn down by then. Soon all that remained of them were cores of tough granite, solidified from molten material that had flowed up into their folds. Often it is this granite that forms the summits of mountains that have been thrust up more recently.

Parts of the Eastern Highlands – notably the Snowy Mountains and Victorian Alps – were pushed up about 65 million years ago. A second phase of general uplift in the east, remarkably gentle, took place within the past 3-7 million years. A probable cause was the slumping of the crust far inland, under the weight of sediments from one ocean or sea after another. The slumped parts, since covered by more recent porous rock, underlie the reservoirs of underground water known collectively as the Great Artesian Basin.

To compensate for this sinking of the crust, land near the east coast gradually rose. It formed tablelands with a barely perceptible slope. Warping to create mountain ranges occurred only in the last stages of uplift, and at the seaward extremity. Similar forces working in the west had a more drastic effect. There the ancient rock shield was pinned down by coastal sediments. It snapped at the point where it emerged, and now its uptilted edge forms a rampart nearly 1000 km long backing the coastal plain on which Perth is centred. The Darling Range is misnamed – it should be the Darling Scarp. But in its influence on climate and vegetation, it acts in much the same way as a mountain system would.

Near-coastal ranges and the coastlines themselves have the freshest and most changeable landforms. All the forces of erosion are seen actively at work. Volcanic activity can be traced. So can the variation of soil fertilities, and the rivalries of plant communities under different climatic regimes. Everywhere, the lie of the land and the look of the landscape are intimately related.

THE OLDEST THING ON EARTH

Electric probing mars a history-making zircon – enlarged 200 times

OUR PLANET was born 4500-4600 million years ago, astronomers believe. It took an unknown time to cool enough to form a solid crust. The most ancient rocks found, in Western Australia and Greenland, are about 3800 million years old. But they are sedimentary – made of something even older.

A clue emerged in 1983 at Mt Narryer, 200 km inland from Carnarvon, WA. Microscopic grains of zircon were discovered in quartzite rocks. Using a new electrical probing technique, scientists measured the proportions of uranium and lead contained as impurities in the zircons.

Uranium loses its radioactivity and turns into lead at a known rate. So the age of the zircons could be calculated. Four of the tiny stones, it seems, must have been formed between 4100 and 4200 million years ago. Until humans venture outside this solar system, they may never handle anything older.

Sun and rain: the great dictators

JUST AS ancient weathering shaped the land, present climates decide its clothing. Sunlight, temperature and moisture determine which trees or shrubs or grasses flourish where. And they govern the likelihood of wildfire – the other factor that sets apart the great plant families of Australia and rules over the appearance of natural landscapes.

Twisting statistics, Australians could boast the world's most generous share of rain. More of it falls, per person, than in any other country. But that is merely a reflection of the sparseness of population. In fact most of the continent is poorly watered and subject to high rates of evaporation. Over a vast sweep between southwestern Queensland and North West Cape, hot sunshine beats down for more than 3500 hours a year.

Mainland Australia straddles the southern hemisphere's belt of greatest air pressure. 'Highs' – cells of descending air as much as 4000 km wide, calm or rotating gently under clear skies – pass from west to east in an almost continuous chain. Troughs separating them, usually at intervals of four or five days, may bring cool changes but seldom much rain. North of the pressurised belt southeasterly breezes – the Trade Winds of sailing ship days – blow steadily from the Pacific. To the south of the belt the air flow is from the west, and much stronger.

The high-pressure belt changes its position seasonally. In winter it is centred over the middle of the continent. Tropical regions, except on the east coast, are parched. The southeasterlies, having deposited their ocean moisture on the coastal ranges, flow on unimpeded and arrive in the northwest dry, hot and dusty.

Southern Australia in winter is swept by a cold westerly air stream. Often this is whipped into chilling southwesterly gales because 'lows' – tight, churning cells of rising and condensing air – intrude from the Southern Ocean. Rain is plentiful, except round the Bight, and the southeastern highlands get snow. But in much of New South Wales and subtropical Queensland, where the westerlies have dried out or do not reach, winter may be sunny.

In summer the belt of high pressure lies over Bass Strait. Rainfall is generally low in southern regions, though clear spells may be broken by squally changes. On most parts of the east coast down to Sydney, however, Pacific moisture is turned into liberal summer rains because the Trade Winds have also moved south.

From November to April, the far north has its 'Wet'. A zone of low pressure, originating over the Equator but shifting in summer to about the latitude of Darwin, sucks in a monsoon of saturated air from the northwest. Thundery showers drench the Kimberleys, the Top End and Cape York Peninsula day after day. In some seasons, but never predictably, the lows pass far enough south to bring flooding rains to Central Australia and outback regions of the southern and eastern states.

Summer is also the season of violent tropical cyclones. Only five or six a year affect the coast, and their destructive power wanes as soon as they pass inland. But the spiralling cloud mass of a decaying cyclone brings heavy rain over an ever-widening area, perhaps for a week or more. Semi-arid regions, particularly in the northwest, receive much of their moisture in this erratic way.

Regardless of average patterns, year-by-year rainfall over most of Australia is notoriously variable. Port Hedland, WA, for example, is listed as having a median annual fall of just over 300 mm. But that figure is merely the product of actual readings as low as 30 mm a year and as high as 1000 mm or more. Apart from the monsoon zone, rainfall is consistently good only in Tasmania, on most of the Victorian, New South Wales and Queensland coasts, and in winter in the extreme southwest of Western Australia. It is no coincidence that all these regions have mountains close to the sea.

Air flowing off sunlit oceans is always loaded with evaporated moisture. But to condense into clouds that precipitate rain, it must be cooled. The usual cause of cooling is elevation: air temperatures drop by about 5°C with each 1000 metres of altitude. A fall in pressure when air flows into a 'low', or a collision of different air masses, can cause the necessary uplift and trigger a storm. However, no one can say exactly where that will happen. Truly reliable rains occur only where moist air flows are blocked and forced upward by steep land.

Australia is not only the flattest of all continents, but also the lowest-lying. Counting mountain ranges, its average elevation is still a mere 300 metres above sea level. That makes it generally warmer than any other land mass in comparable latitudes. Far from being cooled, moist air flowing into many regions is heated up. The longer its journey, the hotter it gets – hence the heat waves that occasionally sear southern cities, including Hobart.

Summer northwesterlies, entering over the Great Sandy Desert between Port Hedland and Broome, have the longest possible low, flat run. If not diverted by atmospheric disturbances they can reach all the way to western NSW – 2500 km. Shade temperatures above 50°C are recorded there, in an arc from Bourke to Wilcannia and White Cliffs, more often than in any other district in Australia.

Superheated air flows hasten the evaporation of soil moisture and the desiccation of plants. In regions perennially short of rain – though with fertile soil – plant life has had to adapt in unusual ways. And where rains in most years are good enough to foster profuse growth, but they occasionally fail, the chance of devastation by fire is abnormally high. Again plants have found ways to cope – and even to benefit.

At the opposite end of the climatic scale, wide tracts of high country in the southeast and Tasmania lie under snow for months each year. Elsewhere, over a surprising area, plants contend with frost in winter and spring. In the south it results from inflows of chilled air after depressions. But frosts also occur well to the north, in places better known for their heat. In the high-pressure belt dominating mid-Australia in winter, cloud cover is rare and ground warmth starts passing into the upper atmosphere as soon as the sun goes down. Alice Springs has more frosty nights than any of the southern capitals except Canberra. On the east coast, the effects of elevation take frosts even farther north. Cooled air, sinking into valleys draining the Great Dividing Range, can ice the ground within 20 km of Cairns.

Parched, sunburnt sandplains reach into NSW at Mungo National Park – once part of a major waterway

Below: Air cooling over Kosciusko National Park, NSW, sinks into the upper Murray Valley, forming a river of cloud

Right: Highland frost and vigorous tree growth join forces to crack capping rock in Girraween National Park, Qld

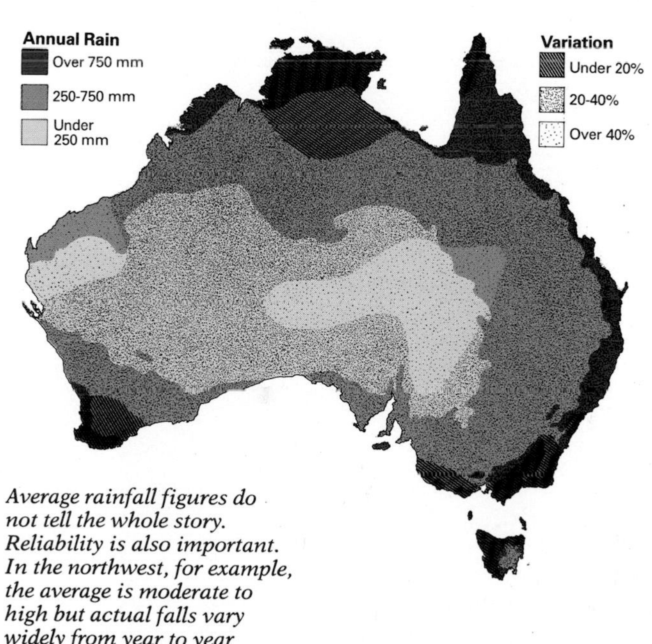

Average rainfall figures do not tell the whole story. Reliability is also important. In the northwest, for example, the average is moderate to high but actual falls vary widely from year to year

Grandeur in the high country

MOUNTAINS are nature's showcases. Bared, they display every type and formation of rock. Erosion can be seen in action, with the effects of rain, wind, frost and chemical change accentuated by the force of gravity. And on vegetated slopes, the temperature gradients created by altitude give plant and animal life their fullest opportunity for variety.

Australia lacks the soaring peaks of the other continents and even of its island neighbours, New Guinea and New Zealand. In compensation, its high country is more accessible and less subject to dangerously sudden switches of weather. Its coastal uplands, especially in Queensland, offer a range of plant communities as wide as any in the world.

Scenically and economically, the Eastern Highlands chain is Australia's most significant mountain system. It curves from Cape York into western Victoria, more or less parallel to the coast, and resumes in Tasmania. Islands in Bass and Torres Straits, along with some off Queensland, are peaks emerging from drowned sections of the same system.

For most of their mainland length the highlands are the more elevated seaward side of a wide belt of tablelands. The Great Divide – where rivers start to flow inland, not to the Pacific Ocean – often occurs at lower altitudes well to the west. That shows how slowly the highlands rose in their final uplift, which was completed about 3 million years ago. Ancient rivers, already flowing east, had time to cut deeper courses as the land tipped up.

Movement was so gentle that buckling to produce ranges of fold mountains was limited to the eastern edge of the belt. Massive tilting of fractured blocks, to raise processions of peaks like the Southern Alps of New Zealand, was virtually non-existent. A spectacular exception is the Bellenden Ker Range, just south of Cairns, Qld. Even the summits of the Snowy Mountains and Victorian Alps are smooth granite tablelands. The Blue Mountains, west of Sydney, were just as flat. Layers of sandstone and shale were pushed up thousands of metres without shifting from their horizontal plane. Today's dramatic pillars, cliffs and ravines are simply the result of weathering – and it is far from finished.

Remnants of huge volcanic systems abound, especially about the Qld/NSW border and to the southwest in the Nandewar and Warrumbungle Ranges. These date from 15-25 million years ago. The later phase of eastern uplift brought new activity, but no big volcanoes were built. Most eruptions were easy upwellings of lava from fissures in the earth's crust.

Left: Glaciers sculpted the jagged peaks and walled lakes of southwest Tasmania

Most of the Great Dividing Range is a tableland cut by rivers – in this case the Shoalhaven River in Morton National Park, NSW

Worn quartzite domes in the Gammon Ranges, SA

Hard basalt from ancient lava flows caps Mt Wilson, 950 metres up in Blue Mountains National Park, NSW

Lava flows continued, in fewer and fewer places, almost to the present day. The last coatings on the western plains of Victoria, where more than 20 000 square kilometres are covered, were laid less than 6000 years ago. Even more of the northern Queensland tablelands was blanketed not long before.

Old volcanoes are often marked now by cylinders of rock jutting into the sky. These are plugs made of the last molten material, solidified before it reached the air. It forms exceptionally hard rock – usually trachyte or rhyolite – that resists erosion while the surrounding cone is worn away.

Molten material that flows out as lava, however, turns into a basalt. Its hardness will vary according to its mineral content. Some basalts, reddish or chocolate brown and rich in iron, remain as protective cappings on tablelands or form thin bands sandwiched in the joints of older rocks. Others, cooling evenly in deep layers, have contracted into clusters of tough hexagonal columns – Melbourne's Organ Pipes, for example.

But many basalts decompose quickly when exposed to air and water. They break down into fine, dark soils containing an unusual abundance of mineral nutrients for plants. It is the prevalence of basaltic – often called volcanic – soils, allied with high rainfall, that allows the Eastern Highlands their luxuriant growth of forests.

Tasmania's heights reveal a much older geological background. The region's main upheaval came 165 million years ago. Enormous tongues of molten material penetrated its original sandstone strata. They cooled as dolerite, which has a columnar 'organ pipe' structure similar to some basalts. Now, with almost all of the sandstone worn away, deep sheets of dolerite cover most of eastern and central Tasmania. Sheer faced crags jut from a tableland so toughly capped that no rivers of significance have managed to cut courses. Instead this is a landscape sculpted by ice. Only in Tasmania can the full effects of glaciation during the last ice age, between 40 000 and 10 000 years ago, be seen. Mountains are chewed away at their sides. Moraines of rock debris trap deep alpine lakes. Countless little tarns, gouged by boulders dragged in a creeping cap of ice, glitter on the plateau.

West of the tableland, Tasmania's ranges have no intrusion of dolerite. They are of softer quartzite, now deeply dissected by gorges. High volumes of water, precipitated almost year-round in rain and snow, seize their chance to find steep courses to the sea between thickly forested slopes. Here are born the island's fast-flowing 'wild rivers', so enticing and precious to white-water adventurers.

No other mountains in Australia stand as tall as the Eastern Highlands, or have soils and rainfall to sustain comparable forest growth. Elsewhere the greatest fascination of higher country usually lies in its stark antiquity. The huge island-mountains of Uluru National Park, for example, or the eroded forms of the Flinders Ranges in South Australia, are individually more haunting than any eastern scene.

Major ranges in Central Australia and the northwest, such as the MacDonnells, the Hamersleys and those in the Kimberleys, are so aged and weathered that their heights lend them little distinction. Instead it is their depths, in the gorges cut by eons-old rivers, which provide the most memorable scenes – and the clearest insights into the structure of the continent.

THIS WAS THE HOTTEST SPOT OF ALL

MOUNT WARNING (left) is the 22-million-year-old central plug of Australia's biggest volcano. Remnants of its rim, straddling the Qld/NSW border across a diameter of about 40 km, survive in the McPherson, Tweed and Nightcap Ranges. All have steep scarps of tough basalt facing in towards Mt Warning, and gently sloping outer flanks.

Scientists can only guess at the original dimensions of the Tweed volcano, but it almost certainly stood taller than Mt Kosciusko is now. Rainforests ringing the rim, largely preserved in a chain of national parks, flourish on rich soils derived from the volcano's outpourings of lava. It is thought to have been active for about 3 million years.

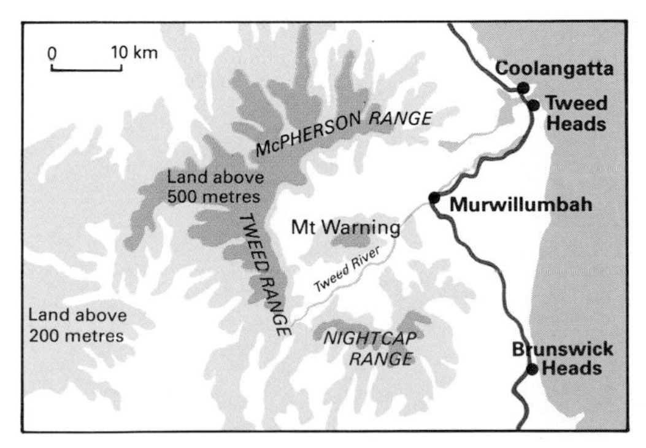

Fresh water: a precious bounty

RIVERS AND LAKES are scarce in Australia. Truly natural ones are even more rare. The Aborigines accepted that most water supplies were sporadic: the movements of the animals they hunted, and their own nomadic lives, were ruled by that fact. But European settlers chose accessible rivers and stayed put. They demanded that the water come to them – tamed.

Dams, weirs and levees were built to eliminate the extremes of drought and flood. Banks were straightened and obstacles removed to aid navigation. Flows were diverted to water livestock and irrigate crops. Supplies were drawn off not just for drinking and washing but also for industrial processes, and lately to fill hundreds of thousands of swimming pools.

Even in remote high country, a century or more ago, streams were altered by erosion of their headwater catchments. Forest logging was to blame. More recently, hydro-electric engineering has regulated many rivers, and created new lakes or raised old ones.

Queensland's Barron Falls, once the year-round tourist highlight of the Atherton Tablelands, now flow only in the wet season when the Tinaroo Dam overspills. The Snowy River is deprived of more than 2 million million litres a year by tunnelled diversion to the Murrumbidgee and Murray. The Murray itself is depleted, and salted by the leaching of minerals from cleared land. The Darling, contributing most of the Murray's water, can no longer fluctuate between a chain of billabongs and a flooding sheet hundreds of kilometres wide. Barrages and storage lakes hold it in check.

Where highland rainforests remain untouched, some unspoilt rivers are still to be found flowing in all seasons. Western Tasmania's are the most celebrated – but also the hardest to reach. Many national parks on the Great Dividing Range, however, give access to streams that spill from scarps in waterfalls or cascades, then plunge into ferny ravines.

Vast floodplains border the Daly River, NT

More indicative of the real nature of most Australian waterways are the braided beds and floodplains of the Channel Country in western Queensland. They are nearly always dry. Even major rivers such as the Diamantina and Cooper Creek are ephemeral, flowing only after prolonged heavy rain. And it takes weeks of the most phenomenal flooding of the Channel Country before the vast salt pans of Lake Eyre are likely to fill.

Monsoon floodplains in the far north are scenes of remarkable annual transformation in plant and animal life. But when it happens, most such districts are inaccessible. The best a traveller can do to appreciate the contrast at Kakadu National Park, for example, is find time for two visits – one just before the wet season, and one as soon as possible after.

Most other national parks in the Northern Terrritory, and all the popular ones to the west from the Kimberleys to Kalbarri, are based on ancient, deeply cut gorges. Their rivers fluctuate seasonally, and in Central Australia most are ephemeral. The attraction for visitors, especially late in the dry season, may be not so much in the watercourses as in the grandeur of their walls. Often the gorges hold pockets of primitive, moist-climate palms and vines – relics of an age long past.

Rivers in the southwest are generally short-flowing and much changed by forest clearance and settlement. Inland, former drainage systems are marked by salt pans, arranged in a horseshoe pattern spanning 500 km. Similar forms extend from north of Lake Eyre to the Flinders Ranges and Eyre Peninsula, SA.

In western NSW, a more recently dried waterway is represented in the Willandra Lakes chain. Mungo National Park's stark lunette walls, like the rims of a moon crater, are built of sands blown from the bed of a lake that held ample water until about 20 000 years ago.

Water storage is so precious now that most natural lakes have been amplified by damming. Australia's deepest, Lake St Clair in Tasmania, was raised to serve power stations on the River Derwent. The greatest of all in area, Lake Argyle in the Kimberleys, was made by damming the Ord River.

Old estuaries, barred by sand ridges, form sizeable coastal lakes in NSW and eastern Victoria. But the streams feeding them are often interfered with, and the lakes themselves modified by settlement or heavy recreational use. Of the few that have been largely spared, outstanding examples are found in The Lakes National Park, Vic, and Myall Lakes National Park, NSW.

The Wimmera River, flowing by Little Desert National Park, gives trees a rare chance in western Victoria

THE HIDDEN RESERVOIRS

ARTESIAN water fell as rain – long ago and very far away. It lies under western Queensland and northwestern NSW, and reaches beneath the Central and South Australian deserts. But all of it came from the Eastern Highlands.

The Great Artesian Basin – really a group of basins separated by underground ridges – is a part of Australia that slumped millions of years ago under the weight of inland seas and their deposits. The sediments formed porous rock, to be capped later by impermeable shales. To balance the slumping, land at the eastern rim rose. Wherever the raised edge of the porous layer has been exposed, it has acted as a conduit for rainwater. Moisture seeps down and collects in a water table, sealed underneath by the old sunken rock.

True artesian water bubbles up under its own pressure if the saturated layer is breached. But bore-sinking for almost a century has lowered the water table; pumping is often needed now. The water is increasingly salty as it ages, and it can have a sulphurous, rotten-egg smell. Most of it is used only for livestock. Where it is pumped from great depths it comes up near-boiling, and can be piped for heating.

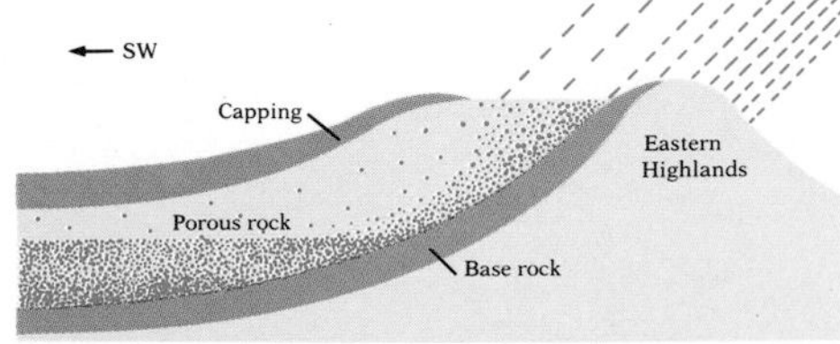

Spongy rock exposed near the Great Divide is sandwiched between layers that water cannot penetrate. Rain sinking into it forms a water table extending more than 1500 km southwestward.

A VICTORY FOR THE WETLANDS

HUNDREDS of wildlife species rely on shallow inland waters for at least part of each year. Without swamps and marshes, many would be poorly distributed – and some extinct. But the shrinking wetlands remain targets for reclamation or water diversion.

The trend has been reversed in central NSW, where the Macquarie River spreads into 40000 ha of meandering creeks and reedy marshes west of Coonamble. The marshes are breeding grounds particularly for ibises, along with more than 150 other species of birds and scores of different amphibians, reptiles and fish.

Upstream, the Burrendong Dam regulates the river. After 1969 the flow was sharply reduced while much of the water went to farms. The river petered out in the marshes, which were impoverished year by year.

Early in the 1980s, a proposed expansion of cotton planting called for even more water to be taken off for irrigation. Protesting conservationists were supported by wheatgrowers and graziers, who had learned that the ibis is a major predator of insects that ruin crops and pastures. The state government heeded their call.

Now the flow to the Macquarie Marshes is almost trebled. Waterfowl habitats are fully flooded, and the river can resume its natural course into the Barwon and on into the Lachlan-Darling-Murray system. The marshes, partly declared as nature reserves and listed by the Heritage Commission, are the likely site of a future national park.

Their waters restored, the Macquarie Marshes come back to life

Left: The last run-off from the summer wet season in the Kimberleys, WA, spills into the Prince Regent River. It flows straight for 80 km along a sandstone fracture

Unspoilt waterways meander through The Lakes National Park, Vic, within easy boating distance of popular Gippsland holiday resorts. The lakes were formed out of estuaries, barred by Ninety Mile Beach

Where the oceans hold sway

TO SEE ALL of Australia's shores at first hand could take a lifetime – or perhaps cost a life. The mainland and Tasmanian coasts, by the most precise measuring method available, extend for more than 30 000 km. Islands on the continental shelf add nearly 18 000 km. Some sections consist of virtually impassable terrain, so far surveyed only from aircraft or boats. Fresh water may not be found for hundreds of kilometres, and the only source of food may be dangerous swamps or seas.

No other country has a coastline so vast, or so pronounced in its contrasts. Shores are backed in some places by deserts, in others by jungles. Towering cliffs and headlands offer seascapes of grandeur; elsewhere the only view may be of mudflats, all the way to the horizon. Ocean currents range from equatorial to subpolar. While seals and Antarctic seabirds breed in the south, warmer waters foster the growth of the world's most massive coral structures.

Australia's coast is noticeably lacking in one respect: for its size, it has very few river outlets. And except near the Eastern Highlands and in the monsoonal north and northwest, rivers have no significant impact on shore formations. There is simply not enough run-off of water or eroded inland rock. Disparity in the supply of material from the hinterland to the coasts, established over millions of years, has led to marked differences in the composition and behaviour of shorelines.

Where plenty of inland material is added to coastal debris, sands are abundant. But they may not stay put. They contain a lot of silica, usually in the form of quartz, so they are slippery. Agitated by waves and winds, they sort themselves until the heaviest minerals – the 'black sands' prized for commercial extraction

Coral backs WA's Houtman Abrolhos Islands – once coastal dunes but now 60 km offshore

Right: Lime-rich dunes on the Bight near Penong, SA

– lie at the bottom of beaches and dunes. Sands above are light, loose and easily torn away by gales and storm waves.

On arid shores, sands are composed more of marine sediments. Their higher content of shell and skeleton fragments makes them rich in calcium – a binding agent. Blown inland, these sands pile up and consolidate. Many wave-eroded limestone cliffs, reefs and offshore stacks originated as calcified dune ridges, built when the sea level was lower.

Not all parts of the coast are being eroded. Some hold their own against the sea, or even gain ground. Normal wave power is far from uniform around Australia. It is determined by global weather patterns and the breadth and slope of the continental shelf offshore, as well as by local geography. Waves are generally strongest in the south and ineffectual on tropical shores – except in cyclones. In the far north, river silts discharged into quiet shallows are caught in mangroves to make new land.

Wave direction is important, especially to the fate of beaches. Strong waves breaking at an acute angle to a beach create a powerful longshore current. Washed-off sand is carried away parallel to the shoreline. Where this happens consistently, beaches are depleted and the coastline gradually recedes.

Southeasterly winds and waves attack the eastern bulge of the continent with a regularity that makes beach recession a fact of life. Foredune stabilisation and restraints on property development can stop it happening more quickly than necessary, but the process is inevitable. Sand movement up the mid-east coast has been relentless for more than 8000 years, since the sea rose after the last ice age.

The outcome, where the longshore currents weaken at last, is seen in the chain of sand islands off Brisbane, in the richly coloured cliffs north of Noosa, and finally in the huge mass of Fraser Island. Most of the material that built them originated in the Great Dividing Range, perhaps as far south as the Blue Mountains. Similar forces worked on the western seaboard; in almost a mirror image, its old limestone coast is recessed in the south and built out towards the Tropic of Capricorn.

Where strong waves consistently meet a

Silt collects in a tropical tangle

THE MANGROVE KINGDOM: LIVING WITH THE TIDES

MANGROVES are trees and shrubs of many different kinds, all adapted to daily flooding by sea water. They restrict their intake of salt by chemical action, or get rid of it through their leaves. Their seeds are spread by the tides.

Australia has nearly 50 species. Most are notable for the aerial root systems that help to anchor them in soft mud. In some, the roots have openings through which the trees breathe when their soils are saturated. Other species send up breathing pegs for metres around each tree.

On northern coasts, communities of 20 of more species form broad, dense forests up to 30 metres tall. Diversity and vigour decline farther south. Around Sydney three or four species form open stands, seldom exceeding 15 metres. In Victoria, South Australia and south of Perth there is only the grey mangrove, stunted and sparsely distributed.

Boat users and resort developers may see mangroves as nuisances. But they stabilise shorelines by trapping silt in their tangled roots. And their fallen leaves start an estuarine food chain on which marine animals – including most commercially harvested fish – depend. Each square metre of tropical mangrove forest yields about 1 kg of organic matter every year.

shore head-on, they can add to the land. They push sand in to form nearshore barriers, sometimes shutting off bays or estuaries. The lagoons that are created eventually fill with silts and windblown sands. Beaches formed of massive barriers occur frequently on the east coast between the Tropic and Wilsons Promontory, and are also found in eastern South Australia and south of Perth.

Tropical Queensland and the Northern Territory, with weaker wave action, have lower barrier beaches less obvious in their origin. Gulfs and landlocked bays in these regions tend to fill as tidal mudflats, backed by broad mangrove beds and salt marshes and sometimes fringed with coral. Open tidal plains, reaching for many kilometres between high and low waterlines, occur widely on each side of North West Cape between Shark Bay and Port Hedland.

Long, open mainland beaches, free of barriers, develop where the general direction of waves is past a shoreline rather than at it. Reefs and rocky sections may give protection, but the sandy stretches predominate. They are common in western Victoria and northern and eastern Tasmania, towards the head of the Bight and in some parts of the southwest.

Headlands interrupt most beach coasts in the southeast, giving shelter and good vantage points. Their bases usually have wave-cut shore platforms, teeming with marine life. Continuously cliffed coasts, however, are rare. The principal ones in accessible areas are immediately south of Sydney – through Royal National Park and beyond – in Otway and Port Campbell National Parks in Victoria, and around most of southeastern Tasmania.

Sheer limestone cliffs give a sharp edge to much of the Nullarbor Plain, and to the desolate western extremity of the continent, north of Kalbarri National Park. The longest rock coast of all skirts the Kimberleys, where red sandstone precipices are cut by fiordlike inlets. Prodigious tides that can range up to 12 metres create channelled currents of freakish violence. And tidal bores – waves that race up rivers – can overturn boats 50 km inland.

Often it is the reefs and islands offshore that most distinguish a coast. They enrich its scenic variety, and give sanctuary to animals and plants rarely seen on the mainland. In spite of Australia's extreme emphasis on seaboard settlement and maritime recreation, landing problems and a lack of fresh water saved many islands. Now an impressive number are fully protected as nature reserves. Others rank among our most celebrated national parks.

Remote island parks, with a controlled flow of visitors, are easily managed. But on closer islands – especially the Queensland islands with fringing coral – the risks of damage are high. The jeopardy of the reef at Green Island, off Cairns, prompted a marine park declaration. That concept of below-the-waterline protection is now applied in defence of almost all of the Great Barrier Reef region.

A scalloped beach line, seen strikingly at Safety Cove on Tasman Peninsula, Tas, results when incoming and receding waves collide and set up an eddying pattern. On a surfing beach, it may indicate dangerous rip currents

The Drum and Drumsticks, off Beecroft Peninsula, NSW, are remnants of an older coastline

The eternal battle of the trees

PLANTS CANNOT RUN from hostile conditions. To survive, they must adapt and diversify. In Australia they have answered with an explosion of species. Flowering plants alone number about 11 000 kinds, from tiny herbs to towering eucalypts. Mosses, ferns, fungi and cone-bearing trees add to the array. And rivalry is intense. Plants struggle not only against climatic setbacks, animal appetites and human ambitions, but also against one another.

Pencil pine grows only in alpine Tasmania

The story of land vegetation starts well over 400 million years ago. Leafless, branching strands of a mossy seaweed crept ashore from the intertidal zone and invaded swamps and marshes. Adapting to more and more exposure to the air, the plants evolved into mosses and colonised firm ground.

Root systems were developed to tap subsurface water. Plants with thick, rigid stems appeared – the ancestors of ferns, club-mosses and horsetails. Competing for light, they reached up on ever-stronger trunks and became the first trees. Forests grew widely, dominated by club-mosses 30 metres tall. Coal deposits are their petrified remains.

Next, more than 250 million years ago, came the conifers – pine trees and their relatives. They broke away from reliance on ground water to disperse reproductive spores; their pollen is produced high in the tree, to be scattered by winds. Another cone-bearing group, short-trunked cycads with palmlike or fernlike fronds, appeared at about the same time. Pines and cycads ruled until 80-90 million years ago.

Flowering plants were taking over by then, especially in warmer climates. Their vivid petals, alluring scents and nectar drew insects, ensuring a more effective transfer of pollen. Magnolias and figs were among the pioneers, and beeches gained early prominence in forests. Palms were soon abundant, and took many forms. The striking thing about the flowering plants was how quickly they produced variations to suit different soils and climates.

The realm of the conifers had been worldwide. But continental isolation was setting in when flowering plants came to the fore. Africa had separated from the southern supercontinent of Gondwanaland, and India and South America were in the process of breaking away. After New Zealand drifted off, about 80 million years ago, Australia's only neighbour – and source of new plants – was Antarctica.

In the last phase of separation, some 60 million years ago, southern Australia and Antarctica shared cool-climate rainforests. Conifers still predominated, among an increasing variety of flowering trees including some beeches. Almost nothing is known of the vegetation of inland and northern Australia, but it can be assumed that the forerunners of nearly all of today's species were established. The only important exceptions, in the far north, came much later from Asia through New Guinea.

Australia's breach with Antarctica was completed about 55 million years ago. The continent began its journey northwestward into warmer latitudes. But world temperatures generally were falling, and patterns of atmospheric circulation changing. Land upheavals and sea incursions modified climates and soils in the east and south. Browsing and grazing mammals and seed-eating birds spread. But plant evolution went on. Now in isolation, it took paths that were to create a uniquely Australian bush.

With the first uplift of the Eastern Highlands completed, about 45 million years ago, beech rainforests entered a long period of dominance

BUILT BY PRIMITIVE PLANTS

CLUMPS like soft rock jut from sand and mud at Hamelin Pool, a shallow arm of Shark Bay, WA. In deeper water they stand in columns up to 3 metres tall. Found in thousands, these are living colonies of single-celled plants bound by secretions of lime.

The microscopic plants, called cyanophytes, represent the earliest form of life after bacteria – and the first to put oxygen into the air. They grow commonly in mats, like algae, and are usually grazed by molluscs. Only at Hamelin Pool are they left alone to build. The outlet is choked, and high evaporation makes the water too salty for molluscs.

Shorn-off cyanophyte mounds, solidified in silica, are found as big white rings in ancient rocks all over the world. Before their organic origin was known they were named stromatolites – 'mattress stones'. Some were built by plants growing 3000 million years ago.

Oddities of western and northern WA. Millstream palms (left) and baobabs or bottle trees – called boabs by locals

at least in the south. The general climate was still moist, but the interior of the continent was already more arid. And plants there were adapting. Trees that had emerged in luxury, enjoying abundant rainfall and rich soils, differentiated to include hardier forms.

Out of the acacia family – the wattles – came an exclusively Australian type with flattened, thornlike stems instead of leaves. From the myrtles, which in tropical America bear a soft, pulpy fruit, came eucalypts with tough, woody capsules. Both groups are thought to have gained some prominence in open forests by 30 million years ago. They and many other flowering trees continued to vary, developing scrubbier forms to survive in the poorest soils.

No one knows when the first alien plants may have arrived, their seeds carried by ocean currents or migratory birds. But intermittently over the past 10 million years, since Australia came into close contact with New Guinea, invaders of Southeast Asian origin have travelled overland. They established themselves with particular success in northern rainforests.

In most of the south, also about 10 million years ago, beech forests suddenly gave way to eucalypts. Some open woodlands and grasslands appeared, though their major expansion did not occur until 3-1 million years ago. By then the world was entering a period – continuing now – in which the climate fluctuated in cycles of glaciation and heating.

Trees advanced or retreated according to their resistance to frost, heat and drought – and increasingly to fire. Expanding populations of browsing animals chewed at them. Through it all, the grasses gained ground. They carpeted alpine plateaux and semi-arid plains, and clung in hummocks in places so barren that not even the scrub eucalypts and acacias could survive.

In a climate steadily more arid, rainforests were forced back to the eastern margins of the continent about 2 million years ago. Since then, in patches within those limits, they have contracted and expanded many times in a to-and-fro struggle with dry-adapted trees. And in tropical rainforests, the component plants have fought among themselves. Different species show up during each phase of resurgence, in fossils taken from the same spot.

Cycads ruled for eons before palms evolved

Fire has been a powerful influence on Australian plant evolution for many millions of years. The fact that so many species benefit from burning and some even rely on it is evidence of that. But charcoal deposits and soil studies show a marked increase in the frequency of fires – and the expansion of grasslands – in the past 40 000 years.

Aborigines used fire to foster the wildlife they hunted. Blazes were started judiciously to keep woodlands clear of litter and encourage grass growth – not too often, yet not so seldom that huge conflagrations were caused. But European settlers anxious for agricultural land burned forests, woodlands and scrublands indiscriminately, and their raging fires bared far more ground than was needed.

Rainforest logging, the substitution of exotic plantations and the spread of introduced pasture grasses and farm crops have all had an obvious impact on native vegetation. More subtle is the conversion of soils by compaction under the hooves of thousands of millions of livestock. Often the bush is damaged by feral animals such as goats and pigs, or supplanted by alien trees and weeds. But on the vast scale of plant evolution, all these are just further complications – and perhaps passing phases – in a battle that never ends.

Rainforests: a squandered heritage

Scores of tree species vie for space and light in the one small patch of tropical rainforest

RAINFORESTS are the scattered relics of an ancient time when most of Australia was moist and fertile. Driven back by a drying climate, they were overtaken by trees better able to resist drought and fire. Before Europeans came, the domain of rainforests was reduced already to less than 1 per cent of the continent's area. Now it is barely a quarter of that. In the main, whatever was most accessible has gone.

Generations of loggers and farmers who felled or burned the trees were largely ignorant of the consequences. They did not realise the extent to which they would trigger off soil erosion and the loss of water yields. They could not foresee a day when the forests would be needed to purify a polluted atmosphere. Least of all could they have understood that they were depleting a genetic store in which some stock – perhaps unseen – might be unique.

Even today it is not always grasped that rainforest species are interdependent. A certain tree may be widely distributed, so its removal from one forest seems harmless. But that could spell the doom of other plants whose habitat is more limited. Simply letting too much light in can kill many species. They may be merely fungi or mosses of no apparent significance. But they could have undiscovered properties important to human survival.

Shade – not just wetness or the types of trees – makes a rainforest. The leaves of the taller trees intermingle to form a canopy. By most botanical definitions, rainforests are at least 70 per cent enclosed under their canopies. Some are totally closed: treetops cannot be seen from the ground, and any light is filtered. Such forests are so humid that hot weather is intolerable – and so dark that walkers may be unable to see hazards.

Left alone, a rainforest recycles the mineral nutrients in dead trees and other fallen material. Decay is so rapid that the soil need not be especially fertile – nearly all the nutrients are stored above ground. But if erosion strips off the litter, or it is burnt and the ash washes away, the forest starves. So the local occurrence of rainforests is related not only to rainfall reliability but also to the least likelihood of fire. Even where eucalypts have come to rule, pockets of rainforest survive in protected gorges and gullies.

Tasmania has the most extensive rainforests – cool spreads of myrtle beech richly carpeted with mosses and ferns. They also occur in limited areas of Victoria. Stands of the closely related negrohead beech occupy high ranges in northern NSW and southern Queensland. Ancestors of these beeches were established before the southern supercontinent of Gondwanaland broke up: kindred trees grow in New Zealand and Chile and are fossillised in Antarctica. Later, beeches were probably the commonest forest trees in most of Australia.

Beech forests are simple in composition. Mature stands grow to a uniform height and have no understoreys made up of other tree species. Tree ferns may grow luxuriantly where the canopy is more open – particularly along riverbanks. But the forest floors are mainly mossy. Epiphytes – plants that attach themselves to others – and parasites, which feed off

Left: Cool-temperate forests of myrtle beech grow widely in Tasmania and in patches in Victoria – such as this one in Wilsons Promontory National Park. Tree ferns abound where the canopy opens along rivers

Negrohead beech, the ruler of temperate rainforests, nears the northern end of its range in Nightcap National Park, NSW

others, are few except for lichens. The beeches may grow to 30 metres, but in the coldest conditions do not exceed 10 metres.

Northern rainforests are much more complex. More than 100 different tree species may be found in one hectare, and none is noticeably dominant. The general height of the canopy is usually 30 metres or so, but here and there an emergent tree stands much taller. And below the canopy are understoreys of shorter trees. Vines climb towards the light, and epiphytes such as orchids and staghorn and elkhorn ferns are abundant. But the forest floor is surprisingly open. Palms and ferns grow fairly sparsely among fleshy-leafed herbs and a few small shrubs and tree seedlings. These seedlings seem never to get any taller – but if adult trees come down, through old age or storm damage, the opening of the canopy brings them shooting up to fill the gap.

Lichen-covered and nearly always buttressed at their bases, the different northern trees are hard to tell apart at ground level. Prized timber species surviving in remote forests include red cedar, coachwood, silky oak, Queensland maple and teak and the imposing kauri, which reaches 50 metres. This great pine, with relatives in New Zealand and New Caledonia, has a lineage even older than the beeches. The northern forests are equally a part of the Gondwanaland legacy.

Forests in the far north have been enriched more recently, however, by Asiatic plants arriving through New Guinea. That heightens a distinction often made between tropical and subtropical northern rainforests. The first kind contain many more species. But the division has nothing to do with the line of the Tropic of Capricorn – it relates to temperature ranges and altitude. Tropical forests in this sense are not found south of Townsville, and even to the north they are replaced by subtropical mixtures in the higher country.

The northern half of Cape York Peninsula has part-time rainforests. Plants here have to cope with months of drought between monsoons. So the forests are dominated by deciduous species that conserve moisture by shedding their leaves at the onset of the dry season. Since roads are open only in the 'Dry', most travellers do not recognise the rainforests. Small patches of similar vegetation occur in the Darwin region, where they are more often called monsoon vineforests.

Beyond their scenic value and their importance as botanical storehouses, rainforests are the busiest havens of wildlife on land. They seethe with the activities of myriads of creatures, at every level from the leaf litter to the topmost flower heads. Rare insects, amphibians, mammals and birds are among the occupants. Whatever threatens rainforests may ring the death knell of these animals.

Starting life as seeds lodged high in other tropical trees, curtain figs send down prop roots – then strangle their hosts

THE PARKS WHERE RAINFORESTS RULE

POCKETS of rainforest are found in the majority of eastern national parks. Those parks where rainforest predominates, or takes up major areas, include:

Cairns region Barron Gorge, Bellenden Ker, Cape Tribulation, Clump Mountain (Maria Creek group), Daintree, Dunk Island, Ella Bay, Graham Range, Green Island, Grey Peaks, Iron Range, Lake Barrine, Lake Eacham, Lizard Island, Mount Hypipamee, Palmerston group, Topaz Road, Tully Gorge.

Townsville region Conway, Eungella, Goold Island (Hinchinbrook Island group), Jourama, Mount Jukes (Mount Blackwood group), Mount Spec, Orpheus Island, Wallaman Falls group, Whitsunday Island.

Rockhampton region Cape Palmerston, Coalstoun Lakes, Fairlies Knob (Mount Walsh group), Kroombit Tops, Mount Bauple, Northumberland Islands.

Brisbane region Bunya Mountains, Burleigh Head, Conondale, Lamington, Maiala (D'Aguilar Range group), Main Range, Natural Arch, Springbrook group, Tamborine Mountain group, The Palms.

NSW northern border region Border Ranges, Dorrigo, Gibraltar Range, Mount Warning, New England, Nightcap, Washpool.

Melbourne region Alfred, Tarra-Bulga, Croajingolong, Mitchell River, Otway, Wilsons Promontory.

Tasmania Cradle Mountain-Lake St Clair, Mount Field, Southwest, Walls of Jerusalem, Wild Rivers.

The forests that welcome fire

TREES MEET nature's harshest terms in Australia's open forests and woodlands. They face the certainty of wildfire. Many have adapted so that they can recover after burning. And some – particularly the eucalypts – now depend on fire for their procreation. They give typical 'gum tree' bushland not only its own look but even its own smell: evaporating oils.

Long before humans arrived to step up the pace of destruction, fires occurred naturally. Lightning strikes were most often the cause. The trees that stood the best chance were those with lignotubers – swellings near the base of the trunk containing latent buds. These come to life if the tree is damaged above. In some species lignotubers are seen as warty lumps on the trunk. But many Australian trees have them underground, extending much like roots.

Eucalypts and some of their companion trees in the open forests developed further defences. They enclosed their seeds in woody cases instead of soft fruits, and many acquired unusually thick bark. But the most successful species went beyond mere survival – they found ways of exploiting fire for their own benefit. They made sure that when a forest was burnt out, it was replaced by their offspring rather than an invading species. Evolution has brought some eucalypts to a point at which, once at least in their seed-bearing lives, they *need* burning down.

The tallest and fastest-growing eucalypts occupy high-rainfall districts. But they rely on strong light. If an overgrown forest becomes too shady, eucalypt seedlings are killed by fungi. Such a forest is waiting for a dry spell followed by a hot, fast-moving fire. Then, at the height of its destruction, it re-seeds itself.

Fed by streamers of peeling bark, flames race up the trunks to the forest canopy. Vaporised leaf oil ignites – sometimes it explodes – drawing the fire even more quickly away from the ground and through the canopy. And from under the vanishing foliage pours a shower of seed capsules – the output of not just one season, but perhaps three or four.

If the fire has moved on quickly enough the seeds are undamaged. (In a furnace test, green capsules protected their seeds for 9 minutes at 440°C.) Germination starts in a bed of ash, holding mineral nutrients in a form that the seedlings can most readily absorb. Their growth is astonishing: some saplings gain 5 metres in a year. In a burnt eucalypt forest, trees of other families have no chance of taking over.

Tall open forests – referred to in older books as wet hardleaf or wet sclerophyll forests – are at their most grand in the extreme southeast and southwest. In Tasmania and Victoria they include the world's tallest hardwood, mountain ash *Eucalyptus regnans,* which can exceed 100 metres. In Western Australia the karri *Eucalyptus diversicolor,* only slightly shorter, is king. Alpine ash, brown stringybark, blackbutt and blue gum are prominent in NSW, and rose gum is characteristic around Brisbane.

These forests are more open at the top than rainforests – canopy coverage is 30-70 per cent – but much leafier below. There is always a dense understorey of shorter eucalypt species and taller shrubs. On rich soils in the moistest areas, some of the understorey plants are rainforest species – on the way to taking over if fire does not come. With tree ferns, lichens and epiphytes abundant, some wet open forests at ground level look much like rainforests. But the trunk bases are not buttressed.

The dominion of eucalypts continues in drier open forests in southern Australia but the trees seldom exceed 30 metres. Fires are more frequent and most species are adapted to resist, then recover through lignotubers. Understoreys are less leafy, with acacias, casuarinas and banksias usually prominent. The most characteristic eucalypt species include peppermint, bloodwood, scribbly gum, stringybark and 'apple' (angophora) in the southeast, and

Heartwood fire dooms a tree – but its scattered seeds and underground tubers are intact

Damage higher up triggers new growth from a charred trunk

Left: A handsome stand of marri, with an understorey of karri oak, in WA's Walpole-Nornalup National Park. Marri grows widely in the southwest where it reaches heights of 30-40 metres. It shares the same range as jarrah and karri and often occurs with them. Its timber does not compare with that of the other two hardwoods – it is marred by gum pockets and rings

DIEBACK: SHARING THE BLAME

COUNTLESS diseases and pests attack eucalypts – especially where natural balances are disrupted. If large numbers of trees are slowly dying, their decline is generally labelled 'dieback'. It is not one problem but many, with different causes.

A soil-borne fungus attacks the giant jarrahs of Western Australia. To limit its spread some state forest areas and national parks are quarantined; there are wash-down facilities to prevent vehicles carrying infected soil from one area to another; road construction and use are restricted.

Dieback in irrigation areas (particularly in the Murray-Murrumbidgee Basin) occurs because of salting and an altered water table: too much water prevents soil aeration and rots tree roots; too little and the trees die of thirst.

Leaf-eating Christmas beetles and other insects are a major cause of eucalypt dieback in the New England district of NSW. Development of pastoral agriculture has provided more food for the beetles' larval stage while removing farmland trees so there are fewer birds to eat increasing numbers of beetles.

River red gum dieback in northwestern Victoria

In the Dandenong Ranges near Melbourne, the problem seems to be too many birds. Dieback has occurred in about 10 per cent of the forest cover because of an infestation by sap-sucking insects called psyllids. These are husbanded by a big population of bellbirds, which eat only the older psyllids and encourage the young to develop. Other birds with less selective appetites are driven away.

messmate, boxes and pink gum near Adelaide. The Perth region has its own group, dominated by jarrah, marri and wandoo.

Casuarinas and acacias rule in many open forests in Queensland, between hoop pine on the wetter seaward margins and cypress pine at the inland limit of forest growth. There are also some eucalypt forests, with grassy floors suggesting that they gained their hold through firing by Aboriginal hunters. Similar grassy eucalypt forests occur in the Darwin region and the Kimberleys, and along the Murray River Valley where they are dominated by the flood-loving river red gum.

Woodlands are distinguished from forests by having a canopy coverage of less than 30 per cent of their area. Often they are simply extensions of forest communities, more widely spaced because they have less soil moisture to share. Grasses are much more common, however. And some non-eucalypt species – melaleucas (paperbarks), for example – take on a prominence not seen in forests. Brigalow, once the most significant of woodland acacias, exists now only in remnants on its range from inland mid-Queensland to northern NSW.

In woodlands as much as in forests, eucalypts remain the most widespread and dominant trees. Their forms range from the snow gums of alpine summits to monsoon species that shed their leaves for the 'Dry'. Counting the stunted types of the outback, there may be more than 500 eucalypt species; botanists are forever making new finds and classifications, and raising or lowering the figure. However many there are, eucalypts represent the plant kingdom's greatest evolutionary triumph – a conquest of every climatic extreme that the continent can offer.

Tree ferns are characteristic of the cooler wet eucalypt forests of the southeast – but never found in those of the west

But the unmistakable aroma of 'gum' leaves, and the blue haze pervading forests in hot weather, are reminders of menace. The layers of oily foliage and the thickly littered floors are incendiary bombs, certain sooner or later to go off. Eucalypts and many of their companions have accommodated to an element against which humans are largely helpless. Fire is a fact of their lives.

Sentinels of the never-never

SCRUB, SPINIFEX and saltbush ... half of Australia is dismissed in three words. Yet in some ways the vegetation of the scorched, parched outback is the most important of all. It sustained the spread of Aboriginal tribes. It afforded the food, shelter and fuel to make the continent traversable – if seldom habitable – by Europeans and their livestock. And in spite of these intrusions, it has ensured the survival of many wildlife species.

Hardly any of the hinterland is absolute desert. Almost anywhere something grows, to make up the world's greatest array of dry-living plants. But two groups of stunted trees, mulga and mallee, have a hold so persistent that their habitats take their names. The Mulga is an immense tract of acacia scrub and sparse shrubland sweeping across Western Australia into the Northern Territory and South Australia, with outliers to the east. The Mallee's parched plains span southwestern NSW, northwestern Victoria and eastern South Australia. Even more mallee country extends west of Adelaide and round the Great Australian Bight to beyond Kalgoorlie, WA.

Mulga denotes one main wattle species, *Acacia aneura*, which on the best soils can reach 15 metres but in its shrub form can be as low as 2 metres. Its many branches, rising steeply from the ground or just above, carry slightly flattened stems – called phyllodes – instead of leaves. These have a hairy, resinous covering and point skyward to minimise heating. Trees go dormant in drought, but revive within four days of receiving moisture in their soil. They do best where there is some chance of rain at any time of year; in regions of strongly seasonal rainfall they tend to be replaced by casuarinas – the so-called oaks.

Spinifex and snappy gums on the Hamersley Range, WA

Aboriginal boomerangs and many souvenir ornaments are made of mulga wood. Livestock prefer browsing the phyllodes – though they are not particularly nutritious – to eating dry grass. Mulga is harvested as emergency fodder in droughts, and sometimes cleared where there is an understorey of edible tussock grasses. But the trees are secure in the driest areas, and where their understoreys are of inedible small shrubs or hummock grasses.

Mallees are ground-branching eucalypts. More than 100 species have been identified. They form a spreading bush, usually 3-9 metres tall, from an underground lignotuber that contains latent buds to regenerate the tree if it is damaged. Six months after a fire, they may have produced up to 70 new shoots. Stem branches are few and leaves are borne only at the tips of the branches. In dense scrub they form a distinctive canopy cover, shallow and almost horizontal.

Since drought-resistant wheat strains were developed, extensive mallee areas have been cleared – with some calamitous consequences. Without the cover of the mallees and their understorey shrubs and grasses, strong winds after long dry spells can rip all of the topsoil away. Millions of tonnes of red dust are dumped in choking storms on towns and cities or into the oceans; some is even blown as far as New Zealand.

On limy or salty soils, both mulga and mallee may merge into country dominated by low chenopod shrubs – saltbushes and their relatives. They are palatable to stock, and when agriculture invaded the outback their territories were the easiest to take. Saltbushes decline with years of grazing: of about 250 chenopod species, more than 20 are expected to disappear from the wild by the end of the century. But the others hold about 6 per cent of the mainland area. Most are in inland South Australia and on the Nullarbor Plain, with an isolated stronghold in western NSW around the dried-out Willandra Lakes.

Spiky hummock grasses dot arid land over a quarter of the continent, from the northwest coast into Queensland and south almost to the Nullarbor. Mostly species of *Triodia*, they are usually called spinifex – though true *Spinifex* exists as a coastal sand-binding plant. To avoid confusion some people call the inland hummock type porcupine grass. It normally occurs in mulga scrub or casuarina woodlands, but on rocky slopes and sandplains it may provide the only ground cover.

Open grasslands of softer, edible tussocks such as Mitchell grass range from south of Arnhem Land and the Gulf of Carpentaria to southwestern Queensland. But most are heavily grazed. Untouched grasslands now are vir-

Poached-egg daisies: the waiting is over

PLANTS THAT HIDE FROM DROUGHT

RAIN in late winter changes the look of arid inland regions with remarkable speed. Unseen in the ground are seeds that can bide their time through years of drought. When conditions favour them they burst into hectic life. Plants shoot in hours and flower in days. Almost as quickly they wither and die, leaving a new generation of seeds to wait once more.

Most such plants – called ephemerals – are members of the daisy or pea families. Their seeds are programmed so as not to be fooled by a passing shower, or by heavier rain at the wrong time of year. As well as searing heat, frost must be avoided. Germination is triggered only by a certain combination of moisture, temperature and light intensity.

Ephemerals have their easiest life near rock outcrops, where they may flourish annually in pockets of run-off moisture. In Central Australia, the seepage of dew from sealed, high-crowned highways is sometimes enough to promote growth along a narrow band at each side. But the most spectacular shows follow heavy rains on flat country. Drab tonings turn green, then explode into vivid colours as far as the eye can see.

Hops and everlastings make the most of run-off

but most do not need to. Their seeds are distributed whenever they are ready – by harvester ants. These seeds all have a tough casing but they bear a soft tail. The ants carry the seeds to their nests, eat the tail, then discard the seeds undamaged. Sometimes they store them in underground galleries. Some 1500 Australian plant species use ants in this fashion, compared with fewer than 300 anywhere else in the world.

Heathlands in the east and south are generally small patches, merging into scrub or woodlands. Most are coastal, on sandy soils. But highland heaths occur in parts of the Great Dividing Range – on soils derived from sandstone or granite – and in Tasmania. In the west, immense tracts of heathland reach east from Albany and north from Kalbarri – not merely along the coast but also on sandplains well inland. It is their predominance that gives Western Australia its well-justified reputation as 'the wildflower state'.

Left: Mallees and pearl bluebush – a kind of saltbush – merge on the sandplains of Nullarbor National Park, SA. Feral camels are often seen

Below: Scrubs at Wyperfeld National Park, Vic, support at least 200 native bird species

tually confined to very wet areas – the high buttongrass plains of southwestern Tasmania, for example, or the swampgrass plains near parts of the NSW south coast.

Heathland plants make up the remainder of the vegetation of the wide-open spaces. In their domain, forest growth is ruled out not by aridity but by soil infertility. In compensation, the flowering shrubs of the heathlands present the most vivid scenes of the bush, and support a profusion of wildlife. Birds such as honeyeaters and parrots are likeliest to catch the eye, but smaller marsupials also feed on nectar and on the insects that swarm in the undergrowth.

Australia's main family of true heaths, the epacrids, has more than 300 species. The best known, common heath with its dangling tubular flowers borne year-round, is Victoria's floral emblem. Lilies and their relatives grow mostly as heath plants, along with thousands of smaller flowering species including ground orchids in a rich variety of forms and colours. But they and the true heaths are dominated by mixtures of taller woody shrubs. The most characteristic family, the proteaceae, includes banksias, grevilleas, hakeas, waratahs and Western Australia's dryandras. Small eucalypts, acacias, paperbarks, tea-trees and casuarinas are also common – but often the most distinctive plants of heathlands are grass trees.

Nearly all species on the fire-prone heathlands can regenerate from underground organs. Some release seed capsules during a fire,

PART TWO
Parks and people

Simple pleasures in a delightful setting: Walyunga National Park on the outskirts of Perth

Running a national park is a balancing act – protecting the environment while letting people enjoy it. Each place has its special problems, with dedicated rangers and backroom staff working to solve them. But a great deal more is up to the public.

Why we have national parks

TAXPAYERS' MONEY goes into national parks, so people are entitled to see some return for it. Where parks provide recreational opportunities close to cities, or where they preserve unusually spectacular scenery, the benefits are clear. The value of protecting wildlife habitats is also widely recognised at last. But in an increasing number of cases, the worth of new parks is far from obvious to the public.

Some are dedicated in places that no one but a scientist would dream of visiting. Western Australia's vast Rudall River National Park, for example, covers a forbidding expanse of rock ridges and dunes between the Gibson and Great Sandy Deserts. It has no roads, and seldom any water. Many parks are sited in high country so rugged that it is penetrated only by expert climbers. Others occupy monotonous stretches of scrub or swampland, offering nothing noteworthy to see or do.

Public benefits are derived in indirect and sometimes unexpected ways. The real importance of a high, forested park may lie in ensuring the adequacy and purity of water supplies to a nearby community. Even without rain, trees shed more moisture than they receive from the air. And they combat air pollution.

Apart from the varying scenic and recreational merits of national parks, and their role in the protection of the environment and wildlife, they can offer four other advantages from which the whole community stands to gain:

Education Field studies by school groups and trainee teachers are given active assistance. Junior ranger programmes encourage children to follow nature interests in their spare time. Advice by parks staff is also offered in courses for private landowners.

Scientific research Professional studies and experiments are permitted in national parks if they cannot be mounted elsewhere and are not unduly destructive. Untouched areas also serve as models, against which scientists can measure what happens when similar environments outside the parks are interfered with.

Schoolchildren find an easy introduction to nature study at Ferntree Gully National Park, Vic

Scientists are still exploring at Rudall River, WA. The public's turn will come much later

Biological banks Without park protection, many plants and animals would no longer exist. Their genetic combinations would be lost to the world. So would the possibility of using them to develop new medicines, food sources and industrial techniques.

Foreign income The fame of many of Australia's national parks is a powerful magnet to overseas visitors. And a major export earner, the fishing industry, depends on the protection of estuarine and island breeding grounds.

If planners had unlimited funds, they would provide many more parks. In the meantime, where population pressures are intense, they encourage passive recreation. They want visitors to relax, look and listen, rather than seek too many artificial amenities and active pastimes. Popular enjoyment has to be balanced against the fragility of natural environments – or else there may be nothing to enjoy later on.

Park administrations bear a responsibility to future generations, not only in Australia but also throughout the world. Our parks and wildlife services belong to an international union, formed under United Nations auspices, and the federal and state governments endorse all of its ideals. But we struggle to live up to them.

The international convention calls for national parks and nature reserves to make up at least 5 per cent of any country's territory. Australia, in spite of many recent additions, falls far short. And the parks are meant to represent every kind of biological community. Again Australia fails: virtually all temperate and subtropical grasslands, for example, have long been transformed by livestock.

Scarcity of land puts environmental aims in conflict with industrial interests. Remaining areas suitable for parks are often earmarked for mining or logging or hydro-electricity generation. Political pressures to continue industrial activity, at least for a time, are usually intense. Sometimes a mixture of uses seems entirely reasonable. But the international agreement requires a nation's 'highest competent authority' to eliminate any exploitation in national parks.

Australia's trouble has been that the highest authority, the federal government, holds absolute power only in Commonwealth territories – the ACT, the Northern Territory, Jervis Bay and some remote oceanic islands. Elsewhere, the federal system gives state governments the right to declare their own reserves and dispose of them as they please. Their older 'national' parks were created under diverse political influences to achieve different goals. Nationwide concerns were never paramount – let alone international responsibilities.

Dissension over such issues as uranium mining, oil prospecting and civil engineering continues to make political battlegrounds of some present and proposed national parks. But in management techniques and planning, at least, Canberra and the states are now in closer accord. Since the mid-1970s all legislatures have passed national parks and wildlife acts along broadly similar lines. Under a council of all the ministers with nature conservation responsibilities, senior officials of the various parks services form a standing committee to co-ordinate policies.

All of Australia's governments today have the benefit of the same high grade of professional advice on nature conservation, considered in the full light of national need. None of them wishes to be seen as environmentally irresponsible, so recommendations for new or expanded parks are usually received sympathetically. Whether enough money can be found to manage them, and provide the right balance of protection and public enjoyment, is altogether another matter.

The Royal: where it all started

Park expansion at Era took in holiday shacks – and herds of imported deer

IDEAS of nature conservation took a back seat in 1879, when Australia's first national park was conceived. The vision was not of a noble wilderness, to be kept sacred, but of a tamed and groomed playground – a Sydney version of London's Hampstead Heath.

Creation of the National Park (its only name for three-quarters of a century) was primarily a public health measure. Sydney's population had doubled in a decade: in some slums, one child in four died before it was five years old. The people needed common land.

Country to the south, cut off by the Hacking River, was about to be opened up by the Illawarra railway. Legislators reserved 7000 hectares for public recreation, and trustees hastened to meet the leisure tastes of the time. Riverside forest was hacked down to make way for lawns and European trees. Deer were brought in, and exotic birds and fish were released. A causeway controlled the river. Pavilions, guest houses and camps sprang up nearby. Cart roads and bridle paths wound into the bush. A tourist village, Audley, had its own vegetable plots, dairy pastures, orchard and blacksmith's forge.

Sports grounds were envisaged – even a horse racing track. In the meantime, undeveloped areas were cleared by the army for manoeuvres and artillery practice. And to recoup the cost of public amenities, the trustees were allowed to license grazing, logging and mining in the park.

Nature lovers were objecting before World War I, and in 1922 they successfully challenged a mining company's right to fell and mill native trees for pit props. But they could do nothing to stem the tide of cars that soon started to swamp the park. The trustees saw it as their duty to provide maximum access.

Motor roads criss-crossed the heathlands and reached the coastal cliffs and bays. People parked, picnicked, camped and cut firewood anywhere. Beach shacks appeared, and during the 1930s Depression the railway side of the park was dotted with humpies put up by jobless men. Some made livings by stealing greenery to supply city florists, or by selling cartloads of timber or soil.

Still more bush suffered in World War II, when the army set up coastal defences and used much of the park for training exercises. Postwar affluence brought a new flood of cars and motor bikes, and the first 'scrub bashers' in off-road vehicles.

The park was granted its Royal prefix in 1955, but to conservationists it seemed a lost cause. Still, it served as an object lesson, readily pointed to by professional ecologists when official policies came under fire in the next decade. After NSW set up Australia's first integrated parks and wildlife service in 1967, the professionals took charge of the mutilated old reserve and set about giving it another chance.

Cars were restricted to a few formed roads and parking zones. Ramshackle buildings were demolished. Maintenance of ornamental gardens and any other attempts to outdo nature were abandoned. The bush came back, season by season, until in its centenary year at the end of the 1970s the Royal National Park could wear its title with some pride.

Imitating an English pleasure garden suited Sydney ideas of ease in Edwardian times

Soldiers took over in World War I, baring the heathlands

Jacks and Jills of all trades

Many ranger tasks are sheer drudgery: emptying garbage bins is not the worst of them

OUTDOOR WORK in a pleasant setting ... that is one part of the picture of a park ranger's life. But another may be writing reports and keeping financial records – or cleaning lavatories. Some tasks entail days and nights of utter solitude. Others require the poise and patience to deal with constant streams of people. Physical demands are high. Rangers have to be dedicated, fit and above all versatile.

Looking after the public constitutes the major part of the workload. Visitors expect easy road access and parking. They want eating facilities, campsites, piped water and sanitation – and nobody else's garbage. They seek information: signposts, leaflets, displays, advice. And they are entitled to safety. Walking routes must be secured and waterways patrolled. People astray in big parks may have to be found and helped, and perhaps given first-aid treatment. But all too often, what park visitors need most is policing.

Enforcement of regulations is the priority role of all rangers. They must keep dogs, cats and firearms out of parks, and make sure that no native plants, animals, rocks or soil are taken without licence. They must try to prevent off-road driving, and any intrusion into areas that are quarantined because plants are regenerating or endangered animals are breeding. Vitally, they have to see that fire restrictions and bans are obeyed.

Every year the parks services report hundreds of prosecutions and fines. Many other infringements are dealt with by a formal caution or just a friendly reminder – sometimes at the risk of abuse or violence. A Sydney Harbour ranger, patrolling by launch, spotted a beach party round an illicit fire. He went ashore to chide the group and was brutally bashed. Even organised crime impinges on parks: rangers in remote districts have had tense encounters with drug smugglers and marijuana growers.

Carpentry skills ease a climb for nature trail parties

Practical work to protect the environment is often sheer hard labour. Firebreaks and trails have to be maintained, and precautionary burns carried out. Most parks are at constant war with noxious weeds, feral animals or soil and sand dune erosion. Many have vandalism to contend with as well, or simply the inevitable wear and tear of heavy visiting. And parks services are increasingly taking over and trying to restore land damaged by other uses.

Rangers' reports form the basis of much of the park information that is distributed to the public. They also contribute to the resource studies and environmental impact assessments that precede major changes in management policies. Rangers may be called on for field observations to establish the numbers and movements of endangered animals, the location of rare plants, or the rate of decay of delicate landforms. Their judgments help decide where visitors are encouraged to go and what they are encouraged to do.

Educating the public is another big role. Some rangers spend much of their time running information and display centres or conducting guided walks. School parties receive special treatment, and rangers also go to schools for classroom talks. Landholders are offered advice on soil conservation, native tree care, wildlife protection, pest control and so on. Public relations addresses are often made to community groups – including some that are opposed to national parks. Hardest to win over are farmers who fear crop raids by animals from nearby parks, local body leaders who resent the loss of ratable land, and people whose livings depend on logging or mining.

Rangers of both sexes are highly trained in emergency procedures: fire fighting, search and rescue, first aid and sometimes flood response. Often they trap or kill animals – in the far north, their tasks may include buffalo musters and crocodile shoots. But little of a ranger's work is so exciting. Much more is mundane: fixing, cleaning and improving facilities, removing refuse, spraying weeds, supervising and informing visitors, issuing permits, collecting fees, answering mail and attending to clerical details.

Winter duties in the Victorian Alps include clearing away snowdrifts so that skiers can get to their slopes – and then retrieving casualties

While tourists shun Kakadu's 'Wet', hard work goes on

THE POWER BEHIND THE PATCH

EMBLEMS patched on every park ranger's uniform are symbols of helpfulness and protection – and firm authority if it is needed. In enforcing certain laws on behalf of their state or territorial services, rangers have powers similar to those of the police. They carry identity cards stating their role as park wardens: their instructions must be obeyed.

Prosecutions for minor breaches of park rules are rare, but offenders who interfere with other people's enjoyment can be evicted. Formal letters of warning may be issued, so a ranger is entitled to ask for a culprit's name and address. To refuse is a further offence.

Under the laws that protect native plants and animals in parks, rangers acting on reasonable suspicion can search vehicles, containers and camps, seize any flora or fauna, and confiscate firearms and other hunting gear. In states where park rangers are also wildlife officers – not Victoria or Western Australia – their powers of search and seizure can extend to private property outside a park.

Positions are so sought after, however, that the parks services can be extremely selective. They usually insist on land management experience, and some states require applicants to hold a diploma in park management, environmental studies or natural sciences. And even that does not guarantee them a job – let alone any choice in where they work. Some busy parks employ a less formally qualified grade of 'park worker', chosen usually for manual skills. But the rangers themselves are expected to be competent and self-reliant in work such as carpentry and mechanical maintenance, along with bushcraft.

Staff with the highest qualifications usually work from regional centres or state head offices. They include architects, designers, lawyers, archeologists and publications specialists. But most are science graduates and technicians, conducting biological and environmental research. A few in each state concentrate on interpretation – the evaluation and explanation of park resources – and planning. This provides the main basis of management policy, which in turn determines how the rangers in the field have to do their work.

Queensland rangers collect data for turtle research

Staying alive in the bush

FIRE IS BY FAR the greatest danger that visitors could face in national parks. When hot winds blow, bushfires can flare with little warning and approach with astonishing speed. But they move on just as quickly. Applying some commonsense safety procedures, no one need be killed or even badly burnt.

In the first place, parks consisting of eucalypt forests, dense scrub or heavily vegetated heathlands are best avoided when fire risks are extreme. They will be stiflingly hot and dusty anyway – hardly enjoyable unless they give access to rivers. Most parks display risk indicators near their entrances. And on the worst days, when total fire bans are declared, they are announced in all radio, newspaper and television weather reports. Check before setting out for a park; if there is a total ban in the district, consider changing your plans.

Fire bans are declared by statewide authorities. But park managements at any time can impose their own rules on the types of fires allowed. These are made clear on signs and in leaflets. Whichever sort of restriction applies, it is enforceable in court. Ignoring it could cost a stiff fine – even jail – or people's lives. For safety's sake alone the rules must be obeyed. And smokers have a particular responsibility to see that matches and butts are extinguished.

The killer in bushfires is not usually flame, but radiated heat. Shield yourself from it. If you are on foot with a fire approaching, don't flee blindly. Look around for the best refuge – in a steep-banked creekbed, or behind a rock outcrop or a fallen log where the vegetation is thinnest. Keep low as you move – crawl if you must – to avoid smoke inhalation. If there is no shelter in sight, lie face down on a bare patch of ground. Scoop out a hollow for yourself if you can, and use loose soil to cover any exposed skin. When the main blaze has passed over you, move to where nothing is left to burn.

If you are in a car, stay there – it is your best possible shield against radiant heat. Cars are unlikely to catch fire, and sealed petrol tanks do not explode. Never try to drive through smoke. Park at the roadside – avoiding thick undergrowth and long grass – and turn on your headlights. Close windows and air vents, and block any chinks with paper or fabric. Get down on the floor and use the mats to cover exposed skin.

SIGN LANGUAGE

AERIAL searchers recognise a code of emergency signals displayed on the ground. Make them at least 3 metres long from wood, fabric or rocks, or by scraping away snow. Your signs will be acknowledged by an aircraft rocking, or flashing a green light. Red flashes, or a full right-hand circuit, mean you are not understood.

I	Serious injury: need doctor
II	Need medical supplies
F	Need food and water
LL	All well
L	Need fuel
□	Need map and compass
X	Cannot proceed
↑	Proceeding this way
K	Show which way to go
Δ	Probably safe to land here
N	No
Y	Yes
JL	Not understood

Bites and stings Never walk far into the bush without long trousers, socks and thick footwear. Take the greatest care where you tread on warm, sunny days, when snakes are most active. If you see a snake in your path, don't try to poke at it – annoyed in that way, it is most likely to strike. But if you stand well clear and make plenty of noise, it will go away.

Most of Australia's 140 snake species are venomous, but only about 15 are capable of killing humans. Unless you are expert in identifying species, however, regard any snakebite as dangerous. Apply a bandage that puts firm pressure *directly on the bitten area* – not a tourniquet. If a limb is bitten, immobilise it with a splint. Then quickly alert a ranger. The park may have its own venom-identification kit and anti-venom supplies.

A lethal species of funnel-web spider (*Atrax robustus*) is a threat to life only in the Sydney region. It is black and big – up to 7 cm across between leg-tips. Treat a funnel-web bite like a snakebite, with pressure bandaging and immobilisation. One other dangerous spider, the redback, may be found anywhere in Australia. Dark, with an orange-red stripe on its back, and measuring 2-3 cm across, its venom is slower-acting and bandaging is unnecessary if medical aid can be obtained quickly.

Bush ticks abound in eastern forests. Tiny when they attach themselves, they burrow into the skin and feed on blood for three or four days, swelling to about 1 cm across. Meanwhile they release a paralysing toxin that can lead to death, especially in children. If you have brushed through dense vegetation, inspect exposed areas of skin for the next three days – and have someone else examine your scalp. A lightly attached tick may be scraped off. One

Rangers and police practise rescue techniques in the Labyrinth at Cradle Mountain-Lake St Clair, Tas

BURNING WITH A PURPOSE

TASMANIAN rangers (pictured below) in Southwest National Park are lighting their own bushfire. It will turn hundreds of hectares into a blackened waste. But these men are making sure that a worse fire will not happen by accident.

The disaster potential of bushfires depends largely on how much fuel they can find. Preventive burning in national parks is ordered before the build-up of litter and undergrowth reaches a dangerous level. Not only the quantity of fuel but also its composition, distribution and moisture content are calculated – in some places with computers.

Frequent burning around the edges of parks is normally done by hand, but bigger tracts inside are more often fired with air-dropped incendiary capsules. Under most fire management programmes, only small sections of each park have to be burnt and closed off for regeneration. In the southeast, for example, preventive burning of as little as 5 per cent each year is enough to keep a whole area safe from full-scale destruction.

embedded more deeply can be killed with kerosene or turpentine, and perhaps prised out with tweezers. If this is not wholly successful, seek medical help. Leeches, which are bigger and less likely to escape notice in the first place, are seldom harmful. They drop out after about five minutes of feeding, or if killed with a burning cigarette end or twig. Don't pull them out – parts left in may cause an infection.

Big, aggressive saltwater crocodiles are increasing in some tropical parks. Remember, they are just as much at home in fresh water. Observe signs warning against swimming and take special care walking on riverbanks. If you find yourself near a basking crocodile, back off quietly. Never place yourself in its path to the water. It may use its tail to knock you out of the way – and one blow from a fullgrown 'saltie' could kill you.

Safety first Unless you are a fit and fully experienced bushwalker, stick to established paths and trails. Don't attempt a long journey through rugged or untracked country unless you have a party of at least three – then if someone is in trouble, another can stand by while the third goes for help. Always carry more water than you believe you will need, along with a first-aid kit and a compass, whistle, knife and waterproof matches. Don't start without obtaining up-to-date maps and telling a ranger of your intentions. And don't fail to report back when the trip is over, if you are asked to. Your negligence could spark a wasteful search operation.

If you are lost, assess your food and water supplies and ration them. Don't waste energy by moving about aimlessly. Seek shelter near an open space where signals can be seen from aircraft, and stay put. If you are forced to keep moving, leave messages along your route or mark it in some way, indicating your direction. To attract attention if other people seem to be nearby, give three whistles, shouts or mirror-flashes at regular intervals, and light a smoky fire of leaves or grass.

Fire-watching from the summit of Mt Lofty becomes a fulltime job during danger periods at Cleland Conservation Park, near Adelaide. Below: Backburning to contain a fast-moving wildfire

How the public can help

IF YOU WOULD enjoy using some spare time to help maintain and improve a favourite national park, just ask. Almost certainly you will be put in touch with a band of volunteers already in action in the district. Most parks – especially those near major population centres – have arrangements with outside groups.

Hundreds of Australians find agreeable fresh-air exercise in voluntary park work at weekends and during holidays. There is room for more. Many tasks are menial: litter removal, weeding and tree planting are typical. But other jobs are highly constructive and add significantly to park amenities. Some are funded by community service clubs and business organisations.

Rapid volunteer response is credited with saving major parts of parks threatened by severe erosion after storm damage. Others, devastated by fire or flooding, have been brought back into public use surprisingly quickly thanks to donated labour. Sometimes a task is long overdue, but simply too hard for the park service to justify on a limited budget. 'Friends of the Prom', for example, trekked back and forth between Melbourne and Wilsons Promontory National Park to remove decades of painted graffiti from rocks at Refuge Cove.

Volunteers with manual trade skills, or experience in plant care on a large scale, are usually most welcome. Others who are adept at dealing with visitors, and can acquire the knowledge to interpret a park's natural features and answer questions, may be enlisted at busy times to help at information centres or take parties on guided walks.

Queensland volunteers pitch in to clear a trail

The Australian Trust for Conservation Volunteers, originating in Victoria but spreading nationwide in 1984, offers mobile squads of young people for national park assignments. These task forces usually camp on the site. Their first big accomplishment, in 1982, was the construction of 4.5 km of rabbit fencing at Hattah-Kulkyne National Park. Since then they have restored jetties, improved tracks, built footbridges and eradicated noxious weeds at various parks – and even cleaned up a disused guesthouse to accommodate visitors.

Members of the public are also entitled to have their say in the planning of national parks – where they should be and what activities should be allowed in them. Management plans are published, and in some states and the ACT the law demands that public comment be invited. Even without such a provision, there is nothing to stop an interested citizen making representations to the appropriate parks service or environment department. A sympathetic MP would probably give assistance.

But individuals have a hard time making themselves heard on national parks issues. Most arguments are too technical, resting on resource evaluations and environmental impact assessments. People seeking to sway government or park management decisions are advised to consult one of the National Parks Associations or a similar organisation.

Outside helpers remove thorn apple, a noxious weed, from a creekbed in Snowy River National Park, Vic

ORGANISATIONS YOU CAN JOIN

PUBLIC organisations in every state and territory work for the establishment of new national parks, and generally to see that natural environments are not only conserved but also enjoyed.

National Parks Associations, which advance detailed cases to governments for the creation of new parks, are based in Sydney, Melbourne, Brisbane and Canberra. Equivalent bodies elsewhere are the SA Nature Conservation Society (Adelaide), the WA Conservation Council (Perth), the Tasmanian Conservation Trust (Hobart) and the NT Environment Council (Darwin).

National Parks and Wildlife Foundations, which conduct fund-raising appeals – such as NSW's annual 'Operation Noah' – to help acquire land for parks and conserve endangered animals, are based in Sydney and Adelaide. The **Australian Conservation Foundation,** with headquarters in Melbourne, focuses attention on wider environmental issues at a national level, but gives particular support to the national parks movement.

National Trusts, besides their work to save items of cultural heritage such as historic buildings, are active in promoting nature conservation. They have offices in all capital cities. The **Wilderness Society,** having triumphed in its No Dams campaign in Tasmania, has set up branches in nearly all mainland capitals.

World Wildlife Fund Australia, based in Sydney, raises money to preserve endangered species in Australia and some nearby Pacific islands. **Environment Centres** in all capitals and in many provincial cities provide public information and administrative facilities for the environmental movement as a whole. They can give you details of hundreds of other local and special-interest groups that may suit your purpose.

NOTE: Addresses at back of book

Making the most of your visit

CREATION of a national park is no guarantee of stunning scenery or exciting activities. Australia's 500-odd parks are meant to preserve widely different environments. Not all may be to your liking. Many will lack the facilities to meet your particular needs. So in planning a visit, make sure you know what to expect.

From information in the regional guide sections that follow, readers can decide for themselves which parks are likely to hold most attraction and how much time they want to spend in them. Descriptions are down to earth – not glamorised. And the interest ratings are equally realistic. If a park rates low in 'day activities', for example, it means there is little to do but look around. There may not be enough to keep children amused for long.

In arranging a tourist itinerary, check on the availability of campsites. If you are interested in visiting several parks it may not be necessary to contact them all in advance – the capital city head office of the National Parks Service should be able to warn you of any difficulty. Queensland has a tourist pre-booking system, operated from Brisbane and regional offices, that covers all of its camping parks.

Consider the time of year and the weather, especially if a long journey outside your home district is involved. Most parks in the tropics, and many others inland, are far from enjoyable in summer. In the bushfire season, or if there have been heavy rains, call the enquiries number before setting out, to make sure that the park of your choice is open and accessible.

If you are travelling with a dog or cat, remember that you cannot take it into a national park. The menace that an escaped cat presents to wildlife is obvious. Few dogs are such efficient hunters – but their mere barking is enough to terrify native animals and disrupt their living patterns for days afterwards.

When you arrive at a park, or at a town office that looks after camping permits, pick up all the explanatory material offered. Anything that heightens your powers of observation will increase your enjoyment. And without full information, you may miss major points of interest. Nearly all parks have general maps. Some have leaflets to aid in bird spotting and plant identification, and special maps for bushwalks and self-guiding nature trails.

Public roads are kept to a minimum in all parks. Be prepared to leave your car in a designated parking area – never drive it into the bush – and see the sights on foot. It is by far the best way. Leaflets or signposts will tell you how long a walk should take, and whether it presents any difficulty.

Knowledge adds interest: an excellent example of park literature from the Northern Territory

The numbat, a rare termite eater, is protected at Dryandra Forest, WA

Scientists are intrigued by Eungella's gastric-brooding frog

Where animals

WERRIKIMBE National Park gained an extra 20 000 hectares of rainforest in 1984 – all for the sake of some mice. They are of a native species found in significant numbers only two years before. Now their home, on the upper Hastings River in northern NSW, should be secure.

Queensland has dedicated one of its national parks solely to preserve the habitat of an endangered species. The northern hairy-nosed wombat survives only at Epping Forest – formerly part of a cattle station on flat, semi-arid woodland west of Gladstone. Fencing keeps out grazing livestock and allows the regeneration of native grasses and scrub on which the wombat colony depends.

Successful husbandry of rare animals – especially those newly discovered – relies on complicated biological research and the scientific monitoring of populations and feeding habits. Only the national parks and wildlife services have the specialised resources for such work, so most conservation efforts are centred on their parks, or on some state parks under their management. Forestry and water catchment authorities play important co-operative roles.

A recent triumph of wildlife conservation has been the saving of the malleefowl in Victoria. It is the world's only mound-nesting bird living in arid regions. Clearing and grazing of its scrub habitats, along with bushfires, had all but wiped it out by the 1950s. But populations flourish

Parks were specially dedicated to rescue the endangered malleefowl. The male spends 8 months every year building a mound in which eggs are buried

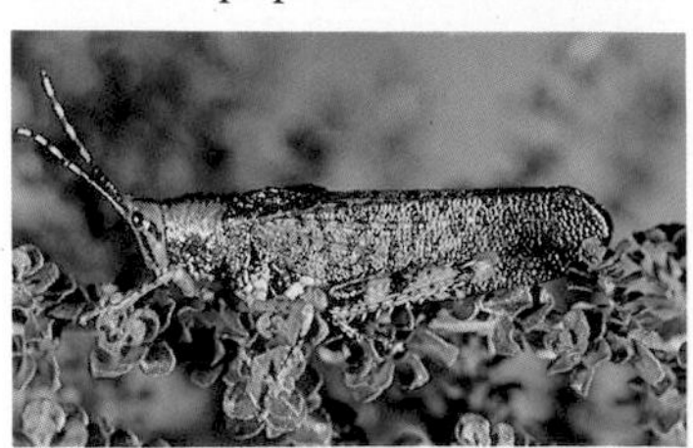

Right: Only Kakadu, NT, has Leichhardt's grasshopper

For half a century the Hastings River mouse was known only from English museum specimens. Now it has a park section all to itself, where researchers are trying to discover its habits

Iron Range, Qld, is a haven for the golden-shouldered parrot

Left: A Queensland ranger examines a ghost bat – our only carnivorous species. Big colonies are seen at Fitzroy Caves and nearby Mt Etna

find safety

now in Little Desert, Hattah-Kulkyne and Wyperfeld National Parks. Mallee Cliffs National Park, in far western NSW, was established with the same aim.

Judging whether a species is truly rare can be difficult in Australia. Much of the fauna is small, secretive and nocturnal in habit. It is hard to find, let alone to count. And fires, floods and prolonged droughts lead to drastic fluctuations in numbers and distribution.

A highly unusual frog, discovered in 1972, disappeared after 1979. It lived in Kondalilla National Park and the neighbouring Conondale and Blackall Ranges of south-eastern Queensland. Called the platypus frog because of its swimming action, it seemed to be the only frog in the world that never left water. And it was the world's only known gastric-brooding vertebrate. Females swallowed fertilised eggs and raised their young in their stomachs – somehow shutting off the production of digestive acids.

Rediscovery was hailed in 1983, when similar orange-coloured gastric-brooders were spotted far to the north in Finch Hatton Gorge, which leads out of Eungella National Park. But a captured specimen, compared with one of the Kondalilla frogs still alive in an Adelaide laboratory, proved to belong to yet another new species. The likelihood of other finds offers medical researchers high hopes of developing a drug to prevent human stomach ulcers.

The task of tallying animal populations is full of such surprises. Camping out in 1982 to count waterfowl, a wildlife officer in northwestern Tasmania made a convincing observation of a thylacine, or marsupial 'tiger'. Most people thought the species was extinct. But this animal's doglike head and black-striped, tawny back were unmistakable. Word of the sighting was withheld from the public for two years. If the breeding grounds of thylacines are traced, they will receive the strictest protection ever known.

Skunk-like in its markings, the striped possum of tropical rainforest parks is also remarkably smelly

Nature gets another chance

WOUNDED LANDSCAPES are hard to heal. Even where full restoration is possible, the cost is often prohibitive. But national parks staff are succeeding, here and there, in turning back the clock. Their techniques were largely developed in old-established parks degraded by decades of heavy visiting. Now they are applied to recently resumed land that has suffered from other uses.

Most new inland parks have been at least partly grazed by livestock. The effect on natural vegetation is compounded by the persistence of feral animals – species that were introduced as domestic stock but now breed in the wild. Goats and pigs do the most widespread damage. Wild rabbits still bare the land in some districts, in spite of the sweeping eradication measures of the 1950s. High-country parks are often scarred by old logging trails or forestry roads, their margins invaded by exotic weeds. Steeper slopes may be subject to soil erosion.

When coastal parks are acquired, they frequently come with a legacy of dune erosion from off-road vehicles and ill-placed walking tracks. Many include old sand mining leases, or quarries where lime or building stone were extracted. Before the usual chores of removing noxious weeds and planting sand-binding grasses can start, the original land contours may have to be rebuilt.

Some park areas have a history of military use. They were taken over still bearing the marks of bombing or artillery practice and infantry exercises. Among the latest acquisitions are the various high headlands that make up most of Sydney Harbour National Park. These would not be available to the public now – suburban housing would have enveloped them – if they had not been reserved for 150 years or more as defence posts. Vantage points are capped with gun emplacements; the sandstone below is riddled with ammunition chambers, snipers' slits and connecting tunnels. The fortifications are worth keeping for their historical value – but their bare surroundings, stripped of soil by wind erosion, were an eyesore. Years of work and substantial funds are going into restoration

Sand mining roads scar a proposed park extension on Nth Stradbroke Island, Qld

Right: Regeneration of grazed land on Bogong High Plains, Vic, is a co-operative venture

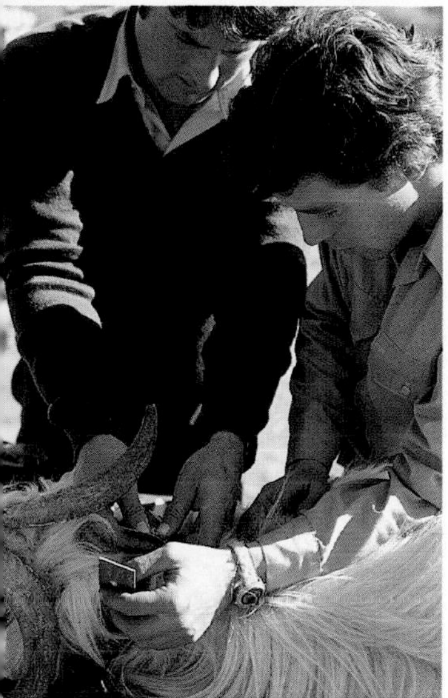

A goat is fitted with a radio collar to track its movements

of the heaths and woodlands that greeted the First Fleet.

Bush regeneration calls for fine judgment, skilled work and inexhaustible patience. Attempts to make dramatic improvements overnight, simply by ripping out alien weeds or dumping new topsoil, are bound to fail. The same weeds – if not worse ones that are even faster-growing – will reappear, and probably work their way deeper into any natural bush nearby. Only a cautious approach, aimed at tipping the balance subtly towards native plants, is likely to succeed.

Managed regeneration of weed-infested bush starts from the least affected area and works towards the most degraded. In weeding, the soil is disturbed as little as possible and surface mulch is put back in place so that any native seeds lie at the proper level. The pace of progress is dictated by the capacity of seedlings to reclaim territory. They must have time to form a dense, diverse community in one zone – and planners must be convinced that it can be kept clear of weeds – before a neighbouring area is touched.

In rainforests the process is complicated by the interaction of plants. The different growth habits of weeds have to be considered, so that they are taken out in the correct order. If tall, leafy vines are removed first, for example, stronger light reaching the forest floor may spur the spread of ground creepers that choke off native seedling growth. Extensive regeneration projects, whether of rainforest trees or of eucalypts and their companions, take many years.

Control of feral animals calls for just as much patience. Little is achieved without a thorough knowledge of how they live in particular habitats. The breeding rate of a species may vary from place to place, depending mainly on climate and the availability of food. Patterns of movement also vary. Some plants and land are more easily damaged than others. All these factors influence a decision on how much control – which usually means killing – is necessary in a park, and what method will work best.

Wildlife suffers heavily from predation by feral cats and dogs and dingoes, and from the competition these and other species create for food, water and shelter. Rabbits and goats strip any vegetation they can reach above ground, and pigs do even worse – they root into the soil with their snouts and leave it fit for nothing but weeds. Water buffalo in the Northern Territory trample and degrade wetlands that are important to tourism and vital to migratory waterfowl. And many feral species are potential carriers of exotic livestock diseases – tuberculosis and brucellosis, for example – that in uncontrolled conditions could be ruinous to the agricultural economy. In their extermination measures, parks services work in close co-operation with farming communities.

THE SCOURGE OF NATIVE WILDLIFE

CATS breeding in the wild are the most efficient of all predators. Their chief impact is on native birds, small mammals and reptiles. Indirectly they can also upset plant life, because they eat many of the animals that control insect pests.

Nearly all feral cats revert to a tabby appearance. Most are greyish, but on red outback soils more are ginger. In forested regions, where food is easily obtained, they are heavier than domestic cats but not noticeably bigger.

But in harsher country, it is survival of the fittest. The most powerful cats get the food – and the biggest toms take all the breeding opportunities. Supercats are evolving. Some stand twice as tall as their ancestors and are many times heavier. One giant shot in the Simpson Desert weighed 12 kg.

Feral pigs lay waste a waterhole at Kinchega, NSW

Trees return to former farmland at Organ Pipes, Vic

Mt Lidgbird on Lord Howe Island rises 777 metres from the edge of a coral-encrusted lagoon. The Lord Howe group, 700 km northeast of Sydney, is regarded as an outstanding example of an island system developed from submarine volcanic activity. Many of its plants and animals are found nowhere else. Much of the main island is protected under NSW national parks and wildlife laws as a 'permanent park'

Below: Forests crowd the deep gorge of the Franklin River in Wild Rivers National Park. This park forms the centre of the western Tasmanian World Heritage area, together with the neighbouring Southwest and Cradle Mountain-Lake St Clair National Parks

An obligation

NATURAL FEATURES of Australia figure importantly as World Heritage sites. Already listed are the Great Barrier Reef, Kakadu National Park, western Tasmania's chain of wilderness parks, the Willandra Lakes region of NSW, the Lord Howe Island group, and the rainforest parks and reserves of northern NSW. Uluru National Park, embracing Ayers Rock, is expected to be added.

Some great national parks overseas, such as Grand Canyon and Yellowstone in the USA, are among the nearly 200 other 'properties' on the list. But the majority are sites of ancient civilisations, or manmade structures of cultural importance. They include many famous cathedrals and palaces — along with the infamous Auschwitz concentration camp.

Inclusion of a natural area is a source of pride to any country. It confers recognition that the area is of world significance because it: represents a major stage of the

THE ANCIENT ROCK ART OF KAKADU

ABORIGINAL sites in Kakadu National Park, occupied for at least 25 000 years, include rock galleries of elaborate prehistoric paintings. Pictured are two from the hundreds seen by visitors to Ubirr (Obiri Rock).

Sand lunettes, windblown from the beds of the dried-up Willandra Lakes, hold evidence of human activity more than 30 000 years ago

to the world

earth's evolution; exemplifies continuing geological processes, biological evolution and human interaction with the environment; contains rare or superlative natural features or areas of exceptional beauty; or supports rare or endangered plants and animals.

But along with pride goes a heavy obligation. When a site is nominated for World Heritage listing, the nation responsible undertakes to ensure 'identification, protection, conservation, presentation and transmission to future generations ... to the utmost of its own resources'. The nominating nation is also obliged to obtain international assistance if it is needed to achieve those aims.

Some loss of sovereignty and secrecy is implied. That may be why the world list is noticeably incomplete: China and the Soviet Union have nothing on it. And in Australia's case the commitment made by the federal government clearly overrides states' rights. That was established in the High Court over the Tasmanian dam argument.

The Great Barrier Reef is the biggest Heritage area of all

Australia's nominations are proposed by the Australian Heritage Commission. Its chairman and six members are part-timers appointed by the federal Environment Minister and drawn from a variety of professions in all states. They also supervise the selection and documentation of other important natural or cultural sites in Australia, and the compilation of a register of what is called the National Estate. Fraser Island, when it was rescued from sand mining, became the inaugural entry on that local list.

World Heritage nominations are received at UNESCO headquarters in Paris. Seventy countries have signed the convention that governs the listing procedure. Nominations go before a committee of 21 national representatives, with a membership that changes frequently so that every country gets a turn. The committee meets to approve listings towards the end of each year.

The roof of Australia: the Great Dividing Range from Kosciusko National Park

PART THREE
A guide to all national parks

Parks are grouped on the basis of their accessibility from major population centres and their proximity to one another. Some other reserves, not classed as national parks, are added because they contain features of unusual interest. In each region a pictorial selection is followed by a directory of all parks.
It gives their location, indicates their character and identifies the public facilities they offer.
Comparative ratings, assessed by parks staff, give recognition to the varied tastes and needs of visitors.
As a further aid, the activities allowed in the parks are listed for each state.

PARK REGIONS

1 ALICE SPRINGS REGION PAGE 48
2 DARWIN REGION PAGE 72
3 DERBY & KUNUNURRA REGIONS PAGE 94
4 CARNARVON & PORT HEDLAND REGIONS PAGE 106
5 PERTH REGION PAGE 116
6 ESPERANCE & ALBANY REGIONS PAGE 142
7 ADELAIDE REGION PAGE 168
8 MELBOURNE REGION PAGE 198
9 LAUNCESTON & DEVONPORT REGIONS PAGE 242
10 HOBART REGION PAGE 258
11 CANBERRA REGION PAGE 280
12 BROKEN HILL & MILDURA REGIONS PAGE 308
13 SYDNEY REGION PAGE 316
14 LISMORE & GRAFTON REGIONS PAGE 348
15 BRISBANE REGION PAGE 368
16 ROCKHAMPTON REGION PAGE 392
17 TOWNSVILLE REGION PAGE 416
18 CAIRNS REGION PAGE 446

DARWIN
2
KUNUNURRA
3
DERBY
NT
PORT HEDLAND
4
1
ALICE SPRINGS
CARNARVON
WA
18
CAIRNS
17
TOWNSVILLE
ROCKHAMPTON
16
QLD
SA
15
BRISBANE
LISMORE
14
GRAFTON
BROKEN HILL
12
NSW
5
PERTH
6
ESPERANCE
ALBANY
7
ADELAIDE
MILDURA
13
SYDNEY
11
ACT
CANBERRA
VIC.
8
MELBOURNE
9
DEVONPORT
LAUNCESTON
TAS.
HOBART
10

ALICE SPRINGS REGION

Hidden oases of the rocky Red Centre

RISING abruptly to stark, jagged crests, the parallel ridges of the MacDonnell Ranges make a wall 400 km long across the very heart of Australia. Though it seldom reaches more than 500 metres above the level of the arid plains of red sand, the barrier looks impenetrable – and forbiddingly dry. Hidden in its folds of iron-stained quartzite, however, are courses cut by ancient rivers. It is 20 000 years since any of them flowed year-round. But in their shady chasms are springs and pools, and lush remnants of once-widespread rainforests.

Aranda Aborigines knew all the water sources but used them sparingly. Most pools were left untouched to sustain plants and wildlife. Bans on drinking and swimming were reinforced by a teaching that the conserved pools harboured monstrous watersnakes. To the Aranda the MacDonnells were *Altjira* – the land that had been there always – and the site of the creation of the first man.

Your access and facilities guide to all national parks in this region is on page 69

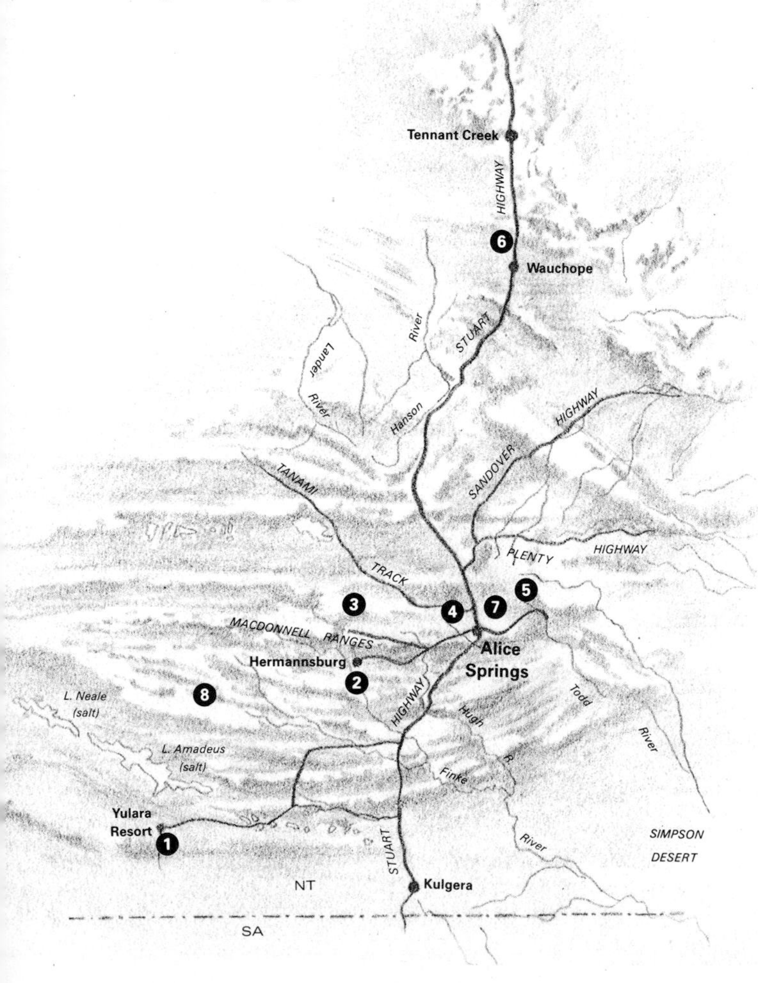

Finding a pass through the MacDonnells became important to Europeans in the 1870s, when an overland telegraph line was laid from Adelaide to Darwin as part of a link between the Australian colonies and Europe. Somehow the wire had to be taken through this hostile region, and a Morse code repeater station must be built there. In 1871 a surveyor found Heavitree Gap – and as a bonus, a bubbling spring in a dry riverbed. He called the river Todd, after his postmaster-general, and the spring Alice, for that dignitary's wife.

Establishment of the telegraph station prompted a surge of further exploration in the ranges, and one by one the many gaps and chasms gave up their secrets. Within a decade they were also giving up their precious waters, and many of their plants, to herds of cattle and sheep that were brought in on pastoral leases.

The retrieval of the MacDonnells' scenic treasures began after World War II when Alice Springs – called Stuart until 1933 – blossomed as a tourist centre. Pastoral leases over the important gap areas were revoked and most by now have been made national parks or nature reserves. But fencing is often needed: in drought the waterholes draw feral cattle and domestic herds from remaining stations, many kilometres away.

In the early days of Central Australian tourism the long side-trip from 'the Alice' to Ayers Rock and the Olgas was a hair-raising adventure – often enough more of a misadventure – that in itself became the high point of many a holiday. Now travellers speed, by air or over a reliable road, to the assured luxuries of an up-to-the-minute tourist village. There are no more surprises – except at the first sight of the great island mountains. In their awesome grandeur, the Rock and the Olgas are still not to be missed.

Featured parks	Pages	Featured parks	Pages
1 Uluru	50-55	5 Trephina Gorge	62-63
2 Finke Gorge	56-59	6 Devil's Marbles	64-65
3 Ormiston Gorge	60	7 Emily & Jessie Gaps	66-67
4 Simpson's Gap	61	8 King's Canyon	68

A ghost gum survives the harsh conditions of the eastern MacDonnell Ranges

Ayers Rock's grooves and holes result from erosion by a considerable rainfall, averaging about 200 mm but nearer 1000 mm in some years. The run-off near the base supports woodland growth with 'desert oak' casuarinas prominent. The Rock is nearly 9 km in circumference at ground level

Uluru National Park

Uluru takes its name from the title that Aborigines gave to Ayers Rock – once thought to be the world's biggest boulder, but identified now as the weathered sandstone peak of a buried range. Its immense bulk, changing in hue with every variation of light intensity and angle, rises from a flat landscape of sandplains, dunes and mulga scrub. Distinct walking tracks encircle the Rock. A route to the summit – 348 metres above the plain – takes most people about 45 minutes. Mt Olga, the highest in a cluster of domes 32 km west of Ayers Rock, rises 546 metres above ground. Climbing is not encouraged – walks into some of the dark gorges between the Olgas are strenuous enough. The formation is known as Katatjuta to the Aboriginal people of the region who are now formal owners of the 132 500 ha park. It is government-managed under a leaseback agreement. Points of mythological and ritual significance, as well as the park's curious geology, are explained on guided tours and in leaflets.

Right: Windblown sands and seeds, caught in hollows, permit some growth of desert grasses and shrubs near the summit of some of the rocks at Katatjuta

Furrowed depressions on a flank of the Rock are called Ngoru – ritual chest scars – by the Aborigines of the area. They occur because some layers of sandstone are tilted so sharply out of the ground that their ends present almost horizontal faces to the weather

Uluru National Park

Perspectives of Ayers Rock
Deceptive distances of the inland: Yulara Tourist Resort is 23 km from the Rock

An aerial view shows the weathering pattern and Uluru set in its landscape

Glowing at sunrise and sunset, on a stormy day the Rock is dark and mysterious, even more a place of ancestral significance

ULURU NATIONAL PARK

Ghost gum, gaining run-off moisture at the base of the Olgas, is one of very few eucalypts found away from rivers in the Northern Territory. Below: Morning light strikes the entrance to the Valley of the Winds, among the Olgas cluster

Tilted strata lines, as well as the vertical grooves of water erosion, can be seen on the Olgas. They are not made of sandstone, in the fashion of Ayers Rock, but of a boulder conglomerate. Both formations were deposited 500-600 million years ago, and thrust up by earth movements some 200 or 300 million years later

'Old Man' forms the northern prominence of Initiation Rock, where youths of the Aranda tribe underwent rituals marking their entry to manhood. By agreement with local Aborigines the rock may be climbed, but not defaced or littered

FINKE GORGE NATIONAL PARK

Arresting rock forms, carved in red sandstone by seasonal floodwaters and windblown sands, greet travellers after an arduous journey south from Hermannsburg and up the sandy bed of the Finke River. They have entered Palm Valley, the pride of a 46 000 ha park that otherwise consists of a sandplain wilderness. Not far up from the junction of Palm Creek with the Finke – both usually seen as strings of waterholes and soaks – stands Initiation Rock. Its intriguing features can be examined on a 500 metre walking circuit. Beyond is a striking ridge-ringed basin, the Amphitheatre.

Upstream the valley walls close in, reducing evaporation by winds and strong sunlight. Cycads and about 3000 specimens of a unique palm line the creekbed – relics of an age when the whole region enjoyed a wetter climate. A walking trail reaches for 7 km up the valley, accompanied for most of the way by a vehicle track.

Facing 'Old Woman', at the other end of Initiation Rock, a bowl of ritual significance is carved in sandstone

Finke Gorge National Park

Palm Valley's Livistona mariae *palms grow nowhere else in the world – though they are related to the cabbage-tree palm common on the east coast. In ancient times when seas invaded Central Australia and the general climate was moister, they were probably widespread.*

Left: Macrozamia cycads grow above Palm Creek, sometimes clinging high on the gorge face. Cycads evolved before the palm family: they bear cones rather than flowers, and individual trees have cones of only one sex

Silver-leaf cassia

Acetosa, an introduced weed run wild

Crumbling rock is colonised

Ormiston Gorge and Pound National Park

Tilted ridges of quartzite, reflecting a dozen colours from the presence of jasper and other silicate compounds, form the high rim of a basin 10 km across. Ormiston Creek and a tributary wander over the basin floor, seemingly puny and often not flowing at all. But in ancient times their floodwaters had the power to breach the western end of the pound, cutting a short but awesome gorge that is the focus of tourist attention in this 4600 ha park.

Sheer faces of red and yellow rock, broken into blocks, hem the boulder-strewn creekbed and a waterhole that is usually suitable for swimming, though not for drinking. There are formed walking tracks at Ormiston. A walk through the gorge – 2.5 km – can be extended into the pound by following the creek upstream. A longer trek east to Mt Giles (1283 metres) entails overnight camping; winter temperatures may fall below freezing point.

River red gums and bloodwoods dot the dry, sandy creekbed, leading out of the pound through a twisting gorge. Euros and wallabies live on the ridges, along with many reptiles

Evening light strikes broken ridges of the Chewings Range, reflecting (left) in a waterhole beneath

SIMPSON'S GAP NATIONAL PARK

Virtually on the outskirts of Alice Springs, this park is heavily used by tourists. The eastern wall of Simpson's Gap itself rises 250 metres above the sandy bed of Roe Creek – usually dry. Here and on Cassia Hill, reached by a 500 metre walk from the park road, travellers whose time is limited gain a reasonable idea of the nature of the MacDonnell Ranges.

A better representation – with some solitude and a chance to see the 31 000 ha park's varied wildlife – is available on the MacDonnell Range Track, leading away to the west from the Cassia Hill carpark. This 7 km walk through shrubland and low hills visits the picturesque Bond Gap. The round trip takes about 5 hours. Hardier walkers, equipped with water and overnight camping equipment, can visit other scenic gaps and a number of interesting waterholes.

Ghost gums (left) and river red gums (below) are thronged year-round by seed-eating birds including the vividly coloured Port Lincoln parrot. Waterfowl come as seasonal migrants

Broken sandstone ledges hold soil for hardy desert plants

Left: Waters of John Hayes Rock Hole, inviting to feral cattle, are often polluted

TREPHINA GORGE

Seasonal tributaries of the Todd River cut two contrasting gorges in a nature park of 1770 ha. Trephina Gorge itself is wide, and sunlight reflecting from its broken red walls – up to 100 metres high – can make it fiercely hot except in the shade of the river red gums growing beside Trephina Creek. John Hayes Rock Hole, formed by another creek in the west of the park, is narrow and shady. Water is held in a deep pool for months after summer rains have passed. Reptiles abound in the rocky environment and many birds of prey hunt overhead. Away from the popular gorges and their picnic areas, quiet vantage points on hills and ridges are easily reached on foot. There are marked walking tracks.

These Eggs of the Rainbow Serpent, as they are called in Aboriginal dreamtime myths, came into being as a single mass formed deep in the earth more than 1500 million years ago. It was cracked into rectangular blocks, then eroded by chemical action as water penetrated all of the joints. Corners took most weathering, so the blocks were slowly rounded. Now the outer layers of the exposed boulders are loosened by daily expansion and contraction. They flake off, leaving cracks in which more chemical erosion starts. In time the Devil's Marbles will be reduced to pebbles

DEVIL'S MARBLES

Huge tors of granite, piled high or strewn among hummock grasses, present a startling landmark on an arid and largely featureless plain of quartz gravel. The Marbles – some measuring 6 metres across – are best seen at sunset, when they glow a deep red. Their shade and dew run-off – winter nights are extremely cold – create a micro-climate in which small plants flourish and birds abound. A conservation park covers 1800 ha.

EMILY AND JESSIE GAPS

Jagged walls of red and white quartzite flank two river-cut openings in the narrowest part of the eastern MacDonnell Ranges, shading near-permanent waterholes. These important gathering places for Aranda Aborigines – Emily Gap has rock paintings on one wall – are also oases for numerous plants and birds. Fairy martins build their side-entry mud nests in rock crannies, and finches and diamond doves flock to river red and ghost gums along the sandy watercourses. Easy walks can be taken from picnic areas at both gaps, and swimming is possible if the creeks are running. The two sites are protected in a nature park of nearly 700 ha.

Desert daisies struggle in a pocket of soil

Early morning sun strikes the west wall of Jessie Gap. The creek's flow is brief but a pool remains for nearly all the year

Plants seize their opportunity around the waterhole at Emily Gap – named, like Jessie Gap, after a surveyor's wife

Left: Sheer quartzite faces, rising behind a ghost gum, were cut in a wetter age when a powerful river found a weak layer in uptilted rock strata

KING'S CANYON NATIONAL PARK

Ancient rivers have carved deep gashes, still sharp-edged, in a curiously domed plateau of the George Gill Range. A park of 76 000 ha, still in the early phase of development, has as its focus a maze of gorges occupied by the seasonal watercourses of King's Creek and its tributaries. These were not fully explored by Europeans until 1960. Rock pools and sandy soaks hold water for all or most of the year, supporting a luxuriant growth of palms, cycads, figs, ferns and cypress pine, attended by prolific birdlife. There is a formed track up to the plateau and its 'Lost City' of domes, some of them pitted with caves. Aborigines sheltered in them until early this century, leaving examples of their rock art. From there on the trail is marked by rock cairns. Visitors may also walk along the floor of the canyon to the base of the waterfall.

Domes studding the plateau surrounding King's Canyon are shaped by differential erosion of a sandstone block that remained horizontal when it was pushed up. Rivers in an age of much higher rainfall dissected its surface, allowing subsequent weathering – by windblown sand more than water – to work down through layers that are progressively harder

PARKS OF THE ALICE SPRINGS REGION

FACILITIES

Cabins

Caravan park

Equipped picnic area

Bush camping allowed

Lavatory building

Established campsite

Campsite but no car access

Note: Popular parks without campsites usually have public camping grounds nearby. If in doubt, call enquiries number.

PARK RATINGS No interest ✗ Some interest ✓ Major interest ✓✓ Outstanding ✓✓✓

Devil's Marbles Conservation Reserve

390 km N. Barkly weather district. Stuart Highway crosses reserve.
DESCRIPTION: Page 65.
BEST TIME: Autumn to spring.
ENQUIRIES: (089) 50 8211.
ADDRESS: NT Conservation Commission, Gap Rd, Alice Springs 5750.

Scenic enjoyment ✓✓✓
Day activities ✓
Family camping ✗
Hard bushwalking ✗

Emily and Jessie Gaps Nature Park

12 km E. Alice Springs weather district. Car access via Ross Highway.
DESCRIPTION: Page 66.
BEST TIME: Autumn to spring.
ENQUIRIES: (089) 50 8211.
ADDRESS: As for Devil's Marbles.

Scenic enjoyment ✓✓
Day activities ✓✓✓
Family camping ✗
Walking, climbing ✓

Finke Gorge National Park

140 km W. Alice Springs weather district. 4WD from Hermannsburg. Last section of access road can flood – check conditions with NT Emergency Services, 52 3833. Coach tours most days.
DESCRIPTION: Page 56.
NOTE: Carry water and all supplies.
BEST TIME: Autumn to spring.
ENQUIRIES: (089) 50 8211.
ADDRESS: As for Devil's Marbles.

Scenic enjoyment ✓✓✓
Day activities ✓✓
Family camping ✓✓
Walking, climbing ✓

King's Canyon National Park

325 km SW. Alice Springs weather district. Car access W from Stuart Highway via Wallara Ranch (unsealed).
DESCRIPTION: Page 68.
BEST TIME: Autumn to spring.
ENQUIRIES: (089) 50 8211.
ADDRESS: As for Devil's Marbles.

Scenic enjoyment ✓✓✓
Day activities ✓✓
Family camping ✓✓
Walking, climbing ✓✓

Ormiston Gorge and Pound National Park

130 km W. Alice Springs weather district. Car access via Larapinta Drive and Glen Helen Road. Park approach road can flood – check conditions with NT Emergency Services, 52 3833. Coach tours available.
DESCRIPTION: Page 60.
NOTE: Carry drinking water.
BEST TIME: Autumn to spring.
ENQUIRIES: (089) 50 8211.
ADDRESS: As for Devil's Marbles.

Scenic enjoyment ✓✓
Day activities ✓✓
Family camping ✓✓
Walking, climbing ✓✓

Simpson's Gap National Park

8 km W. Alice Springs weather district. Car access off Larapinta Drive. Coach tours daily.
DESCRIPTION: Page 61.
NOTE: Total fire ban – gas cooking only.
BEST TIME: Autumn to spring.
ENQUIRIES: (089) 52 3131.
ADDRESS: As for Devil's Marbles.

Scenic enjoyment ✓✓✓
Day activities ✓✓✓
Family camping ✗
Walking, climbing ✓✓

Trephina Gorge Nature Park

75 km E. Alice Springs weather district. Car access off Ross Highway. Coach tours most days.
DESCRIPTION: Page 63.
NOTE: Carry in water.
BEST TIME: Autumn to spring.
ENQUIRIES: (089) 50 8211.
ADDRESS: As for Devil's Marbles.

Scenic enjoyment ✓✓
Day activities ✓✓
Family camping ✗
Walking, climbing ✓

Uluru National Park

450 km SW. Alice Springs weather district. Car access W from Stuart Highway on Lasseter Highway. Entrance fee. Buses, airline flights daily to Yulara Tourist Resort.
DESCRIPTION: Page 50.
NOTE: Camping and accommodation in Yulara Tourist Resort, outside park.
WARNING: Ayers Rock climbers should be realistic about their fitness. Wear rubber-soled shoes and keep to marked track.
VISITOR CENTRE: Yulara Tourist Resort.
BEST TIME: Autumn to spring.
ENQUIRIES: (089) 56 2988.
ADDRESS: ANPWS, Box 119, Yulara, NT 5751.

Scenic enjoyment ✓✓✓
Day activities ✓
Family camping ✗
Walking, climbing ✓✓

(1) Devil's Marbles Conservation Reserve
(2) Emily and Jessie Gaps Nature Park
(3) Finke Gorge NP
(4) King's Canyon NP
(5) Ormiston Gorge and Pound NP
(6) Simpson's Gap NP
(7) Trephina Gorge Nature Park
(8) Uluru NP

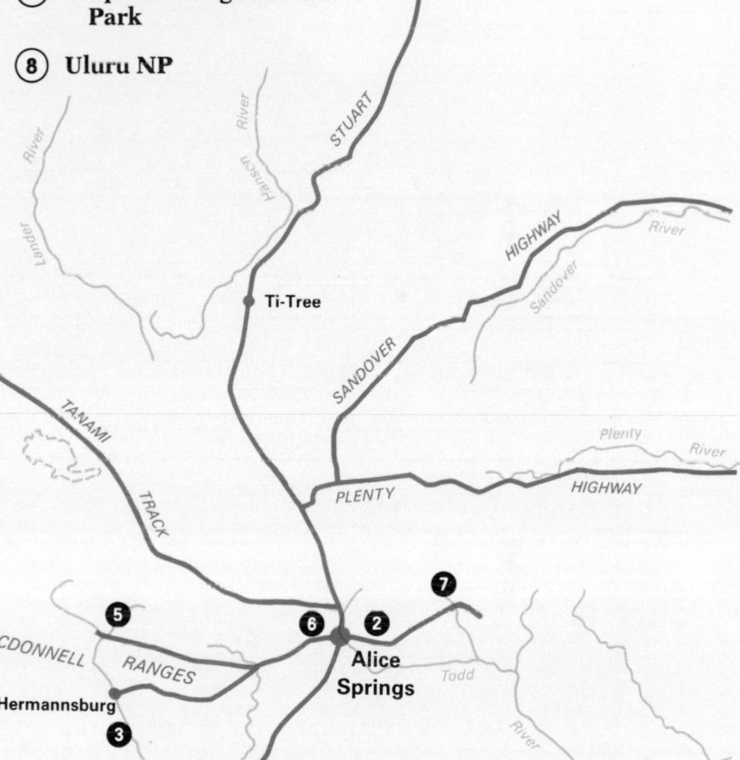

Bearded dragon – mouth agape, beard erect, ready to frighten off its enemies

Juvenile perentie – full-grown specimens average 1.6 metres but can reach 2.5 metres in length

Desert death adder – during the day is usually part-buried in sand and difficult to detect; also unwilling to move, so beware

Reptiles of the inland

Although not 'cold-blooded', most reptiles have low body temperatures. Their warmth must come largely from outside sources; they cannot cope with extreme conditions. After the chill of the night, they are lethargic until warmed by the sun, and as they warm so their colours become lighter. The desired temperature established, they then alternately bask and shelter to maintain it. Such inefficient circulation systems mean that few reptiles can sustain any rapid activity for long.

Thorny devil, Moloch horridus – neither horrid nor devilish, just a tiny slow moving anteater

Central netted dragon – stays on open ground even in high temperatures when others shelter

Centralian blue-tongued lizard – lives among spinifex in sandy desert and has taken on the colouring of the landscape

DARWIN REGION

Midsummer magic in the monsoon wetlands

BULLDUST – clay in particles as fine as talcum powder – billows with every movement on river flats east of Darwin. It is springtime, and no useful rains have fallen since March. But out over the Timor Sea the clouds are building. By November, heat and soaring humidity enforce a lethargy on most forms of life. Birds reduce their activity. Ants are busy, though – moving to higher ground. The Big Wet is on its way.

Late in the month the first storms break, short but violently intense. Sheets of rain blot out any sight except the flicker of lightning. After New Year, storms brew up every few days. Saturated, the clay plains disappear under water – recalling ancient seas that used to lap the Arnhem Land Escarpment. Lilies, rushes and wild rice spread over the shallows. Waterfowl in hundreds of thousands start a squabbling race for nesting sites. Growth is everywhere in four wet months. On firmer margins trees and vines that were leafless – including even a deciduous eucalypt, the white gum – produce foliage of exaggerated size, quickly followed by flowers and fruit. On wooded savannahs out of reach of the floods the grasses appear. Their nodding seed heads may stand 3 metres high, hiding the huge termite mounds that dominated the winter landscape.

The Wet ends abruptly, and often with vehemence. The autumn return of high-pressure weather patterns may be heralded by southerly gales and rains that flatten the grasses, hastening their death and the desiccation that must follow. By May they are ready as fuel for fires that sweep through most Top End woodlands every winter, sparked by dry electrical storms. Meanwhile the wetlands shrink to billabongs, crowding and barely sustaining fish, amphibians, crocodiles and resident birdlife.

This remorseless regime of monsoon and drought militates against successful settlement of the region. Most attempts to grow crops have failed. The season is too short and diseases are rife. Soils are leached by the perpetual cycle of saturation and evaporation. Even the occupation of Darwin is sometimes threatened: tropical cyclones have wrecked it on four occasions.

Europeans have had an impact on the wetlands, however – and brought them close to ecological disaster. Crocodiles were protected only just in time. Their destruction by hunters would have destroyed the natural balance of food supplies. Even more damaging have been the tramplings of vast herds of water buffalo, descended from imported domestic stock. They crush plant roots and convert clear billabongs into mud.

Under control now in Kakadu National Park, buffalo are at last bringing benefits. The Aboriginal owners derive income from a thriving industry based on what is probably the world's most unusual park facility – an abattoir.

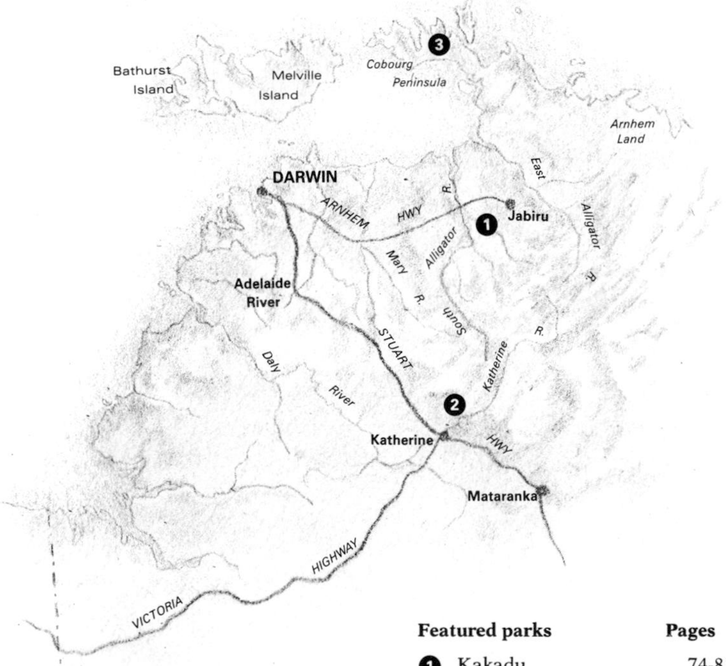

Featured parks	Pages
❶ Kakadu	74-81
❷ Katherine Gorge	82-87
❸ Cobourg Peninsula (Gurig)	88

Your access and facilities guide to all national parks in this region is on page 89

Wetlands of Kakadu – born and reborn in an annual transformation

KAKADU NATIONAL PARK

From the wild heights of Arnhem Land and its forbidding escarpment walls, across the Alligator Rivers floodplains to the mangrove-choked shores of Van Diemen Gulf, the sweep of Kakadu is immense. Proclamation of Stage 2 in 1984, five years after the park was established, more than doubled its size to 1.3 million ha. The biological richness of this area beggars description. Here are well over 900 plant species, nearly 300 kinds of birds, 75 reptiles, 50 native mammals, 30 amphibians, a quarter of all Australian freshwater fish and uncounted thousands of insect species. Kakadu also preserves the most widespread area of very early human culture, with evidence of continuous occupation for well over 20 000 years. Its galleries of intricate and varied prehistoric rock art alone would merit the park's World Heritage ranking.

Development of the Stage 2 area for visitors is expected to be a slow process, and probably a limited one. Tourist movements remain concentrated on the upstream reaches of the East Alligator and South Alligator Rivers and on higher country around Nourlangie Rock. Pressure is heavy on popular scenic and camping areas in the winter months. Solitude can be found on some long walking trails, but routes must be discussed with rangers.

Acacia in an upland forest

The Arnhem Land Escarpment presents a formidable barrier to the east and south. Seasonal creeks flow from the plateau

Right: Angular faces on Nourlangie Rock are evidence of recent falls

KATHERINE GORGE NATIONAL PARK

More than 60 000 people every dry season take boat tours of the beautiful Katherine River, winding between walls of ancient sandstone that tower up to 100 metres high. Private craft are allowed and easily launched. The canyon, cut here and there by the narrow chasms of tributary creeks, reaches for about 12 km upstream before opening into a wider valley dissecting the southernmost reaches of the Arnhem Land Plateau. Ferns and figs cling in moist crevices of the rock walls; paperbarks and pandanus palms take advantage of sandbanked bends. There is no room to walk up the gorge at water level, but trails leading east from a downstream lookout divert into forested gullies that reach the river at points that offer safe swimming. These routes take 1-4 hours one way. Overnight hikers can continue east for two more days. But the most ambitious of them head north through the 180 000 ha park, along the plateau edge overlooking the valley of Crystal and Seventeen Mile Creeks. Then they traverse westward to the swampy headwaters of the Edith River, coming out after five days at Edith Falls.

Tranquil and depleted in the dry season, the Katherine River has whirlpools and 2-metre waves when summer rains flow in

Wind action in the dry season and torrential downpours in the 'Wet' cause a steady crumbling at the edge of the Arnhem Land Escarpment. Its sandstones and conglomerates, laid down about 1500 million years ago, were compacted and pushed up in a bed of fractured blocks 500 metres deep. Slender palms reaching up from the valley floor are isolated relatives of east coast cabbage-tree palms

GURIG NATIONAL PARK

Cobourg Peninsula reaches west from the coastal margins of Arnhem Land, enclosing Van Diemen Gulf. The whole peninsula and its neighbouring islands, with a total area of 220 000 ha, form a national park under legislation guaranteeing the rights of traditional Aboriginal owners. They collect trophy fees from operators of air-charter 'safaris', bringing in tourists from Darwin to shoot water buffalo – formerly domesticated Indian oxen. Also on the peninsula are wild herds of banteng cattle from Bali, rusa deer from Java and ponies from Timor. All were imported to sustain military garrisons at Raffles Bay (1827-29) and Port Essington (1838-49).

Tropical eucalypt forest dominated by Darwin stringybark and woollybutt covers most of Gurig's flat or gently undulating expanses. But there are also patches of monsoon vineforest, kentia palm thickets, swampy paperbark woodlands and highly developed mangrove forests. Each spring the peninsula is the first southern hemisphere port of call for scores of thousands of migratory birds, and its forests abound with resident species. Dugong and turtles frequent nearshore waters along with many fish species – and big saltwater crocodiles.

Creeks discharge high volumes of water long after the wet season, keeping open gaps in the fringing mangroves and maintaining channels where boats can nose in to sandy beaches

Left: Paperbark forest surrounds clay pans. In summer these are swamps, teeming with native and migrant waterfowl

PARKS OF THE DARWIN REGION

FACILITIES

Cabins

Caravan park

Equipped picnic area

Bush camping allowed

Lavatory building

Established campsite

Campsite but no car access

Note: Popular parks without campsites usually have public camping grounds nearby. If in doubt, call enquiries number.

PARK RATINGS No interest ✖ Some interest ✔ Major interest ✔✔ Outstanding ✔✔✔

1. **Cobourg Peninsula Aboriginal Land & Sanctuary (Gurig NP)**
2. **Gregory NP**
3. **Kakadu NP**
4. **Katherine Gorge NP**
5. **Keep River NP**

Cobourg Peninsula Aboriginal Land and Sanctuary (Gurig National Park)

200 km NE. Darwin weather district. Restricted 4WD access through Arnhem Land and Murgenella – **Northern Land Council permit needed.** Road usually impassable December-June. Limited 4WD access within park. Boat access safe only in dry season. Air access from Darwin.

PERMIT NEEDED TO ENTER PARK.

DESCRIPTION: Page 88.

NOTES: Permit needed for bush camping. Water sources limited – area unsuitable for long walking.

WARNING: Do not swim – area infested with saltwater crocodiles. Box jellyfish may be present November-May.

BEST TIME: July to October.

ENQUIRIES: (089) 22 0211.

ADDRESS: NT Conservation Commission, Box 38496, Winnellie 5789.

Scenic enjoyment ✔✔
Day activities ✖
Family camping ✔
Hard bushwalking ✖

Gregory National Park

600 km S, 200 km SW from Katherine on Victoria Highway to Victoria River Crossing or 290 km to Timber Creek. Katherine weather district.

This huge park of more than 1 million ha protects many Aboriginal and some European heritage sites. It is in the early stages of development and facilities and vehicle access are limited. There is an information centre at Timber Creek.

A commercial boat tour explores the spectacular Victoria River Gorge from Victoria River Crossing. Fishing enthusiasts can reach the river at Big Horse Creek landing.

BEST TIME: Winter.

ENQUIRIES: (089) 72 1799.

ADDRESS: NT Conservation Commission, Box 344, Katherine 5780.

Scenic enjoyment ✔✔✔
Day activities ✔✔
Family camping ✖
Hard bushwalking ✔✔✔

Kakadu National Park

250 km E (to Jabiru). Darwin weather district. Car access in all weather by Arnhem Highway to Jabiru. Most internal roads closed in wet season. Check conditions with NT Emergency Services. (84 4455). Air tours from Darwin, Jabiru.

DESCRIPTION: Page 74.

NOTES: Permit needed for bush camping. Billabong water must be boiled before drinking. Bag limits on fishing – no nets or set lines allowed.

WARNINGS: Do not swim – dangerous crocodiles throughout park. Tidal currents and sandbars in East and South Alligator Rivers hazardous to small craft.

VISITOR CENTRE: Near Jabiru.

BEST TIME: May to September.

ENQUIRIES: (089) 79 2101.

ADDRESS: Box 71, Jabiru 5796.

Scenic enjoyment ✔✔✔
Day activities ✔✔✔
Family camping ✔✔✔
Hard bushwalking ✔✔

Katherine Gorge National Park

330 km S. Katherine weather district. Car access by Stuart Highway and sealed road from Katherine, closed only by major floods. Car access to Edith Falls by sealed road turning off 40 km N of Katherine (may be closed in wet season).

DESCRIPTION: Page 82.

NOTE: Permit required for bush camping – must be obtained by 1530. Bush camping not allowed within 8 km of visitor centre.

VISITOR CENTRE: At camping grounds.

BEST TIME: May to August.

ENQUIRIES: (089) 72 1799.

ADDRESS: NT Conservation Commission, Box 344, Katherine 5780.

Scenic enjoyment ✔✔✔
Day activities ✔✔
Family camping ✔✔
Hard bushwalking ✔✔

Keep River National Park

800 km SW. Katherine weather district. Entry 3 km E of NT/WA border on northern side of Victoria Highway.

Highly eroded sandstone bluffs and ridges along the gorge of the Keep River and its tributaries dominate a 26 000 ha park. Tropical woodlands of low eucalypt, native kapok and grevillea grow sparsely in dry, rocky areas. Stringybark and bloodwood are widespread on the valley floors, enormous boabs punctuate the landscape and more luxuriant vegetation fringes pools on seasonal watercourses inhabited by freshwater crocodiles. Weather-worn caverns in the sandstone contain Aboriginal engravings and vividly coloured rock paintings.

NOTE: No water supplies in park.

BEST TIME: Winter.

ENQUIRIES: (089) 72 1799.

ADDRESS: NT Conservation Commission, Box 344, Katherine 5780.

Scenic enjoyment ✔✔
Day activities ✔
Family camping ✔✔
Hard bushwalking ✔✔

Figs and eucalypts crowd Windjana's pools, but sandbanks give walkers some access

WINDJANA GORGE NATIONAL PARK

Kapok bush flower

Jagged walls of limestone – the fossilised coral of a reef that flanked an invading sea perhaps 300 million years ago – frame a narrow canyon where the Lennard River cuts through the Napier Range. The river flows only in the 'Wet', when the 2100 ha park is inaccessible. But cool, deep pools remain in the shade of the walls, which rise as high as 90 metres. Mixed woodlands of river red gums, other eucalypts and many tropical fig species flourish on sandbanks and spread up into crannies of the heavily weathered rock. Caves above shelter examples of Aboriginal art. Beyond the gorge the woodlands soon give way to a savannah of tussock grasses sparsely dotted with eucalypts, bauhinia and an occasional baobab. Harmless freshwater crocodiles are frequently seen in the gorge, living off the fish that abound in its pools. Colourful birds include jabiru, great bowerbirds, three cockatoo species and many herons. Walks are easy in the gorge area and one pool is usually suitable for swimming. The road passes a ruined pioneer homestead where Pigeon, an Aboriginal Ned Kelly, killed a policeman in 1894.

Beyond the gorge, which extends for 4 km through the Napier Range, the Lennard River's dry bed winds across a semi-arid plain. But its grasses are edible tussocks – not spiky 'spinifex'

Left: Vertical grooves in the canyon walls result from trickles of rainwater containing carbonic acid, which dissolves limestone

GEIKIE GORGE NATIONAL PARK

Campers by the tranquil dry-season pool just south of Geikie Gorge can tell at a glance how they would fare here in the summertime 'Wet'. When the Fitzroy River is flowing, it pushes such a volume of water through the narrow canyon that the weathered limestone walls are bleached to heights of more than 16 metres. River red gums and freshwater mangroves bear muddy watermarks

9 metres above the campsite. The mangroves are not the only biological curiosity: the Fitzroy has sawfish and stingray – sea creatures 350 km from any ocean. Their ancestors, like the corals that built the Napier and Oscar Ranges, were inhabitants of seas that reached around the Kimberleys and extended into Central Australia some 300 million years ago. They adapted to a slow transition from salt to fresh water. Also present in big numbers are archer fish, which have mastered the art of shooting down flying insects with jets of water.

Riverbanks in the 3000 ha park are a declared fauna and flora sanctuary. Visitors are not allowed to set foot within 200 metres of the water on either side, except for an open area of the west bank where the camping ground is sited. A short walking trail loops up to the gorge wall, near boat boarding and launching points. Two-hour boat tours, starting at 0900 and 1430 daily, take in 16 km of the gorge. Private boating is allowed but rigidly controlled: craft may head upriver only in the afternoon, in slow procession behind the tour barge. Swimming is permitted, but the sanctuary restrictions apply on going ashore. The fish and crocodiles of the waterholes present no danger to humans.

Mangroves fringe the gorge walls, which show deep weathering (far left) down vertical cracks

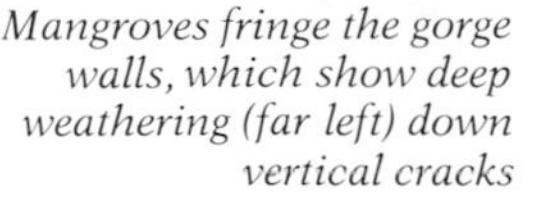

Streamlined for its diving role, a darter rests from fishing. Over 100 bird species seen in the park include kingfishers, herons, great bowerbirds, warblers, parrots and even two kinds of sea eagles

Geikie Gorge National Park

The freshwater crocodile is small, and aggressive only when the female is nesting. This one basks below the mud nests of fairy martins

Annual floodwaters of the Fitzroy River wash the lower gorge walls creamy white, below the stains of decomposed plant matter. The dividing line rises as the canyon narrows, showing how the flow is compressed and forced up. Rainfall in the Fitzroy's catchments is seldom more than 500 mm a year – but they cover an area over half the size of Victoria. The flood peak discharge from Geikie Gorge (pronounced 'Geeky' with a hard 'g') is 29 000 cubic metres a second

Chinks in the limestone near the tunnel entrance throw light on to a pool of spring water

TUNNEL CREEK NATIONAL PARK

The coolest walk in the Kimberleys is not to everyone's taste. Tunnel Creek cuts an underground path for 750 metres through the limestone of the Oscar Range. It is spacious enough – 15 metres wide and never less than 3 metres high. But its clammy darkness can give rise to claustrophobic panic, made more disturbing if the thousands of bats that live here in some seasons are aroused into twittering flight. Walking parties need a powerful torch. They see stalactites descending from the roof in many places, and they may be able to spot Aboriginal paintings. Springs make a permanent flow of water – increased dangerously if the creek itself starts to run.

Halfway along the tunnel the roof has collapsed, allowing bats access to their dark roosting places. At least five species frequent the 90 ha park, including ghost bats and flying foxes (fruit bats)

FACILITIES

Cabins

Caravan park

Equipped picnic area

Bush camping allowed

Lavatory building

Established campsite

Campsite but no car access

Note: Popular parks without campsites usually have public camping grounds nearby. If in doubt, call enquiries number.

PARK RATINGS No interest × Some interest ✔ Major interest ✔✔ Outstanding ✔✔✔

PARKS OF THE DERBY AND KUNUNURRA REGIONS

Bungle Bungle National Park
175 km S of Kununurra. Kimberley weather district. Access off Great Northern Highway 253 km S of Kununurra and 112 km N of Halls Creek on the Spring Creek track. The 55 km to the massif takes about 5 hours. Vehicle access 4WD only. Best viewed from air; flights from both Kununurra and Halls Creek.

Bungle Bungle, gazetted as a national park in 1987, is a spectacular wilderness. It has extraordinary rock formations, unique vegetation, a wealth of wildlife and strong links with Aboriginal culture.

NOTE: Facilities are minimal but a ranger station operates seasonally. Before visiting by road contact the Kununurra office. When in the park advise the ranger of your movements: keep to main tracks. Be self sufficient in all aspects of travel.
BEST TIME: Winter.
ENQUIRIES: (091) 68 0200 or 68 1177.
ADDRESS: As for Windjana Gorge.
Scenic enjoyment ✔✔✔
Day activities ×
Family camping ×
Hard bushwalking ✔✔✔

Drysdale River National Park
350 km NW of Kununurra. Kimberley weather district.
VEHICULAR ACCESS VIRTUALLY IMPOSSIBLE; visits have been made by canoe and by helicopter.

Little was known about this remote park of 440 000 ha until a major expedition in 1975 made its way over rough terrain midway between the Kimberley's humid northwest and the semi-arid eastern region. Scientists collected 600 plant species and noted scores of mammals, freshwater fish, reptiles and birds, as well as over 2000 insect species. Low eucalypt forests and woodlands dominate the vegetation with patches of vine thicket around swamps and along watercourses.
ENQUIRIES: (091) 68 0200.
ADDRESS: As for Windjana Gorge.

Geikie Gorge National Park
280 km E of Derby, 20 km N of Fitzroy Crossing. Kimberley weather district. Car access off Great Northern Highway from Fitzroy Crossing.
DESCRIPTION: Page 98.
NOTES: Boat speed limit 5 knots. Fee charged for launching and for campsites.
BEST TIME: Winter, spring.
ENQUIRIES: (091) 91 5121.
ADDRESS: C/o P.O., Fitzroy Crossing 6765.
Scenic enjoyment ✔✔✔
Day activities ✔✔
Family camping ✔✔
Hard bushwalking ×

1 Bungle Bungle NP
2 Drysdale River NP
3 Geikie Gorge NP
4 Hidden Valley NP
5 Tunnel Creek NP
6 Windjana Gorge NP
7 Wolfe Creek Crater NP

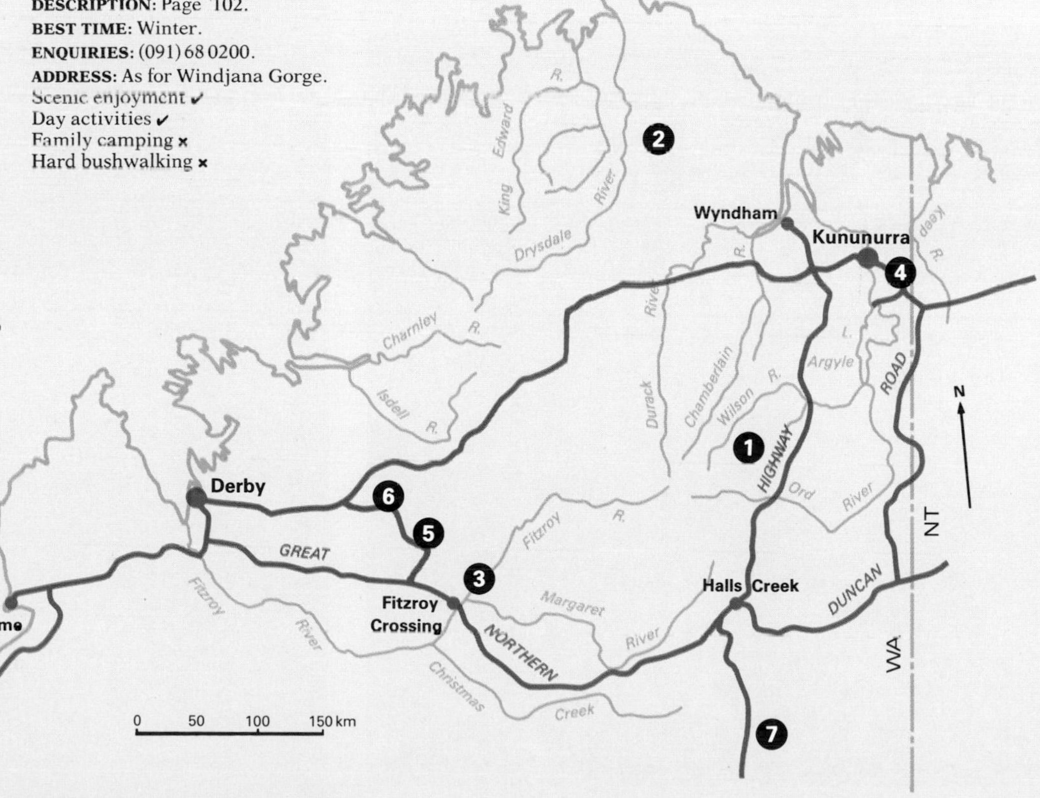

Hidden Valley National Park
3 km E of Kununurra. Kimberley weather district. Car access from town centre.

The road to Hidden Valley drops from Kununurra's outskirts between steep escarpment walls to the broad river flat of Lily Creek. In the dry winter season the creekbed is a stony course dotted with pools fed by permanent springs that trickle from craggy rock faces. Walkers follow a network of interlocking valleys cutting the park's 1800 ha of hilly country. Hummock grasses and scattered baobabs and eucalypts cover stony slopes.
BEST TIME: Winter, spring.
ENQUIRIES: (091) 68 0200.
ADDRESS: As for Windjana Gorge.
Scenic enjoyment ✔✔
Day activities ✔
Family camping ×
Hard bushwalking ✔

Tunnel Creek National Park
180 km E of Derby. Kimberley weather district. Car access off Gibb River road 125 km E of Derby.
DESCRIPTION: Page 102.
BEST TIME: Winter.
ENQUIRIES: (091) 68 0200.
ADDRESS: As for Windjana Gorge.
Scenic enjoyment ✔
Day activities ✔
Family camping ×
Hard bushwalking ×

Windjana Gorge National Park
150 km E of Derby. Kimberley weather district. Car access off Gibb River road 125 km E of Derby.
DESCRIPTION: Page 96.
NOTE: No water supplies in park.
BEST TIME: Winter, spring.
ENQUIRIES: (091) 68 0200.
ADDRESS: CALM regional office, Box 242, Kununurra 6743.
Scenic enjoyment ✔✔✔
Day activities ✔✔
Family camping ✔
Hard bushwalking ×

WARNING
Outback travellers MUST be self sufficient in all aspects of their trip. Their transceivers should preferably have Royal Flying Doctor Service radio frequencies.

Wolfe Creek Crater National Park
510 km S of Kununurra, 150 km S of Halls Creek. Kimberley weather district. Car access off Great Northern Highway 16 km S of Halls Creek.

A huge iron meteorite, exploding with the power of several times its weight in TNT, dug deep into the earth's surface to create a crater 850 metres wide. Arid conditions in the flat desert country of the 1500 ha park have kept erosion at a low level. The crater rim, 50 metres high, retains its gently sloping symmetry, though windblown sand has filled much of the inner dip. The crater is named after a meandering watercourse to the east.
NOTE: No water supplies in park.
BEST TIME: Winter.
ENQUIRIES: (091) 68 0200.
ADDRESS: As for Windjana Gorge.
Scenic enjoyment ✔✔
Day activities ×
Family camping ×
Hard bushwalking ×

Flowers as food

Because of its big variety of nectar-rich native flowering shrubs and trees Western Australia provides a regular banquet, as well as a home, for honeyeaters. The birds feast on the nectar and pollen of banksia, dryandra, grevillea, hakea, kangaroo paw, emu bush, and flowering eucalypts and paperbarks. But not all honeyeaters are of the feathered variety; there is also the honey-possum, unique to the southwest. In some ways this tiny creature seems to mirror some of the nectar-eating birds: it too has a long brush-tipped tongue and, in place of a beak, a narrow, long, pointed snout which it buries in the flower. It then rapidly flicks its tongue in and out to get the pollen – just like the birds.

Banksia grandis

Honey-possum on banksia

Banksia ashbyi

Kangaroo paw

New Holland honeyeater samples bottlebrush

Honeyeaters feed on the flowers of the mighty karri while one race of red-tailed black cockatoo lives in karri forest crown and eats eucalypt seeds

Bloodwood flower Grevillea below

CARNARVON & PORT HEDLAND REGIONS

Miners spur interest in a long-neglected land

PURISTS in conservation may shudder at the very idea of iron-ore mining leases in Hamersley Range National Park, and of surveyors and prospectors roaming in the other parks and reserves of the northwest. The fact is that the miners had prior claims in this harsh, arid corner. Their activities have brought it back to life.

Without the roads, airstrips and water bores built by mining companies and the local knowledge they accumulated, it is doubtful whether ecologists could have gained enough appreciation of the area to judge what was most worth conserving. Certainly, from a public point of view, the unusual natural features of the northwest would have remained unreachable and largely unknown. Touring is a practical proposition only because of the improved communications and other amenities that came with a huge investment in mineral extraction, processing and export facilities.

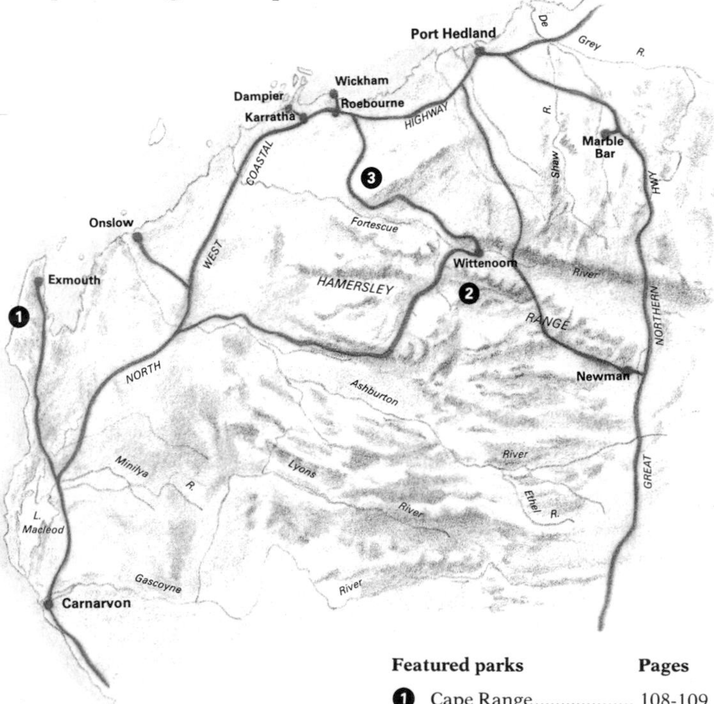

Your access and facilities guide to all national parks in these regions is on page 115

Featured parks	Pages
❶ Cape Range	108-109
❷ Hamersley Range	110-113
❸ Millstream-Chichester	114

Oddly enough, this was the very first part of Australia to be frequented by Europeans. Dirk Hartog commanded the first authenticated landing in 1616, near Carnarvon, and his fellow-Dutchmen came to know the northwest coast well in the following decades. John Brooks, an Englishman, navigated North West Cape waters as early as 1622. William Dampier explored ashore in 1688 and 1699 – first as a pirate, then as a Royal Navy captain.

Every adventurer noted tides of phenomenal range and frightening power. Inland they saw a parched, hostile environment holding no prospect of trade or treasure. Ill-starred attempts in the 1860s to grow cotton and raise beef cattle reinforced that view. Even the frantic military efforts of World War II brought few lasting changes.

The transformation started with oil. Australia's first commercial field was discovered in 1952 at Rough Range, close to what is now Cape Range National Park. This park's only formed roads were built for exploratory surveys; its Shothole Canyon car park was a drilling platform. Nearby Exmouth emerged as the first of the northwestern boomtowns, soon to be eclipsed by port after port to the east. Though their impetus comes from continued development in petroleum and iron ore exploitation, they have become tourist destinations in their own right.

A less publicised industry, salt production, commands attention at both Carnarvon and Port Hedland. Vast evaporation beds, marked by dazzling white storage mounds, are the most efficient on earth. They take advantage of a hot and extraordinarily cloudless climate. The sun beats down for well over 3500 hours in some years. Drenching summer monsoons of the 'Top End' do not reach this northwest corner: its usually meagre rainfalls show slight peaks in both winter and summer. Prolonged heavy rains are rare. Perhaps that is fortunate – they come only with violent tropical cyclones.

Shales and conglomerates of Dales Gorge, in Hamersley Range National Park, were laid down 2000 million years ago

Sheltered by a distant reef, gentle waters wash coral fragments on to Mandu Mandu Beach. The park's coastline reaches for 50 km

Limestone walls screen Yardie Creek's mangrove-lined estuary

CAPE RANGE NATIONAL PARK

Termites take over on heathlands towards North West Cape

From a high spine of limestone running almost to the US Navy communications base at North West Cape, seasonal creeks cut deep gullies to Exmouth Gulf and the Indian Ocean. A park of 50 000 ha occupies the ridge, its seaward slopes and a narrow coastal plain. Though annual rainfall is meagre, cyclonic storms may flood the gullies in summer. Some winter rains can also be expected. But for most of the time the area is parched. Tourists and campers have to plan ahead because the only assured water supply is a bore near Mangrove Creek, about 5 km inside the northern boundary. Both Mangrove and Yardie Creeks are excellent areas for bird watching and botanising.

The park's chief attractions are its fishing camps, strung out along an unsealed road that runs the full length of the ocean boundary. Cross-country walking is not advised, but safe trails are marked along a short section of the range crest, giving good views of the eastern canyons and the gulf. These are reached by two roads turning inland between Learmonth and Exmouth.

Sturt's desert rose, a wild cotton, flourishes in rocky creek gullies, but acacia and eucalypt scrubs predominate

Broken rock litters the shelved walls and floor of Red Gorge, leading west to its junction with three other creek-cut chasms just as deep

Clumps of triodia 'spinifex' deck the heights of Dales Gorge (above and right). Bands of harder rock cross its bed, creating falls and rapids when the creek runs high after the summer wet season, and trapping the cool permanent waters of Circular Pool

HAMERSLEY RANGE NATIONAL PARK

Plunging chasms break the northern scarp of the sun-baked Hamersley Range, creating surprising oases in an arid plateau of spiky hummock grass and mulga. Scree slopes and steep walls – up to 100 metres high – of conglomerates and shales are darkened by deep bands of rich iron ore and seams of blue asbestos. They shade cool, tree-lined creekbeds.

Of 20 major gorges, most of those accessible to visitors have permanent pools. Dales Gorge, a favourite with campers, is noted for its Fortescue Falls and Circular Pool. Yampire and Kalamina Gorges are also popular. But the sight not to be missed in this huge park of more than 600 000 ha is the crossroads of chasms where Red Gorge is joined by Weano, Hancock and Joffre Gorges. There are walking trails into Red Gorge from Weano and Dales campsites; easy trails from all four camping grounds lead into nearby gorges. Energetic walkers can ascend Mt Bruce by a path that takes about 2 hours.

HAMERSLEY RANGE NATIONAL PARK

Seen from north of the park, near Wittenoom, the range rises in flat-bedded layers. They are composed of sediments deposited up to 2000 million years ago

Winter sunshine beats into Weano Gorge. Night temperatures may fall below freezing point

Termite mounds are the most obvious signs of animal life above the gorges. Birds are common but most marsupials and reptiles hide in the daytime

Fed by meagre summer rains, the Fortescue River dries up quickly. But an aquifer of ground water runs beside it, supplying the permanent pools at Millstream through springs. Below: Beyond the Fortescue floodplain is country much more characteristic of the arid Pilbara. The Chichester Range rises in the background

MILLSTREAM-CHICHESTER NATIONAL PARK

Four deep, spring-fed pools in the bed of the Fortescue River, descending in succession like a staircase, make a setting that travellers through the hot and dusty Pilbara find difficult to leave. Forests of river red gum and a tropical paperbark called cajeput reach across mudflats of the river's seasonal floodplain. Here and there are tall fan palms *Livistona alfredii*, a species found only at Millstream and in two localities nearby. Warblers and tree-creepers flock to the trees.

Northeast of Millstream, stony hills rise towards the Chichester Range. It is harsh country, sparsely wooded above a ground cover of hummock grasses. But the range itself, heavily eroded by ephemeral creeks, has some cool, densely vegetated gorges. From Snake Creek – one of two camping sites – a 20-minute walk to Python Pool offers a good sampling of gorge scenery. The park, formed by the enlargement of Millstream's boundaries to join up with the former Chichester Range National Park, has a total area of 200 000 ha. It is no place to roam from established routes without ranger advice.

PARKS OF THE CARNARVON AND PORT HEDLAND REGIONS

FACILITIES

Cabins · Caravan park · Equipped picnic area · Bush camping allowed · Lavatory building · Established campsite · Campsite but no car access

Note: Popular parks without campsites usually have public camping grounds nearby. If in doubt, call inquiries number.

PARK RATINGS No interest ✗ Some interest ✓ Major interest ✓✓ Outstanding ✓✓✓

Cape Range National Park

400 km N of Carnarvon. Pilbara weather district. Car access off Learmonth-Exmouth road or 30 km past Exmouth.

DESCRIPTION: Page 109.

NOTES: Fee charged for camping. Take chemical toilet, gas cooker. Fires prohibited.

WARNING: Terrain rugged, waterless. Temperatures often higher in gorges. Beware of heat exhaustion and do not take long walks without informing other people.

BEST TIME: May to September.

ENQUIRIES: (099) 49 1428.

ADDRESS: Box 55, Exmouth 6707.

Scenic enjoyment ✓
Day activities ✓✓
Family camping ✓
Hard bushwalking ✗

Christmas Island National Park

800 km NW of Port Hedland. Air access by government charter flights weekly from Perth – enquiries (09) 325 4488.

South of Java at the same latitude as Darwin, a park of 1600 ha occupies about one-eighth of an island that has been widely quarried for phosphate. It protects seabird rookeries and tall rainforests along with an unusual variety of landcrabs including the world's biggest – the tree climbing robber crab, weighing up to 3 kg and measuring 1 metre between leg tips. Two walking trails and a 4WD track traverse the park, which has permanent streams in one area. Big southerly swells make its section of the coastline dangerous.

BEST TIME: Autumn to spring.

ENQUIRIES: (062) 46 6211.

ADDRESS: ANPWS, Box 636, Canberra City 2601.

Scenic enjoyment ✓✓✓
Day activities ✓
Family camping ✗
Hard bushwalking ✓

Collier Range National Park

600 km S of Port Hedland. Gascoyne weather district. Great Northern Highway crosses E end of park; dirt access road.

High, deeply eroded ridges and domes dominate a park of nearly 300 000 ha between the headwaters of the Gascoyne and Ashburton Rivers. 'Spinifex' hummock grasses grow sparsely on sandplains and dunes, with mulga, mulla-mulla and some tussock grasses on better soils and eucalypts along creekbeds.

WARNING: Arid, remote area. Travellers far into park must be equipped for outback survival.

BEST TIME: Spring, autumn.

ENQUIRIES: (091) 84 5125.

ADDRESS: CALM, Box 835, Karratha 6714.

Scenic enjoyment ✓
Day activities ✗
Family camping ✗
Hard bushwalking ✓

Hamersley Range National Park

270 km S of Port Hedland. (450 km by North West Coastal Highway, 550 km by Great Northern Highway.) Pilbara weather district. Car access S from Wittenoom and off Newman road 24 km E of Wittenoom.

DESCRIPTION: Page 111.

NOTE: Basic camping in designated areas.

WARNING: Arid, remote area. Ranger must be notified of walks except in gorges and at Mt Bruce.

BEST TIME: Late autumn to early spring.

ENQUIRIES: (091) 89 8157.

ADDRESS: Box 20, Wittenoom 6752.

Scenic enjoyment ✓✓✓
Day activities ✓✓
Family camping ✓
Hard bushwalking ✓

Millstream-Chichester National Park

250 km SW of Port Hedland. Pilbara weather district. Wittenoom road from North West Coast Highway crosses park.

DESCRIPTION: Page 114.

NOTES: No water at Chichester Range camps. Bush camping at Millstream at ranger's direction.

BEST TIME: April to October.

ENQUIRIES: (091) 84 5125.

ADDRESS: As for Collier Range.

Scenic enjoyment ✓✓✓
Day activities ✓
Family camping ✓
Hard bushwalking ✓

Rudall River National Park

450 km SE of Port Hedland. Interior weather district. **NO SAFE PUBLIC ACCESS.**

Dry sand dunes and ridges, salt lakes and the courses of ephemeral streams are protected for scientific study in a park of 1 570 000 ha – Australia's biggest. Visits other than by approved study parties are not encouraged.

ENQUIRIES: (091) 84 5125.

ADDRESS: As for Collier Range.

WARNING

Outback travellers MUST be self sufficient in all aspects of their trip. Their transceivers should preferably have Royal Flying Doctor Service radio frequencies.

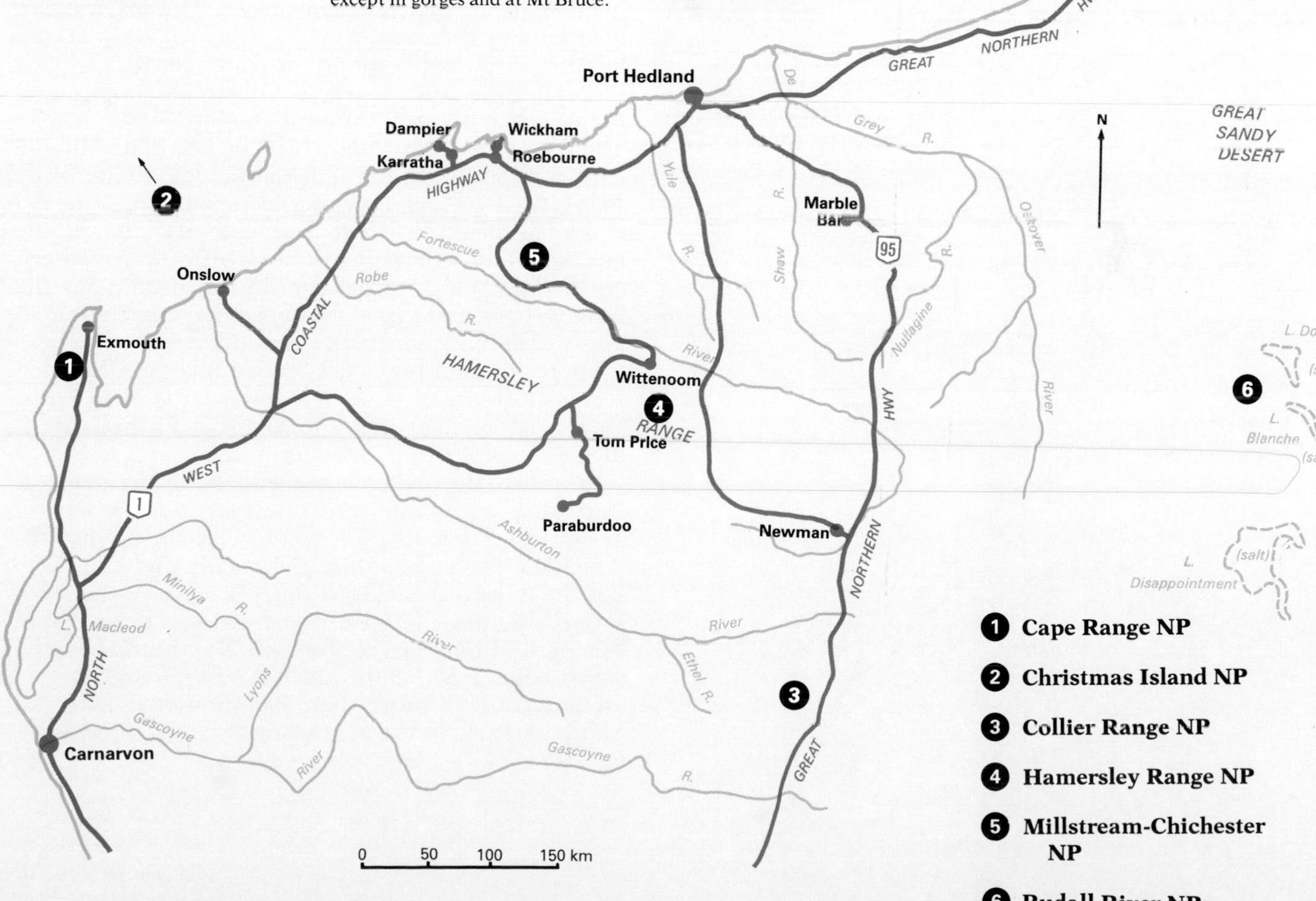

PERTH REGION

Stubborn forests under an alien threat

FORESTS OF the Darling Scarp, giving a priceless margin of greenery to the cleared and developed Swan coastal plain, are dominated by stately jarrah. Reaching 60 metres in height, in defiance of fire, drought and infertile soils, *Eucalyptus marginata* is the west's great survivor. Its timber has long been prized for quality furniture and termite-resistant construction, and jarrah forests were heavily cut over early in the state's history. But for half a century, along with its companion plants in a unique forest community, it has been under threat from an introduced disease.

A microscopic, soil-borne fungus invades the feeder roots and hinders their taking up moisture and nutrients. Called *Phytophthera cinnamomi* or cinnamon fungus, it is thought to have originated in tropical Southeast Asia. In eastern Australia the disease does its most serious damage to mangroves. In the west hundreds of plant species are susceptible – grass-trees, cycads, banksias, dryandras, casuarinas and so on.

Many plants, especially the banksias, are killed quickly. But jarrah in most conditions can fight the fungus for years. Infected trees succumb gradually, losing their outermost leaves in a process called 'dieback'. Between 1940 and 1965, thousands of hectares of forest were wiped out. The disease can also have a dire effect on banksia woodlands and heathlands, notably along the south coast.

For a time, the death of all jarrah forests and many other plant communities seemed inevitable. The west faced scenic deprivation, loss of a valuable timber resource and a dramatic loss of wildlife habitats. In recent years, however, the rate of spread of the disease has declined markedly and the outlook is more hopeful. Armed with improved scientific knowledge of the conditions that favour the fungus, park and forest managers have been able to apply effective quarantine measures.

Spores of the fungus are spread most easily when soil is shifted – often accidentally on vehicle tyres. Park visitors are urged to keep to formed, well-drained roads and to heed any closure signs.

In spite of the presence of dieback the jarrah forest is readily accessible and offers a wide variety of activities in the autumn, winter and spring months – picnicking, bush walking, canoeing and camping. For the more adventurous there is perhaps the most satisfying long-distance forest walk in Australia. The Bibbulmun Track starts at Kalamunda at the scarp edge near Perth and links parks and forests along a route of more than 400 kilometres south to Shannon Park, in the karri forest near Manjimup.

Featured parks	Pages
1 John Forrest	118-119
2 Walyunga	120-121
3 Leeuwin-Naturaliste	122-125
4 Pemberton	126-127
5 D'Entrecasteaux	128-129
6 Nambung	130-131
7 Kalbarri	132-135
8 Kalamunda	136

Your access and facilities guide to all national parks in this region starts on page 137

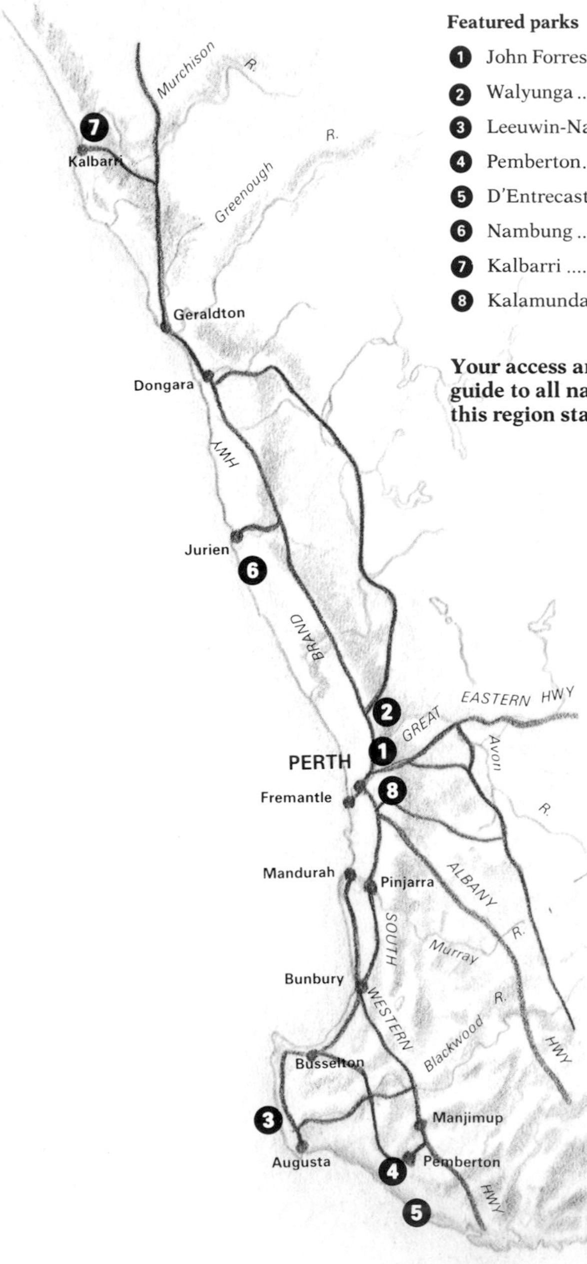

Sandstone grandeur in Murchison Gorge, Kalbarri National Park

JOHN FORREST NATIONAL PARK

Short but hilly walking tracks lead to quiet pools and waterfalls among the eucalypt woodlands of the Darling Scarp. Flanked by outer-suburban development along the Great Eastern Highway, John Forrest is heavily used in warm spring weather and prone to fires in summer. First called Greenmount, it was known from 1900 simply as 'the National Park' – Western Australia's first. Natural features in a park of less than 1600 ha suffered heavily under early policies aimed at taming its streams, particularly Jane Brook, and turning their surrounds into English-style pleasure grounds. One walking route leads along a disused railway line. Gardeners were allowed to take away granite boulders and shingle for landscaping. Nevertheless the trees and wildflowers, and the prolific birdlife they attract, make many charming scenes. High vantage points give good views of the Swan coastal plain.

One-sided bottlebrush (calothamnus) is endemic to Western Australia

Right: Paperbarks shade a peaceful stream. Many of the park's waterways have swimming holes, and Jane Brook is dammed to make a big pool near picnic grounds and restaurants

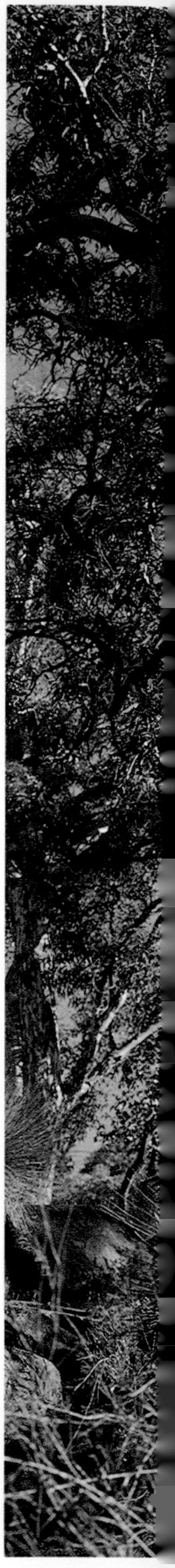

Wandoo dominates a rocky woodland slope

Open woodlands spread along the seaward side of the Darling Scarp. Grass trees surround a granite outcrop

Grey cottonhead, a small herb

Sugarloaf Rock, a deeply weathered granite mound near Cape Naturaliste, is the southernmost breeding site of the red-tailed tropic bird

Wind erosion of dunes behind Quarry Bay, just north of Cape Leeuwin, bares remnants of a limestone bed

Leeuwin-Naturaliste National Park

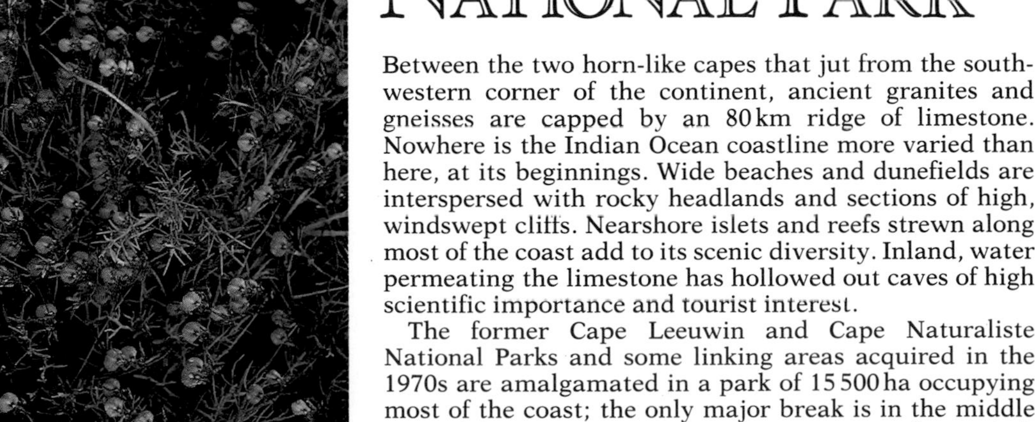

Clematis and hardenbergia

Native violet (Hybanthus calycinus)

Between the two horn-like capes that jut from the south-western corner of the continent, ancient granites and gneisses are capped by an 80 km ridge of limestone. Nowhere is the Indian Ocean coastline more varied than here, at its beginnings. Wide beaches and dunefields are interspersed with rocky headlands and sections of high, windswept cliffs. Nearshore islets and reefs strewn along most of the coast add to its scenic diversity. Inland, water permeating the limestone has hollowed out caves of high scientific importance and tourist interest.

The former Cape Leeuwin and Cape Naturaliste National Parks and some linking areas acquired in the 1970s are amalgamated in a park of 15 500 ha occupying most of the coast; the only major break is in the middle around the Margaret River. Vegetation ranges from wind-stunted heaths and mallee scrubs to eucalypt forests, including tall stands of jarrah in the south.

NAMBUNG NATIONAL PARK

Scaevola: salt-resistant

Spikes and knobs of limestone – many taller than a house, others no bigger than pencils – stud the sands of the Pinnacles Desert. They are the main inland feature of an undeveloped park of 17 500 ha occupying dunefields and sandplains just south of Cervantes township. Other interest in the park is directed towards its 26 km coastline, where sandy beaches are accessible on foot or by four-wheel-drive. Swimming is safe in reef-protected waters and the area has a good reputation for fishing. But the roads can be rough and sometimes sand-drifted. Travellers whose main concern is to see the Pinnacles may prefer to take a bus tour from Cervantes.

The Nambung River makes a chain of waterholes through part of the park before disappearing into a cave system – inaccessible to the public. Woodlands flourish nearby, but visitors see mostly low scrubs and heaths, flowering colourfully in late winter and spring.

Nambung's pinnacles began to form centuries ago when lime-rich sands, blown inland, created high mobile dunes. Rain leached the lime from their upper layers cementing the lower sand into a soft limestone. Stabilising plants spread an acidic layer of soil and humus over the dunes, accelerating the leaching. A hard topping of calcrete formed over the limestone (seen today as a cap on many pinnacles). Plant roots exploited cracks in the calcrete; water seeped down the channels, continuing the subsurface erosion of the limestone. The pinnacles, remnants of that limestone layer, were exposed as the prevailing wind blew away the surrounding quartz sand

An unsealed road takes visitors to a lookout above the Pinnacles Desert, then loops through it for a closer inspection

Watsonia, a South African plant of the iris family, invades the margins of Piesse Brook

Right: Flowering spikes of the common grass-tree attract honeyeaters and bees

Pimelea, a riceflower, favours sandy slopes

KALAMUNDA NATIONAL PARK

Piesse Brook trickles through a hilly little park on the high slopes of the Darling Scarp. Eucalypt woodlands are carpeted with heath plants, blossoming profusely in late winter and spring. The 375 ha park, managed primarily as a plant reserve in an area of spreading suburban development, has no public facilities. But trails connect to make pleasant walks of up to 4 hours. Hikers can cool off in Rocky Pool waterhole if the brook is running.

PARKS OF THE PERTH REGION

1. Alexander Morrison NP
2. Avon Valley NP
3. Badgingarra NP
4. D'Entrecasteaux NP
5. Drovers Cave NP
6. Gooseberry Hill NP
7. Greenmount NP
8. John Forrest NP
9. Kalamunda NP
10. Kalbarri NP
11. Leeuwin-Naturaliste NP
12. Lesmurdic Falls NP
13. Moore River NP
14. Nambung NP
15. Neerabup NP 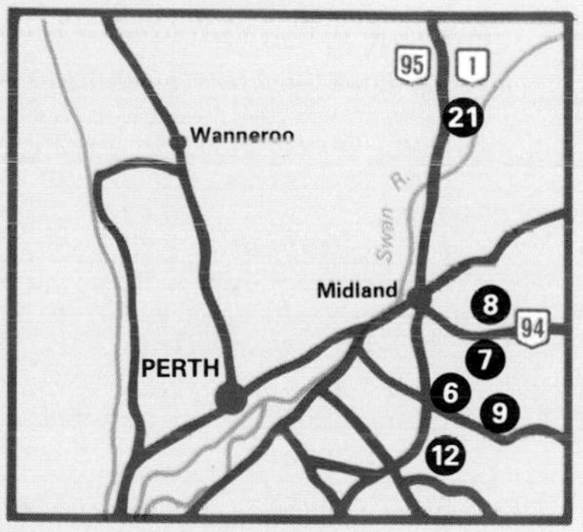
16. Pemberton NPs
17. Scott NP
18. Serpentine NP
19. Sir James Mitchell NP & Shannon Forest Park
20. Tathra NP
21. Walyunga NP
22. Watheroo NP
23. Yalgorup NP
24. Yanchep NP

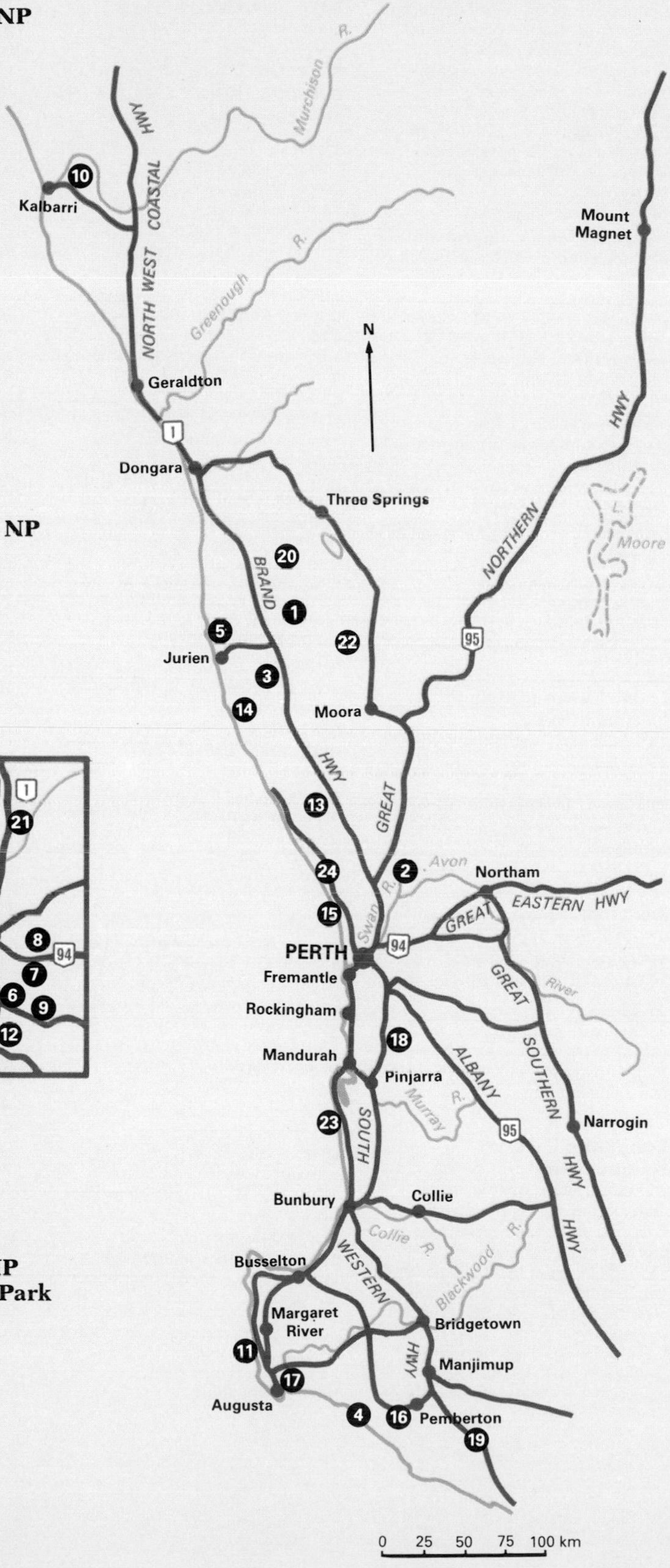

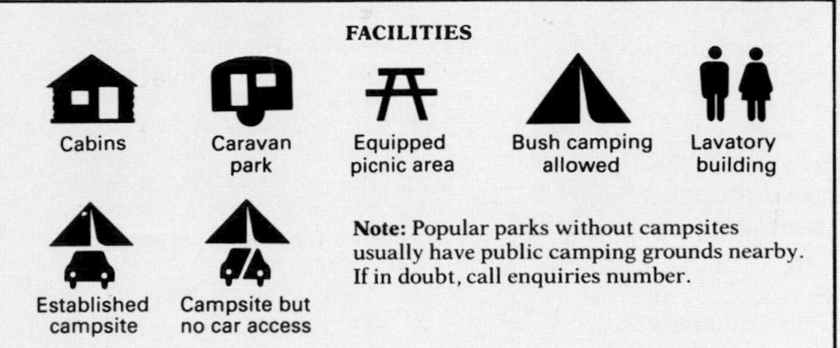

PARK RATINGS No interest ✖ Some interest ✔ Major interest ✔✔ Outstanding ✔✔✔

Alexander Morrison National Park

270 km N. Central West weather district. Car access from Brand Highway 45 km N of Badgingarra, on Coorow road (gravel).

Late-blooming wildflowers flourish on sandplain heathlands covering most of the 8500 ha park, which straddles a little-used road between Coorow and the coast. Birds are abundant on the heaths and in a few areas of low eucalypt woodland and mallee scrub.

NOTE: No water supplies. Park campers must consult ranger.

BEST TIME: Early summer.

ENQUIRIES: (095) 41 1424.

ADDRESS: CALM district office, Box 328, Moora 6510.

Scenic enjoyment ✔✔
Day activities ✖
Family camping ✖
Hard bushwalking ✖

Avon Valley National Park

80 km NE. Lower West weather district. Car access off Toodyay Road via Morangup and Chris Hill Roads (gravel for 19 km).

Bald Hill commands impressive views of the Avon River beginning its descent of the broken Darling Scarp. Emu Spring Brook, a tributary, spills in a 30 metre waterfall after winter rains. Jarrah and marri dominate dry eucalypt forest in a hilly park of nearly 4400 ha, with western Christmas trees and grass-trees prominent in the understorey.

Graded maintenance tracks aid bushwalking. One follows the river downstream, allowing an interesting overnight hike past the Avon's junction with the Brockman River – the two become the Swan – and down into Walyunga National Park. The river is easily crossed in summer and autumn. But the terrain is steep and rocky; sturdy, rubber-soled footwear is needed.

NOTE: Bushwalkers can obtain water at ranger's residence when streams are not running – take container. Campsite fee.

BEST TIME: Spring, autumn.

ENQUIRIES: (096) 26 2540.

ADDRESS: C/o P.O., Gidgegannup 6555.

Scenic enjoyment ✔✔
Day activities ✔✔
Family camping ✔
Hard bushwalking ✔✔

Badgingarra National Park

205 km N. Central West weather district. Car access by Brand Highway (skirts park).

Spring-flowering heaths deck 13 000 ha of gently rolling, sandy country, relieved in places by banksia woodlands. The park is principally a reserve for the rare black kangaroo paw, but its plant communities include many colourful dryandras, hakeas and grevilleas. Some are relics of a wetter climate, having affinities with plants now more common in the southwest.

A 2 km wildflower walk identifies important species. Elsewhere, fire trails lead around and across the park. There are no other tracks, but walking is relatively easy.

NOTES: Permit needed for camping. Take water, gas cooker – fires prohibited.

BEST TIME: August-September.

ENQUIRIES: (095) 41 1424.

ADDRESS: As for Alexander Morrison.

Scenic enjoyment ✔
Day activities ✔
Family camping ✖
Hard bushwalking ✖

PARKS OF THE PERTH REGION

D'Entrecasteaux National Park
350 km S. Southwest weather district. Limited 4WD access off Nannup-Pemberton road 52 km S of Nannup.

DESCRIPTION: Page 129.

BEST TIME: Spring.

ENQUIRIES: (097) 76 1200.

ADDRESS: As for Pemberton.

Scenic enjoyment ✓✓
Day activities ×
Family camping ×
Hard bushwalking ✓

Drovers Cave National Park
250 km N, near Jurien Bay. Central West weather district. 4WD access off Brand Highway-Jurien road.

Caves containing limestone drip formations and important deposits of prehistoric mammal bones are the focus of a park occupying nearly 2700 ha of dry sandplain heathlands and banksia woodlands. It is not developed for general visiting and Drovers Cave itself is kept locked. Experienced cavers may inspect some others by arrangement with the ranger in charge at Nambung.

NOTES: Permit needed for camping. Take water. Fires prohibited.

BEST TIME: Spring.

ENQUIRIES: (095) 45 7043.

ADDRESS: As for Nambung.

Scenic enjoyment ✓
Day activities ×
Family camping ×
Hard bushwalking ×

Gooseberry Hill National Park
25 km E. Lower West weather district. Car access off Lascelles Parade via Williams Street, Gooseberry Hill.

A steep 30 ha patch of wandoo, jarrah and marri woodland high on the Darling Scarp is known in adjoining suburbs as the Zigzag. Embankments and cuttings of a disused switchback railway carry a sightseeing road that descends from a popular lookout. Wildflowers are prolific in spring.

BEST TIME: August-September.

ENQUIRIES: (09) 298 8344.

ADDRESS: As for John Forrest.

Scenic enjoyment ✓✓
Day activities ✓
Family camping ×
Hard bushwalking ×

Greenmount National Park
25 km E. Lower West weather district. Car access off Great Eastern Highway at Greenmount, via Padbury Road, Buses along highway.

Dry eucalypt woodlands occupy 50 ha of a spur of the Darling Scarp, overlooking the Helena Valley and giving good views of Perth. Spring wildflowers attract many visitors.

NOTE: Fires prohibited.

BEST TIME: August-September.

ENQUIRIES: (09) 298 8344.

ADDRESS: As for John Forrest.

Scenic enjoyment ✓✓
Day activities ✓
Family camping ×
Hard bushwalking ×

John Forrest National Park
25 km E. Lower West weather district. Park adjoins Great Eastern Highway between Greenmount and Glen Forrest. Car access at three points on highway (vehicle entrance fee). Foot access also from Swan View or Hovea. Buses along highway.

DESCRIPTION: Page 118.

NOTE: Permit needed for bush camping.

BEST TIME: Winter and spring (August-October for flowers).

ENQUIRIES: (09) 298 8344.

ADDRESS: C/o P.O., Glen Forrest 6071.

Scenic enjoyment ✓✓
Day activities ✓✓✓
Family camping ×
Hard bushwalking ✓✓

Kalamunda National Park
30 km E. Lower West weather district. Car access via Kalamunda to Spring Road and Schipp Road.

DESCRIPTION: Page 136.

BEST TIME: Winter and spring (July-October for flowers).

ENQUIRIES: (09) 298 8344.

ADDRESS: As for John Forest.

Scenic enjoyment ✓✓
Day activities ✓
Family camping ×
Hard bushwalking ✓

Kalbarri National Park
550 km N, 125 km N of Geraldton. Central West weather district. Car access from North West Coastal Highway by Ajana-Kalbarri township road (traverses park). Vehicle entrance fee. Flights Perth-Geraldton-Kalbarri most days. Buses Perth-Kalbarri some days. Bus tours of park from Kalbarri daily (weather permitting).

DESCRIPTION: Page 132.

NOTES: Accommodation of all kinds available nearby in Kalbarri township. Overnight hikers must have written permission from CALM regional office, Box 72, Geraldton 6530 – only groups of 5 or more considered safe in remote areas. No water except from river.

WARNING: Hiking in remoter parts should not be attempted in summer heat.

BEST TIME: Winter and spring.

ENQUIRIES: (099) 37 1140.

ADDRESS: Box 37, Kalbarri 6532.

Scenic enjoyment ✓✓✓
Day activities ✓✓
Family camping ×
Hard bushwalking ✓✓✓

Leeuwin-Naturaliste National Park
265-350 km S. Southwest weather district. Car access from many points along Caves Road.

DESCRIPTION: Page 123.

NOTE: Permit needed for bush camping.

WARNINGS: Crumbling cliff edges are dangerous.

BEST TIME: Spring to autumn.

ENQUIRIES: (097) 52 1677.

ADDRESS: CALM district office, 14 Queen Street, Busselton 6280.

Scenic enjoyment ✓✓✓
Day activities ✓✓
Family camping ×
Hard bushwalking ✓

Lesmurdie Falls National Park
25 km E. Lower West weather district. Car access through Forrestfield or Lesmurdie. Bus along Lesmurdie Road.

Among 50 ha of the dry eucalypt woodlands characteristic of the Darling Scarp, Lesmurdie Creek cascades into a pool surrounded by broad slabs of granite. Steep tracks – eroded and slippery – lead down each side of the falls from a car park near the Lesmurdie entrance. The walk down and back takes about 2 hours. Higher points of the park offer fine views.

BEST TIME: Winter and spring.

ENQUIRIES: (09) 298 8344.

ADDRESS: As for John Forrest.

Scenic enjoyment ✓✓
Day activities ✓✓
Family camping ×
Hard bushwalking ×

Moore River National Park
115 km N. Lower West weather district. Brand Highway passes park.

Rose banksia has its only habitat in this undeveloped park of 17 000 ha, among low woodlands of other banksias, pricklybark and western Christmas tree. Other notable spring-blooming wildflowers are black and golden kangaroo paws and verticordia. The park is a good example of the sandy heathlands of the northern coastal plain, including some dry dune systems and seasonal and permanent swamps. Walkers can take advantage of an extensive network of fire trails.

NOTE: Dry, remote area. All water must be carried in. Camping not permitted.

BEST TIME: Spring.

ENQUIRIES: (095) 61 1004 or 61 1661.

ADDRESS: As for Yanchep.

Scenic enjoyment ✓
Day activities ×
Family camping ×
Hard bushwalking ×

Nambung National Park
245 km N. Central West weather district. Car access by Brand Highway, turning off for Cervantes. Gravel road into park (rough in some sections) starts 2 km from Cervantes.

DESCRIPTION: Page 130.

NOTES: Permit needed for bush camping – usually at Hangover Bay. Fires prohibited. No lavatories in park. Camping and caravan facilities and other accommodation available at Cervantes.

BEST TIME: Spring.

ENQUIRIES: (095) 45 7043.

ADDRESS: Box 62, Cervantes 6511.

Scenic enjoyment ✓✓
Day activities ✓✓✓
Family camping ×
Hard bushwalking ✓

Neerabup National Park
30-45 km N. Lower West weather district. Park adjoins Wanneroo Road, car access by Quinns Rocks road, bisecting park. Foot access to southernmost area from Burns Beach road.

Between Lake Joondalup and Carabooda Lake, a narrow strip of nearly 1100 ha gives an unusually varied representation of coastal sandplain country. In the south the park is wooded with jarrah, casuarina and banksia. In the southeastern corner the limestones of old dune systems outcrop, supporting a dense heath of parrot bush. To the north, woodlands are dominated by massive tuarts with an understorey of heath plants or banksias. Brilliant displays of wildflowers are seen from July to November.

The park has no facilities for visitors but walkers can use fire breaks. The length of the park can be covered in a day.

BEST TIME: July to November.

ENQUIRIES: (095) 61 1004 or 61 1661.

ADDRESS: As for Yanchep.

Scenic enjoyment ✓
Day activities ×
Family camping ×
Hard bushwalking ✓

Pemberton National Parks (Beedelup, Brockman, Warren)
340 km S. Southwest weather district. Car access to main parks from Pemberton via Northcliffe road. Foot access on Bibbulmun Track.

DESCRIPTION: Page 126.

NOTE: Main public facilities are in Warren National Park. Fee charged for Warren River campsites.

BEST TIME: Spring to autumn.

ENQUIRIES: (097) 76 1200.

ADDRESS: Box 35, Pemberton 6260.

Scenic enjoyment ✓✓✓
Day activities ✓✓✓
Family camping ✓✓
Hard bushwalking ✓✓

Scott National Park
330 km S. Southwest weather district. 4WD access off Brockman Highway E of Alexandra Bridge, to Scott River section. Boat access from Augusta or Alexandra Bridge.

A park of nearly 3300 ha protects wetlands and wooded slopes on the east bank of the Blackwood River above its junction with the Scott River, and straddles the Scott for about 3 km upstream. Jarrah, marri and karri are prominent in the woodlands, which have a dense understorey of flowering shrubs. Swamps provide widespread breeding habitats for waterfowl.

The area is entirely undeveloped and difficult to reach except by boat. It is most often seen, unknowingly, by tourists taking scenic launch cruises up the Blackwood River from Augusta.

BEST TIME: Spring to autumn.
ENQUIRIES: (097) 58 1756.
ADDRESS: C/o P.O., Augusta 6290.

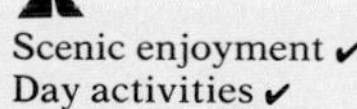

Scenic enjoyment ✔✔
Day activities ✔
Family camping ×
Hard bushwalking ✔

Serpentine National Park
55 km S. Lower West weather district. Car access off South Western Highway by Falls Road or Scrivener Road. Vehicle entrance fee. Gates closed 1800-0900.

Dry eucalypt forests, dominated by jarrah and marri, are preserved in a hilly park of 635 ha. The area has drawn picnic parties since before World War I, when the government was urged to appoint a caretaker to defend it from 'trainloads of excursionists' every wildflower season. The chief attractions originally were the Serpentine Falls and a big granite pool below, where the Serpentine River descends the Darling Scarp. Since the river was dammed upstream in the 1950s, to augment Perth's domestic water supplies, the falls have been seen only in winter. But the pool remains highly popular for swimming in other seasons.

The park has two rare eucalypt species, salmon white gum below the scarp and butter gum on the heights. Wildflowers in the shrub understoreys are no longer particularly prolific – better displays can be seen in parks closer to Perth. Pleasant strolls can be taken along the river above the falls. There are no bush trails, but the ranger will suggest routes for up to a full day's walking over challenging terrain.

NOTE: Booking needed for camping – fee charged.
BEST TIME: Spring to autumn.
ENQUIRIES: (095) 25 2128.
ADDRESS: Falls Road, Serpentine 6205.

Scenic enjoyment ✔✔
Day activities ✔✔✔
Family camping ✔✔✔
Hard bushwalking ✔

Sir James Mitchell National Park and Shannon Forest Park
365 km S. Southwest weather district. South Western Highway Manjimup-Walpole traverses parks, gravel roads lead off. Foot access on Bibbulmun Track.

A token national park area borders the highway to a depth of about 100 metres on each side and for a length of 65 km – less than 1100 ha in all. Of greater consequence is the 60 000 ha forest park that surrounds it for about 20 km. This embraces the Shannon River, from its headwaters north of the highway to its mouth at Broke Inlet.

Hilly forests in the north and centre of the park are dominated by karri, or mixtures of karri, jarrah and marri, usually with dense understoreys of karri wattle. Towards the south, jarrah woodlands and banksias occur at the margins of peaty, seasonally flooded flats supporting sedges and herbs.

Camping and day-visit facilities have been developed near the highway at the old Shannon townsite. Easy trails include a self-guiding interpretative walk and a special route for disabled people. Gravel roads of varying quality – some 4WD only – lead to most parts of the park and fire breaks aid bushwalking. The river is suitable for swimming at many points; it can be negotiated by canoe for 5-10 km upstream from Broke Inlet.

BEST TIME: March to May or September to January.
ENQUIRIES: (097) 71 1988.
ADDRESS: CALM offices, Brain Street, Manjimup 6258.

Scenic enjoyment ✔✔
Day activities ✔✔
Family camping ✔✔
Hard bushwalking ✔✔

Tathra National Park
305 km N. Central West weather district. Car access from Brand Highway by Eneabba-Carnamah road (traverses park – last section unsealed).

Surrounded by agricultural land, Tathra has been left undeveloped as a reseve for the wildflowers of its rolling sandplain heathlands and banksia woodlands. Diverse plant communities in the 4300 ha park include rare species of dryandra and daviesia.

NOTE: Only day visiting permitted.
BEST TIME: Spring.
ENQUIRIES: (095) 41 1424.
ADDRESS: As for Alexander Morrison.

Scenic enjoyment ✔
Day activities ×
Family camping ×
Hard bushwalking ×

Walyunga National Park
40 km NE. Lower West weather district. Car access off Great Northern Highway, turning E 8 km past Upper Swan. Vehicle entrance fee.

DESCRIPTION: Page 121.
NOTE: Permit needed for bush camping.
BEST TIME: Spring to autumn.
ENQUIRIES: (095) 71 1371.
ADDRESS: C/o P.O., Upper Swan 6056.

Scenic enjoyment ✔✔
Day activities ✔✔✔
Family camping ×
Hard bushwalking ✔

Watheroo National Park
235 km N. Central West weather district. Car access through southern sections of park off Midlands Road by Watheroo-Badgingarra road (gravel).

Heathlands in a basin of quartz sands occupy most of an undeveloped park of nearly 45 000 ha. Wildflowers include some rare species, and others that are usually associated with the southwest rather than the dry midlands plains. Small areas are covered by eucalypt woodlands or tall banksia scrub.

NOTE: No water in park. Bush camping may be permitted after consultation with ranger.
BEST TIME: Spring.
ENQUIRIES: (099) 52 5051.
ADDRESS: C/o P.O., Coorow 6515.

Scenic enjoyment ✔
Day activities ×
Family camping ×
Hard bushwalking ×

Yalgorup National Park
130 km S. Lower West weather district. Car access from Old Coast Road S of Mandurah, turning off for Yalgorup township. Buses along Old Coast Road.

Lakes and swamps form a chain between parallel lines of dunes and old limestone ridges, providing breeding habitats and feeding grounds for thousands of waterfowl. More than 100 species have been seen in the 11 500 ha park. Its eucalypt woodlands include tuart, jarrah and marri with banksias, peppermint and casuarina below. Some exposed slopes have coastal heath communities dominated by acacias, dryandras, hakeas and grass-trees.

Short walking trails skirt some of the lakes. Fire breaks aid cross-country walking, but the ranger should be notified beforehand. The park coastline has excellent beaches.

NOTE: Permit needed for bush camping.
BEST TIME: Winter and spring for wildflowers; summer for birdwatching and beach pastimes.
ENQUIRIES: (095) 39 1067.
ADDRESS: Box 406, Mandurah 6210.

Scenic enjoyment ✔✔
Day activities ✔✔
Family camping ×
Hard bushwalking ✔

Yanchep National Park
55 km N. Lower West weather district. Car access by Wanneroo Road (traverses park). Vehicle entry fee to lake and caves area. Perth-Two Rocks bus service.

Big grey kangaroos come out at sundown to graze a golfcourse and sports oval. The scene neatly captures the contradictions of Yanchep, which was intensively developed as a recreational park before it came under national parks management. Much of it was landscaped, and the swampy margins of Yanchep Lake were drained and reclaimed as lawns around what became Loch McNess. Private companies operate guest houses, restaurants, shops and even a licensed inn. Animals, including koalas imported from across the continent, are kept in enclosures by the lake and examples of western wildflower species are displayed in planted beds.

Yanchep does have more natural areas, wooded with marri, jarrah and tuart or banksias and casuarinas, with flowering heaths and grass-trees in the understorey. Numerous fire breaks can be used for up to a day's bushwalking far from the sight or sound of the busy lake area. To the east the 2800 ha park has limestone caves with interesting drip formations. Guided tours are given of Crystal Cave. An entry fee is charged and rubber-soled shoes are needed.

NOTE: Permit needed for bush camping.
BEST TIME: Spring.
ENQUIRIES: (095) 61 1004 or 61 1661.
ADDRESS: C/o P.O., Yanchep 6035.

Scenic enjoyment ✔
Day activities ✔✔✔
Family camping ×
Hard bushwalking ✔

Mammals and reptiles of Western Australia

Western Australia is the ancestral land; its landforms are older than elsewhere on the continent. Separated from the east by vast and inhospitable distances and itself divided north from south by desert, the state has ancient plants and rare and unique animals. Among the animals are the scaly-tailed possum, found only in the northwest Kimberley, the quokka and, today, the numbat. This anteater once lived across South Australia and into western New South Wales but now exists only in pockets in the Stirling Range and Dryandra Forest. As well, distinct western subspecies and geographical races of animals have emerged – as has happened with the black-footed rock-wallaby

Black-footed rock-wallaby – one of a small population at Cape Range

Western grey kangaroo – a protected species

Scaly-tailed possum – only member of its genus

Quokka – once common in the damp southwest, its largest population is now on arid Rottnest Island

Shingle-back lizard – short-legged and slow-moving, it relies on a fierce display to deter intruders

Numbat – predation and burning of habitat have drastically reduced its numbers

Olive python – found in the rocky hills of the northwest

Bungarra lizard – local name for Varanus gouldii, sometimes also known as the racehorse goanna

Australian sea lions – at Cape Le Grand

ESPERANCE & ALBANY REGIONS

The oldest land confronts the stormiest ocean

BOLD CONTRASTS await the traveller here. On one hand, jagged ranges overlook the coast and towering forests crowd sheltered inlets. On the other, windswept sandplains give a foretaste of the Nullarbor. Rainfall – nearly all of it during a chilly winter – declines from a liberal 1000 mm or more a year in the west to less than 300 mm in the east and north.

But the regions have their unities. Wildflowers, their species numbered in thousands, mount delightful spring displays in forest understoreys and on the most unpromising of heathlands. And everywhere the worn granite shield of the earliest Australia shows itself. It covers more than a third of the continent – but only here does it meet the sea.

Along most of the coast the shield forms low, tough headlands to take the brunt of boisterous Southern Ocean gales. Bays and landlocked havens strung between include King George Sound, the roomiest harbour in all Australia.

Dutch navigators, exploring this coast as early as 1627, kept cautiously out to sea after rounding Cape Leeuwin. They failed to spot the sound, or Esperance Bay, or any of the well-watered, wooded havens such as Nornalup Inlet. The best location found by Pieter Nuyts, the first explorer, was near Ceduna at the parched eastern end of the Bight. Even that was seriously proposed as the site of a Dutch colony, long before the British staked any claim on the continent. If Nuyts or the compatriots who followed him, such as Abel Tasman, had discovered just one of the better-favoured harbours to the west, the course of Nieuw Hollandt history might have been very different.

Rivers in these regions are the shortest-running in Australia, seldom originating more than 50 km from the coast. Those farthest east are seasonal trickles, most of them draining into saltmarshes before they can reach the ocean. Depressions in the hinterland plateau, marked on many maps as lakes, are salt pans that rarely receive water.

Tourist emphasis falls understandably on the coastal playgrounds, the forests of karri and other giant western eucalypts, and the rugged scenery of the Stirling and Porongurup Ranges. But the parks of the regions give an excellent sampling of a wide variety of other environments, including the semi-arid northern plains. Together they serve to protect many plants and animals that are found nowhere else in Australia.

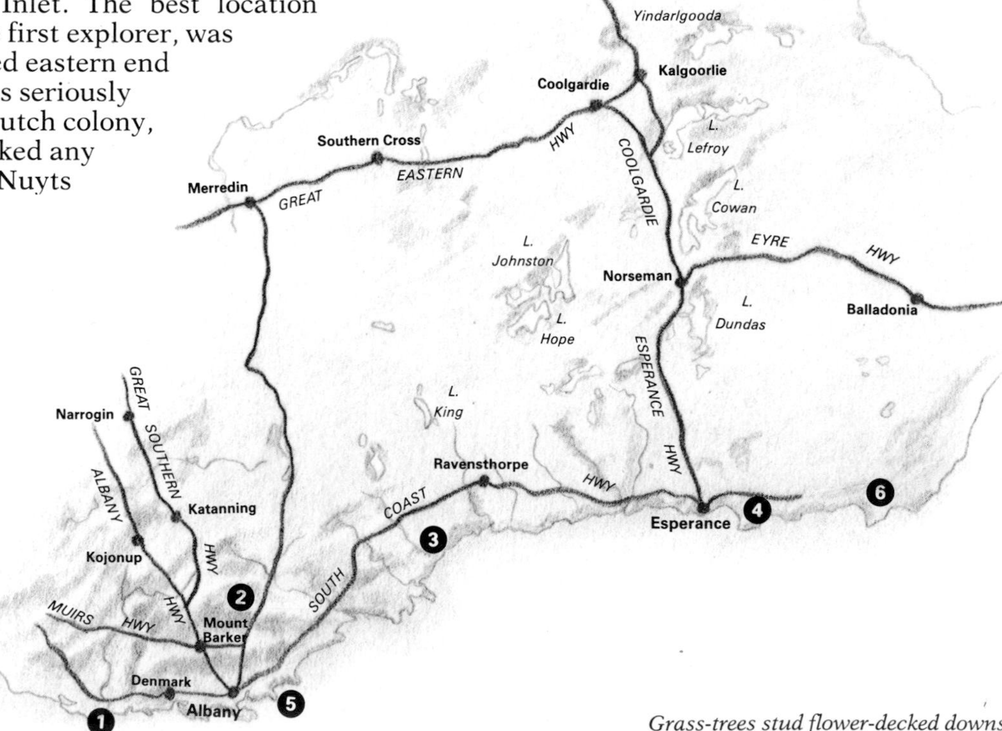

Featured parks **Pages**

1. Walpole-Nornalup..... 144-147
2. Stirling Range........... 148-151
3. Fitzgerald River......... 152-155
4. Cape Le Grand........... 156-157
5. Two Peoples Bay and Mt Manypeaks........ 158-161
6. Cape Arid.................... 162-163

Your access and facilities guide to all national parks in these regions starts on page 164

Grass-trees stud flower-decked downs between Mt Manypeaks and Two Peoples Bay

WALPOLE-NORNALUP NATIONAL PARK

Warren cedar overhang a flood-prone bend of the Deep River (left). Rainfall in the park and the catchments of its rivers averages more than 1000 mm a year. Karris (right), the mightiest trees of the west, flourish in the moist conditions and flowering shrubs grow profusely in the forest understoreys. But this region remains susceptible to fire: WA has no closed-canopy rainforest trees

Left: Granite boulders are strewn in the Frankland River

Above: Though badly burnt, this regenerating giant is identifiable as a red tingle – few eucalypts have this broadened, buttressed base

Eucalypt woodlands are carpeted with low shrubs and heaths. More than 800 flowering species are found in the park – some of them unique, and confined to certain peaks in the range

Blue-flowering Stirling Range smokebush

Pink mountain bell – unique

Paper-heath – found in the far south

Stirling Range National Park

Kingia – 'black gin' – grass-trees grow to 5 metres

Hovea is a woody shrub of the pea family

Dryandra is peculiar to Western Australia

Rose coneflower – common on heathlands

Mountain pea grows nowhere else

Salty flats surround the upper reaches of Hamersley Inlet, which is usually flushed out by river waters in winter. To the west, quartzite peaks of the Mid Mt Barren group slope steeply to a lonely coast

FITZGERALD RIVER NATIONAL PARK

Intermittent streams flowing from the Barren Ranges feed sand-barred inlets along a 100 km coastline between the fishing settlements of Bremer Bay and Hopetoun. East of the Fitzgerald River, which cuts across the centre of the 240 000 ha park, the flanks of Mid Mt Barren (457 metres) and other peaks drop directly to the Southern Ocean, forming sea cliffs or steep scree slopes. But most of the coast has beaches of dazzling quartz sands, backed by dunes and sandplains. Inland the Fitzgerald and Hamersley Rivers have cut narrow gorges with tall, colourful cliffs. Their valleys and some other watercourses have woodlands of mallee eucalypt, melaleuca and a eucalypt called swamp yate. On the sandy heathlands, mallee scrub has a dense and diverse understorey of flowering shrubs.

Access within the park is very limited. Four-wheel-drive tracks may be closed in wet months to control the spread of dieback disease.

Right: Dense heaths stabilise dunes beside Fitzgerald Inlet, which is usually cut off from the ocean by a sand bar

Left: Binding grasses protect Fitzgerald Beach from wind erosion. Rip currents are frequent along this coast – would-be swimmers should seek a ranger's advice on the safer sections, and never venture far out. Rock anglers must be wary of freakish 'king' waves

Hibiscus withstands exposure on windy coastal sites

FITZGERALD RIVER NATIONAL PARK

Leaves of royal hakea last for up to five years, their colour steadily growing richer

Lambertia attracts butterflies

WA has its own tea-tree species

Heathland shrubs grow in an almost bewildering profusion among mallee eucalypts (left and below). Fitzgerald River was the first area in WA to be internationally listed as a biosphere reserve. It is managed so that its plant and animal communities serve as a model against which changes in similar areas can be judged

Blossom of the bell-fruited mallee, a heathland eucalypt

Southern plains banksia

A weathered granite tor stands sentinel over Thistle Cove, where waves of the Southern Ocean swing in (right) to create fine conditions for swimming and rock fishing

CAPE LE GRAND NATIONAL PARK

Purple enamel orchid, one of a ground-growing group found only in the southwest

Humped outcrops of bare granite and gneiss mark the eastern limits of Esperance Bay. Coves indenting the headland are the most popular destinations in a 31 000 ha park. Agreeable beaches allow safe swimming, fishing and boating. Short scenic walks can be taken through richly flowering sandplain heaths to hilly mallee scrublands commanding good views of the coast and the Recherche Archipelago. Birds abound and native bees nest in the shelter of rock caves and overhangs. Energetic visitors can tackle a 15 km, full-day trail linking the coves between Le Grand Beach and Rossiter Bay. The western half, skirting Mt Le Grand (345 metres) to Hell Fire Bay and Thistle Cove, is hard going and requires experience.

Frenchman Peak (262 metres) is easily climbed by a track up the eastern flank

Silver tea-tree – recently rediscovered after a century

White spider orchid

Downy stackhousia

Tumbled sandstone boulders frame the mouth of the Waychinicup River, which flows out at Hassell Beach, to the east of Mt Manypeaks

Two Peoples Bay and Mt Manypeaks

Efforts to preserve the rare noisy scrub bird have focussed attention on two areas of outstanding scenic merit. **Two Peoples Bay Nature Reserve** was created on the Point Gardner headland after the bird was rediscovered there in 1961. Part of its 3600 ha is closed to the public and vehicles are not allowed to the south towards Cape Vancouver, but Moates and Gardner Lakes and the southern coast are open. Not far east, between Normans Beach and the Waychinicup River, **Mount Manypeaks Nature Reserve** was declared in the 1970s to provide a less fire-prone home for the scrub bird colony and for western bristlebirds. Its trackless 1300 ha, including Mt Manypeaks (565 metres), pose a test for expert bushwalkers.

Oxylobium blooms among tors of granite. Smooth outcrops of the ancient rock occur strikingly (below) on colourful heathlands overlooking Two Peoples Bay

Scarlet banksia is common on sandy soils

Curry flower is named for its scent

Leschenaultia

Southern cross, a perennial herb

Prickly bitter pea

Bald Island is a sanctuary for the quokka, a short-tailed wallaby. Uncommon on the mainland, its only other stronghold is Rottnest Island, not far from Perth.

Two Peoples Bay and Mt Manypeaks

CAPE ARID NATIONAL PARK

Beaches of Yokinup Bay make a sandy sweep of 20 km from the mouth of the Thomas River to a granite headland capped by Mt Arid (356 metres). An hour's climb from a coastal track, the peak gives superb views of a complex shoreline and dozens of islets of the eastern Recherche Archipelago. Easier vantage points are gained near the rivermouth camping ground at Belinup Hill, which has a self-guiding nature-circuit of 1 km. Behind dunes and swampy clay flats, this area is well vegetated with colourful heath plants and banksia, acacia and mallee eucalypt scrub. Inland, the 280 000 ha park consists mostly of sandplains. But in the north it is dominated by the wooded Russell Range, where razorback Mt Ragged rises to 585 metres.

Mt Ragged, standing out on the distant skyline, can be reached along a four-wheel-drive road. Fingers of granite shelter shallow, sandy bays (right) where swimming and fishing are popular

PARKS OF THE ESPERANCE AND ALBANY REGIONS

PARK RATINGS No interest ✖ Some interest ✔ Major interest ✔✔ Outstanding ✔✔✔

Boorabbin National Park
465 km NW of Esperance. Goldfields weather district. Park reaches for 20 km on both sides of Great Eastern Highway between Southern Cross and Coolgardie.

A narrow roadside park of 26 000 ha in rolling country protects tracts of sandplain heath. In spring, the low shrubs and smaller plants present a dazzling spectacle of colour and variety.

BEST TIME: Spring.
ENQUIRIES: (090) 21 2095.
ADDRESS: CALM, Box 366, Kalgoorlie 6430.
Scenic enjoyment ✔
Day activities ✖
Family camping ✖
Hard bushwalking ✖

Cape Arid National Park
125 km E of Esperance. Eucla weather district. Car access from Fisheries Road E of Esperance (last 18 km gravel, suitable for caravans) to main camping area. 4WD needed to reach other camping areas.

DESCRIPTION: Page 162.
NOTES: Campers must take water. Pack campers are advised to inform ranger of intentions – much of park is waterless.
WARNING: Swimmers need advice on safe beaches.
BEST TIME: Spring for wildflowers, summer for water sports.
ENQUIRIES: (090) 75 0055.
ADDRESS: East Mail Run, Esperance 6450.
Scenic enjoyment ✔✔✔
Day activities ✔✔✔
Family camping ✔✔✔
Hard bushwalking ✔✔

Cape Le Grand National Park
50 km SE of Esperance. Southern Coastal weather district. Car access from Merivale Road or Fisheries Road (fair gravel surfaces within park).

DESCRIPTION: Page 156.
NOTES: Pack campers are advised to notify ranger at park entrance. All campers should take wood or gas stove. Fee charged at established camping areas at Lucky Bay and Le Grand Beach.
BEST TIME: Spring, summer.
ENQUIRIES: (090) 75 9022.
ADDRESS: Box 706, Esperance 6450.
Scenic enjoyment ✔✔✔
Day activities ✔✔✔
Family camping ✔✔✔
Walking, climbing ✔✔✔

Eucla National Park
930 km E of Esperance. Eucla weather district. Eyre Highway passes park near WA/SA border.

Literal high point of the park is Wilson Bluff, reached from the highway by 4WD track. It gives impressive views of the sheer sea cliffs of the Great Australian Bight. Mallee scrub and heaths cover most of the 3340 ha park. Nearby, the abandoned Eucla telegraph station, dating from the construction of the original transcontinental telegraph line, is part-buried among encroaching sand dunes.

BEST TIME: Spring.
ENQUIRIES: (090) 71 3733.
ADDRESS: CALM, Box 234, Esperance 6450.
Scenic enjoyment ✔✔
Day activities ✔
Family camping ✖
Hard bushwalking ✖

Fitzgerald River National Park
185 km NE of Albany, 250 km W of Esperance. Southern Coastal weather district. Car access to Mylies Beach and Barrens Beach picnic area from Ravensthorpe or Hopetoun, and to Gordon Inlet off Highway 1 via Bremer Bay Road. 4WD needed for all other park tracks.

DESCRIPTION: Page 152.
NOTES: No water except at Twin Bays. Pack campers should report to ranger before starting walk.
WARNINGS: Swimmers need advice about safe areas. 'King' waves may endanger anglers. Shale cliff edges may be unstable.
BEST TIME: Spring, summer.
ENQUIRIES: (098) 35 5043.
ADDRESS: Box 33, Jerramungup 6337.
Scenic enjoyment ✔✔✔
Day activities ✔✔
Family camping ✔
Hard bushwalking ✔✔

Frank Hann National Park
230 km NW of Esperance. Goldfields weather district. Car access through park by Norseman-Lake King road (gravel – part rough).

A park of nearly 50 000 ha straddles the road for a stretch of 55 km. It provides a variety of habitats from sand heaths to mallee scrub and eucalypt woodlands – surprising in an area of low rainfall. Among flowers in spring, the red rapier feather flower is particularly striking.

WARNING: Area remote and waterless – travellers must be equipped for outback survival.
BEST TIME: Spring.
ENQUIRIES: (090) 71 3733.
ADDRESS: As for Eucla.
Scenic enjoyment ✔
Day activities ✖
Family camping ✖
Hard bushwalking ✖

WARNING
Outback travellers MUST be self sufficient in all aspects of their trip. Their transceivers should preferably have Royal Flying Doctor Service radio frequencies.

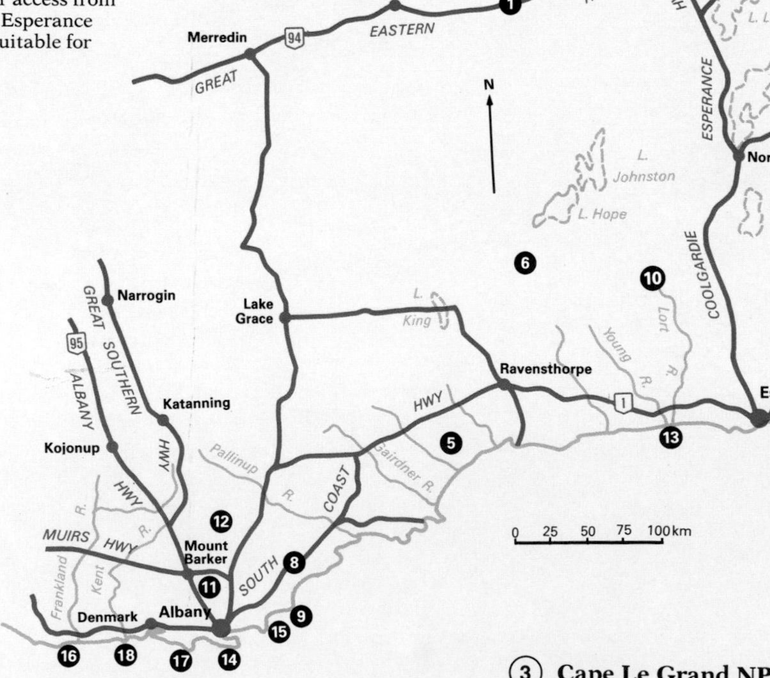

① Boorabbin NP
② Cape Arid NP
③ Cape Le Grand NP
④ Eucla NP
⑤ Fitzgerald River NP
⑥ Frank Hann NP
⑦ Goongarrie NP
⑧ Hassell NP
⑨ Mount Manypeaks Nature Reserve
⑩ Peak Charles NP
⑪ Porongurup NP
⑫ Stirling Range NP
⑬ Stokes NP
⑭ Torndirrup NP
⑮ Two Peoples Bay Nature Reserve
⑯ Walpole-Nornalup NP
⑰ West Cape Howe NP
⑱ William Bay NP

Goongarrie National Park
515 km N of Esperance, 100 km N of Kalgoorlie. Goldfields weather district. Car access from Kalgoorlie to Menzies road (gravel, fair condition).

Mulga, at the southern edge of its range, meets mallee scrub and York gum woodlands in a park of almost 50 000 ha. Emu bush (also called poverty bush) and acacias are prominent shrubs over a ground cover of speargrass. Wildflowers bloom as ephemerals if soaking rain falls.

WARNING: Area remote, dry – travellers must be fully equipped for outback survival.
BEST TIME: Winter and spring, after good rains.
ENQUIRIES: (090) 21 2095.
ADDRESS: As for Boorabbin.

Scenic enjoyment ✔
Day activities ×
Family camping ×
Hard bushwalking ×

Hassell National Park
50 km NE of Albany. Southern Coastal weather district. Car access through park on South Coast Highway between Albany and Bremer Bay.

A roadside reserve, merely some 150 metres wide, extends for 34 km. Its 1260 ha are dense with wildflowers in spring and early summer. Among birds in the tall shrubs are red wattlebirds and New Holland, white-necked and singing honeyeaters.

NOTE: No water.
WARNING: Snakes are common.
BEST TIME: Spring.
ENQUIRIES: (098) 41 7133.
ADDRESS: CALM, 44 Serpentine Road, Albany 6330.

Scenic enjoyment ✔
Day activities ×
Family camping ×
Hard bushwalking ×

Mount Manypeaks Nature Reserve
50 km E of Albany. Southern Coastal weather district. Car access from Hassell Highway near Many Peaks township or 11 km farther to track along Waychinicup River.

DESCRIPTION: Page 158.
NOTE: No fires allowed.
WARNING: Swimming safe only at Normans Beach
BEST TIME: April-May and September-October.
ENQUIRIES: (098) 46 4276.
ADDRESS: As for Two Peoples Bay.

Scenic enjoyment ✔✔
Day activities ×
Family camping ×
Hard bushwalking ✔

Peak Charles National Park
185 km N of Esperance, 100 km SW of Norseman. Goldfields weather district. Car access from Kumarl on Coolgardie-Esperance Highway by good gravel road degenerating into track (impassable after rain).

Two granite outcrops, Peak Charles and Peak Eleanora, dominate mallee-covered sandplains, eucalypt woodlands and vast salt lakes in the 40 000 ha park. Precipitous cliffs of Peak Charles (658 metres) are broken into numerous boulder-strewn shelves with curved gorges. Nestling into the walls of the peak are small meadows where several varieties of orchid and unusual species of darwinia and one-sided bottlebrush are found.

Only experienced bushwalkers should make the one-hour climb to the top of Peak Charles. A trail ends halfway up, then scrambling up some steep sections is necessary.

NOTES: Camping allowed only at the foot of Peak Charles. Take water.
BEST TIME: Spring, autumn.
ENQUIRIES: (090) 71 3733.
ADDRESS: As for Eucla.

Scenic enjoyment ✔✔
Day activities ✔
Family camping ×
Walking, climbing ✔✔

Porongurup National Park
50 km N of Albany, 20 km E of Mount Barker. Southern Coastal weather district. Car access from Porongurup township; from Woodlands Road off Mount Barker to Porongurup Road; or from Millinup Road off Chester Pass Road from Albany.

High rainfall attracted by the Porongurup Range, 12 km long and up to 670 metres high, enables karri forest – once widespread in the area – to survive on the higher slopes. Below the giant trees flourish native wisteria, water bush, hazel trees and blue-flowered hovea trees. Farther down, jarrah and marri grow above meadows of wildflowers.

In this park of 2400 ha, western grey kangaroos and brush wallabies are common. Wedge-tailed eagles hover overhead, using up-draughts from the peaks, and scarlet and yellow robins, western rosellas, white-tailed black cockatoos and tree martins are plentiful. Rufous tree-creepers are cheeky foragers of crumbs around picnickers, and the karri trees in flower attract flocks of purple-crowned lorikeets, heard but seldom clearly seen.

A scenic drive gives views of the distant Stirling Range, and three walking tracks (2-3 hours return) lead to peaks, past sculptured rocks and a huge balancing boulder. Bare granite domes and some sheer cliffs appeal to rock climbers.

NOTE: Walkers should carry water and wear sturdy shoes.
WARNING: Snakes are common in summer.
BEST TIME: May to October.
ENQUIRIES: (098) 53 1095.
ADDRESS: RMB 1112, Mount Barker 6324.

Scenic enjoyment ✔✔
Day activities ✔✔
Family camping ×
Walking, climbing ✔✔

Stirling Range National Park
80 km N of Albany. Great Southern and Southern Coastal weather districts. Chester Pass Road from Albany (sealed) crosses park. Access roads from Cranbrook, Kendenup and Mount Barker and roads within park are unsealed (good surface).

DESCRIPTION: Page 148.
NOTES: Bush campers and rock climbers should sign books at registration posts near Bluff Knoll turnoff or at park headquarters. Fee charged at established camping area.
VISITOR CENTRE: At Toolbrunup turn-off.
BEST TIME: August to November.
ENQUIRIES: (098) 27 9230, 27 9218.
ADDRESS: Amelup via Borden 6338.

Scenic enjoyment ✔✔✔
Day activities ✔✔✔
Family camping ✔✔✔
Walking, climbing ✔✔✔

Stokes National Park
86 km W of Esperance. Southern Coastal weather district. Car access via good gravel road from South Coast Highway.

The tranquil waters of Stokes Inlet provide opportunities for fishing, sailing and wind surfing, and safe bathing for small children. The ocean beaches offer pleasant walking and a trail (2 hours return) runs along the escarpment overlooking the inlet, but most of the 10 700 ha park is untouched and visitors must make their own way to see the wildflowers and coastal formations.

NOTES: Take water and gas stove.
BEST TIME: Spring, summer.
ENQUIRIES: (090) 76 8541.
ADDRESS: WMR, Esperance 6450.

Scenic enjoyment ✔✔✔
Day activities ✔✔
Family camping ✔✔
Hard bushwalking ✔

Torndirrup National Park
15 km S of Albany. Southern Coastal weather district. Car access via Frenchman Bay Road.

Chasms, cliffs, blowholes and beaches between rugged headlands rim a 3870 ha park reaching east to Flinders Peninsula, the southern flank of King George Sound. Heavy seas funnelling up a crevice in the granite occasionally drench visitors on a viewing platform 25 metres above the sea at the Gap, and sealed roads lead to other vantage points. Shelving slopes of rock tempt fishermen, but 'king' waves have caused several drownings.

Experienced and energetic walkers can make their way along a poorly defined track through prickly parrot bush to Bald Head, the most easterly point of the promontory. The return trip of 4-5 hours gives the visitor views of the ocean, the islands in the sound, and Albany, 10 km to the north. What early explorers took to be dead coral in the sand on top of Bald Head are calcified roots of shrubs. Among the birds in the stunted coastal scrub which includes a local bottlebrush with deep red flowers, New Holland honeyeaters are abundant.

WARNING: Heed notices about wave danger.
BEST TIME: Spring.
ENQUIRIES: (098) 44 4090.
ADDRESS: Box 904, Albany 6330.

Scenic enjoyment ✔✔✔
Day activities ✔
Family camping ×
Hard bushwalking ✔

Two Peoples Bay Nature Reserve
40 km E of Albany. Southern Coastal weather district. Car access to picnic area along Two Peoples Bay Road from Lower King. Access to one part of the reserve is entirely prohibited.

DESCRIPTION: Page 158.
NOTES: Walkers attempting Mt Gardner or Cape Vancouver trails are advised to notify reserve officer. No fires allowed.
WARNING: Snakes frequently encountered.
VISITOR DISPLAY: At picnic area.
BEST TIME: August to January.
ENQUIRIES: (098) 46 4276.
ADDRESS: Via Albany 6330.

Scenic enjoyment ✔✔
Day activities ✔✔
Family camping ×
Hard bushwalking ✔✔

Walpole-Nornalup National Park
120 km W of Albany. Southwest weather district. Car access from Walpole, or from Peaceful Bay Road off South Coast Highway at Bow Bridge.

DESCRIPTION: Page 144.
NOTE: Fee charged at established camping areas.
BEST TIME: Spring.
ENQUIRIES: (098) 40 1026, 40 1066, 40 1090.
ADDRESS: Box 17, Walpole 6398.

Scenic enjoyment ✔✔✔
Day activities ✔✔✔
Family camping ✔✔✔
Hard bushwalking ✔

West Cape Howe National Park
30 km W of Albany. Southern Coastal weather district. Car access from Lower Denmark Road and Hortons South Road (good gravel). All other access 4WD only.

Main features are Shelley Beach, Torbay Head, West Cape Howe and Bornholm Salmon Holes beach. The coastline is backed by coastal heathland and swamps with a small area of karri forest near the main park entrance on Torbay Hill.

Popular with fishermen, hang gliders, naturalists and rock climbers.

WARNING: Beware of dangerous waves.
BEST TIME: Spring, summer.
ENQUIRIES: (098) 44 4090.
ADDRESS: Box 904, Albany 6330.

Scenic enjoyment ✔✔
Day activities ✔
Family camping ✔
Walking, climbing ✔✔

William Bay National Park
70 km W of Albany. Southwest weather district. Car access from South Coast Highway 14 km W of Denmark. Bus services pass park.

Less spectacular than other coastal parks in the region, the 1900 ha park nonetheless has much to offer. The narrow sandy beaches and low headlands – pleasant fishing spots – are backed by high rolling sand dunes from which granite tors jut out. A small area of petrified forest was caused by shifting sand which buried tall trees and then moved on, leaving the trunks still upright. Between the dunes grow thickets of stunted Western Australian peppermint, and away from the coast there is a small tract of karri forest. To the west Parry Inlet provides a breeding ground for waterfowl.

BEST TIME: Spring, summer.
ENQUIRIES: (098) 40 9255.
ADDRESS: Box 180, Denmark 6333.

Scenic enjoyment ✔
Day activities ✔
Family camping ×
Hard bushwalking ✔

Visitor activities in the national parks of Western Australia

Bird watching
Coastal parks, Geikie Gorge, Stokes, Yalgorup.

Bushwalking
All national parks but particularly Cape Le Grand, Hidden Valley, Porongurup, Stirling Range.

Camping
Cape Le Grand, Cape Range, Hamersley, Walpole-Nornalup.

Wild camping
Bungle Bungle, Walpole-Nornalup (Nuyts Wilderness).

Canoeing/boating
D'Entrecasteaux, *Kalbarri, Walpole-Nornalup, Walyunga.

Car touring
Hamersley Range, Nambung, Stirling Range, Walpole-Nornalup.

Caving
Leeuwin-Naturaliste, Tunnel Creek.

Cave tours
Leeuwin-Naturaliste, Yanchep.

Cycling
John Forrest, Leeuwin-Naturaliste, Torndirrup, Yanchep.

Wind blows a fine spume off the waves as a solitary fisherman waits for the telling twitch at his line

A chandelier of stalactites is one of the sights of Yanchep caves

Fishing, ocean
Cape Le Grand, Cape Range (Ningaloo), D'Entrecasteaux, Leeuwin-Naturaliste, Nambung, Stokes, Torndirrup.

Fishing, freshwater
Geikie Gorge, Millstream-Chichester, Pemberton (Warren River).

Geological studies
Cape Arid, Fitzgerald River, Geikie Gorge, Hamersley, Leeuwin-Naturaliste, Millstream-Chichester, Nambung, Stirling Range, Windjana Gorge, Wolfe Creek, Yalgorup.

Horse riding
John Forrest.

Photography
Bungle Bungle, Fitzgerald River, Geikie Gorge, Hamersley, Hidden Valley, Kalbarri, Leeuwin-Naturaliste, Nambung, Stirling Range, Torndirrup.

Picnicking
John Forrest, Porongurup, Serpentine, Walyunga, Yanchep.

Power boating
Cape Range (Ningaloo), Scott River, Walpole-Nornalup.

Orienteering
Avon Valley, John Forrest, Walyunga.

Rafting
Avon Valley, *Kalbarri, Walyunga.

There is the opportunity to photograph wildlife in most parks

Rock climbing
Porongurup, Stirling Range, West Cape Howe.

Scuba diving/snorkelling
Leeuwin-Naturaliste, William Bay.

Surfing
Leeuwin-Naturaliste.

Swimming
Cape Le Grand, Cape Range, Leeuwin-Naturaliste, Millstream-Chichester, William Bay.

Walking along coastal tracks and beaches
Cape Arid, Cape Le Grand, Cape Range, Leeuwin-Naturaliste.

Wildflower studies
Alexander Morrison, Badgingarra, Cape Le Grand, Fitzgerald River, Kalbarri, Stirling Range.

Windsurfing
D'Entrecasteaux, Leeuwin-Naturaliste, Walpole-Nornalup.

Wildlife observation
Cape Range, Geikie Gorge, Yanchep.

*The Murchison River flows infrequently and is dangerous in full flood. Permission must be obtained from ranger beforehand.

Wild camping in the new Bungle Bungle National Park

Surfing off Leeuwin-Naturaliste National Park

Signs like these mean business. They are NOT tourist souvenirs as some irresponsible people seem to think. Always heed warnings and take special care in crocodile country.

Hikers reach a vantage point overlooking the Murchison River in Kalbarri National Park

CAMPING

Wild camping — away from it all, no facilities other than those you create.
Camping — a pit toilet and a tap but no other facilities.
Family camping — established camping ground with showers, toilets, barbecue areas and where you can probably take a caravan, but check beforehand.

ADELAIDE REGION

Where an artist found wonder in wastelands

SETTLERS from Britain were slow to see any beauty in sun-scorched, dusty lands and lonely eucalypts. They signified hardship and despair. But early this century a German-born painter opened Australian eyes. Working mainly in the Flinders Ranges, Hans Heysen mastered the intensity of light in the dry outback, catching contrasts of form and tone in watercolours of haunting power.

He is remembered fittingly in the Heysen Trail, now being developed by the South Australian government. A system of connected walking and horse-riding tracks will reach from the northernmost heights of the Flinders to the ocean shores of Fleurieu Peninsula. Sections completed, spanning about 500 km, take in the state's best-known inland parks – including the scraps of forest that survive on the Mt Lofty Ranges just east of Adelaide.

Densely wooded country is rare in this generally semi-arid climate. The raised plain and steep scarps of the Mt Lofties catch just enough winter rain. But land reserved here, so close to the capital, suffered heavily from recreational use. Under strict international principles adopted in the early 1970s, some old national parks were stripped of their status. Many such areas are now called conservation parks – a designation that means priority is given to the conservation of wildlife and plants and preservation of the natural landscape. Some conservation parks, such as Cleland, Black Hill, Seal Bay, Naracoorte and Deep Creek, have good visitor facilities. When restored to a more natural condition, enlarged and with extra amenities, they may emerge as national parks.

Away from the ranges, parks within easy reach of Adelaide are chiefly appreciated for their coastal scenery and the maritime activities they allow – especially fishing. Their sparse vegetation may be less appealing, but it provides habitats for a surprising diversity of wildlife. Adelaide is also the most convenient capital from which to make a journey to parks in the arid hinterland of NSW, or even to Simpson Desert National Park in the 'corner country' of Queensland.

Climate bears importantly on a choice of destination. Winter on or near the coast is likely to be cold and wet, and summer almost anywhere may be fiercely hot. Winter and spring are the most suitable seasons for visits to the Flinders Ranges and the far northeast. Parks west of Adelaide are at their best in spring and autumn. Midsummer travelling should be limited to the coastal parks of the southeast and Kangaroo Island, which are also pleasant from late spring until well into autumn. South Australia has a general bushfire risk period from November to April. Total fire bans are automatically imposed in some parks for all or most of that time.

Featured parks	Pages
1 Cleland	170-171
2 Black Hill	172-173
3 Flinders Chase	174-175
4 Seal Bay	176-177
5 Mt Remarkable	178-179
6 Flinders Ranges	180-183
7 Coffin Bay	184
8 Lincoln	185
9 Canunda	186-187
10 Coorong	188

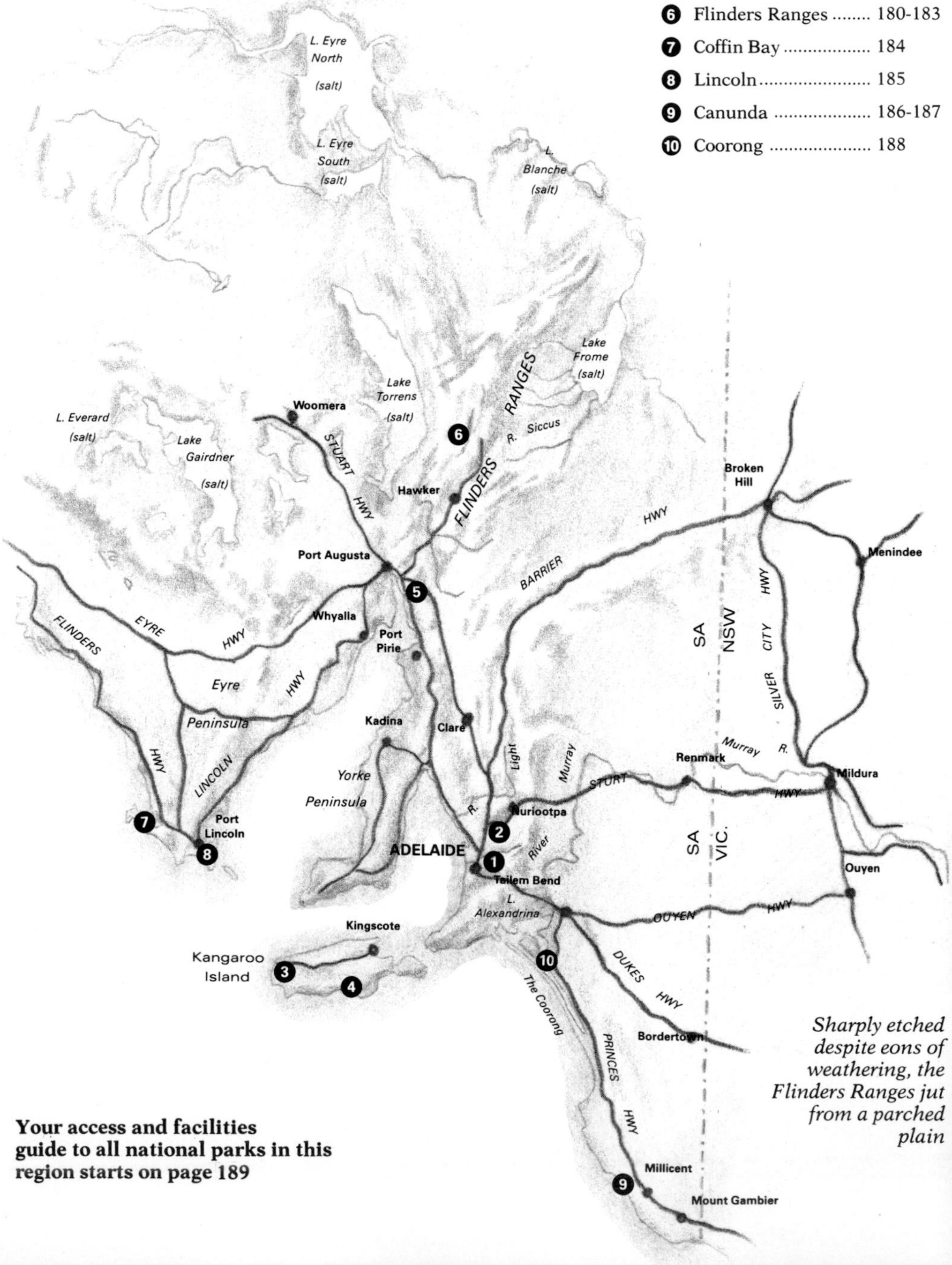

Your access and facilities guide to all national parks in this region starts on page 189

Sharply etched despite eons of weathering, the Flinders Ranges jut from a parched plain

Flowering peas surround a burnt slope where eucalypts are growing back. The blossoms are not native, but relics of Cleland's farming past

CLELAND CONSERVATION PARK

Timbered ridges overlooking Adelaide run west from the summit of Mt Lofty (725 metres) to the rocky gorge of Waterfall Gully. Eucalypt forests and woodlands cover most of Cleland's 890 ha, but king ferns can be found in a few peat bogs. The ferns are relics of a much moister South Australian climate, and are confined now to isolated spots in the Mt Lofty Ranges. There is an excellent network of walking tracks. The pride of Cleland – though largely manmade – is its central native fauna zone. Some exhibits are enclosed, but kangaroos and emus wander freely. Artificial lakes and swamps support waterfowl species rarely seen at such close quarters.

Grass-trees, called yakkas here, border another stand of regenerating eucalypts

Cool creek gullies make for pleasant walking – but alien weeds are common so close to the city

A yakka stands sentinel over introduced butterfly iris

Paterson's curse

Everlasting pea

Eucalypt woodlands crowd to the edges of tilted blocks of sandstone on the windy heights

BLACK HILL & MORIALTA CONSERVATION PARKS

The 1300 ha of these abutting parks in the Adelaide foothills create a major conservation as well as recreation area close to the city. Grasslands merge into woodlands of river red gum and yellow gum in the northernmost part of Black Hill, but most of the combined area is clothed in eucalypt forests and woodlands dominated by stringybark, on a rough terrain of ridges and steep, rocky gorges. Morialta is noted for its many waterfalls – seen at their best after good rains. Two falls on the Fourth Creek cascade more than 30 metres.

The Black Hill section includes a native plant park and nursery where educational walks can be taken in any season. Other walking tracks cover about 50 km in and between the two main sections; suggested routes take from 45 minutes to 2½ hours. Rock faces in the gorge of Morialta Creek are regarded by climbers as the best within easy reach of Adelaide. But they are dangerous, and call for experience and good equipment. Climbers must be members of approved organisations.

Heavy rain has fed a gushing waterfall in the Morialta section, among steep rock faces that challenge expert climbers

Remarkable Rocks, a richly coloured outcrop on the southwestern shores of Kangaroo Island. Deeper reds are the natural hues of ironstone; vivid orange comes from lichen growth. Some of the most striking coastal scenery is concentrated near Cape du Couedic

FLINDERS CHASE NATIONAL PARK

Picnic grounds are fenced at Rocky River – not to hold people in but to keep animals out. Cape Barren geese and big kangaroos are boldly insistent in their demands for handouts of food, and possums after dark are ready to help themselves. Flinders Chase is South Australia's most important wildlife refuge. The grassy floors of its eucalypt woodlands were never raided by rabbits, and alien predators such as foxes and dingoes did not reach Kangaroo Island. The major native predator is Rosenberg's goanna. Some mammals and many bird species have been introduced from the mainland to ensure their survival. Native birds include the rare western whipbird and the glossy black cockatoo – the latter found nowhere else in the state, although far from rare in eastern Australia.

The park of 73 662 ha occupies a southward-tilting plateau at the western end of the island. It has a rugged coastline of abrupt rocky cliffs and wave-eroded limestone and ironstone formations. Beaches are seldom safe for swimming. Three major rivers dissect the plateau; they flow year-round and their ravines support dense forests. Vehicle tracks radiate from the park headquarters at Rocky River, giving access to some parts of the coast. Marked walking trails, taking 1-3 hours return, reach secluded rivermouths and coves.

Melaleucas and banksias form dense coastal scrubs. Farther inland the park has mallee and stringybark woodlands, and forests dominated by sugar gum

Nobby Island juts from Vivonne Bay, to the west of Seal Bay. Erosion by powerful waves has carved it from the main landmass. Sea lions breed among rocks in the foreground, where visitors are forbidden to walk

SEAL BAY CONSERVATION PARK

Sea lions retreat in hundreds from the waterline at Seal Bay on colder days, to shelter in the sandhills. Beyond a mild gaze, they show no concern at the approach of visitors. But these huge marine mammals are not tame – an attempt to touch them will risk a savage bite. The Kangaroo Island colony at Seal Bay accounts for a tenth of the total population of Australian sea lions, and nowhere else are they so easily and reliably seen. They breed in a cycle of about 18 months, after bulls weighing up to 300 kg have fought on the beach for control of harems of cows. Pups are born and nursed in rocky coves at each end of the beach – off-limits to the public.

Bales Beach, to the east, has no restrictions on walking. The water is not suitable for swimming as white pointer sharks frequent this coast. Fishing is forbidden, to protect the sea lions' food stocks. Heaths and mallee woodlands back the eroded limestone cliffs of the 700 ha park and provide a habitat for small and large marsupials.

Zierra, a relative of boronia

White-bellied sea-eagles hunt in flight or from perches

Black-eyed Susan

Guinea flower

A sea lion cow is ready to defend her unweaned pup

Sloping ridges enclose a fertile basin (left) where sheep grazed until the 1960s. Mambray and Alligator Creeks flow quietly through deep gorges (below and right) cut into the sandstone heights. The fancifully named Alligator Creek used to be called Ally's Creek, probably after an Aboriginal stockman

Mount Remarkable National Park

Deep gorges, tree-lined and cool, dissect tilted outcrops of red-brown quartzite sandstone forming the southern Flinders Ranges. Mambray and Alligator Creeks share an oval basin rimmed with sharp ridges – a foretaste of what is seen to the north at Wilpena Pound. Mt Remarkable itself occupies a separate section of the 8649 ha park and is the least visited. But at 995 metres it caps a range that is chiefly responsible for reasonably reliable rains in this district, in contrast to the baked lowlands to the west and south along Spencer Gulf.

River red gums and white cypress pines dot the valleys of the basin, among grasslands where wildflowers bloom brilliantly in early spring. Ridges are wooded with tall sugar gums, distinguished by their piebald grey-and-salmon trunks, and blue gums. Marsupials are abundant along with more than 100 bird species and many reptiles, including the big lace monitor.

Pultenaea

Finger flower

Mallee

COFFIN BAY NATIONAL PARK

At the heel of Eyre Peninsula a T-shaped platform of limestone and granite juts defiantly into the heavy westerly swells of the great Australian Bight. Coffin Bay Peninsula gives visitors a choice between boisterous surf and gentle, landlocked waters. Swimming and diving are safe at several sandy beaches on either side of the isthmus. Fishing is popular from the shore and from boats, which can be launched at Coffin Bay township or at Point Avoid, where tuna and abalone boats shelter. Coastline features of the 30 380 ha park include striking limestone cliffs, shelving outcrops of smooth granite, active dunefields and scrub-covered dune ridges. Woodlands and richly flowering heathlands surround the quiet inner bays of Port Douglas.

The low granite mass of Golden Island, off Point Avoid, resists the constant pounding of Bight seas. But soft formations of limestone and siltstone on the shore (left) are eroding quickly

Angular pigface in bloom

Thistle Island, rising beyond smaller islands off Memory Bay in the south of the park, shelters much of the east coast from heavy seas curving round the peninsula

LINCOLN NATIONAL PARK

Pimelea

Seaside pastimes are the popular attractions of Lincoln, which occupies most of Jussieu Peninsula at the south-eastern end of Eyre Peninsula. Visitor activity is concentrated on the northern shores, facing across quiet waters to Port Lincoln, and at Taylors Landing on the island-sheltered east coast. These parts have the only roads suitable for conventional vehicles, and the only beaches where safe swimming, fishing and boating are assured. Few travellers see the arresting coastal scenery of the wave-battered south, and fewer still know much of the sandy, scrub-covered interior. Most of the 17 372 ha park has no overland walking trails because it fills the role of a nature reserve. Its merging of semi-arid and coastal vegetation and bird habitats is of high scientific interest. Among birds of the scrub are some at the eastern limit of a range that extends to Western Australia.

Templetonia retusa

CANUNDA NATIONAL PARK

'Live' sand dunes, drifting inland under the remorseless pressure of westerly winds off the Southern Ocean, uncover and rebury ancient history at Canunda. Old stone dwellings near the resort town of Southport have disappeared. Still older Aboriginal campsites, with fireplaces and shell dumps, have appeared. Where the shifting sands expose former dunes, now solidified, these become low sea cliffs to take the brunt of the ocean's power.

Waves and winds built all of this park, which forms a narrow sand barrier reaching for 40 km between Cape Buffon and Cape Banks. Trapped behind it are flood-prone lowlands and the shallow fresh waters of Lake Bonney. The strip of 9000 ha, averaging about 2 km in width, is a miniature version of the Coorong.

Dense coastal heaths clothe clifftops and stable dunes; swamp plants fringe the wetlands behind. The park is principally a refuge for seabirds, waterfowl and heathland species including the endangered orange-bellied parrot and the seldom-seen rufous bristlebird. Beaches and cliffs are suitable for fishing, but swimming is extremely dangerous from all the beaches. Walking finds little favour: the dunes make hard going.

Eroded limestone remnants of ancient dunes dot nearshore waters at the northern end of the park, providing roosts and nesting grounds for seabirds

Forlorn stumps remain where trees have been swamped and killed by drifting sand. Heavy mineral particles, sinking as the sediments are churned and sifted, make a dark layer at the base of the dune. Below: Salt-tolerant plants colonise an old, solidified dune ridge exposed by winds

Heaths and scrubs crowd a little freshwater lake perched among dunes. But plants growing too close were killed by flooding

Melaleucas fringing the inland side of the Coorong near Woods Well are bowed by the insistent force of winds off the Southern Ocean. These winds also push up the barrier dunes of Younghusband Peninsula, seen in the background

Pelicans and silver gulls hunt for crustaceans. The book and film Storm Boy*, about an Aboriginal youth's affinity with a pelican, were set in this area*

COORONG NATIONAL PARK

Heavy ocean surf and placid lagoon waters are seldom more than 2 km apart along 60 km of coast reaching south from the Murray River 'mouth'. The flow of the depleted river is so feeble, in comparison with the inward thrust of waves and marine sands, that it rarely finds an outlet without help from bulldozers. Instead its silted and salted waters spread sluggishly in Lakes Alexandrina and Albert and down the shallow Coorong, creating perfect wetland habitats for waterfowl.

The park of 38 000 ha, including the Coorong waters as well as the dune barrier of Younghusband Peninsula, embraces a game reserve of nearly 9000 ha where eight wild duck species may be hunted in season. Fishing is popular off the ocean beach and in the Coorong, where conditions are ideal for small boats. A short nature trail near the park headquarters car park, south of Salt Creek, explains the changes in vegetation and in sand dune formation that visitors find in the park.

PARKS OF THE ADELAIDE REGION

FACILITIES

Cabins

Caravan park

Equipped picnic area

Bush camping allowed

Lavatory building

Established campsite

Campsite but no car access

Note: Popular parks without campsites usually have public camping grounds nearby. If in doubt, call enquiries number.

PARK RATINGS No interest ✘ Some interest ✔ Major interest ✔✔ Outstanding ✔✔✔

Belair Recreation Park

13 km S. Central weather district. Car access off Upper Sturt Road, Glenalta. Open 9 am till sunset.

Residential development thins around Belair as Adelaide's suburbs begin to climb into increasingly rugged terrain of the Mt Lofty Ranges. Gentle slopes of the 800 ha park's western section are a major recreation reserve for the city, with sports fields, a golf course, adventure playground, tennis courts and a kiosk. River red gums and peppermint box dominate the remnants of natural vegetation, while extensive stands of mature exotic trees ornament avenues and picnic grounds. Governors of South Australia favoured the area as a summer refuge in the mid-1800s. Their residence has been restored and is now open as a museum.

Deep valleys dissect the park's less disturbed eastern section. Stringybark forests interspersed with pink, blue and manna gum provide a natural environment where walkers see spring wildflowers at their best.

BEST TIME: Spring.
ENQUIRIES: (08) 278 5477.
ADDRESS: Box 2, Belair 5052.

Scenic enjoyment ✔
Day activities ✔✔✔
Family camping ✔✔
Hard bushwalking ✘

Black Hill and Morialta Conservation Parks

12 km NE. Central weather district. Car access off Morialta Road, Rostrevor, and Gorge Road, Athelstone. Closed to cars at sunset.

DESCRIPTION: Page 172.
BEST TIME: Spring, autumn.
ENQUIRIES: (08) 336 3966.
ADDRESS: 115 Maryvale Road, Athelstone 5076.

Scenic enjoyment ✔✔
Day activities ✔✔
Family camping ✘
Hard bushwalking ✔✔✔

Canunda National Park

400 km SE, 26 km W of Millicent. Southeast weather district. Car access off Princes Highway via Southend. Limited park roads for conventional vehicles; full length for 4WD.

DESCRIPTION: Page 186.
NOTES: Permit required for camping. Carry drinking water.
WARNING: Swimming dangerous.
BEST TIME: Spring to autumn.
ENQUIRIES: (087) 35 6053.
ADDRESS: C/o P.O., Southend 5280.

Scenic enjoyment ✔✔
Day activities ✔✔
Family camping ✘
Hard bushwalking ✔

Cleland Conservation Park

9 km SE. Central weather district. Car access off Summit Road, Crafers, and off Waterfall Gully Road, Greenhill. Bus Adelaide-Greenhill Road.

DESCRIPTION: Page 170.
BEST TIME: Spring, autumn.
ENQUIRIES: (08) 339 2581.
ADDRESS: Box 245, Stirling 5152.

Scenic enjoyment ✔✔
Day activities ✔✔✔
Family camping ✘
Hard bushwalking ✔

Coffin Bay National Park

720 km W, 50 km W of Port Lincoln. Western Agricultural weather district. Car access off Flinders Highway 32 km W of Port Lincoln.

DESCRIPTION: Page 184.
NOTES: Permit required for camping. Bush camping restricted to designated sites.
BEST TIME: Spring, autumn.
ENQUIRIES: (086) 85 4047.
ADDRESS: C/o P.O., Coffin Bay 5607.

Scenic enjoyment ✔✔✔
Day activities ✔✔
Family camping ✔
Hard bushwalking ✘

Coorong National Park

210 km SE, 60 km S of Meningie. Southeast weather district. Car access off Princes Highway along inland boundary. Two crossings bridge the Coorong to ocean beaches: 42 Mile Crossing passable year-round; Tea Tree Crossing may be covered by water up to half a metre deep in winter.

DESCRIPTION: Page 188.
NOTES: Acces to some islands in Coorong prohibited. Licence required for duck shooting. Permit required for camping.
WARNING: Ocean beaches south of Tea Tree Crossing unsafe for swimming.
BEST TIME: Spring to autumn.
ENQUIRIES: (085) 75 7014.
ADDRESS: Private Bag 43, Meningie 5264.

Scenic enjoyment ✔
Day activities ✔✔
Family camping ✘
Hard bushwalking ✘

Deep Creek Conservation Park

110 km S. Central weather district. Car access off Main South Road at Delamere.

Bushwalkers must be prepared for steep descents as trails through deep valleys of the Mt Lofty Ranges drop to meet the Southern Ocean at the southern end of Fleurieu Peninsula. Sandy pocket beaches just outside the park boundary are reached by walking trails from the major campsites, but most of the park's coastline consists of rocky shores and high cliffs sculpted by relentless ocean swells.

Camping in this 4000 ha park is restricted to undeveloped sites in the tall inland forests of brown stringybark and messmate. The dense scrub understorey contains silver banksia, tea-trees and grass trees. Towards the coast persistent, salt-laden winds stunt the trees: messmates grow in a mallee form and heath plants and pink gum predominate.

NOTES: Permit required for camping. No water supplies in park. Fire ban December-March.
BEST TIME: Spring, autumn.
ENQUIRIES: (085) 59 2263.
ADDRESS: C/o P.O., Delamere 5204.

Scenic enjoyment ✔✔✔
Day activities ✔
Family camping ✘
Hard bushwalking ✔✔

Flinders Chase National Park

210 km SW, 100 km W of Kingscote, Kangaroo Island. Central weather district. Car access off Playford Highway via West End Highway. Car ferry and flights Adelaide-Kangaroo Island; bus Kingscote-Flinders Chase.

DESCRIPTION: Page 175.
NOTES: Permit required for camping; fee charged. Bush camping restricted to designated sites. Fire ban November-March.
WARNINGS: Swimming unsafe. Waves dangerous to walkers at Remarkable Rocks.
BEST TIME: Spring to autumn.
ENQUIRIES: (0848) 37 235.
ADDRESS: Private Bag 246, Rocky River, Kangaroo Island 5223.

Scenic enjoyment ✔✔✔
Day activities ✔✔✔
Family camping ✔✔✔
Hard bushwalking ✔✔

Flinders Ranges National Park

470 km N, 55 km N of Hawker. Northern Agricultural weather district. Hawker-Blinman road crosses park; sealed to Wilpena.

DESCRIPTION: Page 181.
NOTES: Permit required for camping; fee charged. Fire ban November-March. Boil all creek water before drinking.
BEST TIME: Autumn to spring.
ENQUIRIES: Oraparinna section (086) 48 0017; Wilpena section (086) 48 0048.
ADDRESS: Private Bag 22, Hawker 5434.

Scenic enjoyment ✔✔✔
Day activities ✔✔
Family camping ✔✔✔
Hard bushwalking ✔✔✔

Gammon Ranges National Park

680 km N, 265 km N of Hawker. Northeast Pastoral weather district. Car access via Hawker and Copley to Balcanoona.

From the grounds of a former sheep station homestead bushwalkers cross grasslands and pounds dotted with eucalypts, blue-grey mulga and casuarinas to reach rugged cliffs and gorges in the Gammon Ranges. From a distance there seems little relief from the 100 000 ha park's horizon of arid, rocky slopes sparsely dotted with yakkas, cypress pine and hummock grasses. Higher rainfalls on the crest of the main range, however, support dense scrubland dominated by mallee, melaleucas and acacias. In the gullies and gorges semi-permanent creeks foster stands of river red gum and attract a diverse bird population. Parrots move along the tree-lined creeks in big flocks. The gorges also provide an important habitat for yellow-footed rock wallaby colonies, which had to compete for food with feral goats until a control programme in the early 1980s drastically reduced the goats' numbers.

NOTES: Fee charged for camping. Carry drinking water.
BEST TIME: April-October.
ENQUIRIES: (086) 42 3800.
ADDRESS: SANPWS district office, Balcanoona via Copley 5732.

Scenic enjoyment ✔✔
Day activities ✔
Family camping ✘
Hard bushwalking ✔✔✔

Innes National Park

300 km W, 145 km S of Ardrossan. Cental weather district. Car access off Highway 1 at Port Wakefield via Ardrossan, Minlaton and Warooka.

A repetitive musical song coming from the dense heath and mallee scrub at the tip of Yorke Peninsula alerted ornithologists in 1965 to the presence of the rare western whipbird. Establishment of a 9000 ha park was principally to preserve the bird's habitat, but it also secured a natural environment around the rugged, cliff-lined coast and its string of popular beaches.

Mallee woodland covers most of the park, enclosing grassy patches and scattered stands of casuarinas and cypress pine. Along the northern shores ridges of stabilised dunes are interrupted by huge sand blowouts drifting inland towards salt marshes and an open growth of tea-tree and cutting grass around a chain of salt lakes. Stunted heath clings to the slopes and headlands exposed to powerful winds blowing off the Southern Ocean.

Surfaced roads ring the park, linking clifftop lookouts, launching ramps, campsites and sheltered bays favoured by anglers and swimmers.

NOTES: Fee charged for camping. Carry drinking water.
WARNING: Clifftops are eroded and may crumble underfoot.
BEST TIME: Spring to autumn.
ENQUIRIES: 011 ask for Stenhouse Bay 12.
ADDRESS: P.O., Stenhouse Bay 5577.

Scenic enjoyment ✔✔✔
Day activities ✔✔✔
Family camping ✔✔✔
Hard bushwalking ✔

PARKS OF THE ADELAIDE REGION

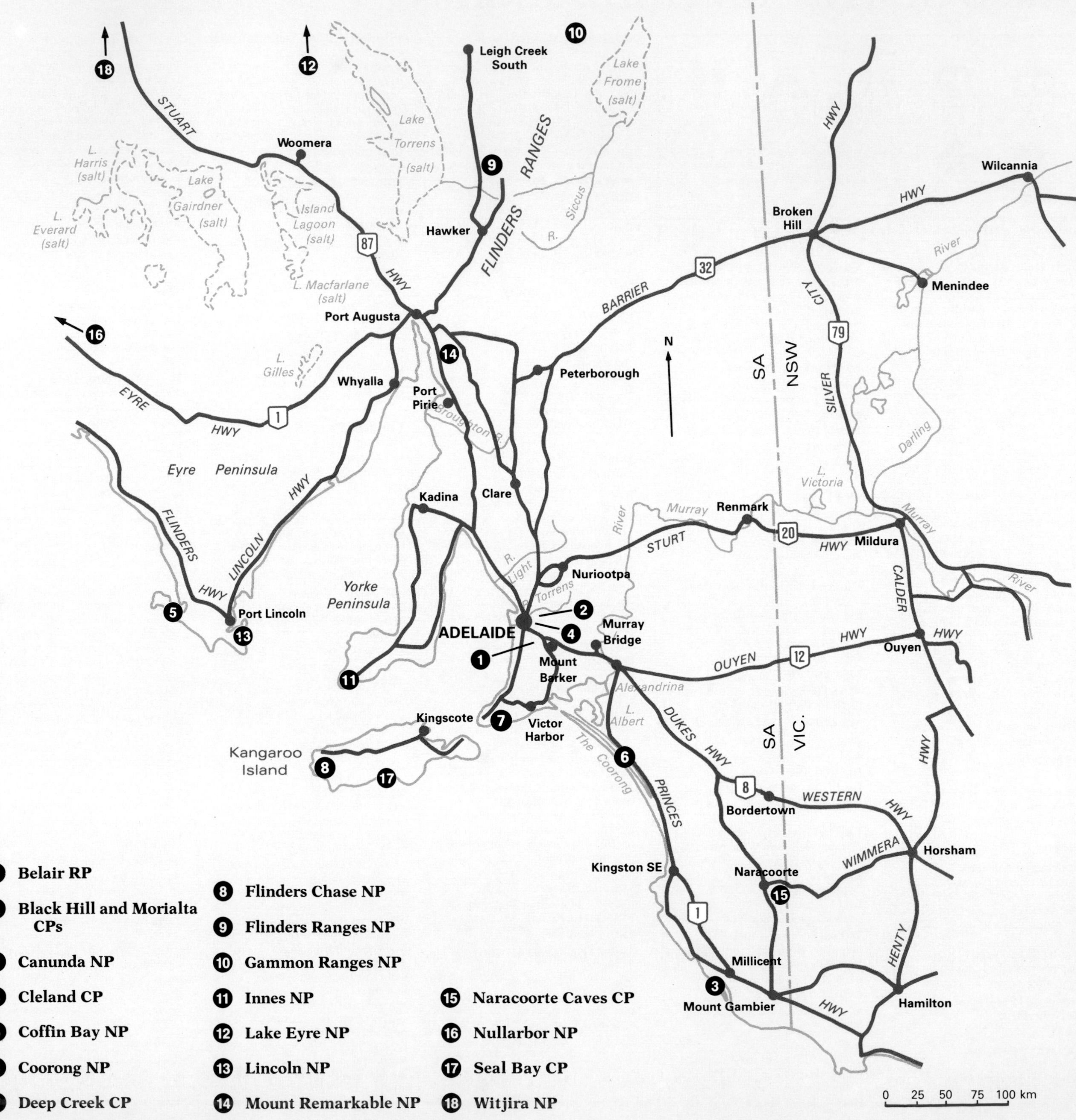

1 Belair RP
2 Black Hill and Morialta CPs
3 Canunda NP
4 Cleland CP
5 Coffin Bay NP
6 Coorong NP
7 Deep Creek CP
8 Flinders Chase NP
9 Flinders Ranges NP
10 Gammon Ranges NP
11 Innes NP
12 Lake Eyre NP
13 Lincoln NP
14 Mount Remarkable NP
15 Naracoorte Caves CP
16 Nullarbor NP
17 Seal Bay CP
18 Witjira NP

Lake Eyre National Park
900 km N, 100 km NW of Marree. Northeast Pastoral weather district. 4 WD access only.

This vast new park of 1.228 million ha was declared in 1986. The legendary 'inland sea' is both a great salina (dry salt lake) and a great playa lake (one that is occasionally flooded). As salina, its surface was used for the setting of a world land speed record in 1964; as playa, it fills with fish and waterbirds – gulls, pelicans, cormorants, black swans, pink ducks.

The contrast between its two faces is dramatic, but a visit to the region is only for those with a sense of adventure, a love of space and solitude, and a fascination with the sort of wildlife and plants that exist under Eyre's extreme conditions.

Typical vegetation is samphires, saltbush, bluebush and spinifex. The area is home to many species of dragon lizards, geckos and snakes; to tiny marsupial hunters like the mulgara, kowari and dunnart; it is the territory of the wedge-tailed eagle, falcons and harriers.

NOTE: Camping permit required.
WARNING: Visitors must be fully equipped for outback survival. Carry all water and fuel supplies, spare parts and radio transceiver. There are no facilities.
BEST TIME: Cool weather after outback rains. Dangerous in summer.
ENQUIRIES: (086) 75 2499.
ADDRESS: Box 34, Leigh Creek 5731.

Scenic enjoyment ✔✔
Day activities ✖
Family camping ✖
Hard bushwalking ✖

Lincoln National Park
695 km W, 27 km S of Port Lincoln. Western Agricultural weather district. Car access off sealed road 14 km S of Port Lincoln. Internal roads unsealed.
DESCRIPTION: Page 185.
NOTES: No water supplies in park. Permit required for camping.
WARNING: Parts of coastline unsafe for swimming.
BEST TIME: Spring.
ENQUIRIES: (086) 82 3936.
ADDRESS: 90 Tasman Terrace, Port Lincoln 5606.

Scenic enjoyment ✔✔
Day activities ✔✔✔
Family camping ✔✔
Hard bushwalking ✔

Mount Remarkable National Park
270 km N, 50 km N of Port Pirie. Northern Agricultural weather district. Car access to Alligator Gorge off Main North Road at Wilmington; to Mambray Creek off Highway 1, 45 km N of Port Pirie.
DESCRIPTION: Page 178.
NOTES: Permit required for camping: fee charged; bookings recommended for long weekends. Bush camping restricted to designated sites (elsewhere with permission of ranger). No bush camping during total fire ban November-April. Carry drinking water on walks.
BEST TIME: Autumn to spring.
ENQUIRIES: Mambray Creek section (086) 34 7068; Alligator Gorge section (086) 67 5181.
ADDRESS: Private Bag 7, Port Germein 5495.

Scenic enjoyment ✔✔✔
Day activities ✔✔
Family camping ✔✔✔
Hard bushwalking ✔✔✔

Naracoorte Caves Conservation Park
355 km SE, 14 km S of Naracoorte. Southeast weather district. Car access off Naracoorte Penola road 9 km S of Naracoorte.

Beneath the limestone rock of Cave Range, delicate calcite structures decorate the ceilings and floors of about 60 caves. Three caves with electric light are open daily for guided tours. As well as conical stalactites and stalagmites, waters slowly dripping into the caves have left calcite deposits in thick columns, long hollow tubes and in thin sheets called shawls. Erratic capillary action has formed striking, star-shaped helictites.

Excavations in part of Victoria Cave have uncovered skeletons of many extinct species, including several types of giant marsupial which roamed the region before the cave mouths were blocked by sand some 10 000 years ago. A display has been set up in the cave so that specimens and excavation can be seen together.

Above ground the caves section of this 300 ha park is clothed in forests of brown stringybark and blackwood with an understorey of tea-tree, banksias and wattle. River red gums grow profusely along the banks of Mosquito Creek in the southern part of the park, but the area is regularly inundated in winter and has little attraction for bushwalkers.

NOTES: Permit required for camping; fee charged. Fee charged for entry to caves; tours 9.30-16.00 daily.
VISITOR CENTRE: At park headquarters.
BEST TIME: Year-round.
ENQUIRIES: (087) 62 2340.
ADDRESS: Bax 134, Naracoorte 5271.

Scenic enjoyment ✔✔✔
Day activities ✔✔
Family camping ✔✔
Hard bushwalking ✖

Nullarbor National Park
1100 km W, 300 km W of Ceduna. Western Agricultural weather district. Eyre Highway crosses park; rough tracks branch off to coastal cliffs.

Few travellers speeding to distant destinations along the Eyre Highway expect great scenic enjoyment from the vast plain of the Nullarbor. Those who are attracted by signs indicating coastal lookouts, however, are rewarded by stunning views of sheer, high cliffs along the Great Australian Bight. Mallee scrub is patchily distributed in the 230 000 ha park's coastal region, but elsewhere low rainfalls support only a low ground cover of bluebush and saltbush. Grasses and wildflowers appear ephemerally after rains at any time of year, but most frequently in winter.

Subsurface erosion through the plain's level strata of marine limestone has created a number of cave systems. In the absence of trees and heavy vegetation many birds and mammals rely on the caves' shelter to nest and rear their young. Most species, including an important population of hairy-nosed wombats, are nocturnal, emerging in the evening when temperature and humidity are at levels which help contain the loss of body moisture by evaporation.

WARNING: Crumbling cliff edges and strong winds are dangerous along the coast.
BEST TIME: Autumn to spring.
ENQUIRIES: (086) 76 1098.
ADDRESS: SANPWS district office, C/o P.O., Streaky Bay 5680.

Scenic enjoyment ✔✔
Day activities ✔
Family camping ✖
Hard bushwalking ✖

Seal Bay Conservation Park
170 km SW, 60 km SW of Kingscote, Kangaroo Island. Central weather district. See Flinders Chase for island access. Car access off South Coast Road.
DESCRIPTION: Page 177.
NOTE: Fishing prohibited – nearshore waters are a marine reserve.
BEST TIME: Spring to autumn.
ENQUIRIES: (0848) 22 381.
ADDRESS: Box 39, Kingscote 5223.

Scenic enjoyment ✔✔
Day activities ✔✔
Family camping ✖
Hard bushwalking ✖

Witjira National Park
1400 km NNW, 200 km NE of Oodnadatta. Northeast Pastoral weather district. 4 WD access only.

Declared in 1986, the 779 500 ha park extends from the western stony tablelands east to the sand dunes of the Simpson Desert; and from north of Macumba to the flood plains of the Finke River. It protects a unique complex of mound springs.

These are like oases in the desert; permanent sources of water in a land where rainfall is scarce and summer temperatures extreme. The springs are natural outlets for waters from the Great Artesian Basin. As the water evaporates, the minerals it held crystallise and are left behind as solids. Over time they have combined with the ancient sand and clay to form mounds around the spring outlets.

The springs are home to rare fish and amphibia. Because there is permanent water the area has a large and varied bird population.

Traditionally this is the land of the Lower Southern Aranda people. The springs, floodplains and sand dunes are all part of their mythology. Each spring has connection with different ancestors. There are a number of major ritual centres around the Finke.

NOTE: Camping permit required.
WARNING: Visitors must be fully equipped for outback survival. Carry all water and fuel supplies, spare parts and radio transceiver. There are no facilities.
BEST TIME: Cool weather after outback rains. Dangerous in summer.
ENQUIRIES: (086) 75 2499.
ADDRESS: Box 34, Leigh Creek 5731.

Scenic enjoyment ✔✔
Day activities ✖
Family camping ✖
Hard bushwalking ✖

Tammar wallaby – lives in coastal scrub or mallee thicket, feeds at nig

Fat-tailed dunnart – superb adapter which lives anywhere from the coast to Lake Eyre

Bearded dragon Amphibolorus vitticeps – creature of the inland

Short-beaked echidna – in arid areas active only at night

South Australian wildlife

In spite of the flatness, aridity, high temperatures and sparse vegetation of much of the state it is home territory to an abundance of wildlife. Creatures have adapted to a life with little fresh water and little shelter; most forage at night and shelter in scrub or among rocks during the day. Yellow-footed rock wallabies live where there is apparently no water source; the tammar wallaby is able to drink seawater; birds and various other species do not breed in times of severe drought.

Yellow-footed rock wallaby – inhabitant of dry country it is prey of the wedge-tailed eagle

Wedge-tailed eagle nest – in drought years the birds may not breed

Western grey kangaroos – unlike the eastern grey do not carry a dormant embryo in the uterus while a joey is in the pouch

Birdlife

Peregrine falcon – uses the abandoned nests of other birds

Rock parrot – lives in coastal shrubland and on the islands

Red-rumped parrot – ground-feeding seed-eater

Little penguin – only penguin to breed in Australia

Little corellas – strip the roost tree of all leaves

Pink cockatoo – feeds in branches or on ground on seeds, nuts, fruits and roots

Straw-necked ibis – breeding colonies may contain 200 000 birds

Osprey – young ospreys learn to fish within a week of leaving the nest

Visitor activities in the national parks of South Australia

Abseiling (with permits)
Black Hill, Flinders Ranges.

Bird watching
Canunda, Coorong, Deep Creek, Flinders Chase, Flinders Ranges, Gammon Ranges, Innes, Lincoln, Mount Remarkable.

Bush camping
Canunda, Coffin Bay, Coorong, Deep Creek, Flinders Ranges, Gammon Ranges, Innes, Lake Eyre, Lincoln, Mount Remarkable, Nullarbor, Witjira.

Bush walking, including day walks
Black Hill, Cleland, Flinders Chase, Flinders Ranges, major feature at Deep Creek, Gammon Ranges, Mount Remarkable.

Camping
Flinders Chase, Flinders Ranges, Mount Remarkable, Naracoorte.

Canoeing/boating
Coffin Bay, Coorong.

Car touring
Flinders Ranges, Nullarbor. Limited touring in Flinders Chase, Gammon Ranges, Innes, Coorong. With well equipped 4WD at Lake Eyre, Witjira.

Caving (experienced people, with permit)
Naracoorte (a special feature), Nullarbor.

Cave tours
Naracoorte (major attraction).

Cycling
Belair (limited).

Fishing, beach/ocean
Canunda, Coffin Bay, Coorong, Innes (major feature), Lincoln.

Geological studies
Flinders Ranges, Gammon Ranges, Mount Remarkable.

Historical studies
Belair (limited), Flinders Ranges, Gammon Ranges, Innes.

Horse riding (on specified tracks)
Belair, Flinders Ranges.

Photography
Coffin Bay, Coorong, Deep Creek, Flinders Chase, Flinders Ranges, Gammon Ranges, Innes, Lincoln, Mount Remarkable.

Picnicking
Belair, Black Hill, Cleland.

Orienteering (organised groups)
Belair.

Rock climbing (with permits)
Black Hill, Flinders Ranges.

Wind surfing
Coffin Bay (limited), Coorong.

Yachting
Coffin Bay, Coorong (small yachts; not fo beginners), Lincoln.

Wildlife observation
Cleland, Flinders Chase, Seal Bay – speci feature of these three parks.

Birdwatchers at Innes National Park, home of the rare western whipbird

South Australian parks provide bush walking for the fit and less demanding walks for those who merely want to wander and enjoy nature

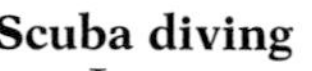

Scuba diving
Innes.

Snorkelling
Innes.

Surfing
Innes (major feature).

Survival skills/journey testing
Lake Eyre, Witjira.

Swimming
Coffin Bay, Coorong, Innes, Lincoln.

Tennis
Belair.

Walking along coastal tracks and beaches
Canunda, Coffin Bay, Flinders Chase, Innes, Lincoln, Seal Bay.

Wildflower studies
Black Hill, Deep Creek, Flinders Chase, Flinders Ranges (spring and after rain).

Rock climbing in Morialta Gorge, wh faces are as testing as any in the cou

CAMPING

Bush camping — away from it all, no facilities other than those you create.
Camping — a pit toilet and a tap but no other facilities.
Family camping — established camping ground with showers, toilets, barbecue areas and where you can probably take a caravan, but check beforehand.

The Coorong is a breeding ground for waterbirds and its ocean beach a haunt for fishermen

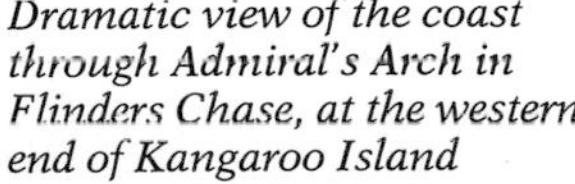

Dramatic view of the coast through Admiral's Arch in Flinders Chase, at the western end of Kangaroo Island

Surfing off Pondalowie Bay at Innes National Park

The native fauna centre at Cleland Conservation Park draws visitors like a magnet. There they may have close-ups of many native animals and birds, but the most popular display is always the koalas

Proud achievements in park acquisition are crowned in the Grampians

MELBOURNE REGION

Forests hold their ground in a crowded corner

VICTORIA is the most densely populated Australian state, and the most intensively farmed. In spite of that nearly a third of its natural bushland remains. Most is mountainous: the Great Dividing Range marches across the state, its outlying ridges pushing to the Bass Strait coast. No other mainland region is so dominated by high country.

National parks in the northeast preserve the lofty plains of the Victorian Alps, snow-covered in winter, but grassy and sprinkled with wildflowers at other times. Parks in the east include wooded upland wildernesses at Croajingolong and Snowy River, temperate rainforests and subtropical remnants at Tarra Valley and Bulga, and an unsurpassed variety of plant communities around the granite peaks of Wilsons Promontory. Ranges in the west are backdrops for remarkable coastal scenery at Otway and Port Campbell. And spacious areas are reserved in highlands fringing Melbourne itself.

With the dedication in 1984 of Grampians National Park, Victoria attained an admirable mark in conservation: more than 5 per cent of its territory is protected in national parks or other professionally managed reserves. In hectares alone the target was not difficult – more than enough mountain terrain lay unused. Finding a representative range of other habitats was harder, but the will was found after a political storm in the late 1960s.

The row centred on obscure sandplains in the remote northwest. Even now they are little visited. A scheme for agricultural expansion threatened one of the last habitats of the malleefowl. The volume of public outcry – and a staggering by-election result – shook the state government. It abandoned the farming plan and proclaimed a vast extension of Little Desert National Park. More significantly, it conceded that piecemeal ways of resolving conflicts over crown land use were not good enough.

A Land Conservation Council was set up in 1970 to plan for the preservation of ecologically important or scenically valuable areas and to meet future needs for public leisure and recreation. Its recommendations, accepted with very little demur by succeeding governments, have led to a dramatic increase in the extent and variety of parks on public land. Completion of the council's programme, to include a few types of natural habitats still missing from the state's array of parks and reserves, calls for the costly resumption of private lands. Shortage of funds is a stumbling block. But Victoria's achievements already are the envy of other states, and of many countries overseas.

Featured parks	Pages
1 Brisbane Ranges	200-201
2 Otway	202
3 Kinglake	203-205
4 Organ Pipes	206
5 Cape Schanck	207
6 Wilsons Promontory	208-213
7 Tarra-Bulga	214-216
8 Hattah-Kulkyne	217
9 Croajingolong	218-219
10 Mt Buffalo	220-221
11 Bogong	222-223
12 Port Campbell	224-225
13 Lower Glenelg	226
14 Mt Eccles	227
15 Grampians	228-231

Your access and facilities guide to all national parks in this region starts on page 232

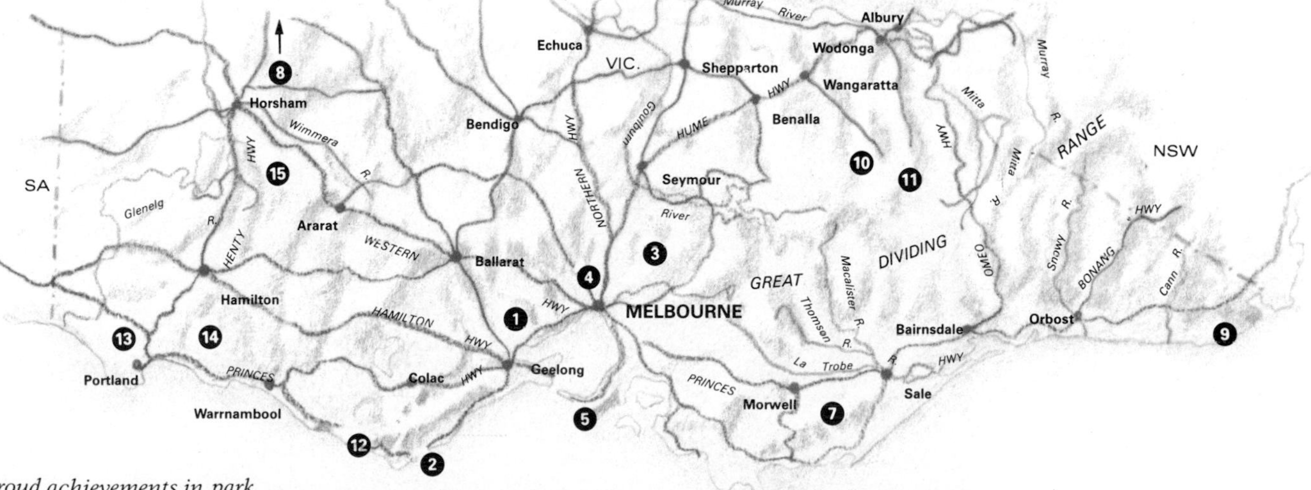

Grassy glades among forests on the moister slopes may owe their origins to a gold boom at nearby Steiglitz in the 1860s. Many trees were felled to make mine props

Koalas are commonly seen – their natural numbers have been boosted by introductions from Phillip and French Islands in Western Port Bay, east of Melbourne. Kangaroos, wallabies, possums and echidnas also live in the park, with about 150 species of birds

Steiglitz grevillea

Everlastings bloom on a rocky slope of Anakie Gorge, where a river now represented by Stony Creek cut through the ancient slates and shales of the escarpment

Southern grass trees – members of the lily family – thrive on sandy soils. Often they delay putting up their sweet-scented flowering spikes until a bushfire has singed them

Bush peas form a dense mat in spring

BRISBANE RANGES NATIONAL PARK

Victoria's richest displays of spring wildflowers are seen here, little more than an hour's drive from Melbourne. The park's 420 native plant species include the unique Brisbane Ranges or steiglitz grevillea and many others that are rare, or cut off from their normal habitats. The unusual geology of the ranges seems to have preserved relics of an age when plants were differently distributed.

A steep scarp forms the eastern edge of the 7500 ha park. It marks the Rowsley Fault, along which the lands of the Port Phillip basin subsided about 1 million years ago. Deep, rocky gullies such as Anakie Gorge now cut into the scarp. To the west the park consists of a gently undulating plateau where eucalypt woodlands have a dense understorey of heaths. Low forests occur on some shale-derived soils.

Curving spurs of the Otway Range reach the westernmost shores of Bass Strait, giving shelter to the Parker River and allowing the sediments it carries to form a delta

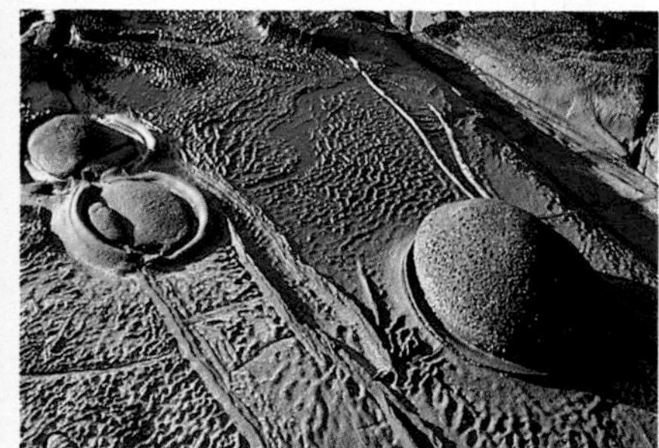

Waves and spray working on sandstone of varying hardness produce intriguing shapes on a shore platform

OTWAY NATIONAL PARK

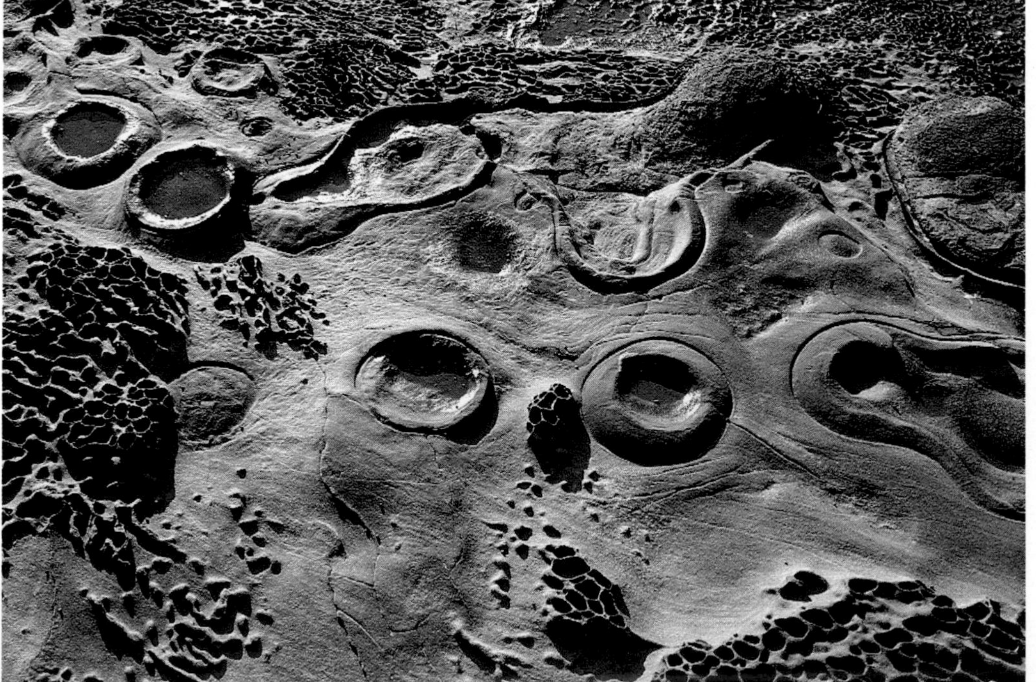

Broad platforms of wave-worn sandstone skirt cliffs along the Bass Strait shore east of Cape Otway. They make a fascinating pathway for walkers beginning a journey round the cape and along uninhabited Southern Ocean beaches reaching towards Port Campbell. This is a coast of bitter gales and heavy seas, but given fair weather and a fortunate timing of the tides, about 60 km can be traversed, at or near the waterline, in four or five days.

The eastern section of the 12 750 ha park includes an inland wedge taking in the catchments of the Calder, Parker and Elliott Rivers in the Otway Range. A high rainfall supports towering forests of mountain ash on protected slopes, and gullies of myrtle beech rainforest with thick undergrowths of mosses and tree ferns. Short forest walks can be taken from Maits Rest on the Great Ocean Road. Wallabies and possums are commonly seen. Bower birds and king parrots are among many species of birds in the park.

KINGLAKE NATIONAL PARK

Cool, fern-filled gullies contrast agreeably with slopes of dry eucalypt forest running towards Melbourne from the Kinglake ridge, where the Great Dividing Range curves closest to the city. North-south spurs 400-500 metres high are separated by the valleys of streams that drop sharply – cascading after good rains – to the lowlands before joining the Yarra River. Each of the three sections of the 11 400 ha park, which has been pieced together from land long since deserted by farmers, miners and timber getters, offers at least half a dozen different walks that sample the varying scenery. Some have steep pinches, but they command excellent views over the foothills and plains surrounding Melbourne. Lyrebirds are numerous, though not often seen; the males can be heard practising their mimicry in winter.

More than 30 species of ferns have been identified in the steep, damp gullies of Kinglake

Goodenia ovata can grow up to 2 metres in mountain forests

Musk daisies thrive in gullies, often emerging over tree ferns

Double-tails orchid

KINGLAKE NATIONAL PARK

Left: Wombelano Falls plunges from densely forested heights in the park's northern section – the most challenging area for bushwalkers

Tall eucalypts crowd a well-watered hillside – but the bracken floor indicates a recent fire

ORGAN PIPES NATIONAL PARK

Plants grow readily in the rich Keilor Plains soils on and around the Organ Pipes, but weeds are a problem – the area was cleared and used for grazing for 130 years

Towering columns of basalt were formed from a million-year-old lava flow that filled a river valley, then split as it cooled and shrank. A later earth movement tilted the structure, and now the valley wall that concealed it has been stripped away by the action of Jacksons Creek. Close views are gained on an easy walk of about 800 metres. Other features of the 85 ha park seen on longer walks include Rosette Rock, where columns radiate like the spokes of a wheel, and the Tessellated Pavement, where the creek has worn other columns down to ground level and left what look like hexagonal tiles.

Wave erosion on a southern tongue of Cape Schanck eats at soft rock behind a more resistant pillar. Eventually it will stand alone as a nearshore stack. Right: Wind-driven spray and sand etch flowing contours in layered sandstone. But its capping of limestone, from an ancient dune, wears at a far slower rate

CAPE SCHANCK COASTAL PARK

Clifftops and dunes backing a string of noted surfing beaches are reserved for public recreation along almost all of the Bass Strait side of Mornington Peninsula, from Portsea to beyond the Cape Schanck lighthouse. It is a windswept coast, frequently battered by heavy seas. Woodlands once ran to the cliff edges, but the area was cleared and grazed before 1870. The scrubs that have taken over since are stunted and sparse, and where they are damaged there are serious problems of soil erosion and dune movement. Rock formations provide the natural highlights of the 1095 ha park. Short walks are described in leaflets. Experienced walkers can cover the 28 km length of the park in one or two daily stages – but camping is not permitted.

Mt Bishop is a typical granite tor, formed of upthrust molten material and now exposed by the erosion of softer overlying rock

Tannin from decaying plant matter stains Tidal River, near the main camping area

WILSONS PROMONTORY NATIONAL PARK

Seaweeds swish in gentle currents at Waterloo Bay

'The Prom' is so popular with Victorians that holiday cabins must be balloted for, and a permit system operates to control the numbers taking overnight hikes. Solitude is possible, however, around remote bays and inlets. Six peaks stand above 500 metres. More than 80 km of marked walking tracks crisscross the 49 000 ha park. Most of them lead to sandy beaches in the shelter of striking headland formations.

Plant life is exceptionally varied. Many of the 700 species of flowering plants and ferns are uncommon, or found elsewhere only in Tasmania. Eucalypt forests dominate the high country, and include some tall mountain ash. Protected east-facing slopes have temperate rainforest zones, with myrtle beech in some gullies. Exposed slopes support eucalypt or banksia woodlands. There are also grasslands and extensive swamps. Corner Inlet even has a scattering of stunted mangroves – the southernmost in the world.

Lichen-coated granite boulders defy the elements at Picnic Point. Islands of the Glennie group, visible in the distance, are included in the park along with a dozen others close to 'The Prom'. Left: A flat beach at Whisky Bay makes a take-off runway for terns after a feast of fish and crustaceans. Nearby islands are important breeding grounds for many species of seabirds, including penguins. The promontory is also a resting place for many other birds on their north-south migratory routes

Wilsons Promontory National Park

A chilly midwinter sea, calm in the shelter of Waterloo Bay, laps dazzling sands eroded from granite rich in quartz and feldspar

Mist conceals the peaks of the Wilson Range, rising steeply behind sandy beaches at Tidal River. The river has its outlet in a tightly sheltered corner of Norman Bay, halfway down the western side of the promontory. Boulders on the intertidal fringe (below) are coated with moss

Casuarinas and ferns, including uncommon gleichenia or coral fern (left foreground), crowd a deep, wet gully beside the track to Waterloo Bay

Wilsons Promontory National Park

Granite tors studding the slopes of Mt Boulder (500 metres) orginated more than 300 million years ago as magma thrusting up into sedimentary rock

Tarra-Bulga National Park

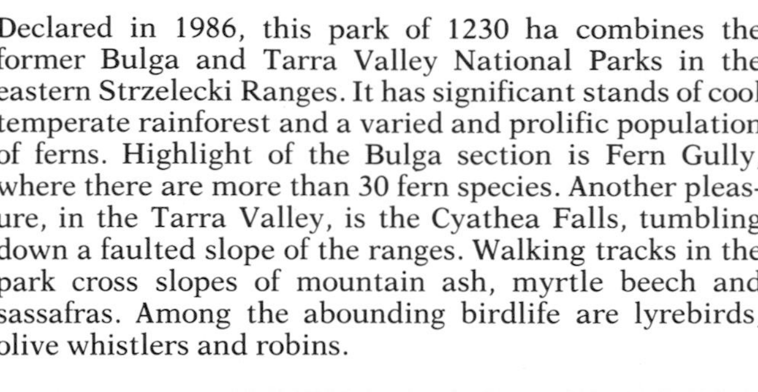

Declared in 1986, this park of 1230 ha combines the former Bulga and Tarra Valley National Parks in the eastern Strzelecki Ranges. It has significant stands of cool temperate rainforest and a varied and prolific population of ferns. Highlight of the Bulga section is Fern Gully, where there are more than 30 fern species. Another pleasure, in the Tarra Valley, is the Cyathea Falls, tumbling down a faulted slope of the ranges. Walking tracks in the park cross slopes of mountain ash, myrtle beech and sassafras. Among the abounding birdlife are lyrebirds, olive whistlers and robins.

Filmy ferns

Leaves of myrtle beech

Among Bulga's profusion of ferns are the kangaroo fern (left), an epiphyte that attaches itself to trees, and soft tree ferns (below). Along the scenic track skirting the north side of the park (right), tall eucalypts emerge from a dense understorey of rainforest character

Constant moisture at the Cyathea Falls fosters luxuriant fern growth. Rainfall is high, and sunlight and drying winds rarely penetrate the gully

Hattah-Kulkyne National Park

In contrast to its ending at the Coorong, the Murray River is master upstream of Mildura. At Hattah its periodic flooding has created an oasis of leafy woodlands among the semi-arid grasslands and sand ridges of north-western Victoria and far western NSW. Floodwaters spill west along Chalka Creek to replenish a system of intermittent wetlands and a dozen lakes, securing the breeding grounds of scores of waterfowl species.

River red gums crowd the lake shores and sometimes grow among black box on higher ground, where extraordinary floods of the past have allowed them to seed. Other trees characteristic of the 40 000 ha park are buloke casuarina, eumong acacia and white cypress pine. Wildflowers, abundant in spring, have replaced some forest stands that were cleared for timber and grazing. A short self-guided nature walk starts near the park entrance and takes no more than 45 minutes.

Gracefully twisting river red gums line the Murray, which forms a winding eastern boundary to the park. These trees thrive on flooding – but here it endangers them because powerful currents erode the bank and expose their roots

Winds eat a path through dunes behind Point Hicks, which is thought to have been the first Australian landfall on James Cook's exploratory voyage in 1770. Sand-binding plants in the foreground are true spinifex – their name is wrongly given to hummock grasses of arid hinterland regions

Sands pushed in by powerful waves make a lagoon of the Thurra River's estuary. Storm surges and spring tides break the barrier periodically, flushing out the waterway. Scrubs and heaths on the dunes make ideal habitats for the rare eastern bristlebird and ground parrot

CROAJINGOLONG NATIONAL PARK

Naturalists rank Croajingolong as one of the most interesting parks in Victoria, and among the most significant in Australia. In 86 000 ha it has elements of three widely differing vegetation types: cool-temperate communities like Tasmania's, soft-leafed subtropical plants in common with coastal NSW, and species adapted to fierce drought and fire regimes.

The range of animal life is correspondingly wide. Contrasts in scenery are bold. Steep, forested ridges and gullies – the catchments of dozens of streams – run south from a dissected tableland to an intricate coastline of cliffs, vast dune systems, lakes and tightly enclosed inlets, moulded by the persistent wave power of Bass Strait.

A seaboard of 100 km, from the NSW border to Sydenham Inlet, is of chief interest to holidaymakers. It has Victoria's mildest year-round climate – though a peculiarity of the district is its dry electrical storms in summer. Gale-driven bushfires did extensive damage in 1983, but little is evident round the inlets where visitors concentrate their activities. The park skirts the busy boating and fishing resort at Mallacoota Inlet and extends to quieter spots to the west, reached by unsealed roads.

Dry forests of eucalypts and angophoras cloak Croajingolong's steep inland ridges

Waves working on a cliff base of folded, tilted rock near Mallacoota Inlet are slowly creating an archway. Mallacoota was a reserve as early as 1909, along with Wingan Inlet. Small national parks in these two localities, and Captain James Cook National Park at Point Hicks, were absorbed into Croajingolong in 1979

Mountain gentian, blooming in February

Mountain gums force open a rock cleft that was created by frost

Crystal Brook flows tranquilly towards the Eurobin Falls in summer. But the wear on the boulders tells of a violent torrent when the snows melt each spring

The sheer plateau walls to be found in Mt Buffalo National Park – where many rocky peaks exceed 1500 metres – offer some of the hardest climbs in Australia

Paper daisies

Mount Buffalo National Park

Massive bluffs and towering, near-vertical, granite walls punctuate the extensive Buffalo Plateau, soaring 1000 metres above the Ovens Valley. Granite tors stud the tops which are snow-covered in winter; in the 1930s, Buffalo became Victoria's first skiing playground. At the southern edge, a rocky pyramid reaches 1723 metres. Called the Horn, it puts the finishing touch to the animal silhouette that prompted early explorers to give the plateau its name. Many other peaks in the 31 000 ha park exceed 1500 metres. Buttresses and almost sheer walls – especially at the Gorge, above Eurobin Falls – offer rock climbers some of the most varied and challenging faces in Australia.

Wildflowers deck the alpine grasslands and heaths in summer, among woodlands of snow gum. Eucalypt forests on the lower slopes include candlebark, mountain gum and alpine ash. Walkers can choose from 140 km of tracks. They include nature trails at the Gorge, Dicksons Falls and View Point – all accessible on a brief visit. Canoeing is popular on Lake Catani.

Alpine heaths struggle for survival on the rocky edge of the Bogong plateau

BOGONG NATIONAL PARK

Eleven of Victoria's 12 highest summits cluster here, in the state's biggest tract of alpine country. Mt Bogong (1986 metres) stands supreme in the northernmost corner of the 81 200 ha park. Most of it is tablelands, offering cross country skiers unrivalled scope in winter. Falls Creek and Mt Hotham, alpine resorts, are outside the park but practically enclosed by its boundaries.

Flowers blossom brilliantly on grassy upland slopes and bogs in summer, above a belt of snow gum woodlands. Mountain gum and alpine ash dominate lower forests, with black sallee and dense fern understoreys in some gullies. Marsupials and native birds are abundant. Walks of varying difficulty cover most of the park.

Blossoms of the alpine strawflower and hairy cutleaf daisy (far right) ornament the high plains late in summer

Seen from above, columns of basalt look like paving stones. They are made of volcanic lava that shrank and split as it cooled. At the Ruined Castle (right) later earth movements have snapped the columns

Horizontal layers of limestone stand out clearly in Island Arch. Waves and spray have found a weak spot in the middle and are eating out a hole. This formation is just offshore from Loch Ard Gorge, which was named after the most disastrous of six shipwrecks near Port Campbell. Of 54 people aboard the Loch Ard in 1878 only two survived – an 18-year-old cabin boy and a girl passenger of the same age. The boy, Tom Pearce, scaled the gorge to fetch help. Four victims are buried on the clifftop

PORT CAMPBELL NATIONAL PARK

Limestone is no match for the wave power of the Southern Ocean. Travellers on the Great Ocean Road, for about 12 km on either side of Port Campbell, see a coastline in rapid retreat. It is carved in an erratic pattern of gorges, archways, blowholes and sheer cliffs where huge slabs, undercut by the tides and weakened above by rain seepage, have collapsed and been pulverised. Seas boil around tougher remnants, isolated as nearshore stacks.

Excellent vantage points are gained by side roads or on foot from marked points on the highway. A self-guided 'discovery walk' taking 1½ hours starts near Port Campbell beach. Smaller beaches are accessible at Loch Ard Gorge, Sherbrooke River and below Gibson Steps. Coastal scrubs and heaths cloak clifftops and gorges in the 1750 ha park. A big seabird population may include penguins, and shearwaters nest on Muttonbird Island.

London Bridge, off the western end of the park towards Peterborough, will eventually collapse and two separate stacks will be left. The Twelve Apostles (some seen at right) are probably remnants of a bigger formation that went through a similar process. The ocean is claiming back what it created some 25 million years ago, when this part of the continental mass lay under water. Marine deposits of shell and skeletal debris built a paving 250 metres thick. When the land rose later, this became a limestone plateau – now all too easily eroded

LOWER GLENELG NATIONAL PARK

Nearing the end of its 400 km course from the Grampians, the Glenelg River cuts a deep gorge through the limestone of an ancient sea bed. The gorge and its bordering eucalypt forests are protected for a length of 35 km. In the eastern part of the 27 300 ha park, the Kentbruck Heath is noted for spring wildflowers, including more than 50 species of ground orchids.

Unsealed roads and walking tracks reach a variety of ferny gullies, river and gorge viewing points and a coastal lookout. The river is accessible at many spots; swimming and fishing are popular and small boats are easily launched. Many cave systems have been discovered deep in the limestone. The Princess Margaret Rose Caves, 15 km north of Nelson, are open daily for tours.

Acacias and eucalypts overhang the Glenelg River above its entry to the gorge. The river is a breeding ground for many ocean fish. Anglers make good catches of bass, black bream, mulloway and Australian salmon between October and May. Left: Moleside Creek, a swift-running tributary of the Glenelg, originates in the low hills of the colourful Kentbruck Heath

Lake Surprise, ringed with eucalypt woodlands, seems to be fed by underground springs. Its level falls each summer but returns during the winter to a maximum depth of 13 metres. Swimming and boating are allowed, but boats have to be carried down a steep stairway

Hot gases once poured from this vent in the crater flanks, giving the volcano a safety valve. Later such fissures provided shelter for Aboriginal hunting parties, or roosts for insect-eating bats

MOUNT ECCLES NATIONAL PARK

Manna gum woodlands end abruptly on the stony cliffs rimming Lake Surprise. Tranquil green waters fill a cavity like a giant bathtub, more than 700 metres long and 180 metres wide. Below are the blocked vents of one of Australia's most recent volcanoes, active between 10 000 and 6000 years ago.

Mt Eccles, a rounded cone prominent above the south-eastern edge of the craters, is not itself a volcano. It is a heap of debris, windblown from successive eruptions. The slopes – dangerously unstable to walk on – are of scoria, a light rock made from bubbly lava.

Safer walks, taking from 20 minutes to 2 hours, lead around the cliffs and the wooded edges of the lake. Along the route of an old lava flow at the northern end is a cave of basalt, big enough to enter. Solidified drips of lava hang from the ceiling like stalactites. No greater variety of volcanic forms can be so easily seen as in this park 5470 ha in area.

Dry eucalypt forests crowd a tough ridge of sandstone in the Serra Range. Peregrine falcons nest in its crannies

GRAMPIANS NATIONAL PARK

Victoria gained its biggest – 167 000 ha – and most imposing national park in 1984. In the former Grampians State Forest, forestry and grazing were already tightly zoned, and much of the area was handed over in a natural state with public amenities such as camping grounds and picnic areas widely provided. Motorists and bushwalkers alike have unrivalled scope to roam among striking landforms and richly diverse vegetation on the westernmost heights of the Great Divide.

Folded sandstones form a series of weathered ranges running north-south for about 100 km. The highest point, Mt William in the east, is 1168 metres and many other summits exceed 800 metres. Most of the ranges have steep scarps on their eastern sides but slope gently to the west. The park surrounds three sizeable reservoirs where boating and fishing are popular, and includes countless creeks and streams. There are numerous walking tracks to all the major scenic features; the Wonderland area, near Halls Gap, is the most fascinating and accessible.

Eucalypts dominate the forests and woodlands, but sightseers are especially attracted to the high heaths and their brilliant floral displays between August and November. Nearly 900 flowering species – including 100 orchids – are found in the park and several are found nowhere else. Over 200 bird species have been recorded. Mammals include the endangered brush-tailed rock wallaby.

The Balconies, near Halls Gap, command sweeping views south

Aboriginal paintings decorate Flat Rock Shelter. Tribes from both north and south shared occupation of the Grampians

Below: Sandstone faces of the Grand Canyon are deeply etched by rain and chemical action

A rich pocket of iron succumbs to water erosion

Eucalypts on dry slopes (left) suffer frequent fire damage, but tree ferns (right) survive as rainforest relics in deep gullies

GRAMPIANS NATIONAL PARK

The Broken Falls, on the McKenzie River, are formed from an intrusion – called a dyke – of porphyritic rock. It is volcanic in origin, and much harder than the usual sandstone of the Grampians

PARKS OF THE MELBOURNE REGION

FACILITIES

Cabins

Caravan park

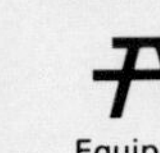
Equipped picnic area

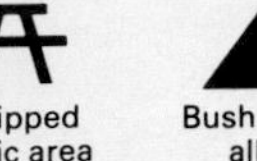
Bush camping allowed

Lavatory building

Established campsite

Campsite but no car access

Note: Popular parks without campsites usually have public camping grounds nearby. If in doubt, call enquiries number.

PARK RATINGS No interest ✗ Some interest ✓ Major interest ✓✓ Outstanding ✓✓✓

Alfred National Park

470 km E, 18 km E of Cann River. East Gippsland weather district. Princes Highway crosses park.

Bushfires badly damaged much of this rare enclave of Victorian warm-temperate rainforest when they swept through the 2300 ha park in 1983. It will take many years before the complex balance of vegetation in the deep, moist gullies is regained. More than 40 fern species have been identified in the park. They include the rare oval fork fern and prickly tree fern.

Short trails will help visitors avoid dense, leech-infested undergrowth on walks around rainforest pockets. Fire trails lead to a granite ridge which caps the park with the three peaks over 400 metres. The surrounding forest, seen from the highway, is dominated by eucalypts growing over a profusion of wattles.

NOTE: No camping in park.

BEST TIME: Year-round.

ENQUIRIES: (051) 58 6351.

ADDRESS: Park office, Princes Highway, Cann River 3889.

Scenic enjoyment ✓✓
Day activities ✓✓
Family camping ✗
Hard bushwalking ✗

Baw Baw National Park

200 km E, 60 km N of Moe. West Gippsland weather district. Car access off Princes Highway via Thomson Valley Road north of Erica (last 13 km unsealed).

Snow gum woodland and a dense understorey of flowering shrubs grows to the highest ridges and peaks of the Baw Baw Plateau, a mountainous block at the southern end of Victoria's high country. Extensive treeless tracts of sub-alpine bog and peaty swamps form on poorly drained, lower-lying ground where a number of major rivers begin their courses to steep, heavily forested gullies at the edge of the 13 300 ha park.

Short walking trails into the park meet a 20 km section of the Apline Walking Track traversing the plateau from north to south past Mt St Phillack (1566 metres) and Mt Erica (1524 metres). Above 1200 metres snow covers the ground from July to September and many summer hiking tracks become cross-country ski touring routes. The Alpine Village, a downhill skiing centre outside the park and approached via Drouin, can be used as a starting point.

NOTES: Carry snow chains in winter and ensure car radiators contain anti-freeze. Permit required for walking in Mount Whitelaw area. Bush camping not permitted in Mount Whitelaw area. All bush campers should contact park ranger before setting out. Licence required for trout fishing.

WARNING: Severe weather changes occur suddenly. Ski tourers and bush campers must be adequately equipped to cope with emergencies.

BEST TIME: Year-round.

ENQUIRIES: (051) 65 3481.

ADDRESS: Box 63, Rawson 3825.

Scenic enjoyment ✓✓✓
Day activities ✓✓
Family camping ✓✓
Hard bushwalking ✓✓✓

Bogong National Park

375 km, 93 km SE of Myrtleford. Northeast weather district. Car access off Ovens Highway via Mount Beauty to Falls Creek or via Harrietville to Mount Hotham. Coaches to Falls Creek and Mount Hotham in ski season.

DESCRIPTION: Page 222.

NOTES: No camping within 200 metres of public roads or within 30 metres of streams. Overnight walkers should carry tents: huts may be full or difficult to find. Licence required for fishing.

WARNING: Severe weather changes occur suddenly; carry adequate clothing and emergency rations.

BEST TIME: Year-round (summer for flowers).

ENQUIRIES: (057) 57 2693.

ADDRESS: Box 180, Mount Beauty 3699.

Scenic enjoyment ✓✓
Day activities ✓
Family camping ✓✓
Hard bushwalking ✓✓✓

Brisbane Ranges National Park

105 km W. Central weather district. Car access off Western Freeway along Ballan-Geelong road.

DESCRIPTION: Page 201.

NOTES: Bookings required for the small campsite. Bush camping in designated areas only.

BEST TIME: Autumn to spring.

ENQUIRIES: (052) 84 1230.

ADDRESS: C/o P.O., Anakie 3221.

Scenic enjoyment ✓✓
Day activities ✓✓
Family camping ✓
Hard bushwalking ✓

Burrowa-Pine Mountain National Park

420 km NE. Northeast weather district. Car access off Murray Valley Highway to Cudgewa or off Tallangatta-Corryong road. Cudgewa-North Walwa road (dry weather) passes through park.

The isolated dome of Pine Mountain (1062 metres) with its exposed faces of red granite rises steeply from the Murray River plain. Like most areas in the 17 600 ha park, the mountain's summit can only be reached by walkers trekking through trackless bush. But the effort is rewarded with panoramic views to the Snowy Mountains in the north and to the mountainous block around 1300 metre Mt Burrowa in the south.

Broad valleys cleared for farming surround the park which consists of two mountainous blocks linked by an L-shaped corridor. Snow gums grow around Mt Burrowa on peaks where snow may lie for several weeks in winter. Red cypress pines and kurrajong predominate on the dry slopes of Pine Mountain, and the area is noted for a number of rare plants, including the phantom wattle and Pine Mountain grevillea. A short walking track leads from the picnic and camping area at the end of Falls Road (off Cudgewa-North Walwa Road) to the impressive Cudgewa Bluff Falls.

NOTES: Water scarce in summer.

BEST TIME: Autumn and spring.

ENQUIRIES: (060) 77 4284.

ADDRESS: Box 74, Cudgewa 3705.

Scenic enjoyment ✓✓
Day activities ✓✓
Family camping ✓
Hard bushwalking ✓✓

Cape Schanck Coastal Park

90 km S. Central weather district. Car access off Nepean Highway between Rosebud and Portsea. Vehicle entrance fee in summer. Buses Frankston-Portsea.

DESCRIPTION: Page 207.

NOTES: No camping in park. Surf patrols at Gunnamatta Beach and Portsea Back Beach during weekends and holidays in summer.

BEST TIME: Spring to autumn.

ENQUIRIES: (059) 84 1586.

ADDRESS: Box 117, Sorrento 3943.

Scenic enjoyment ✓✓
Day activities ✓✓
Family camping ✗
Hard bushwalking ✓✓

Churchill National Park

32 km SE. Central weather district. Car access off Stud Road, Rowville. Buses along Stud Road daily.

Though less than 200 ha in area, Churchill preserves a fine sample of plant species typical of Dandenong foothills woodland. A small patch of messmate and narrow-leafed peppermint forest grows on high ground along the northern boundary, but most of the fenced-in park is covered by open woodland dominated by swamp gum, manna gum, black wattle and dogwood. These species have been able to recolonise the area after clearing for electricity transmission lines, stone quarrying and the ravages of bushfires.

Many small mammals have survived in the park, but they are mostly nocturnal. Visitors are more likely to see kangaroos, wallabies and wombats reintroduced to the park after the original populations died out. A bend in one of the walking trails is noted for its colony of bellbirds, recognised by the bell-like notes of their song.

NOTE: No camping in park.

BEST TIME: Spring to autumn.

ENQUIRIES: (03) 700 4700.

ADDRESS: C/o P.O., Rowville 3178.

Scenic enjoyment ✓
Day activities ✓✓
Family camping ✗
Hard bushwalking ✗

1. Alfred NP
2. Baw Baw NP
3. Bogong NP
4. Brisbane Ranges NP
5. Burrowa-Pine Mountain NP
6. Cape Schanck Coastal Park
7. Churchill NP
8. Cobberas-Tingaringy NP
9. Croajingolong NP
10. Fern Tree Gully NP
11. Fraser NP
12. Grampians NP
13. Hattah-Kulkyne NP
14. Kinglake NP
15. Lind NP
16. Little Desert NP
17. Lower Glenelg NP
18. Mitchell River NP
19. Morwell NP
20. Mount Buffalo NP
21. Mount Eccles NP
22. Mount Richmond NP
23. Organ Pipes NP
24. Otway NP
25. Port Campbell NP
26. Snowy River NP
27. Tarra-Bulga NP
28. The Lakes NP

(29) **Wilsons Promontory NP**

(30) **Wonnangatta-Moroka NP**

(31) **Wyperfeld NP**

Cobberas-Tingaringy National Park

450 km NE, 80 km N of Buchan. East Gippsland weather district. Car access north of Buchan along roads to Suggan Buggan and Bonang.

Mountainous terrain cut by fast-flowing, rapids-strewn rivers and the narrow gorges of their tributaries make up much of this 107 000 ha park. A great variety of rock types, and altitudes ranging from 160 metres to 1838 metres at Mt Cobberas, ensure an ever-changing landscape with panoramic views from ridges and mountain peaks. Diverse vegetation includes alpine herbfields and grasslands, slopes of cypress pine and white box in drier areas, sheltered gullies of mountain rainforest and alpine woodlands of snow gum.

Snow covers the high plains and ridges in winter, providing excellent opportunities for cross-country skiing. In summer hikers take extended bushwalks along fire trails and undeveloped though well-used wilderness routes. Wide sandy beaches along the Snowy River near Mackillop Bridge are suitable for swimming, while rapids upstream, challenge experienced canoeists.

WARNING: Snowy River may rise rapidly, becoming dangerous to swimmers and canoeists.

BEST TIME: Spring to autumn.

ENQUIRIES: (0648) 8 0277.

ADDRESS: Deddick via Bonang 3888.

Scenic enjoyment ✔✔✔
Day activities ✔
Family camping ✔✔
Hard bushwalking ✔✔✔

Croajingolong National Park

500 km E, 20 km S of Cann River. East Gippsland weather district. Car access off Princes Highway between Cann River and Genoa. Train Melbourne-Bairnsdale, bus Bairnsdale-Mallacoota.

DESCRIPTION: Page 219.

NOTES: Bookings and fee required for all four campsites. Licence required for fishing.

BEST TIME: Spring to autumn.

ENQUIRIES: (051) 58 6372.

ADDRESS: As for Alfred.

Scenic enjoyment ✔✔✔
Day activities ✔✔✔
Family camping ✔✔✔
Hard bushwalking ✔✔

Fern Tree Gully National Park

34 km E. Central weather district. Car access off Burwood Highway. Vehicle entrance fee. Trains Melbourne-Upper Ferntree Gully.

A network of easy walking tracks with abundant picnic facilities and views of Melbourne and Port Phillip Bay makes Fern Tree Gully a major weekend attraction in the Dandenong Ranges. More than 300 000 people visit the 460 ha park each year.

A thick growth of eucalypts and tree ferns has been re-established along Fern Tree Gully Creek with the help of intensive weed control and fencing. A stepped path follows the creek's course down One Tree Hill (503 metres), which was cleared last century.

Poorer soils on slopes and ridges away from the main gully support a low eucalypt forest dominated by red stringybarks, long-leafed box and peppermint.

NOTE: Gates close at 8 pm in summer, sunset in other seasons.

BEST TIME: Year-round.

ENQUIRIES: (03) 758 1001.

ADDRESS: Box 21, Upper Ferntree Gully 3156.

Scenic enjoyment ✔✔
Day activities ✔✔✔
Family camping ×
Hard bushwalking ×

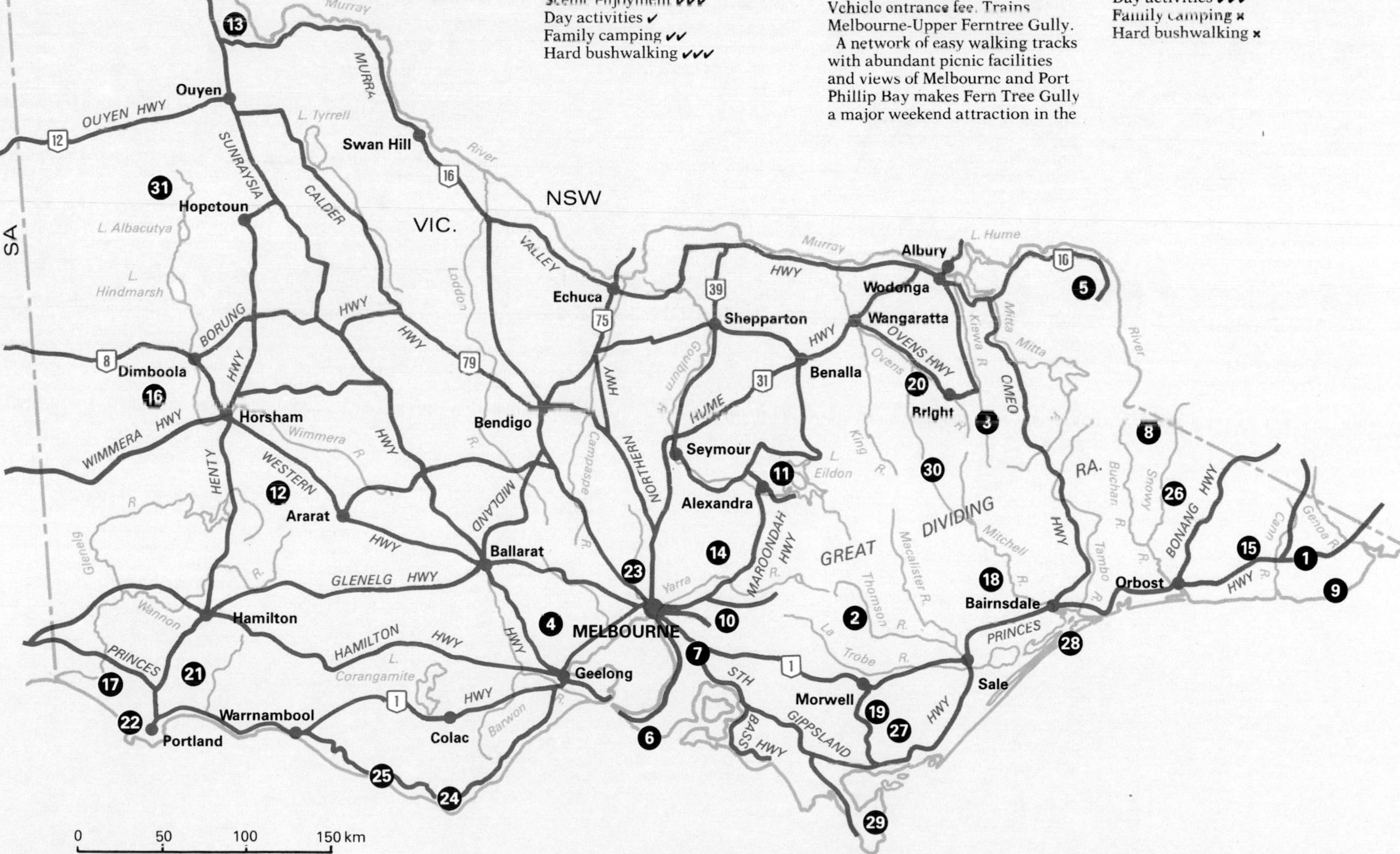

Fraser National Park

165 km NE, 17 km E of Alexandra. North Central weather district. Car access off Goulburn Valley Highway.

A number of farms disappeared when the valleys of the Goulburn and Delatite Rivers were flooded in the early 1950s to create Lake Eildon to provide extra irrigation for the lower Goulburn Valley. Fraser National Park was established in 1957 on former grazing land on the western shore of Lake Eildon.

Hillsides surrounding the lake have been extensively cleared, both by farmers and by the gold prospectors who came before them. In the absence of grazing, forests of red stringybark, narrow and broad-leafed peppermint, red box and silver wattle are returning.

The 3750 ha park is generously equipped with lakeshore camping and picnic facilities for the convenience of visitors mostly interested in swimming, canoeing and power boating. The regenerating forests can be explored along a web of formed tracks climbing spurs and gullies to commanding ridge-top lookouts.

NOTES: Fee charged for camping. Bookings required during holidays. Licence required for fishing.

BEST TIME: Spring to autumn.

ENQUIRIES: (057) 72 1293.

ADDRESS: Box 153, Alexandra 3714.

Scenic enjoyment ✔✔
Day activities ✔✔✔
Family camping ✔✔✔
Hard bushwalking ✔

Grampians National Park

280 km W, 25 km SW of Stawell. Wimmera weather district. Car access off Western Highway from Stawell, Ararat and Horsham; off Glenelg Highway from Dunkeld.

DESCRIPTION: Page 228.

NOTES: Camping not permitted in water catchment or scientific reference areas and Wonderland section. Booking required for camping at Zumstein; fee charged. Fourteen other areas available – no booking or fee. Licence required for fishing.

WARNINGS: Severe weather changes occur suddenly; bushwalkers should carry adequate warm clothing. Rock slides may occur in broken or steep areas.

BEST TIME: Late winter and spring.

ENQUIRIES: (053) 56 4381 or 82 5011.

ADDRESS: Box 18, Halls Gap 3381.

Scenic enjoyment ✔✔✔
Day activities ✔✔✔
Family camping ✔✔✔
Hard bushwalking ✔✔✔

Hattah-Kulkyne National Park

430 km NW, 39 km N of Ouyen. Mallee weather district. Car access off Murray Valley Highway 4 km E of Hattah.

DESCRIPTION: Page 217.

NOTES: Bush camping restricted to designated sites with permission of ranger. Carry water supplies. NSW licence required for river fishing; Victorian licence for lakes.

VISITOR CENTRE: Park entrance.

BEST TIME: Autumn, spring.

ENQUIRIES: (050) 29 3253.

ADDRESS: RSD Hattah 3501.

Scenic enjoyment ✔✔
Day activities ✔✔✔
Family camping ✔✔✔
Hard bushwalking ✔✔

Kinglake National Park

65 km NE. Central weather district. Car access off Yarra Glen-Yea road and Steels Creek road north of Yarra Glen.

DESCRIPTION: Page 203.

NOTES: Bookings and permit required for camping. Fee charged at Masons Falls picnic area.

BEST TIME: Spring to autumn.

ENQUIRIES: (057) 86 5351.

ADDRESS: National Park Road, Pheasant Creek 3757.

Scenic enjoyment ✔✔✔
Day activities ✔✔✔
Family camping ✔✔
Hard bushwalking ✔✔

Lind National Park

425 km E. East Gippsland weather district. Car access off Princes Highway 20 km W of Cann River.

The scenic drive along Euchre Creek Valley, once part of Princes Highway, passes through a gully of warm-temperate rainforest so dense in places that the nearby creek is totally obscured from view. Kanooka, blackwood and lilly pilly tower above an understorey of tree ferns and vines, with striking displays of wildflowers in spring and scattered crimson splashes of Gippsland waratahs in summer.

Highway realignment in the early 1960s has made a peaceful haven of the 1160 ha park and its creek-side rest area. A 4 km walking trail climbs away from picnic grounds along a ridge to the new highway, where a tall eucalypt forest dominated by silvertop ash overlooks the speeding traffic.

BEST TIME: Spring to autumn.

ENQUIRIES: (051) 58 6351.

ADDRESS: As for Alfred.

Scenic enjoyment ✔✔
Day activities ✔
Family camping ✖
Hard bushwalking ✖

Little Desert National Park.

365 km NW, 8 km S of Kiata. Wimmera weather district. Car access of Western Highway at Kiata.

Soils unsuited to 19th-century agriculture gave the Little Desert its name, but average annual rainfalls of 400 mm support a variety of vegetation types. Sandy plains dominated by mallee and stringybark eucalypts extend west through the 35 300 ha park from woodlands of river red gum and black box on the Wimmera River flood plains. Smooth-barked yellow gums grow on isolated clay pans, and patches of reddish soils among the sand dunes foster broombrush and stringybarks.

Heath plants growing with the mallee produce impressive displays of wildflowers in winter and spring, attracting nomadic birds such as lorikeets and honeyeaters. Over 200 native bird species have been sighted in the park, including malleefowl. Its abandoned nesting mounds of sand and litter can be seen on one of the short nature trails that have been developed to sample the park's distinctive features.

NOTE: Water is scarce – visitors should carry their own.

BEST TIME: Spring (for wildflowers) and autumn.

ENQUIRIES: (053) 89 9218.

ADDRESS: RMB 389, Nhill 3418.

Scenic enjoyment ✔
Day activities ✔
Family camping ✔✔
Hard bushwalking ✔

Lower Glenelg National Park

400 km SW, 40 km NW of Portland. Western weather district. Car access off Princes Highway or Portland-Nelson road.

DESCRIPTION: Page 226.

NOTES: Bookings required for all camping in park. Fee charged for campsites and cabins at Caves camping ground.

VISITOR CENTRE: Princess Margaret Rose Caves, open daily.

BEST TIME: Spring (for wildflowers) to autumn.

ENQUIRIES: (087) 38 4051

ADDRESS: C/o P.O., Nelson 3292.

Scenic enjoyment ✔✔✔
Day activities ✔✔✔
Family camping ✔✔✔
Hard bushwalking ✔

Mitchell River National Park

300 km E, 60 km NW of Bairnsdale. East Gippsland weather district. Car access off Princes Highway via Fernbank.

This new national park of 11 900 ha, declared in 1986, incorporates the former Glenaladale National Park. The extension puts the focus in the park on the Mitchell River gorge which has some of Gippsland's most spectacular scenery.

The Den of Nargun, a rocky cave figuring in Aboriginal legends, stretches across the deep rainforest gully of Woolshed Creek as it descends to the steep, rapids-strewn gorge of Mitchell River. The creek may dry in summer, but when flowing it veils the 20 metre wide cave mouth with a fine curtain of water falling to a pool 3 metres below. Stalactites hang from the dripping roof and tall stalagmites grow to met them from the cave floor.

The steep-sided gully protects a warm-temperate rainforest of tall kanookas, pittosporums and lilly pillies shading a mass of ferns, orchids and tangled wood vines. Away from the cool humidity of the gully, drier soils in the park support magnificent stands of kurrajong, silvertop and box trees.

Short walking trails encircle the creek in one corner of the park, taking in a lookout bluff and branching off north along the Mitchell River below steep reddish cliffs. The park has some of the best white-water canoeing in Victoria.

NOTES: Limited camping – sites in gorge are restricted to canoeists and walkers in transit; bookings recommended. Licence required for fishing. Fires permitted only in authorised fireplaces.

BEST TIME: Year-round.

ENQUIRIES: (051) 52 6277.

ADDRESS: CFL Bairnsdale Region, 210 Main Street, Bairnsdale 3875.

Scenic enjoyment ✔✔
Day activities ✔✔
Family camping ✖
Hard bushwalking ✔

Morwell National Park

165 km SE, 16 km S of Morwell. West Gippsland weather district. Car access off Midland Highway between Churchill and Boolarra.

Rapid subdivision and development in surrounding forests in the 1960s prompted the former owner of Morwell to offer it for conservation. Gullies and ridges covering 280 ha in the southern foothills of the Strzelecki Ranges were not totally untouched, but one of the last patches of natural Gippsland forest was in good condition. In particular the area is a habitat of the rare butterfly orchid *Sarcochilus australis*, a small tree-clinging plant that in summer sends out a drooping stem clustered with yellow-green flowers distinguished by a tongue of red and yellow markings. The orchid grows on sheltered trees in gullies where southern blue gums and mountain grey gums tower over tree ferns and tall shrubs.

One of the two short walking trails established around the main gully climbs to ridges and spurs dominated by stringybark forest in the park's western section.

BEST TIME: Spring and early summer (for wildflowers).

ENQUIRIES: (051) 22 1478.

ADDRESS: Box 19, Churchill 3842.

Scenic enjoyment ✔✔
Day activities ✔
Family camping ✖
Hard bushwalking ✖

Mount Buffalo National Park

320 km NE, 96 km SE of Wangaratta. Northeast weather district. Car access off Ovens Highway at Porepunkah. Vehicle entrance fee.

DESCRIPTION: Page 221.
NOTES: Bookings required for campsites during holidays. Camping ground closed late May to early November. Licence required for fishing. Cars must carry chains in winter; radiators need anti-freeze. Motel, lodge and guesthouse accommodation available.
WARNING: Severe weather changes occur suddenly throughout the year.
VISITOR CENTRE: Keown Lodge, open in summer and over Easter.
BEST TIME: Year-round (winter for skiing).
ENQUIRIES: (057) 55 1466.
ADDRESS: Mount Buffalo 3745.

Scenic enjoyment ✔✔✔
Day activities ✔✔✔
Family camping ✔✔✔
Walking, climbing ✔✔✔

Mount Eccles National Park
335 km W, 42 km S of Hamilton. Western weather district. Car access off Hamilton-Port Fairy road at Macarthur.
DESCRIPTION: Page 227.
NOTES: Fee charged for campsites; bookings required at Easter. Special facilities are available for disabled people.
BEST TIME: Spring and autumn.
ENQUIRIES: (055) 76 1014.
ADDRESS: RMB 1160, Macarthur 3286.

Scenic enjoyment ✔✔
Day activities ✔✔
Family camping ✔
Walking ✔

Mount Richmond National Park
390 km SW, 33 km W of Portland. Western weather district. Car access off Portland-Nelson road.

Swamps and wet heathland around the base of Mt Richmond (229 metres) are fed by water that has seeped down through the hill's sandy soil and porous core. It is a hardened cone of volcanic ash, dust and pumice, covered by wind-blown sands from the shifting dunes of Discovery Bay. Rainwater sinks in instead of running off the surface to form streams.

Correas, heaths, wattles and bush peas are well suited to these conditions. Over 400 flowering plants have been recorded in the 1700 ha park, providing impressive displays of wildflowers year-round, but particularly in spring.

Walking tracks allow visitors the fullest access to heathlands and swamp areas and to the summit of Mt Richmond, where a lookout platform towers over forests of brown stringybark and manna gum for views of coastal and inland scenery.
BEST TIME: Spring (for wildflowers).
ENQUIRIES: (055) 23 3232.
ADDRESS: CFL Portland Region Office, Port and Heath Roads, Portland 3305.

Scenic enjoyment ✔✔
Day activities ✔✔
Family camping ✘
Hard bushwalking ✘

Organ Pipes National Park
25 km NW. Central weather district. Car access off Calder Highway at Sydenham. Train Melbourne-Sydenham (3 km from park).
DESCRIPTION: Page 206.
BEST TIME: Year-round.
ENQUIRIES: (03) 390 1082.
ADDRESS: C/o P.O., Diggers Rest 3427.

Scenic enjoyment ✔✔
Day activities ✔✔
Family camping ✘
Hard bushwalking ✘

Otway National Park
200 km SW, 14 km S of Apollo Bay. Western weather district. Car access off Great Ocean Road Bus Melbourne-Apollo Bay.
DESCRIPTION: Page 202.
NOTES: Visits to Cape Otway lighthouse must be pre-arranged.
BEST TIME: Spring to autumn.
ENQUIRIES: (052) 37 6889.
ADDRESS: Box 63, Apollo Bay 3233.

Scenic enjoyment ✔✔✔
Day activities ✔✔
Family camping ✔✔✔
Hard bushwalking ✔✔✔

Port Campbell National Park.
270 km SW. Western weather district. Great Ocean Road passes through park between Princetown and Peterborough.
DESCRIPTION: Page 225.
NOTES: Fee charged for campsites; bookings required in holiday periods.
WARNING: Dangerous waves along shoreline below cliffs.
VISITOR CENTRE: Port Campbell.
BEST TIME: Late spring to autumn.
ENQUIRIES: (055) 98 6382.
ADDRESS: Tregea Street, Port Campbell 3269.

Scenic enjoyment ✔✔✔
Day activities ✔✔✔
Family camping ✔✔✔
Hard bushwalking ✘

Snowy River National Park
450 km E, 135 km NE of Lakes Entrance. East Gippsland weather district. Car access along Bonang road off Buchan-Jindabyne road; turn off Princes Highway at Nowa Nowa for Buchan.

Diversion and flow regulation in the upper reaches of the Snowy River have reduced the frequency of both flooding and drought along the river's deep valley. But heavy rains still cause sudden rises in the water level, particularly in gorges south of Mackillop Bridge, where the Snowy enters this 26 200 ha park. Boulders strewn across narrow passages become dangerous white-water rapids demanding great skill and endurance for canoeists. Trips from Mackillop Bridge take 3-4 days to the Buchan River junction.

Walkers also follow the Snowy Valley south, but at Tulloch Ard Gorge the river is pinched between rock walls towering over a surging torrent. Hikers must be prepared to swim through the gorge to continue farther south. Less daunting walks include the Silver Mine Track, from Mackillops Bridge, which leads to an old mining area and provides scenic views of the Snowy River.
BEST TIME: Summer and autumn.
ENQUIRIES: (0648) 8 0277.
ADDRESS: As for Cobberas-Tingaringy.

Scenic enjoyment ✔✔✔
Day activities ✔
Family camping ✔
Walking, canoeing ✔✔✔

Tarra-Bulga National Park
195 km SE, 43 km S of Traralgon (Bulga 190 km SE, 38 km S of Traralgon). West Gippsland weather district. Car access off Princes Highway at Traralgon.
DESCRIPTION: Page 214.
NOTE: No camping in park.
BEST TIME: Year-round.
ENQUIRIES: (051) 96 6127.
ADDRESS: Balook via Yarram 3971.

Scenic enjoyment ✔✔✔
Day activities ✔✔
Family camping ✘
Hard bushwalking ✘

The Lakes National Park
300 km E, 60 km E of Sale. East Gippsland weather district. Car access via Longford and Loch Sport off Princes Highway at Sale. Rotamah Island accessible by boat, or on foot along Ninety Mile Beach.

Long sandspits, low sand islands and the narrow stretch of dunes along Ninety Mile Beach, pushed up in the past 9000 years, enclose what was previously an immense bay in the Gippsland Lakes area. River silts have partly filled it, dividing it into a chain of freshwater lakes which could break out into Bass Strait only after exceptional flooding. But after a navigation channel was cut near Lakes Entrance in 1889, the level of the lakes fell by almost half a metre and the waters became brackish. Salt-marsh plants have colonised the widened lake margins, backed by paperbark scrublands, heaths and low woodlands of banksias and eucalypts.

Although relatively remote by road from a string of nearby holiday towns, the natural bushland of the 2400 ha park is only a short boat trip away. Facilities for picnics and camping are generous. A bird hide at Lake Killarney, on one of the many walking tracks, allows visitors to study black swans, pelicans, grebes, ducks and cormorants without disturbing their feeding and breeding.
NOTES: Fee charged for camping at Emu Bight. Bookings required for camping in holidays.
BEST TIME: Spring to autumn.
ENQUIRIES: (051) 46 0278.
ADDRESS: C/o P.O., Loch Sport 3851.

Scenic enjoyment ✔✔
Day activities ✔✔✔
Family camping ✔✔✔
Hard bushwalking ✘

Wilsons Promontory National Park
230 km SW, 62 km S of Foster. West Gippsland weather district. Car access off South Gippsland Highway.
DESCRIPTION: Page 209.
NOTES: Fee charged for all camping. Campsites must be booked for holiday periods. Permit required for bush camping; numbers strictly limited. No wood fires November to April. Lodges and cabins also available.
VISITOR CENTRE: Tidal River.
BEST TIME: Spring to autumn.
ENQUIRIES: (056) 80 8538.
ADDRESS: Tidal River, via Foster 3960.

Scenic enjoyment ✔✔✔
Day activities ✔✔✔
Family camping ✔✔✔
Hard bushwalking ✔✔✔

Wonnangatta-Moroka National Park
340 km NE, 140 km N of Sale. North East weather district. Car access of Heyfield-Mansfield road at Licola.

High peaks of the Great Dividing Range dominate the northern part of this 107 000 ha park and create a watershed for scores of rivers and streams which cut deep valleys and narrow gorges through the surrounding plateau of high snow plains. Strictly controlled grazing is allowed in certain limited areas and will be phased out elsewhere in 1991. Selective logging in forests of mountain gum and alpine ash is permitted until 1988. Neither activity interferes much with the enjoyment of bushwalkers, ski tourers, deer hunters, trout anglers and four-wheel-drive enthusiasts, for whom the rugged terrain has long been a popular destination.
NOTE: Licences required for fishing and deer hunting.
WARNING: Severe weather changes occur suddenly.
BEST TIME: Year round (winter for cross country skiing).
ENQUIRIES: (051) 74 6166.
ADDRESS: CFL Traralgon Region, 71 Hotham St, Traralgon 3844.

Scenic enjoyment ✔✔✔
Day activities ✔
Family camping ✘
Hard bushwalking ✔✔✔

Wyperfeld National Park
450 km NW, 100 km N of Dimboola. Mallee weather district. Car access off Henty Highway at Hopetoun.

Camping ground and short nature walks are centred on a chain of dry lakes that fill only on rare occasions when the Wimmera River floods north through the vast, sandy park. Mature stands of river red gum and black box lining the old watercourses testify to past floodings; their seeds will not germinate without plentiful ground moisture.

Most of the 100 000 ha park, however, is dominated by vegetation types adapted to little change from their semi-arid conditions. Heaths grow on isolated claypans; sandy ridges support tea-trees, mallees and cypress pines.
NOTES: Permits required for bush camping. Fee charged for camping sites. Fires permitted only in authorised fireplaces. Carry drinking water on all walks in park.
BEST TIME: Midwinter and spring.
ENQUIRIES: (053) 95 7221.
ADDRESS: RMB 1465, Yaapeet 3424.

Scenic enjoyment ✔
Day activities ✔
Family camping ✔✔
Hard bushwalking ✔✔

Victoria's wildlife

More than any other state Victoria is dominated by high country. But as it sweeps south to the coast from the Alps and the semi-arid grasslands of the northwest it takes in many different types of landscape and habitat – high plains, great rock outcrops, temperate rainforest, heathlands, mallee, fern-filled gullies. Because of these varied environments it also has a wide range of plants and wildlife.

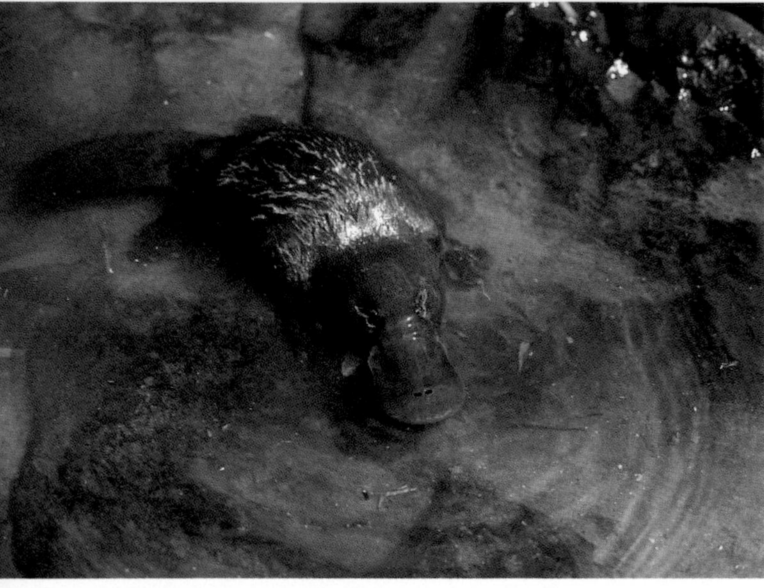

Platypus – receptors in the sensitive skin of the bill tell it about the underwater surroundings

Mountain pygmy-possum – may store seed as a food reserve for the alpine winter

Common wombat – in summer this forest-dweller seldom emerges from its burrow except at night

Wallaroo – shaggy dark grey hair differentiates it from the western subspecies

Little penguins – wait until dark before coming ashore in groups to roost in crevices or burrows

Australian shelduck – also known as the mountain duck, it prefers lowland areas and lives by brackish lakes

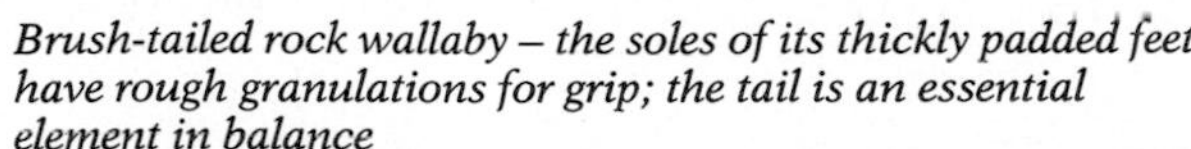
Brush-tailed rock wallaby – the soles of its thickly padded feet have rough granulations for grip; the tail is an essential element in balance

Malleefowl – the male is responsible for maintaining the mound nest and keeping it at the right temperature

Victoria's birds and flowers

Australian king parrot – feeds among the outer branches of forest trees, particularly on eucalypts and acacias

Flame robin – coats the outside of its cup-shaped nest with cobwebs or dry moss

Superb lyrebird – has a powerful voice that is unmatched for repertoire and mimicry

Australian pelican – groups sometimes swim slowly in formation to drive fish into the shallows

Grampians National Park *has almost 900 species of flowering plants, seen at their best from August to November. Among the orchids are: l, small helmet orchid; cl, slaty helmet orchid; b, mayfly orchid*

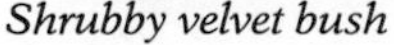

Shrubby velvet bush

Grampians thryptomene

Common heath – state emblem

Many of Baw Baw's summer hiking tracks become touring routes for cross-country skiers in winter

Cycling in thin winter sunshine on the nature drive at Wyperfeld

A walk in the fresh air to spark the appetite and then a sizzling sausage from the barbecue

Paddling along a tidal river in Wilsons Promontory National Park

Visitor activities in the national parks of Victoria

Bird watching
Churchill, Little Desert, The Lakes (special bird hides).

Bush camping
Baw Baw, Bogong, Brisbane Ranges, Cobberas-Tingaringy, Croajingolong, Grampians, Mitchell River, Otway, Snowy River, Wilsons Promontory.

Bushwalking
Alfred, Baw Baw, Bogong, Brisbane Ranges, Churchill, Cobberas-Tingaringy, Croajingolong, Fern Tree Gully, Fraser, Grampians, Kinglake, Lind, Little Desert, Lower Glenelg, Mitchell River, Morwell, Mount Buffalo, Mount Eccles, Mount Richmond, Organ Pipes, Otway, Port Campbell, Snowy River, Tarra-Bulga, The Lakes, Wilsons Promontory, Wonnangatta-Moroka.

Camping
Fraser, Grampians, Kinglake, Little Desert, Lower Glenelg, Mount Buffalo, Mount Eccles, Otway, Port Campbell, Snowy River, The Lakes, Wilsons Promontory, Wonnangatta-Moroka.

Canoeing/boating
Cobberas-Tingaringy, Croajingolong, Fraser, Grampians, Lower Glenelg, Mitchell River, Mount Buffalo, Otway, Snowy River, The Lakes, Wonnangatta-Moroka.

Car touring and 4-W driving
Baw Baw, Bogong, Brisbane Ranges, Cobberas-Tingaringy, Croajingolong, Grampians, Snowy River, Wonnangatta-Moroka.

Cave tours
Lower Glenelg.

Cycling
Bogong, Churchill, Fern Tree Gully, Wilsons Promontory.

Deer hunting
Wonnangatta-Moroka.

Fishing, ocean
Cape Schanck, Croajingolong, Otway, Port Campbell, The Lakes, Wilsons Promontory.

Fishing, freshwater
Baw Baw, Cobberas-Tingaringy, Croajingolong, Fraser, Grampians, Little Desert, Lower Glenelg, Mitchell River, Otway, Snowy River, Wilsons Promontory, Wonnangatta-Moroka.

Geological studies
Mount Eccles.

Croajingolong, with its wide variety of plant, animal and bird life in inland areas, and its great stretches of unspoiled coastline, is magnificent territory for hikers

Historical studies
Brisbane Ranges, Port Campbell.

Horse riding (in specified areas)
Baw Baw, Bogong, Cape Schanck, Cobberas-Tingaringy, Grampians, Kinglake, Lower Glenelg, Mount Buffalo, Snowy River, Wonnangatta-Moroka.

Photography
Alfred.

Picnicking
Alfred, Baw Baw, Bogong, Brisbane Ranges, Cape Schanck, Churchill, Croajingolong, Fern Tree Gully, Fraser, Grampians, Kinglake, Lind, Little Desert, Lower Glenelg, Mitchell River, Morwell, Mount Buffalo, Mount Eccles, Mount Richmond, Organ Pipes, Otway, Port Campbell, Tarra-Bulga, The Lakes, Wilsons Promontory.

Power boating
Fraser, Lower Glenelg, Wilsons Promontory.

Orienteering
Churchill.

Rafting, white water
Cobberas-Tingaringy, Mitchell River, Snowy River.

Rock climbing
Grampians, Mount Buffalo.

Scenic driving
Lind, Mount Buffalo, Otway, Port Campbell, Tarra-Bulga, Wilsons Promontory.

Skiing, cross country/downhill
Baw Baw, Bogong, Cobberas-Tingaringy, Mount Buffalo, Wonnangatta-Moroka.

Scuba diving
Wilsons Promontory.

Snorkelling
Wilsons Promontory.

Surfing
Cape Schanck, Otway, Wilsons Promontory.

Swimming
Cape Schanck, Cobberas-Tingaringy, Croajingolong, Fraser, Grampians, Mount Buffalo, Port Campbell, Snowy River, Wilsons Promontory.

CAMPING

Bush camping — away from it all, no facilities other than those you create.
Camping — a pit toilet and a tap but no other facilities.
Family camping — established camping ground with showers, toilets, barbecue areas and where you can probably take a caravan, but check beforehand.

Tobogganing
Mount Buffalo.

Walking along coastal tracks and beaches
Cape Schanck, Croajingolong, Otway.

Water skiing
Fraser, Lower Glenelg.

Wildflower studies
Brisbane Ranges, Churchill, Grampians (best area in Victoria), Little Desert, Mount Richmond – all outstanding in spring.

Windsurfing
Fraser.

Yachting
Fraser, The Lakes, Wilsons Promontory.

There is good beach fishing from many of the state's national parks

LAUNCESTON & DEVONPORT REGIONS

Reminders of an age when ice ruled the land

ALPINE SCENERY presents its boldest face in the Tasmanian highlands. Peaks and bluffs towards the north coast stand in sharper relief than any to be seen on the mainland Great Divide. Their craggy profiles were carved by glaciers about 20 000 years ago, during the last ice age. Creeping rivers of ice chewed at the flanks of brittle dolerite outcrops. The debris formed moraines that now pen high lakes, or it slipped into valleys to make stony wastelands of their floors. Boulders dragged over the central plateau gouged holes to be filled by hundreds of glittering tarns.

Even now, in a climate far milder, winter frosts crack more rock and spring thaws move the rubble down the slopes. Alpine heaths and gnarled, low-growing shrubs have to withstand months under snow. And visitors must beware of the onset of severely cold, wet weather at any time of year.

Launceston and Devonport, northern Tasmania's principal entry points for air travellers and car-ferry traffic respectively, have ready access to the most arresting mountain scenery. The state's best skifields, on the high massif of Ben Lomond, are only 50 km from Launceston. In summer the moorlands are an untracked wilderness of flowering heaths, and the 'organ pipe' dolerite columns of the surrounding bluffs make an unforgettable sight.

Outstanding examples of glaciated landforms are concentrated at Cradle Mountain, two hours or so from Devonport. Peaks in the national park – or the Reserve, as Tasmanians often call the district – create a jagged skyline above lakes of icy clarity and deeply carved, rock-strewn valleys. A picture-postcard snow scene in winter, it has a bleak majesty all its own after the thaw.

In contrast to the nearby highlands, easily accessible parks on the north coast enjoy mild climates and markedly lower rainfall, but they lack much scenic distinction. Freycinet, even more sheltered and sunny on the east coast, offers the greatest diversity in its peaks and sea cliffs of granite and its long white beaches. But motorists will see little: Freycinet is a park for walking and boating.

Mainlanders visiting any of the national parks in these regions – except Ben Lomond and Cradle Mountain in the winter sports season – will notice an unusual freedom from population pressures. Traffic is light and facilities are seldom over-used. Natural surroundings can be appreciated in northern Tasmania with the least likelihood of human distraction.

Featured parks **Pages**

(1) Ben Lomond 244-245
(2) Freycinet 246-247
(3) Cradle Mountain-Lake St Clair 248-249
(4) Rocky Cape 250-251
(5) Hellyer Gorge................ 252-253

Your access and facilities guide to every national park in these regions starts on page 254

Tarns fill glacial scars on the plateau east of Cradle Mountain

Frost-resistant plants cling precariously in thin soils capping each column of dolerite. The rock was formed in the same way as columnar basalt, from the cooling of magma that intruded into sedimentary rock. But it is less rich in silica, and more than 100 million years older than most basalts found on the mainland

BEN LOMOND NATIONAL PARK

Half an hour from Misery Bluff, cross-country skiers reach the Plains of Heaven. Pressing on, they find Little Hell. Ben Lomond's lofty plateau, bristling with the colourful names beloved of skiers, is Tasmania's premier snow-sports area. A commercial alpine resort perches on the flanks of the tallest peak, Legges Tor (1572 metres). Out of season the 16 500 ha park offers adventure – without marked trails – to walkers and climbers prepared to brave a chilly climate. Deep beds of dolerite, bared by eons of erosion of overlying sedimentary rock, were smashed and scoured by the movement of glaciers in the last ice age. Above 1250 metres, frost action is still breaking down the rock. Gravity moves the debris into valleys where it builds blockfields – barren or sparsely vegetated areas where chunks of rock cover a layer of peat. But the alpine moors are fertile: creeping cushion plants appear through melting snow, and heaths flower brilliantly in summer. Celery-top pine and a stunted, deciduous beech called tanglefoot – both peculiar to Tasmania – grow at sub-alpine levels, above eucalypt woodlands.

Broken rock slides down the flanks of Stacks Bluff (1527 metres) on the southernmost edge of the plateau. Glaciers tore at the dolerite columns for thousands of years. Now frost carries on the destruction, shrinking and cracking the rock

An icy dawn breaks over moorlands between Lake Youl (foreground) and Lake Baker. Far to the east are the peaks of the Tower Hill Range

FREYCINET NATIONAL PARK

Roads reach only 6 km into a mountainous park of nearly 11 000 ha. Visitors prepared to continue on foot find tracks winding over or round the four-peaked ridge of the Hazards to a low, marshy isthmus bordered by Hazards Beach and Wineglass Bay – each with a campsite. A circuit of the Hazards can be made in half a day. To the south, hardy walkers can traverse most of the western coast of Freycinet Peninsula and its high central spine, dominated by Mt Freycinet (620 metres). The full round trip takes two days, with a camp at Cooks Beach to break the journey. Schouten Island, accessible only by boat, has a camp but no tracks. Coastal scrubs and heaths, flowering profusely in spring, make up most of the vegetation. Birds and small marsupials are abundant.

Schouten Island, seen from the south between Taillefer Rock and Freycinet Peninsula, is split by a clear faultline. The near side consists of mostly bare granite; timbered heights beyond were formed separately, from dolerite. Left: To the north of the peninsula, the steep faces of the Hazards jut into Thouin Bay. Mt Dove (485 metres) is on the left

Granite cliffs (left) line Lemon Bight at Cape Forestier, on the northeastern corner of Freycinet Peninsula. The coastline veers sharply westward to Wineglass Bay (above), where swampy heathlands back a waterline walking route. Swimming can be dangerous from the eastern side of the park, exposed to Tasman Sea swells. Sandy beaches on the opposite side, fronting Great Oyster Bay, are safe and highly popular in late summer

Cradle Mountain's dolerite peaks tower over the icy waters of Lake Dove

A slow-moving sheet of ice covered this plateau between 20 000 and 15 000 years ago. The glacier tore rocks from the flanks of outcrops such as Barn Bluff (background); dragged along in the ice, they gouged out countless hollows that are now lakes and tarns

CRADLE MOUNTAIN-LAKE ST CLAIR NATIONAL PARK

Mountain scenery of stark, unforgettable grandeur unfolds itself to walkers with a week or more to spare for the north-south traverse of Tasmania's most famous park. The going is fairly easy on the Overland Track, but side-track climbs are much harder. And bitter weather can strike at any time – warm clothing and waterproofs should be carried. Many shorter walks, taking about half a day, are available on tracks starting near the access roads at each end of the 132 000 ha park.

In the north, Cradle Mountain and Barn Bluff dominate a landscape of open moors and heathlands, dotted with lakes and tarns. Peaks ringing the park's central plain include Mt Ossa, Tasmania's tallest at 1617 metres. Valleys to the south, squeezed between the Du Cane and Traveller Ranges, funnel into the long, deep basin of Lake St Clair, which is the source of Hobart's River Derwent.

Vegetation ranges from beech rainforests to alpine grasses, snow gums and ancient species of pines. Wildlife includes echidnas, platypuses, marsupial 'cats', Tasmanian devils and wombats.

Sailing boats can be launched into Lake St Clair

Tiny beaches at Rocky Cape gain shelter from tongues of tough quartzite reaching into Bass Strait. Waters are usually calm and safe to the east of the cape but the area has one notable shipwreck – an early steamer that lost its way in blinding bushfire smoke

Rocks off the cape are tilted almost vertically from their original bedding planes. The district has a complicated history of earth movements involving folding, faulting, tilting, dolerite intrusion and volcanic eruptions, along with glacial striation – the scratching effect of boulders dragged in ice

ROCKY CAPE NATIONAL PARK

Cassinia (right), one of the paper daisies, and coast tea-tree (below) cope well on poor, sandy soils. Common heath (bottom right), widespread from NSW to SA, was first found at Rocky Cape

Wooded slopes of the Sisters Hills back a jagged coastline littered with reefs and islets and pitted with water-worn caves. Aborigines used some of the caves for at least 8000 years: archeological interest was the chief reason for the park's proclamation in 1967. Remains from the feasting of generations of hunters and seafood gatherers can be seen in two caves open to the public near the western end of Sisters Beach, and in two more on Flagpole Hill, at Rocky Cape itself.

Easy, well-marked walking trails cover most of the 3000 ha park. Some lead to little pocket beaches between headlands jutting into Bass Strait; rock pools and crevices hold a fascinating range of marine life. Other tracks climb the hills, where two lookouts offer impressive coastal views. Scrubs and flowering heaths are dominant but the inner slopes have peppermint eucalypts and patches of stringybark forest. Sea eagles, roosting on promontories and in some of the taller trees, are among more than 90 bird species seen in the park.

Silver banksia

Scented paperbark

Orchids growing on the bark of old rainforest trees beside the Hellyer River

Flood-worn boulders border a cascading tributary stream

Tree ferns (above) and epiphyte fishbone ferns (below) grow densely in the wet gorge

Hellyer Gorge

Chilling rains are frequent in the steeply winding gorge of the Hellyer River. But given any luck with the weather, travellers on the lonely Murchison Highway south from Somerset could find no more delightful wayside stop. A state reserve of 570 ha straddles the road each side of the Hellyer Bridge, offering picnic grounds screened by big tree ferns. A short but sometimes slippery track leads to the river through a rainforest of tall myrtle beech, encrusted with mosses, fungi and epiphyte orchids. Similar forests once covered hills to the north and east, now planted with exotic trees. Swift-running streams feed the Hellyer, which is itself a major tributary of the Arthur River, the most important waterway of northwestern Tasmania. Henry Hellyer, an explorer-surveyor for the Van Dieman's Land Company, made the first European ascent of Cradle Mountain in 1831.

PARKS OF THE LAUNCESTON AND DEVONPORT REGIONS

Asbestos Range National Park

60 km NW of Launceston, 40 km E of Devonport. Central North and Midlands weather district. Car access from Launceston on West Tamar Highway and Badger Head Road, or from Devonport on Frankford Road and Bakers Beach Road. Approach roads gravel.

Coastal heathlands merge into dry eucalypt woodlands in a park of nearly 4300 ha extending from Port Sorell to Greens Beach, on the western edge of Port Dalrymple. Two long, sandy beaches are separated by the humped mass of Badger Head. Swimming is popular at both, though the western end of Bakers Beach has strong currents.

Many easy walks can be taken on the coast or into the foothills of the Asbestos Range. A hide for waterfowl observation is provided at a freshwater lagoon behind Bakers Beach, half an hour's walk from a car park. Birds of the heaths and woodlands are also abundant. Wallabies and wombats are particularly common and forester kangaroos, which died out here last century, have been successfully reintroduced.

BEST TIME: Spring to autumn.
ENQUIRIES: (004) 28 6277.
ADDRESS: NPWS head office, Box 210, Sandy Bay 7005.

Scenic enjoyment ✔
Day activities ✔✔✔
Family camping ✔✔
Hard bushwalking ✗

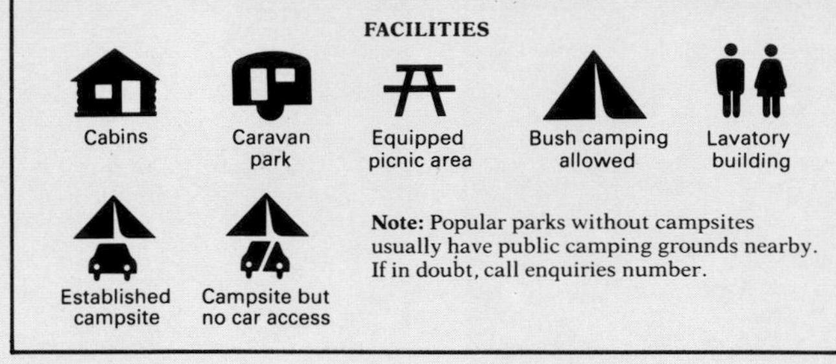

PARK RATINGS No interest ✗ Some interest ✔ Major interest ✔✔ Outstanding ✔✔✔

Ben Lomond National Park

50 km SE of Launceston. East Coast weather district. Car access on Launceston-Ben Lomond road. Entrance fee in ski season. Risky bends on ascent to ski village; chains should be carried in winter. Snowfalls may close road. Buses from Launceston in ski season.

DESCRIPTION: Page 245.
NOTE: Alpine resort accommodation privately arranged through Northern Tasmanian Alpine Club.
BEST TIME: Skiing June-September, walking November-April.
ENQUIRIES: (003) 41 5312 or (003) 99 3414 (ski season only).
ADDRESS: As for Asbestos Range.

Scenic enjoyment ✔✔✔
Day activities ✔
Family camping ✗
Hard bushwalking ✔✔✔

Cradle Mountain-Lake St Clair National Park

85 km S of Devonport. Central Plateau and Upper Derwent Valley weather district. Car access to Cradle Valley end via Forth or Gowrie Park; last 30 km gravel. Snowfalls may close road. Lake St Clair end accessible by car or bus from Hobart (170 km) on Lyell Highway to Derwent Bridge.

DESCRIPTION: Page 249.
NOTE: Fees charged for hut use and for the Overland Track.
WARNING: Severe weather possible even in summer. Walkers should register plans with ranger.
BEST TIME: November-March.
ENQUIRIES: Northern end (003) 63 5187, southern end (002) 89 1115.
ADDRESS: As for Asbestos Range.

Scenic enjoyment ✔✔✔
Day activities ✔
Family camping ✗
Hard bushwalking ✔✔✔

Freycinet National Park

180 km SE of Launceston. East Coast weather district. Car access via Lake Leake and Coles Bay. Car and bus access from Hobart (200 km) via Tasman Highway. Entrance fee.

DESCRIPTION: Page 246.
NOTE: Camp bookings required midsummer, Easter.
WARNING: Carry water on longer walks.
BEST TIME: Summer-autumn.
ENQUIRIES: (002) 57 0146.
ADDRESS: Via Coles Bay 7215.

Scenic enjoyment ✔✔
Day activities ✔✔✔
Family camping ✔✔✔
Hard bushwalking ✔✔

Hellyer Gorge State Reserve

100 km W of Devonport. Northwest Coast weather district. Murchison Highway from Somerset passes through reserve.

DESCRIPTION: Page 253.
BEST TIME: Spring to autumn.
ENQUIRIES: (003) 41 5312.
ADDRESS: As for Asbestos Range.

Scenic enjoyment ✔✔✔
Day activities ✔
Family camping ✗
Hard bushwalking ✗

1 **Asbestos Range NP**
2 **Ben Lomond NP**
3 **Cradle Mountain-Lake St Clair NP**
4 **Freycinet NP**
5 **Hellyer Gorge State Reserve**
6 **Mount William NP**
7 **Rocky Cape NP**
8 **Strzelecki NP**
9 **Walls of Jerusalem NP**

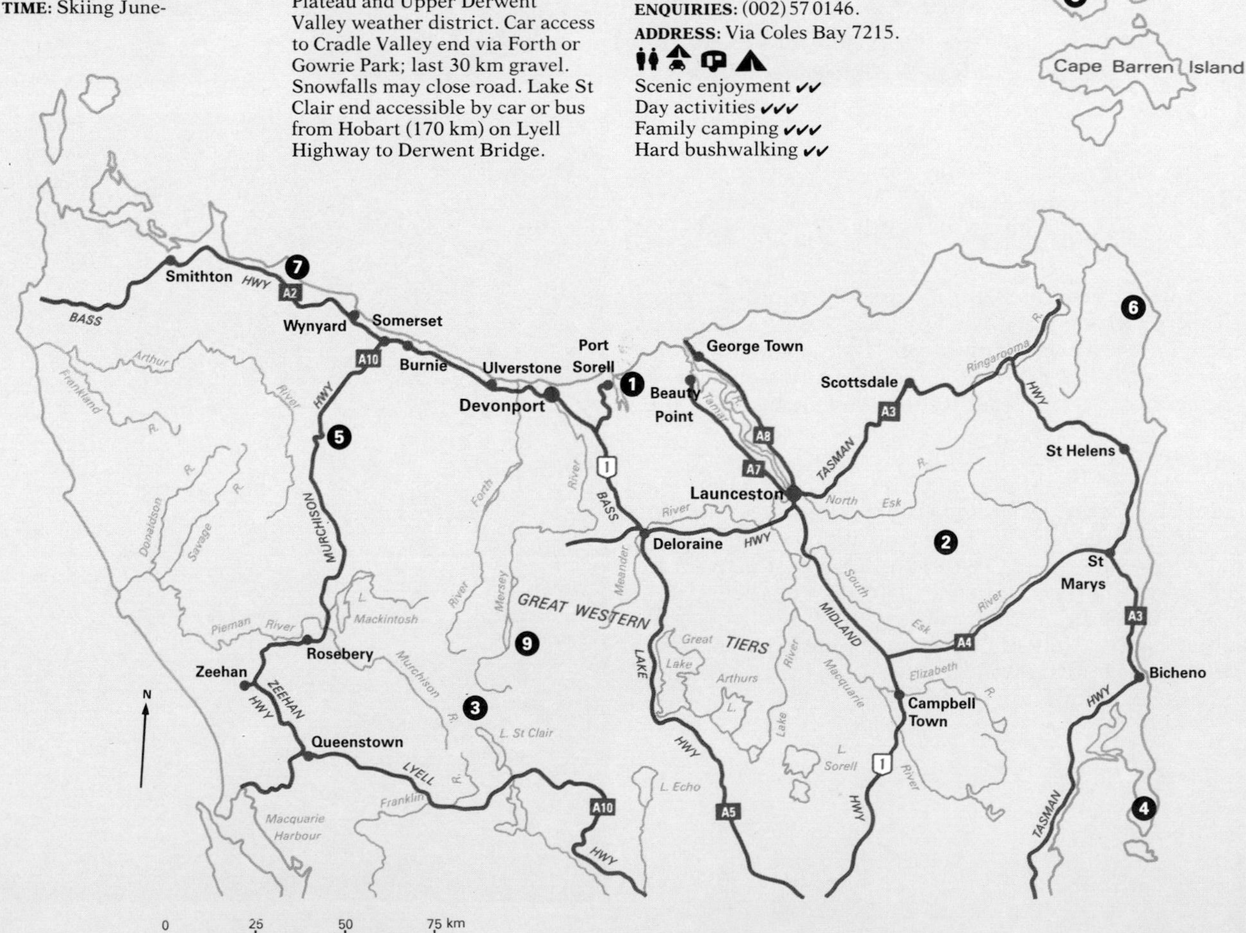

Mount William National Park

160 km E of Launceston. Northeast weather district. Car access via Tasman Highway and Herrick-Gladstone road; unsealed roads in park.

Long, open bays each side of Cape Naturaliste have sandy beaches popular for swimming and fishing. Dunes and coastal heathlands in a park of nearly 14 000 ha contrast with timbered inland slopes leading up to Mt William (216 metres) and Baileys Hill. They make up the biggest protected area of dry eucalypt forest in Tasmania.

The park is managed principally as a wildlife reserve, giving sanctuary to forester kangaroos, Bennett's wallabies, echidnas, pademelons, wombats, marsupial 'cats' and Tasmanian devils. Seabirds are abundant along with scores of forest and heath species.

NOTE: Bore water available near campsites.

BEST TIME: Summer.

ENQUIRIES: (003) 57 2108.

ADDRESS: As for Asbestos Range.

Scenic enjoyment ✓
Day activities ✓✓
Family camping ✓✓
Hard bushwalking ✓

Rocky Cape National Park

100 km W of Devonport. Northwest Coast weather district. Car access via Bass Highway, turning off for Sisters Beach 12 km past Wynyard, or Rocky Cape 30 km past Wynyard. Burnie-Stanley buses pass park.

DESCRIPTION: Page 251.

BEST TIME: November-March.

ENQUIRIES: (003) 41 5312.

ADDRESS: As for Asbestos Range.

Scenic enjoyment ✓
Day activities ✓✓
Family camping ×
Hard bushwalking ✓

Strzelecki National Park

165 km NE of Launceston. Northeast and Flinders Island weather district. Air access only: Launceston-Whitemark daily, Hobart-Whitemark Mon., Wed., Fri. Cars, bicycles for hire – 7 km to park entrance.

Granite peaks of the Strzelecki Range, topped by Mt Strzelecki (800 metres), dominate a park of 4200 ha at the southwestern corner of Flinders Island. The area is mostly undeveloped but a track leads up to the mountain to reveal excellent views of the island and others in the Furneaux group. The climb takes 4 hours.

Behind coastal heathlands are slopes of dry eucalypt forest and valleys supporting dense stands of moisture-loving species such as blue gums and peppermints. Tree ferns are prolific in some gullies. Wildlife does not differ markedly from mainland Tasmania but a local wombat, classed as a subspecies, is smaller and softer-furred than the usual type and more active by day.

BEST TIME: Summer.

ENQUIRIES: (003) 59 2148.

ADDRESS: As for Asbestos Range.

Scenic enjoyment ✓✓
Day activities ✓✓
Family camping ✓✓
Hard bushwalking ✓✓

Walls of Jerusalem National Park

110 km W of Launceston, 115 km S of Devonport. Central Plateau and Upper Derwent Valley weather district. Car access on Bass Highway to Deloraine, then via Mole Creek and Mersey Forest road (unsealed).

Sheer dolerite cliffs rise forbiddingly to the northwest of the central plateau – what Tasmanians call the Lake Country. In the lower valleys of the 11 500 ha park, groves of pencil pines surround glacier-carved lakes and tarns, and grassy expanses are decked with wildflowers in early summer. Sub-alpine heaths and wet grasslands share the plateau. Gnarled snow gums cling to rocky ridges near the Walls. A big population of marsupials includes wallabies, potoroos, wombats, possums and native 'cats'. Parrots are prominent in a wide variety of birds.

A well-defined walking track ascends to the plateau from the Fish River. It penetrates the Walls through Herod's Gate and passes Lake Salome at the base of the tallest cliff, West Wall (1490 metres). Mt Jerusalem (1458 metres) stands not far south. Two shelter huts are provided. Rock climbers find ample opportunities, and parts of the plateau in winter are suited to cross-country skiing.

WARNING: Sudden changes of weather.

BEST TIME: Summer.

ENQUIRIES: (003) 41 5312.

ADDRESS: As for Asbestos Range.

Scenic enjoyment ✓✓✓
Day activities ×
Family camping ×
Hard bushwalking ✓✓✓

THE OVERLAND TRACK:
Cradle Mountain-Lake St Clair

Enough sidetracks to keep hikers and climbers occupied for weeks lead off the 80 km trail linking craggy Cradle Mountain with forested hills around the placid expanse of Lake St Clair. Walks of five days or more sample diverse moorland, mountain and gorge landscapes.

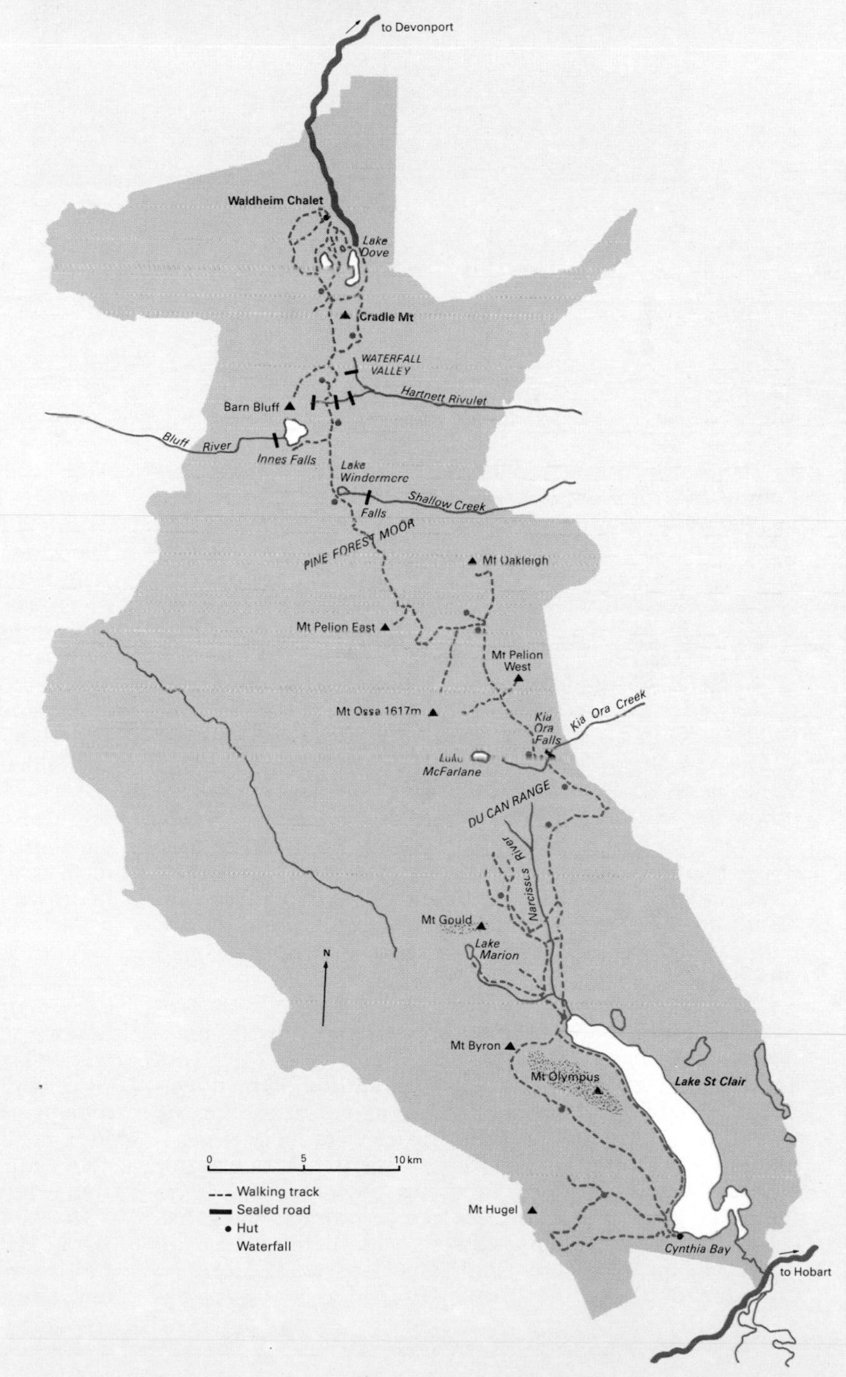

How the west was won

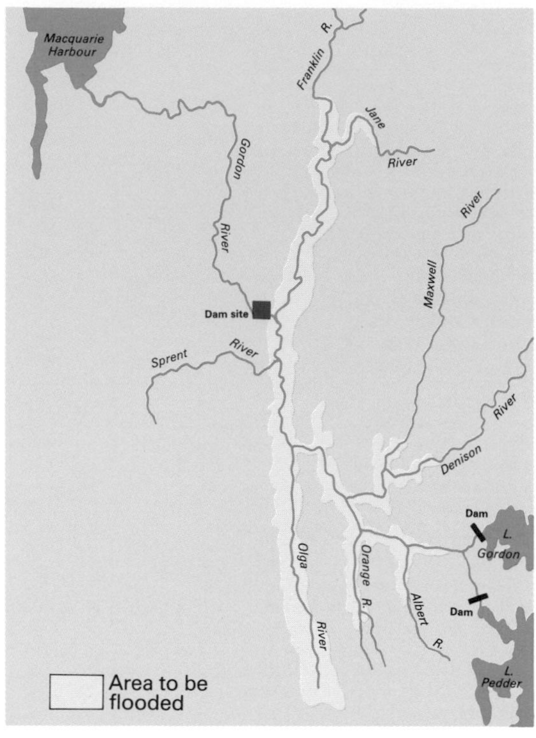

Waters backing up from the dam would have flooded 37 km of the Gordon Valley, 33 km of the Franklin Gorge, and parts of seven tributaries. The power station was to have had an average annual output of 172 megawatts. The whole scheme was expected to take 9½ years at a cost of $136 million, with a peak workforce of 1200

TASMANIA'S Gordon River dam conflict redrew the battle lines of environmental debate in Australia. What started in 1980 as yet another 'greenie' protest ended three years later in a constitutional showdown that changed the face of federal-state relations. Along the way, 1272 opponents of hydro-electric exploitation of the western rivers were arrested and 447 were imprisoned. But the real casualties were politicians.

'No Dams' campaigners drew strength from their frustration a decade earlier, when the pent-up waters of Lake Pedder engulfed a national park. Opposition marshalled then – too late – formed the nucleus of the Tasmanian Wilderness Society. Knowing that the next target of power generation planning would be the Gordon River, and that the Franklin would probably be involved as a major tributary, the society built its case well in advance. Films and photographs were assembled to depict the wild beauty of the two rivers and their gorges. Lectures and publications were prepared. Mainland and international support was enlisted.

Late in 1979 the state Hydro-Electric Commission proposed a dam on the Gordon immediately below its junction with the Franklin, flooding the valleys of both rivers and part of seven others. A power station 1 km downstream would meet Tasmania's estimated needs for the rest of the century. Other possibilities were more expensive and less productive. With both of the state's major political parties wedded to cheap power as a way to industrial growth, the HEC seemed certain to win again.

But local and national dissent was mobilised on an unprecedented scale in 1980. The Australian Heritage Commission placed the Tasmanian wilderness on its register of the National Estate. Yielding, the Labor state cabinet chose an alternative: the Gordon would be dammed higher up, at its junction with the Olga River. The Franklin, untouched, would be the focus of a new Wild Rivers National Park. The state's upper house, however, insisted on the HEC's Franklin scheme.

Fresh force was lent to the anti-dam argument in 1981 by the discovery that caves along the wild rivers, crammed with Aboriginal artefacts, had been occupied before and during the glacial phase of the last ice age. By then the government was committed to resolving its parliamentary deadlock by referendum. Premier Douglas Lowe was deposed and his successor, Harry Holgate, presided over a poll in which the only formal choice was one dam or other. A third of voters spoiled their ballots – most wrote 'No Dams' – but a clear majority consented to drowning the Franklin.

Early in 1982 the federal government nominated the western Tasmanian wilderness parks for World Heritage listing. But the state Liberal opposition leader, Robin Gray, claimed that he was assured of commonwealth loan funding for the power scheme. The Holgate government fell and the Liberals enjoyed a record success at the ensuing elections. Laws were quickly passed to start the dam project and to revoke parts of Wild Rivers National Park needed by the HEC. And in anticipation of physical confrontations, the police were given the power of on-the-spot arrest for trespass.

On the mainland, a Tasmanian application to have the World Heritage nomination withdrawn was rejected by the federal government. The Labor opposition caucus formally opposed any damming in western Tasmania –

contradicting the state ALP policy. In an outer-Melbourne by-election 40 per cent of voters wrote 'No Dams'. In Paris the World Heritage listing was proclaimed. That signalled the start of the active blockade. Executing a long-hatched plan, protesters swarmed into the west to obstruct HEC site preparation and the movement of equipment. Their quixotic exploits, and the soaring toll of arrests, were chronicled daily in the national media.

Late in January 1983 Prime Minister Malcolm Fraser offered $500 million to finance a coal-fired power station instead of the hydro project. Premier Gray refused, and Mr Fraser repeated that his government could not intervene against the state's will. A few days later he called a general election. Labor under Bob Hawke won a sweeping victory, and quickly passed regulations forbidding HEC activities in the World Heritage area. On 1 July 1983 the High Court confirmed that the federal government's World Heritage obligations entitled it to override state powers. A year later the Tasmanian government accepted a compensatory offer from Canberra of $277 million.

Blockaders wait in a picket line of inflatable dinghies to challenge barges bringing bulldozers up the Gordon River. More than 2600 people signed up to take part in the blockade, which lasted nearly three months. Charges against those arrested – and often jailed for not accepting bail conditions – were eventually dropped

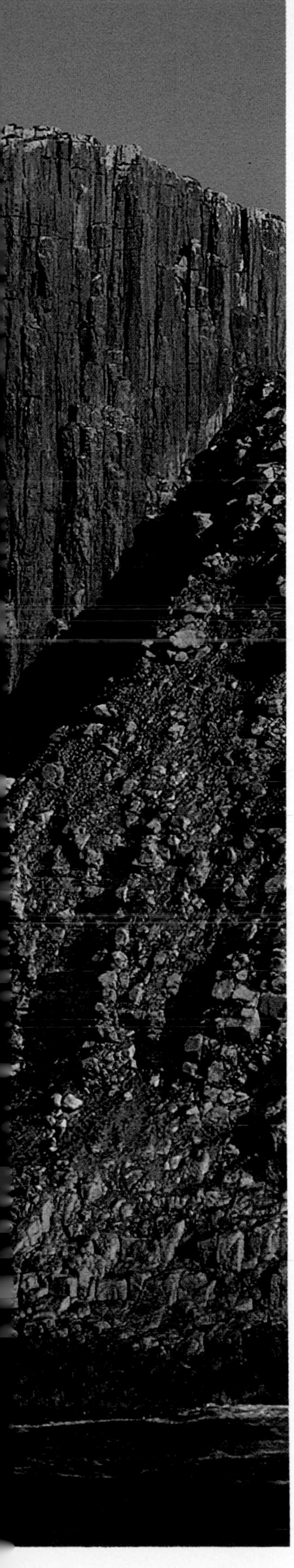

HOBART REGION

Seaside splendour and a challenging wilderness

EVEN IN the heart of Tasmania's capital, lonely landscapes are evoked. The River Derwent draws its flow from sources as far-flung as the northern Great Lakes, the glacier-chiselled central plateau, the chilling depths of Lake St Clair and the forested ranges west towards Mt Field. On their way to Hobart these waters drive the turbines of a dozen power stations – symbols of the conflict between industrialisation and conservation that splits Tasmanian society.

Downstream, the broadening Derwent estuary is shielded from Storm Bay by a hooked string of ridged peninsulas, unconvincingly linked by low sandspits. The same formation occurs again and again around the wilder coast beyond: Bruny Island, Tasman and Forestier Peninsulas, Maria Island, Freycinet Peninsula. At the lip of Storm Bay, Cape Raoul defies the Tasman Sea with jagged walls of dolerite. They signify the colossal upsurge of magma under half of Tasmania, emerging after eons of surface weathering to give it a special look.

Crags of dolerite even cap Mt Wellington, 1270 metres above the city's western outskirts. From the Pinnacle lookout tourists see not only the winding course of the Derwent and the intricacies of the coast, but also a seemingly endless series of timbered ranges receding to the west.

That fact was brought home savagely to city people in 1967, when bushfires swept over and round the mountain; 51 lives were lost and factories and hundreds of homes were destroyed.

Mt Field, the national park most accessible from the capital, is also the best in the range of forest and alpine plant communities it has on show in a relatively small area. Parks and reserves to the east of Hobart offer striking coastal scenery and ample opportunity for maritime diversions. Lake Pedder, vastly enlarged to the horror of ecologists, makes an aquatic playground in the northern part of Southwest National Park.

Few people other than the most determined walkers and climbers experience more of Southwest, or much of Wild Rivers National Park. Together these two, and Cradle Mountain-Lake St Clair, constitute a true wilderness of a size and quality that thoroughly merit its World Heritage listing. Here adventurers find Australia's best rafting rivers and its most celebrated system of mountain-and-ocean walking trails. The principal route, spanning 180 km from Lake Pedder to Port Davey on the west coast and around to Catamaran in the far south, is a trudge of at least eight days. The reward is a matchless variety of unspoilt scenes.

The untamed southwest virtually starts here, above Hobart.

Featured parks **Pages**

1 Wild Rivers 260-263
2 Southwest 264-265
3 Mount Field 266-267
4 Maria Island 268-269
5 Tasman Peninsula 270-271
6 Truchanas Reserve 272

Your access and facilities guide to every park in this region is on page 273

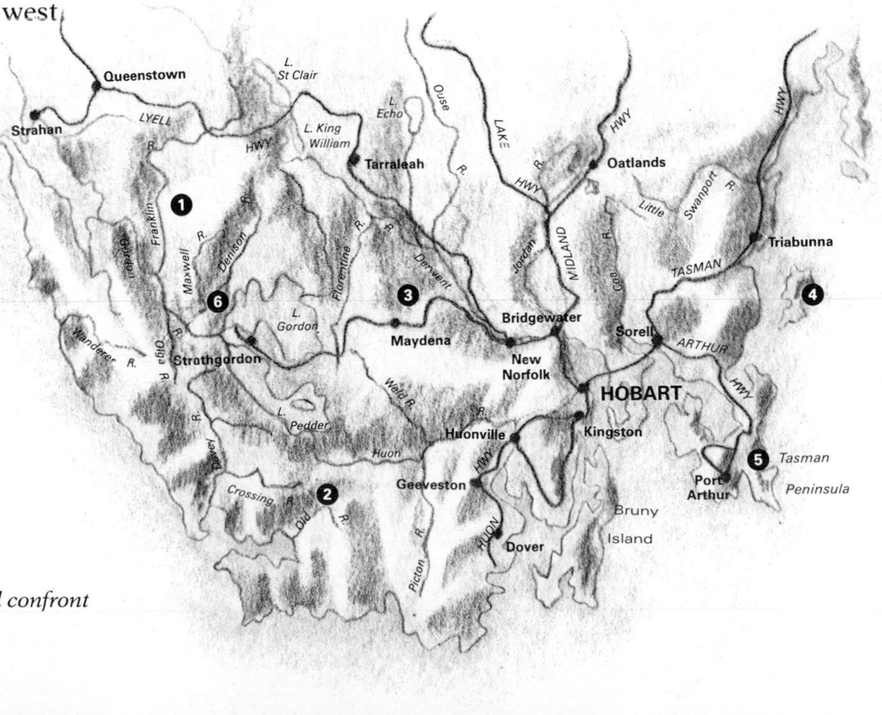

Dolerite clusters 165 million years old confront the ocean at Cape Raoul

On Frenchman's Cap, in the Deception Range, a glacier-cut quartzite face rising 300 metres challenges rock climbers

High rainfall in the catchment ranges keeps tributaries such as the Alma River (above) running full year-round to supply the Franklin (right). Myrtle beech crowds the steep flanks of the Franklin Gorge, which offers canoeists and rafting parties the longest white-water adventure in Australia

Grass triggerplants grow on lower forest slopes

Shiny tea-tree occurs in the rockiest areas

WILD RIVERS NATIONAL PARK

'No Dams' confrontations and political ructions in the early 1980s made Gordon and Franklin household names. But few Australians see these rivers, let alone their catchment ranges. Franklin-Lower Gordon Wild Rivers National Park covers nearly 200 000 ha of midwestern Tasmania. It links two older parks, Cradle Mountain-Lake St Clair and Southwest, and absorbs a third, Frenchman's Cap, to complete a continuous band of high-country wilderness with a westward arm down the Gordon to the coast at Macquarie Harbour.

Rainforests are dominated by myrtle beech but they contain some Huon pine. There are eucalypt forests on drier slopes as well as high heaths, buttongrass plains and boglands. Scores of bird species nesting in the park include the endangered orange-bellied parrot. Possums are the most prominent marsupials, but Tasmanian devils and native 'cats' may also be seen at night.

Boats from Strahan take scenic cruises up the lower Gordon, and motorists on the Lyell Highway can sample the upper Franklin bush along a 2 km track starting 4 km south of the Collingwood bridge. Deeper penetration of the park, by raft or canoe or by hard walking and climbing, should be attempted only by seasoned and well-equipped parties in consultation with rangers.

Near the end of its journey to Macquarie Harbour, the Gordon River takes a tortuous course through the Elliott Range

Quartzites and schists of the Arthur Range were twisted and folded eons ago, then jaggedly carved by glacial action during the last ice age

SOUTHWEST NATIONAL PARK

Lake Pedder's lucid waters, raised in the early 1970s for hydro-electric storage, swallowed one national park but became the centrepiece for another, far bigger. Embracing the enlarged lake, the 440 000 ha of Southwest reach out beyond the Frankland and Arthur Ranges to the west and south coasts through a wilderness of rocky ridges and deep, forested valleys. Visitors restricted to car travel can reach the northwestern and southeastern shores of the lake, where boating and trout fishing are popular. Swimming is possible but the water is always cold. The rest of the park poses stern tests for the most serious bushwalkers and climbers. Tracks radiating from an access route south of the lake reach Port Davey and other points on a rugged, lonely coast.

Precipitous Bluff (1120 metres) presents a challenge to rock climbers in the far south of the park. Dense rainforests of myrtle beech surround the outcrop. Southwest also has extensive alpine moorlands of heath and stunted scrub, and buttongrass meadows at lower levels

MOUNT FIELD NATIONAL PARK

Mountain heath

Towering examples of *Eucalyptus regnans*, the world's tallest hardwood, guard the entrance to an astonishing kingdom of trees. The road in winds from 100 metres above sea level to more than 1000. Moorlands and ridges climb still higher beyond Lake Dobson, culminating in Mt Field West (1434 metres). Every type of inland Tasmanian tree community is represented in a park of 17 000 ha: rainforest species, varied stands of eucalypts and stunted alpine scrubs. Curiosities include wind-bent 'horizontal scrub', the bane of bushwalkers, and pandani, the world's tallest heath. It grows to 9 metres and looks more like a palm. *Athrotaxis*, a genus of conifers peculiar to Tasmania, grows in two widely different forms, King Billy and pencil pine.

Bird and animal life is as diverse as the plants. Half of all Tasmania's bird species have been seen here. Furtive, nocturnal marsupials may include the thylacine or Tasmanian tiger – the last in captivity was trapped nearby in the 1930s.

Contrasting nature walks can be taken from the road to Russell Falls, just inside the park, and at two points higher up. A further easy track encircles Lake Dobson. Steep slopes just west of the lake are popular skifields in winter. Snow usually lies on the high moors until November. Cross-country ski trails lead west and north. After the thaw, strenuous walks taking up to a day each way are available. But rainfall is high throughout the year and bitterly cold snaps are frequent.

Below: Dicksonia tree ferns – 'manferns' – frame Russell Falls

Filmy fern colonises mossy spots on rotting logs

Gentianella favours wet alpine soils

Eucalypts and pines share the shores of Lake Dobson

Left: Eucalyptus regnans *can exceed 100 metres in height. Widely known as mountain ash, here it is called swamp gum – and its timber is sold as Tasmanian oak*

TASMAN PENINSULA

Storm-torn bluffs and cliffs, reaching for 25 km down the eastern side of Tasman Peninsula, present travellers on the approach to Eaglehawk Neck with the most arresting view of a wild coast to be seen in all Australia. Famous features such as the Tessellated Pavements, the Blowhole, Tasman's Arch and the Devil's Kitchen are within easy reach near the isthmus. Farther afield over forested hills, eroded clusters of columnar dolerite form extraordinary sea cliffs. They are equally impressive at Cape Raoul (page 258), Cape Pillar and Cape Hauy, where some columns stand needle-like offshore. Sheltered beaches are found south of Port Arthur and in Fortescue Bay, north of Cape Hauy. A scenic walking track between Fortescue and Waterfall Bays takes six hours each way.

Boulders carried by an ancient glacier are embedded in the sedimentary layers of a bluff at Fortescue Bay. Grooves in the face indicate a recent collapse, through undercutting by wave action

Tidal erosion of a shore platform at the northern end of the Eaglehawk Neck isthmus has exaggerated the cracks between blocks of vertically jointed sandstone. The tiled appearance inspired their name: the Tessellated Pavements

Plants in Tasmania's parks

Cut off from the mainland quite recently, in geological time, Tasmania is a world of its own. Developing in isolation, some of its plants and animals are unique, while others have developed differently from their mainland relations. Still others are all that remain of species which once flourished in other states. In its World Heritage area is one of the world's last great temperate wildernesses. Because of the wealth of trees and water, forest species of animals and plants are abundant; in summer the coastal heathlands attract birdlife – honeyeaters, scrub wrens pink robins and others busy themselves among the tea-tree and flowering plants.

Although it looks tropical, Richea pandanifolia is a heath unique to Tasmania. Growing to 12 metres it is one of the world's tallest

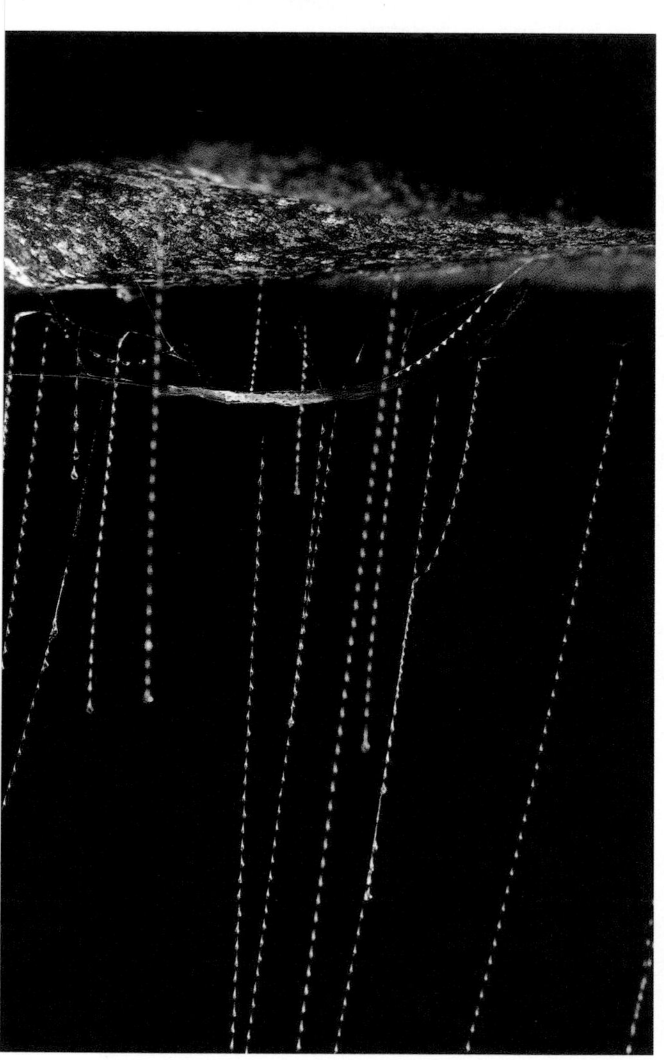

Glow-worms' sticky threads trap food

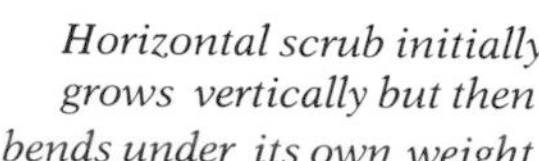

Horizontal scrub initially grows vertically but then bends under its own weight

Bellendena montana, mountain rocket, another Tasmanian native

Correa reflexa, the native fuchsia

Diplarrena moraea is a member of the iris family

Pink robins inhabit the undergrowth and fern-filled gullies of temperate rainforest

Hairy leek orchid

Broad-lip leek orchid,

Visitor activities in the national parks of Tasmania

Abseiling
Freycinet.

Bird watching
All national parks.

Bush camping
All national parks.

Bush walking
All national parks.

Camping
All national parks.

Canoeing/boating
Asbestos Range, Freycinet, Maria Island, Mount William, Rocky Cape, Southwest, Strzelecki, Wild Rivers.

Car touring
Asbestos Range, Ben Lomond, Mount Field, Mount William, Rocky Cape, Southwest.

Fishing, ocean/beach
Asbestos Range, Freycinet, Maria Island, Mount William, Rocky Cape, Southwest, Strzelecki.

Fishing, freshwater
Cradle Mountain-Lake St Clair, Mount Field, Walls of Jerusalem.

Geological studies
Ben Lomond, Cradle Mountain-Lake St Clair, Freycinet, Hartz Mountains, Maria Island, Mount Field, Rocky Cape, Southwest, Strzelecki, Walls of Jerusalem, Tasman Arch and Blowhole.

Hartz Mountains in winter: in spring and summer the moorlands are a sea of wildflowers

Historical studies
Historic sites and Maria Island.

Horse riding
Asbestos Range, Mount William.

Orienteering
Asbestos Range, Ben Lomond, Cradle Mountain-Lake St Clair, Freycinet, Hartz Mountains, Maria Island, Mount Field, Mount William, Rocky Cape, Strzelecki, Wild Rivers.

Photography
Asbestos Range, Tasman Arch and Blowhole.

Picnicking
Asbestos Range, Hellyer Gorge, Tasman Arch and Blowhole, Walls of Jerusalem.

Power boating
Asbestos Range, Freycinet, Maria Island, Mount William, Rocky Cape, Strzelecki.

Rafting
Wild Rivers.

Dense forests in the lower levels of Mount Field National Park contrast with the sparse shrub cover above the treeline where a ski area has been developed

Eddystone Lighthouse in Mount William National Park was built in 1889. It is sometimes open to visitors

Rock climbing
Ben Lomond, Cradle Mountain-Lake St Clair, Freycinet.

Skiing, cross country/downhill
Ben Lomond, Cradle Mountain-Lake St Clair, Mount Field, Walls of Jerusalem.

Scuba diving
Freycinet, Maria Island, Mount William, Rocky Cape, Strzelecki.

Snorkelling
Asbestos Range, Freycinet, Maria Island, Mount William, Rocky Cape, Strzelecki.

Surfing
Mount William.

Swimming
Asbestos Range, Cradle Mountain-Lake S Clair, Freycinet, Maria Island, Mount Willia Rocky Cape, Strezelecki.

Tobogganing
Ben Lomond, Mount Field.

Walking along coastal tracks and beaches
Asbestos Range, Freycinet, Maria Island Mount William, Rocky Cape, Southwest, Strzelecki, Tasman Arch and Blowhole.

Day walking near Lake Pedder in Southwest National Park

Southwest, largest of the parks, is mostly remote wilderness where small, fully equipped walking parties camp out to get to know and understand the state's great forests and the creatures that live in them

Water skiing
Asbestos Range, Freycinet, Mount William, Rocky Cape.

Wildflower studies
All national parks.

Wildlife observation
Asbestos Range, Cradle Mountain-Lake St Clair, Freycinet, Maria Island, Mount Field, Mount William.

Windsurfing
Asbestos Range, Freycinet, Maria Island, Mount William, Rocky Cape.

Yachting
Asbestos Range, Cradle Mountain-Lake St Clair, Freycinet, Maria Island, Mount William, Rocky Cape, Strzelecki.

CAMPING

Bush camping — away from it all, no facilities other than those you create.
Camping — a pit toilet and a tap but no other facilities.
Family camping — established camping ground with showers, toilets, barbecue areas and where you can probably take a caravan, but check beforehand.

Mount William has sweeping beaches for riding or walking and the waters offshore provide good fishing

CANBERRA REGION

Abundant choice where the seasons point the way

THE AUSTRALIAN Capital Territory waited until 1984 for its own national park, Namadgi – but Canberra people could hardly feel deprived. Most of the parks in southern NSW and some in northeastern Victoria are reached far more easily from the national capital than they can be from Sydney or Melbourne.

Choices are wide, for no other region offers greater contrasts in climate, altitude, landforms and plant life. Nearly all of the parks are suitable for active recreation. For visitors to make the most of their opportunities, however, they must have regard to the time of year.

Kosciusko National Park, with its vast area extending from west of Canberra to the Victorian border, commands most public attention because of the sporting potential of its winter snowfields. Skiers based in the capital are enviably close to Australia's most highly rated slopes and facilities – they can be up and back in the same day if they wish. But Kosciusko's off-season appeal is often overlooked. In summer the high plains are refreshingly cool, and alpine meadows bring forth a profusion of plants found nowhere else.

Forests to the east, on the contorted and dissected edge of the Great Dividing Range, throw down a gauntlet to the toughest bushwalkers. Traversing the steep ridges and ravines of parks such as Morton and Deua calls on all their skills and stamina. To see much, other than on foot, usually requires four-wheel-drive transport – and perhaps a guide. Winter storms here, and heavy rains at any time, are best avoided.

The escarpment falls away to richly fertile lowlands backing the NSW south coast, which people from the ACT have made virtually their own playground. Arresting rock forms, pleasant beaches, lagoons and heathlands are preserved in a string of maritime parks where the climate is mild year-round. Summer is naturally favoured for swimming, but fishing and boating enthusiasts follow their pursuits at any time unless South Tasman gales churn the ocean.

To the northwest, travellers from Canberra are within reasonable distance of parts of NSW to which Sydneysiders rarely venture. They include national parks of surprising diversity – rock gorges, oases of open forest and woodland on the pastoral plains, and finally a hint of the central deserts in the sandy wastes of Willandra. Out here the time to travel and camp is winter, under sunny skies, but free of fierce heat, flies and mosquitoes.

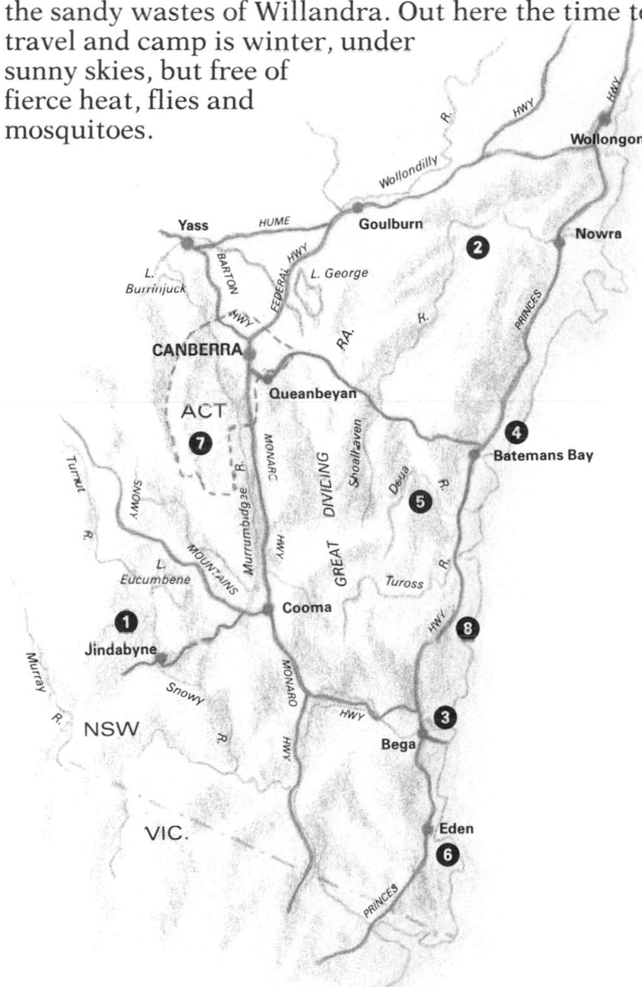

Featured parks	Pages	Featured parks	Pages
(1) Kosciusko	282-289	(5) Deua	296-297
(2) Morton	290-291	(6) Ben Boyd	298-299
(3) Mimosa Rocks	292-293	(7) Namadgi	300-301
(4) Murramarang	294-295	(8) Wallaga Lake	302

Frost-cracked granite litters a stream on Mt Kosciusko's flanks

Your access and facilities guide to the national parks in this region starts on page 303

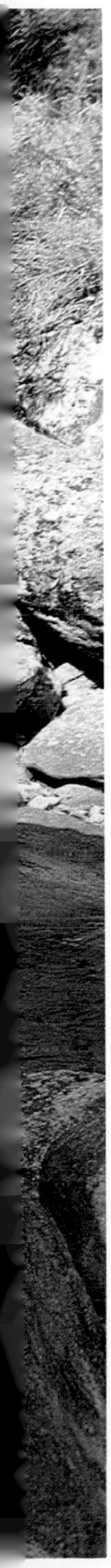

Left: Broken granite blocks are worn into rounded boulders by a swift-flowing alpine stream. The lack of moss indicates an open, sunny position – intensely cold in winter

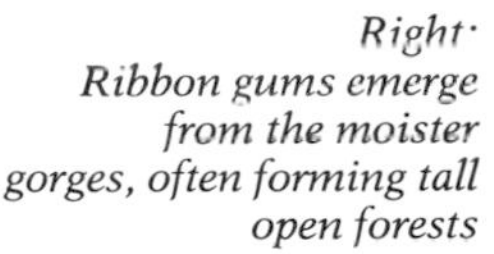

Right: Ribbon gums emerge from the moister gorges, often forming tall open forests

Below: Alpine daisies flourish on boggy soil beside the Lakes Walk, near Charlotte Pass

KOSCIUSKO NATIONAL PARK

Australia's biggest alpine region, with ten summits above 2100 metres, is embraced by this immense park. Most winters about a sixth of its 646 893 hectares are snow-covered. Skiers come in tens of thousands, creating an ever-growing demand for resort facilities and mechanical aids that sit uneasily with principles of nature conservation. However, in 1986 an understanding was signed by the Commonwealth, ACT, Victoria and NSW for co-operative management of the Australian Alps national parks. A co-ordinated approach should help achieve a balance between the vital need to protect catchment areas and water resources, and recreation demand.

Few of the heights are noticeably peaked. Most are broad plains or slopes where glacial tarns and alpine herbs, grasses and bog plants appear colourfully when the snow melts. Open woodlands of snow gums reach to the tree line at 1850 metres, surmounting forests of taller eucalypts. Many trails are mapped for high-altitude walks in summer or exploring below the snow line at any time of year. North of Kiandra, four of the 60 Yarrangobilly Caves are open at weekends for inspection of their remarkable limestone formations.

Kosciusko National Park

Stunted snow gums define the tree line north of Charlotte Pass. Only windswept tussock grasses and herbs grow on the higher granite slopes, cut by the beds of streams that flow in the spring thaw

Button daisies bloom on boggy meadows

A butterfly pollinates snow daisies

A lon
unde

Eons of physical and chemical weathering have broken granitic tors northwest of Thredbo (above and left) into smaller and smaller fragments. Rock-strewn herb fields like this are the favourite habitat of the mountain pigmy possum

Kosciusko National Park

Snow gums shed their bark each year, but their thick, leathery leaves remain. Lines of trees (right) form sheltering corridors for the winter movement of small birds, reptiles and marsupials

Snow stays unmelted only on the most exposed tops, and seldom for more than three months

Sandy soils above the Fitzroy Falls support heath-leafed banksia while rainforest species (right) emerge beneath

MORTON NATIONAL PARK

Making the memorable foot descent beside the Fitzroy Falls, from the most easily accessible part of Morton National Park, visitors not accustomed to wet bush are likely to have their first encounter with leeches. They are harmless and soon drop off. The falls, plunging 80 metres, are characteristic of the high but deeply dissected sandstone plateau that makes up the northern parts of the 152 949 ha park. Rims of the river gorges command fine views, especially on walks leading from the Nowra-Moss Vale road and southeast of Bundanoon. The major area of the park to the south, however, is a wilderness of forested razorback ridges and steep ravines. Walkers are urged not to attempt a cross-country trip without notifying the park office at Nowra of their proposed route and exit date.

Barrengarry Creek flows placidly towards the Belmore Falls. Tall eucalypt forests grow to the very edges of the sandstone plateau

The Yarrunga Valley, running a thickly forested course southwest from the Fitzroy Falls, is typical of the walled gorges that fast-flowing streams have cut through Morton's original high tabeland

A stormy day dawns at Pretty Beach. O'Hara Island, in the distance, represents a submerged outlier of the Murramarang Range, which backs the narrow coastal park

Grey kangaroos nibble the fresh shoots of grasses introduced to bind foredunes at Depot Beach. Given such a delicacy, they ignore the tougher natural tussocks and sedges

MURRAMARANG NATIONAL PARK

Oyster catchers and other wading birds in thousands probe busily along sheltered beaches and lake shores below the steep slopes of the Murramarang Range. Eastern spurs of this partly drowned range remain as rocky headlands with wave-cut shore platforms jutting into the Tasman swell. The park's three sections, totalling less than 1610 ha and never more than 2 km wide, reveal coastal landforms and vegetation in an unexpected diversity. Nearshore islands and stacks, included in the park, add to its scenic interest.

Behind low dunes, the flowering heaths and banksia and casuarina scrubs quickly give way to tall eucalypt forests. These include some pure stands of spotted gum. Rainforest shrubs occur in a few sheltered gullies. Big mobs of grey kangaroos emerge from cover at dusk to feed on dune grasses. Wallabies are also common.

Ebbing tides leave shallow sheets of water on the flat shore platforms south of Depot Beach. Small marine animals and plants abound, and mosquito larvae are collected to feed aquarium fish

Macrozamia cycads, commonly called burrawangs, form the entire understorey in a stand of spotted gum behind Richmond Beach

BROKEN HILL & MILDURA REGIONS

Sands yield the secrets of an Aboriginal Eden

A CHAIN of massive, crescent-shaped dunes juts eerily from the parched plain between the lower Darling and Lachlan Rivers. Their barren heights suggest the walls of moon craters, rather than anything associated with earthly life. Yet these dunes, called lunettes, hold some of the world's most important evidence of ancient human culture and the impact of a changing climate. They stand on the site of a prehistoric paradise.

More than 40 000 years ago, the Lachlan carried so much water from the Eastern Highlands that it spilled into a vast system of linked overflow basins – the Willandra Lakes. They remained amply supplied for about 15 000 years, teeming with fish, crustaceans and shellfish. Birds would have flocked there. The abundant marsupial population included a giant kangaroo, 3 metres tall.

People, anatomically identical to modern humans, led well-fed lives beside the waters. But as the last ice age deepened, rainfall became less dependable and lake levels varied. With the return of warmer conditions came the start of the dry climatic phase that continues today. Lake Mungo, at the downstream end of the chain, has been empty for 15 000 years.

The lake-dwellers first turned to grinding seeds to eke out their food supply, then drifted away to better water sources. Winds tore out the dried sediments of the lake beds, piling them on the eastern shores. Under the solidifying lunettes, traces of settlement lay buried and preserved.

Discovery of the Willandra culture began only in 1968 when a geologist working there noticed stone artefacts and bones. Early the following year a scientific party went to the area to investigate. In the eroding Mungo lunette, a scientist noticed an accumulation of mussel shells – the remains of a feast. Radiocarbon dating showed them to be 32 000 years old. Fragmented bones, found in a pit, proved to be those of a young woman of about 26 000 years ago. Her body had been burnt, the bones smashed, then burnt again – the world's oldest example of ritual cremation.

A later excavation established the use of red ochre in ceremonial burials 30 000 years ago. Other finds have included stone cutting and scraping tools, seed grinders and fireplaces. Stone cannot be dated, but shells found with some of the artefacts are 40 000 years old. Cautious investigations are continuing in Mungo National Park, which forms a relatively small part of the Willandra Lakes entry in the World Heritage list.

Not far away at Kinchega National Park, the long-dead Willandra scene is brought to life for travellers. The bountiful lakes at Kinchega, fed by the Darling, are regulated now by engineering and provide a permanent aquatic playground for the people of Broken Hill. In origin and formation, however, they are virtual replicas of the Willandra system. It is not hard to imagine the contentment of the people on whom nature smiled so many millennia ago.

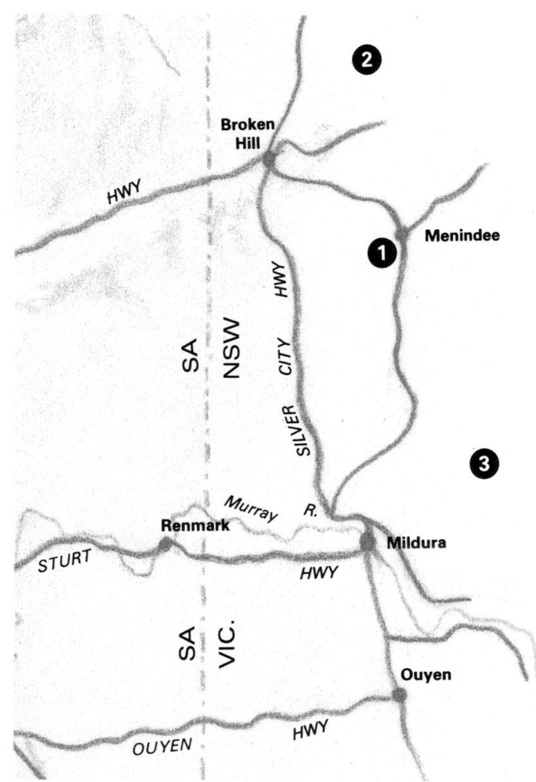

Featured parks	Pages
① Kinchega	310-311
② Mootwingee	312-313
③ Mungo	314

Your access and facilities guide to national parks in this region is on page 315

Kinchega National Park has typical arid landforms but its lakes, overflows from the Darling River, are breeding, nesting and feeding grounds for large numbers of waterbirds.

A shingleback adopts a threatening posture in self-defence. Slow-moving and harmless, it is related to bluetongue lizards

Kinchega National Park

Regulated overflow lakes of the once-erratic Darling River form centrepieces for a park of 44 182 ha, set among black river flat soils, red sandplains and stark lunette dunes. River red gums and flooded box fringe the Darling and the two saucer-shaped, connected lakes, Menindee and Cawndilla. Woodlands of black box thrive on the alluvial soils. On the sandplains there is little but bluebush, prickly wattle and canegrass – until good rains come and ephemeral flowering plants shoot up. Waterfowl frequent the lakes and red kangaroos, grey kangaroos and euros are common. Two self-guiding nature walks are available, the longer taking 2 hours. The river and lakes are usually suitable for swimming or fishing.

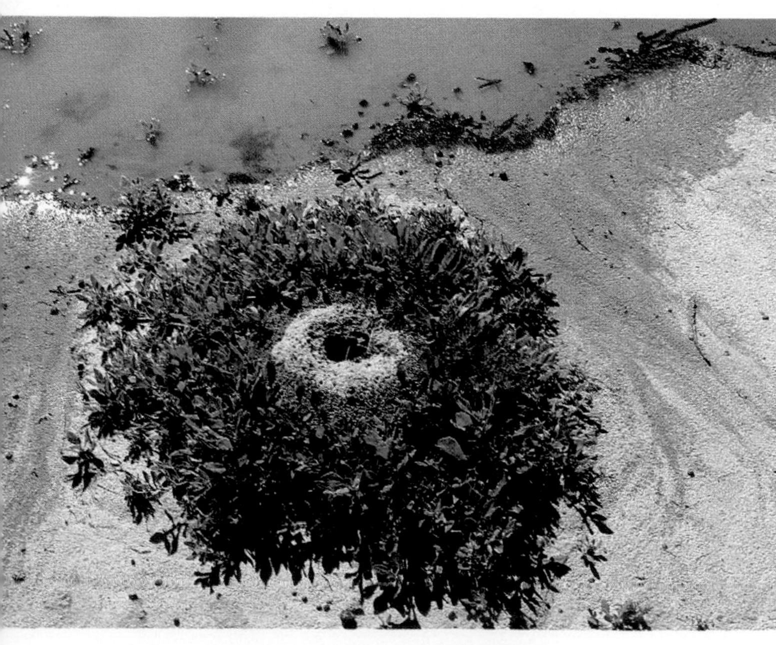

Drowned trees in Lake Cawndilla, artificially flooded, remain as waterfowl roosts. Left: Ephemeral plants shoot from seeds stored by harvester ants

Flowering dock (left) blooms at any time of year after soaking rains or an overspill from the lakes. Below: Floodwaters, moving south after freakish downpours in Queensland, engulf a black box eucalypt

A wind-blasted eucalypt struggles for existence on a broken lower ridge of the heavily eroded Bynguano Range

Broadleaf hopbush

MOOTWINGEE NATIONAL PARK

Nearly all of NSW's remaining yellow-footed rock wallabies are protected by the acquisition of 68 912 ha of former grazing properties between Broken Hill and White Cliffs. During 1984 the area was closed for management planning. The resulting park has old Aboriginal camps, stone arrangements, implements and hundreds of rock paintings, stencils and engravings made around waterholes in valleys of the Bynguano Range: many designs are filled by pecking (chipping) to give a solid irregular surface in contrast to the smooth rock.

Watercourses beneath the range's steep bluffs support river red gums, and wildflowers blossom after rains. Beyond, in a parched belt where Australia's highest temperatures are recorded, lie sandplains and gibber. Rabbits and feral goats compete with kangaroos for saltbush among mulga and cypress pine.

Nutambulla Creek is more often a string of billabongs

Wind erosion attacks soft rock under a capping of harder conglomerate. The process has eaten out many caves where Aborigines found shelter and practised their arts

Prickly solanum (top left), pimpernel (right), sponge fruit (above) and silver tails

MUNGO NATIONAL PARK

Crumbling sands in the Walls of China, which curve for more than 30 km round the north and east sides of dry Lake Mungo, hold complete evidence of what may be the world's oldest site of human culture. People lived here, feasting royally, at least 40 000 years ago. Much later, with the onset of the last ice age, the lake waters dwindled and became increasingly salty. Windblown sands from the drying margins piled up in a crescent dune – called a lunette. The last muddy sediments were added as a crust of salty clay. Now saltbush spreads over the lake bed. Belah, a leafless casuarina, is dominant on the old shores.

Erosion by occasional rains cuts deep grooves in the soft, layed sediments of the Mungo lunette – the Walls of China. Each of the Willandra Lakes, which together make up a World Heritage area, has a similar windblown formation. Left: Saltbush dying from root exposure as erosion destroys its habitat

PARKS OF THE BROKEN HILL AND MILDURA REGIONS

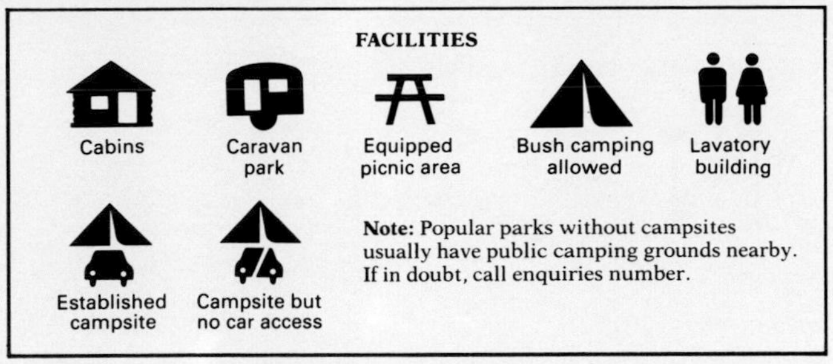

FACILITIES

Cabins

Caravan park

Equipped picnic area

Bush camping allowed

Lavatory building

Established campsite

Campsite but no car access

Note: Popular parks without campsites usually have public camping grounds nearby. If in doubt, call enquiries number.

PARK RATINGS No interest × Some interest ✔ Major interest ✔✔ Outstanding ✔✔✔

Kinchega National Park

110 km SE of Broken Hill. Lower Western weather district. Car access off Broken Hill-Menindee road at Menindee.

DESCRIPTION: Page 310.

NOTES: Licence required for fishing. Permit required for boating.

BEST TIME: Autumn and spring.

ENQUIRIES: (080) 88 0253.

ADDRESS: Box 459, Broken Hill 2880.

Scenic enjoyment ✔✔
Day activities ✔
Family camping ✔✔
Hard bushwalking ✔

Mallee Cliffs National Park

30 km E of Mildura. Lower Western weather district.

Before bushfires in the mid-1970s this 57 969 ha tract of relatively undisturbed mallee woodland preserved the most extensive natural habitat of malleefowl in NSW. The land reverted to the crown after leases expired in 1975, but private properties surround it. Fencing and access restrictions were expected to foster regeneration of both the vegetation and the malleefowl population. The birds are reluctant, however, to nest in burnt areas for as long as 13 years after a fire, and the extent of the setback to their numbers has not yet been surveyed.

NOTE: 4WD recommended.

ENQUIRIES: (050) 23 1278.

ADDRESS: NSWNPWS district office, Box 318, Buronga 2648.

Mootwingee National Park

130 km NE of Broken Hill. Upper Western weather district. Car access via Silver City Highway and White Cliffs road (unsealed – difficult when wet).

DESCRIPTION: Page 312.

NOTE: Advisable to carry water as supplies limited.

ENQUIRIES: (080) 88 0253.

ADDRESS: NSWNPWS district office, Box 459, Broken Hill 2880.

Mungo National Park

110 km NE of Mildura. Lower Western weather district. Car access from Mildura off Arumpo road, from Ivanhoe off Gol Gol road, from Balranald off Gol Gol road (all unsealed – impassable after rain). Bus Mildura-Mungo some days.

DESCRIPTION: Page 314.

NOTES: Visitors should inform ranger of intention to camp. Nearest petrol Mildura, Pooncarie, Penarie.

VISITOR CENTRE: Near Mungo woolshed.

BEST TIME: Autumn to spring.

ENQUIRIES: (050) 23 1278.

ADDRESS: As for Mallee Cliffs.

Scenic enjoyment ✔✔✔
Day activities ✔
Family camping ✔
Hard bushwalking ×

Sturt National Park

340 km N of Broken Hill. Upper Western weather district. Car access on Silver City Highway to Tibooburra (unsealed and often impassable after rains).

Pastoral properties acquired to form this 310 634 ha park in the early 1970s range across floodplains on the edge of the Bulloo overflow to rolling downs of mitchell grass, and gibber plains merging with the high red sandhills of the Strzelecki Desert. In the middle of the park isolated flat-topped mountains of the Grey Range rise up to 150 metres above the gibber plains. Known as the 'jump-up' country, the range is a bluff formation of mesas with deep gullies on their steeper side.

Removal of sheep from the area has helped restoration of natural vegetation. Mulga and saltbush communities dominate the sandplains, but little other than isolated clumps of lignum grows in the harsh environment of scattered claypans. River red gums define the courses of seasonal creeks. Wildflowers and grasses quickly follow rains that sometimes fill lakes and attract a diverse birdlife to the area. In normal dry conditions kangaroos, emus and euros evade the heat in whatever shade they can find, emerging to feed in the evening.

Four short nature walks have been established within the park and in dry conditions visitors have around 300 km of serviceable unsealed roads for touring. A pastoral museum is housed near a former homestead at Mt Wood, and Golden Gully recreates the workings of an 1880s goldfield.

NOTE: Enquire about local road conditions before setting out.

WARNING: Visitors must be equipped for outback survival. Carry extra water, fuel and spare parts.

VISITOR CENTRE: Tibooburra.

BEST TIME: April-September.

ENQUIRIES: (080) 91 3308.

ADDRESS: NSWNPWS district office, C/o P.O., Tibooburra 2880.

Scenic enjoyment ✔✔
Day activities ✔✔
Family camping ✔
Hard bushwalking ×

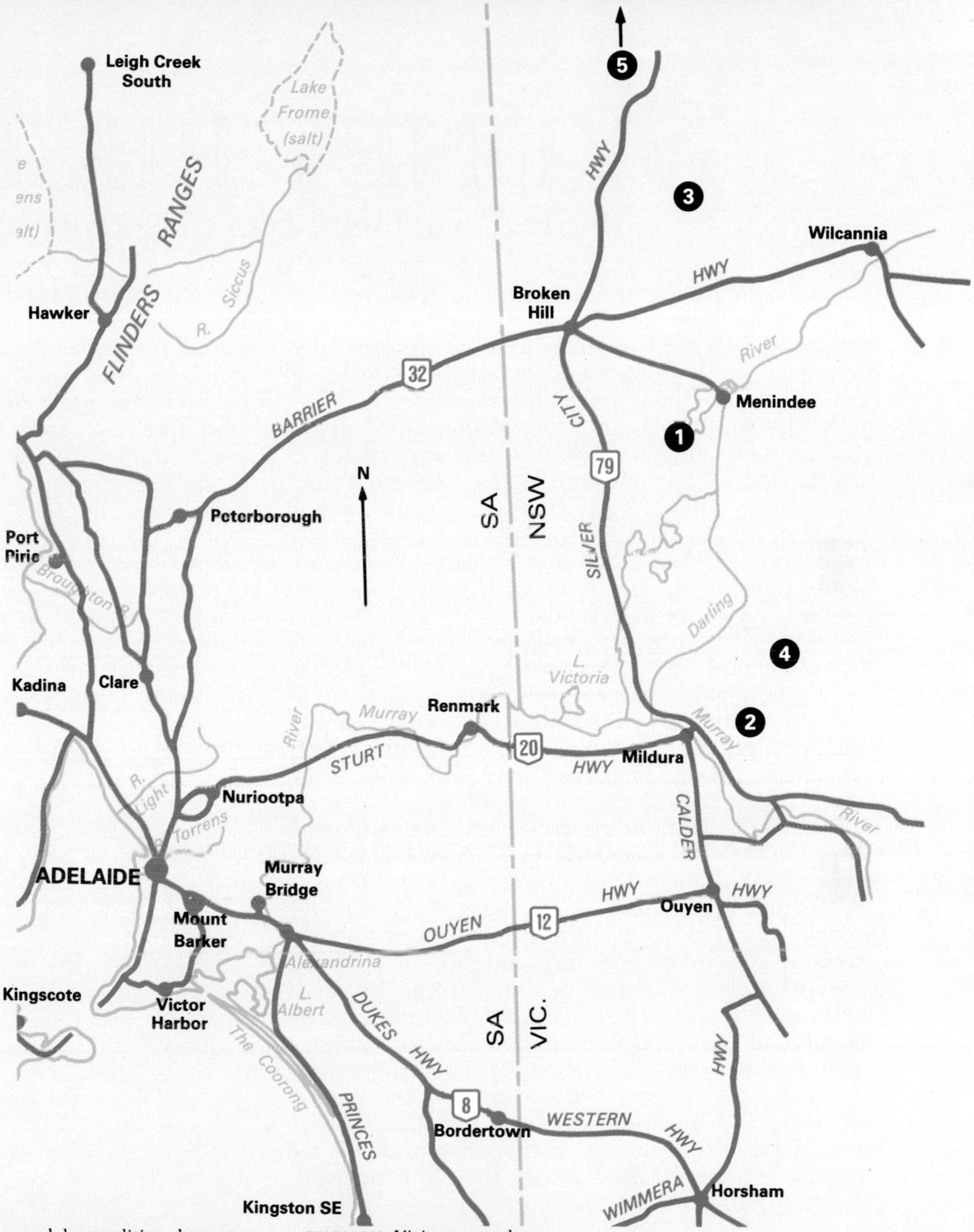

1 Kinchega NP
2 Mallee Cliffs NP
3 Mootwingee NP
4 Mungo NP
5 Sturt NP

SYDNEY REGION

A city blessed with breathing space to spare

CELEBRATED ocean beaches and no less than six far-reaching harbours bring Sydneysiders visual delight and an unusual amount of room for relaxation. Add the liberal access they enjoy to bushland and they seem almost too well treated.

To the south, and in a broad cordon from the west to the north, outer suburbs and satellite towns are flanked by big national parks. These embrace unspoilt sea cliffs and sandy bays, lofty ridges and plunging gorges, rushing streams and placid backwaters. Flowering heaths and eucalypt woodlands clothe most of them, along with some rainforest patches and mangrove stands.

Agreeable settings are easily found for a picnic or a stroll, especially in the oldest parks – the Royal and Ku-ring-gai Chase – and the newest, on the Port Jackson headlands opened after generations of military occupation. In the coastal parks and on the highlands, striking vistas are so readily gained that the eye starts to take them for granted.

But the bush still holds mysteries. Limitless challenge invites the energetic and the adventurous. Kanangra-Boyd, Wollemi, Marramarra and Dharug are virtual wildernesses. They and even the developed parks are not without hazards. Scarcely a weekend goes by without a rescue call.

By whatever measure – within 50 km, 100 km or 200 km of the city centre – Sydney has many more hectares of parkland per head of population than any other metropolis in the world. This endowment is not due to any greater wisdom on the part of early leaders – it is more a reflection of their frustration. Much of the country at their disposal was too hard for settlers to penetrate, or the sandstone soils were too poor for them to farm.

Later preservation of these lands, in the face of road and railway expansion and an exploding demand for home sites and building materials, is mainly to the credit of bushwalking groups. Their efforts, starting before World War I, instilled the idea that unexploited country could be an asset rather than a nuisance.

Walkers set up a National Parks and Primitive Areas Council in 1932 to pinpoint districts of special value and prod the sensibilities of governments. Their campaigns won support from a growing body of people who may never have shouldered a pack or pitched a tent, but who saw the merit of saving natural landscapes. Sydney, the city most beset by the pressures of population and industry, became the leader in environmental awareness.

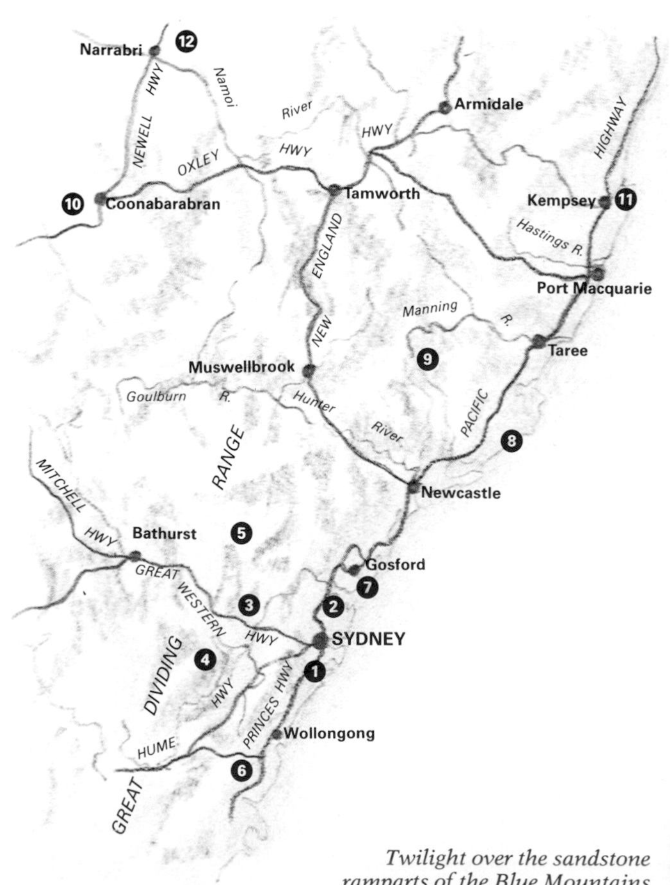

Twilight over the sandstone ramparts of the Blue Mountains

	Featured parks	Pages
1	Royal	318-321
2	Ku-ring-gai Chase	322-323
3	Blue Mountains	324-327
4	Kanangra-Boyd	328-329
5	Wollemi	330
6	Budderoo	331
7	Bouddi	332-333
8	Myall Lakes	334

	Featured parks	Pages
9	Barrington Tops	335
10	Warrumbungle	336-337
11	Hat Head	338-339
12	Mt Kaputar	340-341

Your access and facilities guide to every national park in this region starts on p 342

Windswept heaths crown the headlands guarding peaceful Wattamolla Bay. Navigators George Bass and Matthew Flinders, saved from a storm in 1796, gratefully called it Providential Cove

ROYAL NATIONAL PARK

Sydney's southern playground for more than a century, the Royal presents a tamed, altered face to people who rely on cars. But natural scenery in a surprising variety awaits those prepared to walk. A coastal track diverts from high moors to shady gullies and sheltered bays with little-used beaches. It is 30 km – a two-day trek – but easily broken up because many inland trails link the coast with the park's central roads, the railway stations on its western boundary, and the ferry wharf at Bundeena. Walkers need never retrace their steps.

The Hacking River originates in the south of the 15 014 ha park and flows out to Port Hacking past the visitor centre at Audley. Rainforest survives upriver, especially in the steep tributary gorges. On the sandstone heights towards the coast, eucalypt woodlands give way to heaths that blossom vividly in spring, attracting scores of bird species. Between Marley and Garie, high sea cliffs overhang shore platforms and wave-eaten caves. To the south the sandstone scarp recedes and slopes of the underlying shale are exposed. Palms, vines and subtropical shrubs grow in dense profusion on moist, chocolate-brown soils.

Cabbage-tree palms in Black Gin Gully, leading down to Little Garie Beach, flourish on shale soil – rare in a sandstone region. Understorey trees and shrubs, soft-leafed but spiky, grow so densely that this relic of a wetter climate is almost impossible to penetrate

ROYAL NATIONAL PARK

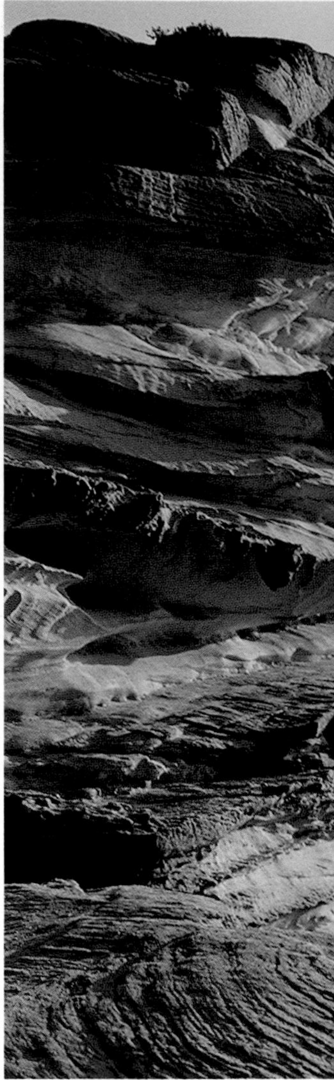

Cliff faces at Boy Martin Point, Wattamolla (top left), and near Curracurrang (above and left) are relentlessly eaten out by winds and rain. Often they overhang because the topmost layer of sandstone is hardened. Soils built up over millions of years support heath plants on the clifftops but the faces are too exposed for growth – except for ferns struggling in a few crevices

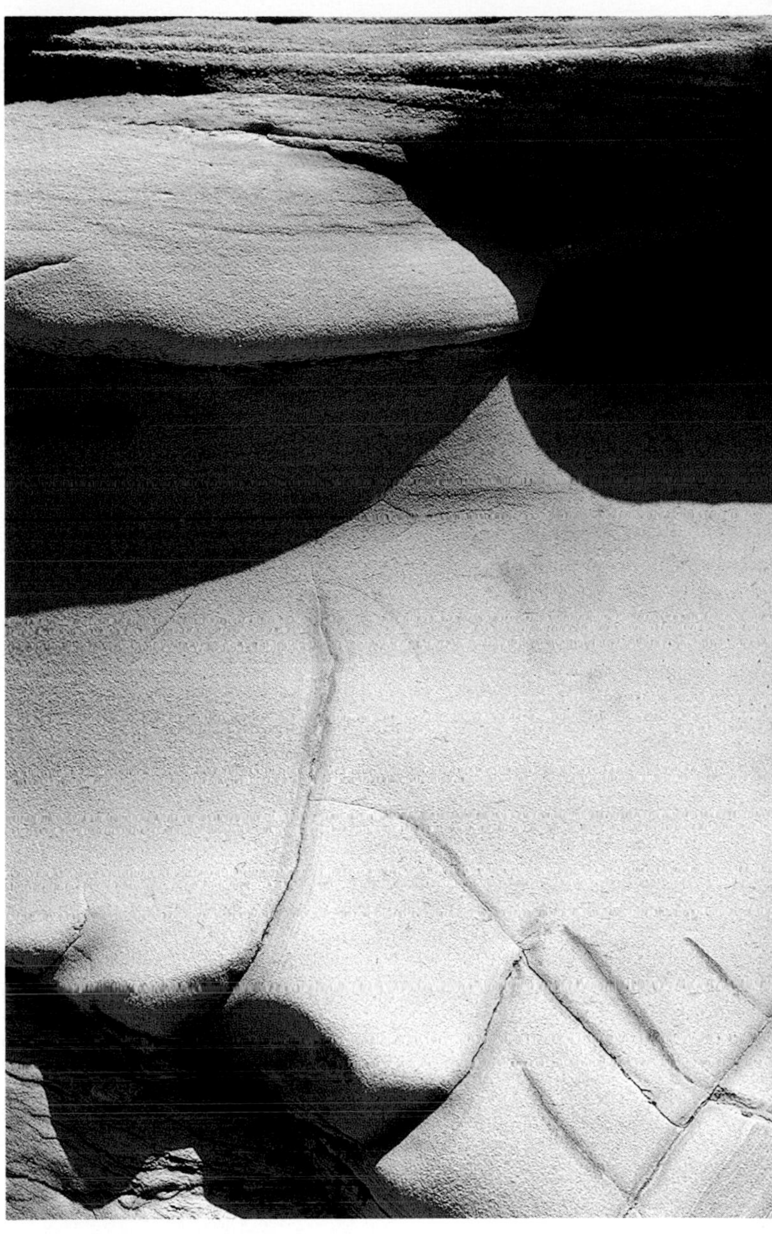

Softly flowing sculptures are created by tidal erosion of a cliff base (above). Sandstone strata of varying hardness recede at different speeds. Brittle rock in a shore platform (left) has been cracked by the expansion and contraction due to the sea's day-and-night temperature fluctuations. Water eats into the cracks and other points of weakness

KU-RING-GAI CHASE NATIONAL PARK

Tidal waterways carve deeply into the high sandstone plateau between Sydney's upper north shore suburbs and Broken Bay. Good roads reach six waterside picnic grounds, shark-netted swimming areas, and an exceptional viewing point at West Head. Boating opportunities abound along 120 km of navigable shoreline. Tracks off the West Head road lead down – often steeply – to quiet beaches on Pitt and Cowan Waters. Gentler nature walks are provided near the 14 591 ha park's two visitor centres. Cross-country hikers can enter from the Pacific Highway.

Soils are mostly dry and impoverished, but flowering heaths and shrubs brighten the plateau scrubland in spring. Some slopes are more heavily wooded with eucalypts, acacias and casuarinas, and rainforest communities are found in a few moist gullies. More than 100 bird species may be seen, but the reptiles and small mammals are furtive. Many exposed sandstone surfaces bear the traces of engravings by Aborigines of the Guringai group, who fished and hunted in this area until about 1850.

Steep slopes above the waterways descend in steps, formed by broad, flat rocks called floaters. These retain soil for vigorous woodland growth and provide basking spots for reptiles

Lion Island dominates the view of Broken Bay from a West Head walking track. Little penguins nest on the island, a nature reserve

Vivid plants of Ku-ring-gai Chase's high heaths include hakea (left) and delicate rock orchids

Cascades in McCarrs Creek, by the park's southeastern entrance, are a rare sight in sandstone country. Beds are usually cut back more sharply to make sheer waterfalls

Storm clouds clear over the Grose Valley, looking northeast from Govetts Leap. Floors of the park's walled valleys lie more than 600 metres below the rims of the old plateau

BLUE MOUNTAINS NATIONAL PARK

Glimpsed from near Sydney, the western walls of the Cumberland Basin are indeed blue. The optical effect of distance is intensified by a haze of evaporating eucalypt oils. But the heights are not mountains. They are ridges left from a collapsing plateau that has been split and undercut by rivers. A generation of explorers failed to grasp that. One after another they probed the forested valleys, to be confronted each time by sandstone precipices. Not until 1813 did they skirt around to climb the lower ridges and find links to the fertile western slopes.

Highways and a railway following those paths now embrace Australia's most photographed landscapes. Side roads and short walks among a maze of secondary ridges bring visitors to the brink of plunging rock walls and waterfalls. Isolated remnants of the high tableland – more than two-thirds destroyed since it was pushed up about 3 million years ago – stand as eye-catching pinnacles and crags. Hundreds of metres below lie the valley floors.

Two of the three major walled valleys are excluded from the 215 970 ha park. The Megalong is farmed and the Jamieson is developed for tourism, with a scenic railway and cableway near Katoomba as well as a Giants' Stairway foot descent. The main park area for walkers is the Grose Valley, east of Blackheath. Other marked trails start near Glenbrook. Wilderness areas lie north of Bells Line of Road and in the southernmost section of the park, most of which is a city water catchment that cannot be entered without a permit.

Vegetation varies widely. Heaths struggle on the dry, infertile ridge tops, while swamp plants grow on poorly drained parts of the plateau. Ferns colonise wet ledges on the cliff faces, and rainforest patches are found at the bases. But eucalypts predominate in scores of forms ranging from tall blue gum, peppermint, scribbly gum, black ash and white ash to stunted mallees. Mammals are seldom seen, but birds abound in more than 100 species.

Heaths persist on poorer soils

Boronia: brilliant in spring

Insect-eating sundews crowd a native violet on boggy ground

Right: Sunlight reflects from the still-fresh rock face left by a landslide near Cyclorama Point, Katoomba, in 1931

BLUE MOUNTAINS NATIONAL PARK

This hardy heath plant appears to grow out of nothing. It is colonising rock that has been softened on the surface by the chemical action of lichens

Cataracts on Kedumba Creek, above Wentworth Falls, are buffered from the dry eucalypt forest by an inviting zone of soft-leafed shrubs and herbs

Rainwater washing over Mt Wilson's basalt capping – a legacy of lava flows from ancient volcanoes – has cut channels along weaker seams

Right: Plants cling in crevices on the wind-worn faces of the Three Sisters – remnants of a plateau cut by river action. The pillars are tough, but too brittle for safe climbing

Flame robins hunt insects on a seed-shedding dead banksia

Kanangra-Boyd National Park

Kanangra Plateau juts like a peninsula of rock in a sea of forest. Flanked by walls that look impossible to scale, it could be Conan Doyle's 'Lost World'. In fact the climb is not unduly difficult: a walk of about 45 minutes from the end of the park's only road is rewarded by panoramic views as good as any in the Blue Mountains district. A shorter walk in the opposite direction – with a steep pinch at the end – leads to the impressive Kanangra Falls. Mossy glades and naturally grassed clearings near the road are pleasant to explore. Elsewhere this 68 276 ha reserve is a wilderness for seasoned bushwalkers. Eucalypt woodlands occupy most of the higher country, while taller forests grow in moist gullies and on volcanic soils. Birds and marsupials are abundant.

Cascading gently in a dry spell, the Kanangra Falls spill over in a mighty torrent after good rains

Resistant rock stands out at Kanangra Walls, in bold contrast to the deeply cut ranges just north. The plateau is made not of sandstone but of a pebbly conglomerate, like the boulder in the foregound.

WOLLEMI NATIONAL PARK

Protection of the Wollemi wilderness has been hailed as one of the great triumphs of Australian nature conservation. The park contains the country's biggest area of unaltered forests — more than 486 400 hectares. And in the Colo River it has the last major unpolluted waterway in NSW. Its unity and vast size should ensure a safe future for its diverse plant and animal communities — especially since the development of public facilities will be restricted to the perimeter.

The park is centred on the Colo catchment, which includes the Wollemi, Wolgan and Capertee Rivers. On sandstone country similar to that of the Blue Mountains, they have carved a complex of cliffed canyons and steep, forested gorges. Tall eucalypts predominate, but other vegetation includes snow gums, mallees, swamp plants and pockets of rainforest in gullies and on some basalt-capped heights. Wollemi poses a challenge to the most expert bushwalkers and canoeists, who are urged to consult with rangers about access points and routes.

Sheer-walled sandstone forms, characteristic of the Blue Mountains system, continue north into the Wollemi wilderness and tower over its eucalypt forests

Patches of rainforest occur on basalt-capped peaks and in moist gullies. But this one, on the western edge of the park near Breakfast Creek, is suffering by its proximity to the boundary road. Introduced weeds (left foreground) are invading

BUDDEROO NATIONAL PARK

Spray fills the narrow, rock-strewn gorge of the Minnamurra River where it spills 50 metres from the abrupt edge of the Illawarra Escarpment. Incessant dampness fosters the growth of a small subtropical rainforest dominated by figs that are thickly overgrown with vines, staghorns, ferns and orchids. The nature trail up from the road is an easy half-hour climb. Guided walks with explanations of the plants and wildlife can be arranged.

Buttressed trunks on the bigger trees beside the falls track identify them as subtropical rainforest species – among the southernmost in Australia. Their uneven size results from logging late last century

Water spilling from the Illawarra Escarpment cuts a cavernous course into Minnamurra's dark volcanic rock. The area forms part of Budderoo National Park, and includes a rainforest nursery for regeneration of previously cleared sections

BOUDDI NATIONAL PARK

Buzzing insects make the loudest sound likely to be heard on the wooded slopes that descend from the spine of Bouddi (pronounced Boody) Peninsula to a choice of peaceful beaches. Grass trees and burrawang cycads crowd the tracks, shaded by eucalypts and banksias. Lookouts give extensive views of the 1161 ha park's succession of headlands and rocky shore platforms. In creek-fed gullies towards the foot of the coastal range, patches of subtropical rainforest reach to the beaches.

Swimmers and anglers rank the Tallow and Little Beach campsites among the most pleasant in the state – though gear and supplies have to be carried all the way down. Only the Putty Beach camp has vehicle access. Maitland Bay offers the most spacious area for picnics, sheltered swimming and exploration of rock pools. But fishing of any sort is forbidden. Waters in and beyond the bay, out as far as the Maitland Bombora reef, are protected as a marine extension of the park.

Tracks crossing the forested heights above Maitland Bay command vistas westward along the deeply indented coast of Bouddi Peninsula. Lion Island, Broken Bay and Ku-ring-gai Chase lie beyond

Shore platform erosion reveals a freakish structure near the Putty Beach campsite. Water, swirling over rock that was already cracked and worn, repaved each block with fine sediments laid in circles. Now they are being worn down again. A similarly patterned boulder at Maitland Bay (left) seems to have been carried there by the sea

MYALL LAKES NATIONAL PARK

Unusual peace pervades the Myall waterways and woodlands, sheltered in a bowl formed by high coastal dunes and forested inland hills. Three big lakes, linked by twisting narrows, together extend for about 50 km. Rough roads give motorists access to three lakeside camps – one of which, Mungo Brush, is only 10 minutes across the dunes from the ocean beach. But nearly half of the 31 190 ha park consists of quiet, easily navigable water: the fullest enjoyment comes from boating. All three camps have ramps for private boats. Houseboats and small launches can be hired outside the park, and canoes are available at the Bombah Point camp. Waterborne visitors have no difficulty finding secluded landing spots. The lakes, fresh or somewhat brackish, offer fair fishing and prawns are usually prolific.

Pelicans throng the lakes, roosting on low islets and reaping a rich harvest of fish. Left: A backwater of Boolambayte Lake, lined with casuarinas and melaleucas, typifies the stillness of the 'Murmuring Myalls'. Yet they lie only a short walk from the boisterous Tasman Sea surf

Mosses and microbes work rapidly to recycle plant nutrients in the humid climate of the Tops. Frequent fogs rolling up from the east, along with rain and snow, keep the beech forests almost continually moist

BARRINGTON TOPS NATIONAL PARK

Snow gums and alpine grasses are reminders that severe weather can strike suddenly on the two 1500 metre plateaux – Barrington Tops and Gloucester Tops – that crown this heavily forested park. Snowfalls occur fairly often from autumn to spring, and drenching rains and fogs may come at any time. The 39 114 ha reserve covers most of the catchments of the Manning and Hunter Rivers. The flanks of the linked plateaux fall away steeply and vegetation is highly diverse because of wide variations in altitude, exposure and soil types. There are sheltered stands of subtropical rainforest as well as cool-temperate beech forests and eucalypt communities. Birdlife is prolific, and sightings may include lyre birds, bower birds and brush turkeys. Walking is the main activity: trails of varying length and difficulty reach most parts of the park and reveal impressive highland scenery.

Belougery Spire (1060 metres), is formed of resistant trachyte – molten material that solidified in the throat of an expiring volcano

Cypress pine marks the point where inland plants take over

Phebalium clings in a crevice

Volcanic plugs on the Grand High Tops rim forested amphitheatres where 180 species of birds have been seen

WARRUMBUNGLE NATIONAL PARK

For 5 million years, this western spur of the Great Dividing Range was hell on earth. A unique skyline testifies to its chaotic phase of violent explosions and massive lava flows, between 17 and 13 million years ago. Spires, domes and pinnacles, jumbled over an area of 19 651 hectares, reach nearly twice the height of the surrounding hills. But these are merely worn-down remnants, made from the last cooling lava that choked the dying volcanoes. The real heights are long gone.

All the curious landforms of the Warrumbungles can be seen at a distance from lookouts, and tracks of varying length and difficulty take walkers close to the main features. Most can be climbed but a permit is needed from the visitor centre; numbers are controlled to protect delicate structures and plant cover. Experienced walkers can also penetrate the deep gorges that split the park.

Vegetation is unusually diverse because the range has two climates: wet on the southern flanks and in the gorges, dry in the north. Eucalypt forests and woodlands give way to hinterland plant communities dominated by cypress pine *Callitris*. High sandstone patches support heaths that blossom vividly in spring. Grey kangaroos, wallaroos and wallabies may be seen, and the prolific birdlife includes a third of all Australia's parrot species.

Hovea in brilliant bloom

Parallel lines of dunes back the long arc of Hat Head Beach, seen from rainforested heights near Smoky Cape

Kennedia, a vigorous creeper that flowers in summer, helps to stabilise the dune sands

HAT HEAD NATIONAL PARK

Of all the national parks on the NSW north coast, only Hat Head has been spared the ravages of sand mining. It remains a perfect example of the constructive power of waves, pushing up sediments to fill a 16 km strip between two former islands – now Smoky Cape and Hat Head. A walk inland in the south of the park reveals the progression of sand colonisation by plants. Behind a barrier beach and naked frontal dunes are binding grasses and creepers, then banksia and tea-tree scrubs, swamp sedges and wet heaths, eucalypt woodlands and finally forested ridges. The inner dunes hold small freshwater lagoons, some of them perched well above sea level. Hawks, falcons and sea eagles hunt over the 6355 ha park, and other birds including honeyeaters flock there when the heaths flower in late winter and spring.

White 'honeysuckle' banksia, sheltered by the frontal dunes, exceeds 10 metres in height

Fine-grained rock of volcanic origin forms cracked shore platforms at the northern end of the park. Marine animals and plants abound in hundreds of small, tide-washed pools

PARKS OF THE SYDNEY REGION

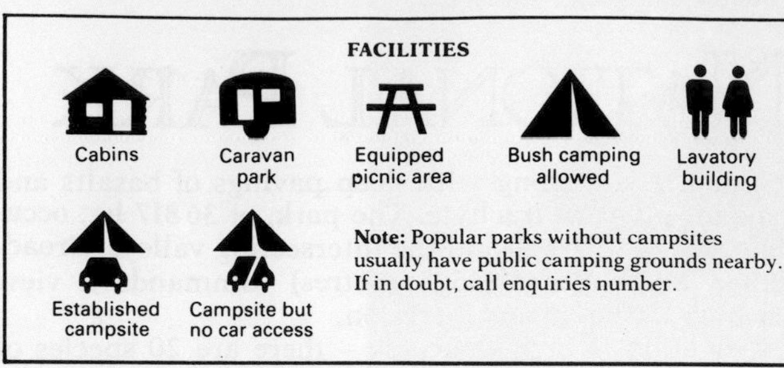

PARK RATINGS No interest ✖ Some interest ✔ Major interest ✔✔ Outstanding ✔✔✔

Barrington Tops National Park
320 km N, 40 km W of Gloucester. Hunter weather district. Car access to Gloucester River camp and Tops from 10 km S of Gloucester (unsealed — creek crossings may flood). Mostly sealed access to Barrington section via Dungog and Salisbury; continuation to Williams Top unsealed and steep. 4WD access to northern parts of park October-May except in wet weather.
DESCRIPTION: Page 335.

WARNING: Sudden weather changes — take adequate clothing.
BEST TIME: Summer.
ENQUIRIES: (049) 87 3108.
ADDRESS: NSWNPWS district office, Box 270, Raymond Terrace 2324.

Scenic enjoyment ✔✔✔
Day activities ✔
Family camping ✔✔
Hard bushwalking ✔✔✔

Blue Mountains National Park
100 km W. Central Tablelands weather district. Car access to northern section off Bells Line of Road, to southeastern section off Great Western Highway at Glenbrook, Woodford, Wentworth Falls. Vehicle entrance fee (Glenbrook area only). Trains Sydney-Blackheath.
DESCRIPTION: Page 324.
NOTES: Access prohibited within 3 km of Lake Burragorang and

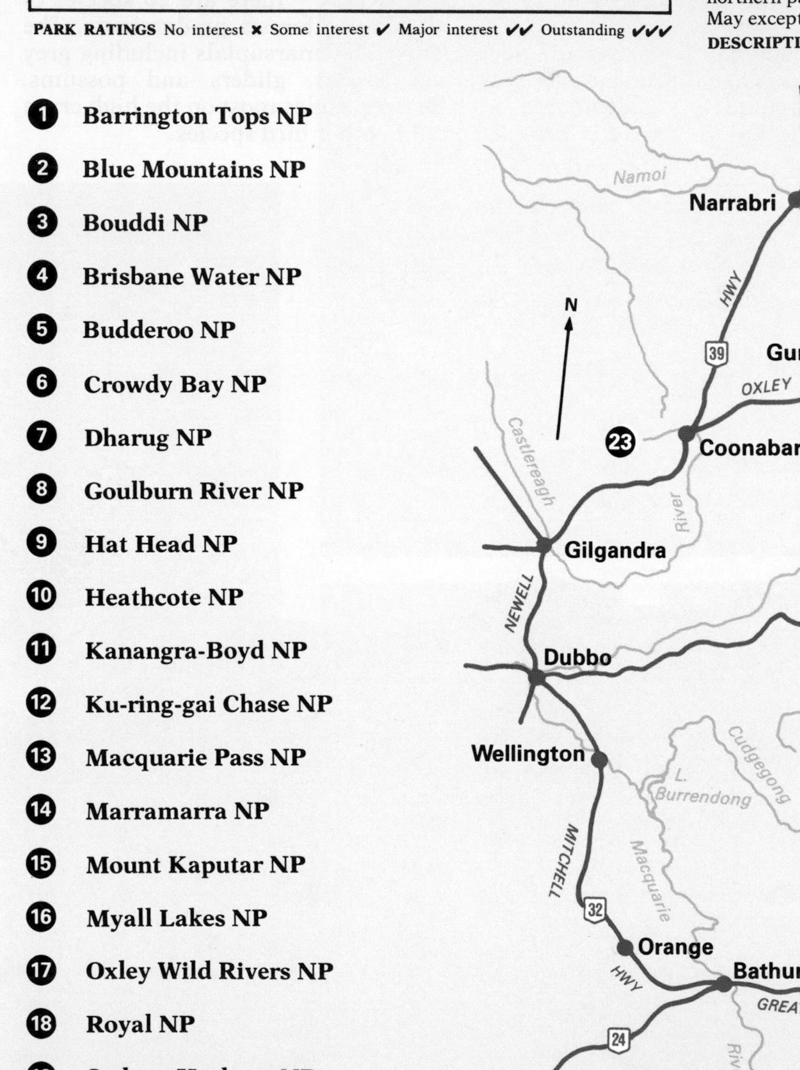

1 Barrington Tops NP
2 Blue Mountains NP
3 Bouddi NP
4 Brisbane Water NP
5 Budderoo NP
6 Crowdy Bay NP
7 Dharug NP
8 Goulburn River NP
9 Hat Head NP
10 Heathcote NP
11 Kanangra-Boyd NP
12 Ku-ring-gai Chase NP
13 Macquarie Pass NP
14 Marramarra NP
15 Mount Kaputar NP
16 Myall Lakes NP
17 Oxley Wild Rivers NP
18 Royal NP
19 Sydney Harbour NP
20 Thirlmere Lakes NP
21 Tomaree NP
22 Warrabah NP 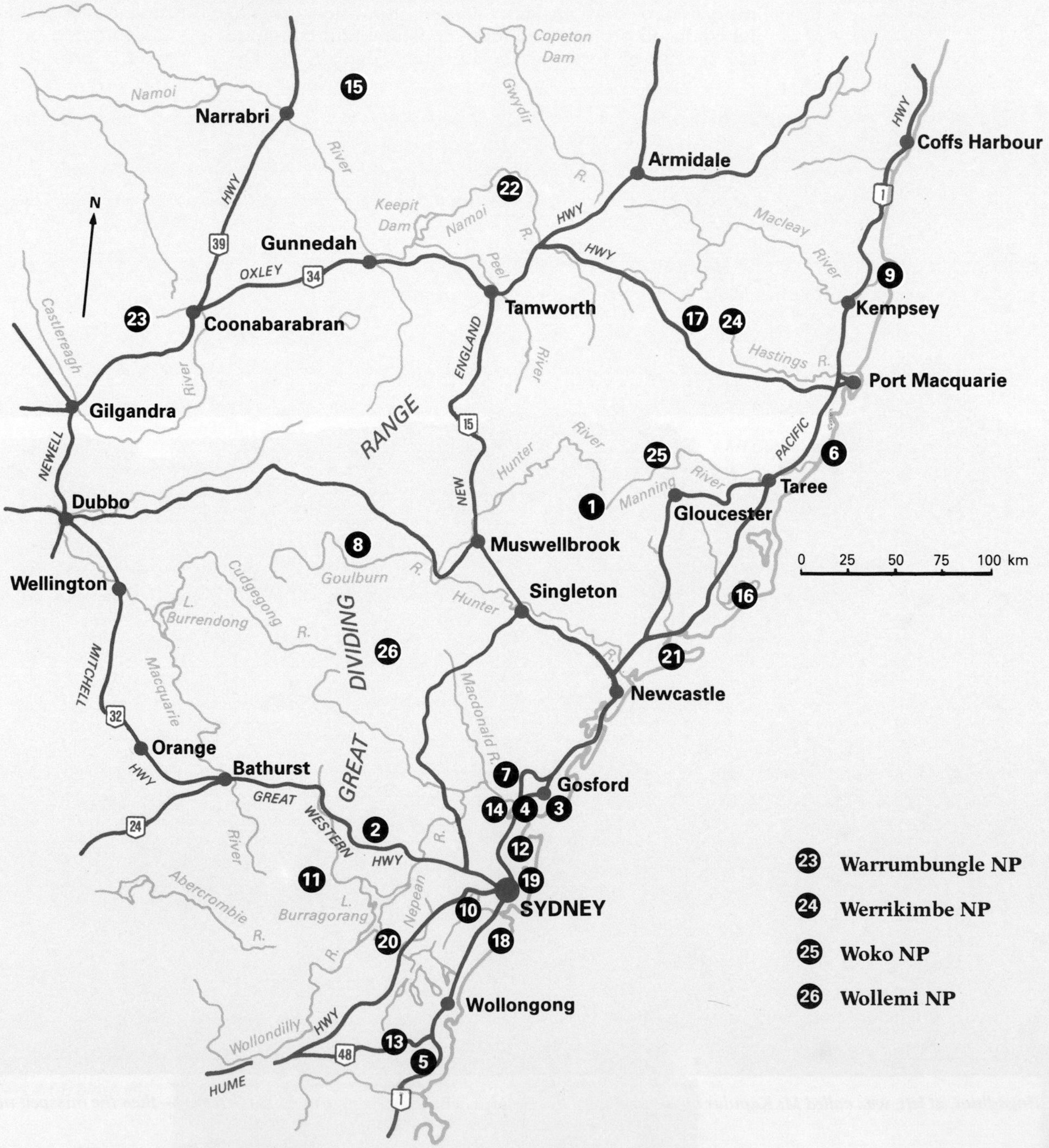
23 Warrumbungle NP
24 Werrikimbe NP
25 Woko NP
26 Wollemi NP

Warragamba Dam; permit needed to enter rest of metropolitan water catchment area (for southern section). Camping ground bookings and permit needed.

WARNING: Avoid remote areas if fire risk is high.

VISITOR CENTRES: Blackheath, Glenbrook.

BEST TIME: Spring to autumn.

ENQUIRIES: Northern section (047) 87 8877; southern section (047) 39 2950, weekend only.

ADDRESS: NSWNPWS district office, Box 43, Blackheath 2785.

Scenic enjoyment ✔✔✔
Day activities ✔✔✔
Family camping ✔✔✔
Hard bushwalking ✔✔✔

Bouddi National Park

100 km N, 20 km SE of Gosford. Metropolitan weather district. Car access from Pacific Highway via Gosford and Kincumber or via Woy Woy and Rip Bridge; five entry points between Kincumber and Killcare. Trains Sydney-Gosford; buses to park once or twice daily.

DESCRIPTION: Page 332.

NOTES: Bookings needed for camping grounds. No drinking water at Maitland Bay.

BEST TIME: Spring to autumn.

ENQUIRIES: (043) 24 4911.

ADDRESS: NSWNPWS district office, Box 1393, Gosford Sth. 2250.

Scenic enjoyment ✔
Day activities ✔✔
Family camping ✔✔
Hard bushwalking ✔

Brisbane Water National Park

75 km N, 10 km SW of Gosford. Metropolitan weather district. Car access from Pacific Highway at Girrakool or via Woy Woy and Pearl Beach. Trains Sydney-Woy Woy or Wondabyne; buses Woy Woy-Patonga.

Streams and long tidal inlets cut the sandstone plateaux between Broken Bay and the northwestern reaches of Brisbane Water. Higher parts of the 14 000 ha park have predominantly eucalypt woodland with an understorey of heathland plants. Some steep-sided gullies have subtropical rainforest pockets. Scrub or swamp wallabies, possums and koalas may be seen and birdlife is prolific.

An Aboriginal rock engraving site is open at Girrakool. Mooney Mooney nature trail (4 hours return) offers good scenery and longer walks are possible. Several lookouts command high views within an easy walk of car parks and picnic grounds. The outstanding vantage point is the Warrah lookout, above Patonga and Broken Bay.

VISITOR CENTRE: Girrakool.

BEST TIME: Late winter-early spring for wildflowers.

ENQUIRIES: (043) 24 4911.

ADDRESS: As for Bouddi.

Scenic enjoyment ✔✔
Day activities ✔✔
Family camping ✘
Hard bushwalking ✔✔

Budderoo National Park

130 km S, 15 km W of Kiama. South Coast and Illawarra weather district. Car access along sealed road from Jamberoo. Vehicle entrance fee.

This new park, dedicated in 1986, incorporates the Minnamurra Falls area and adjoins the Barren Grounds Nature Reserve. It protects about 20 km of the Illawarra escarpment south from the falls. Bringing in this area will help conserve the rare and endangered ground parrot and the eastern bristlebird, and also rainforest communities below the cliff-line.

DESCRIPTION: Page 331.

WARNING: Touching leaves of giant stinging trees causes painful irritation.

BEST TIME: Year-round.

ENQUIRIES: (044) 21 9969.

ADDRESS: NSWNPWS district office, Box 707, Nowra 2540.

Scenic enjoyment ✔✔
Day activities ✔✔
Family camping ✘
Hard bushwalking ✘

Crowdy Bay National Park

380 km N, 45 km NE of Taree. Mid-North Coast weather district. Car access off Pacific Highway at Moorland or Laurieton (gravel).

Heathland occupies most of the 7420 ha park, behind low dunes and a surfing beach. Some open woodland occurs near the Diamond Head camping ground. Eucalypt stands include the southernmost needlebarks.

The heaths, mostly flowering in late winter, attract honeyeaters and ground-dwelling birds such as quail. Tortoises, goannas, lizards and snakes abound in spite of predation by hawks and falcons from nearby forests. Mammals include red-necked and swamp wallabies and grey kangaroos.

NOTE: No drinking water at Diamond Head.

BEST TIME: All year.

ENQUIRIES: (065) 83 5518.

ADDRESS: NSWNPWS district office, Box 61, Port Macquarie 2444.

Scenic enjoyment ✔
Day activities ✔✔
Family camping ✔✔✔
Hard bushwalking ✘

Dharug National Park

75 km NW. Metropolitan weather district. Car access off Wisemans Ferry-Spencer Road or Old Northern Road.

From steep sandstone bluffs overlooking the north bank of the Hawkesbury River ridges, spurs and deep gullies extend into a park covering 14 785 ha of virtually untouched bush. The main vehicle access is to picnic spots and camping grounds in the Mill Creek area, 5 km east of Wisemans Ferry. Short walking tracks are provided there. Cross-country walking is possible but a ranger should be notified.

Heights above the Hawkesbury support forests of eucalypts and angophoras. Coachwood, sassafras and twining vines shade creeks dissecting the plateau behind, while acacias, flannel flowers and heaths occupy more open country. Honeyeaters and small marsupials are attracted in large numbers, and waterfowl flock wherever the creeks spread in marshy areas. Wallaroos and wombats are commonly seen around Mill Creek.

NOTE: Permit and bookings needed for camping.

BEST TIME: Spring.

ENQUIRIES: (043) 24 4911.

ADDRESS: As for Bouddi.

Scenic enjoyment ✔✔
Day activities ✔✔
Family camping ✔✔
Hard bushwalking ✔

Goulburn River National Park

360 km N, 35 km S of Merriwa. Hunter weather district. Car access (gravel) by Merriwa-Bylong Road.

Multi-hued sandstone cliffs, pitted with caves, frame the broad, sandy bed of the Goulburn River as it meanders for 65 km through open woodlands of cypress pine and eucalypts. Where tributary creeks join the river, rocky bluffs jut out to give exciting views. Many are close to the only road through the 67 600 ha park. A lookout just east commands views of most of the western section.

No trails have been made, but the sand flats of the riverbed allow for easy walking. Patches of quicksand exist, but are not dangerous. The river is safe for swimming, and rock climbers find a challenge in the gorge. Wildflowers add attraction to the ridges above in winter and spring. Kangaroos, wallaroos, wombats and many native birds are abundant.

Important Aboriginal campsites have been located and many more are expected to be found – the river seems to have been a major east-west travelling route. All sites are protected by law, and no artefacts may be taken.

BEST TIME: Spring.

ENQUIRIES: (065) 43 2274.

ADDRESS: NSWNPWS district office, Box 351, Muswellbrook 2333.

Scenic enjoyment ✔✔✔
Day activities ✔
Family camping ✘
Hard bushwalking ✔✔

Hat Head National Park

480 km N, 20 km E of Kempsey. Mid-North Coast weather district. Car access from Pacific Highway via Smoky Cape Lighthouse road or Gladstone-Hat Head road.

DESCRIPTION: Page 338.

NOTE: No drinking water.

BEST TIME: Year-round (summer for swimming).

ENQUIRIES: (065) 83 5518.

ADDRESS: As for Crowdy Head.

Scenic enjoyment ✔✔
Day activities ✔✔
Family camping ✔✔
Hard bushwalking ✔

Heathcote National Park

40 km S. Metropolitan weather district. Car access from Princes Highway 3.5 km S of Waterfall. Sealed road along park edge to Woronora Dam – no public roads in park.

Heathcote is classed as a wilderness park: facilities shown below are just outside, at Woronora Dam and Sarahs Knob. Most of the 2250 ha park consists of low sandstone ridges cut by gullies. Wildflowers make colourful spring displays among dry eucalypt woodlands and low heaths. Grass trees are common, and unusual plants to be found include the gymea lily and fern-leafed grevillea.

Sandy beaches line some accessible parts of the Heathcote and Woronora Rivers. Swimming is a principal recreation, along with bushwalking. The Bullawaring track offers an easy walk of about 2 hours.

NOTES: Permit needed for bush camping; take own water supplies.

BEST TIME: Spring (wildflowers), summer (swimming).

ENQUIRIES: (02) 521 2230.

ADDRESS: NSWNPWS district office, Box 44, Sutherland 2232.

Scenic enjoyment ✔✔
Day activities ✔✔
Family camping ✘
Hard bushwalking ✔

Kanangra-Boyd National Park

180 km W. Central Tablelands weather district. Car access from Jenolan Caves 16 km mostly unsealed, some steep and corrugated.

DESCRIPTION: Page 328.

NOTE: River water only at camp – supply may dry up.

WARNING: Avoid remote areas when fire risk is high.

BEST TIME: Spring to autumn.

ENQUIRIES: (047) 87 8877.

ADDRESS: As for Blue Mountains.

Scenic enjoyment ✔✔✔
Day activities ✔✔
Family camping ✔✔
Hard bushwalking ✔✔✔

Ku-ring-gai Chase National Park

30 km N. Metropolitan weather district. Car access to Bobbin Head section from Pacific Highway at Turramurra or Mount Colah; to West Head section from Mona Vale Road at Terrey Hills. Vehicle entrance fee. Buses to Bobbin Head from Turramurra station; walking trails from near Mount Ku-ring-gai, Berowra and Cowan stations; ferry to Basin camp from Palm Beach.

DESCRIPTION: Page 322.

VISITOR CENTRES: Kalkari (near Bobbin Head), West Head.

BEST TIME: Year-round (spring for wildflowers).

ENQUIRIES: (02) 457 9322.

ADDRESS: NSWNPWS district office, Bobbin Head, Turramurra 2074

Scenic enjoyment ✔✔
Day activities ✔✔✔
Family camping ✔✔
Hard bushwalking ✔

Macquarie Pass National Park
115 km S, 33 km SW of Wollongong. South Coast and Illawarra weather district. Car access from Princes or Hume Highways via Illawarra Highway (Robertson-Albion Park). Train Moss Vale-Mount Murray (request stop).

Forests and woodlands flank the steep gorge of Macquarie Rivulet in its descent of nearly 700 metres from the Illawarra Escarpment. Hairpin bends on the Illawarra Highway, traversing the 1060 ha park, make for tense motoring. An unsealed road, branching off to the south about halfway down, leads 3 km to the start of a walking track to Rainbow Falls. Former logging trails provide unmarked routes to other waterfalls and swimming spots.

Eucalypts predominate, but the park has some gullies of subtropical rainforest. Parts were logged last century but are regenerating: some regrowth of red cedar can be seen. Lyrebirds, satin bowerbirds and smaller marsupials are among a diverse animal population. Eels and small fish inhabit some creeks.

BEST TIME: Spring to autumn.
ENQUIRIES: (044) 21 9969
ADDRESS: NSWNPWS district office, Box 707, Nowra 2540.

Scenic enjoyment ✓✓✓
Day activities ✓
Family camping ×
Hard bushwalking ✓

Marramarra National Park
55 km NW. Metropolitan weather district. Car access to park boundary by Canoelands Road (off Old Northern Road between Glenorie and Wisemans Ferry) or from Wisemans Ferry by Laughtondale Gully Road.

Short trails from the boundary access roads take bushwalkers through eucalypt woodlands to quiet streams feeding the Hawkesbury River and Berowra Creek. Marramarra Creek, the major waterway inside the 11 500 ha park, is navigable by canoe. Mangroves crowd the mouth, 8 km north of Berowra Waters, and casuarinas overhang the banks upstream. But some grassy flats make good camping sites. Waterfowl abound, and grey kangaroos and red-necked wallabies may be seen in the wooded areas.

NOTE: Fresh water in tributary creeks unreliable.
BEST TIME: Spring to autumn.
ENQUIRIES: (02) 457 9322.
ADDRESS: As for Ku-ring-gai Chase.

Scenic enjoyment ✓✓
Day activities ✓
Family camping ×
Hard bushwalking ✓

Mount Kaputar National Park
620 km NW, 53 km E of Narrabri. Northwest Slopes and Plains weather district. Car access (not caravans) to Dawsons Spring and Bark Hut camps by mostly unsealed road from Narrabri. Access to Sawn Rocks from Narrabri-Bingara Road.

DESCRIPTION: Page 341.
NOTE: Bookings required for Dawsons Spring cabins.
WARNINGS: Dangerous cliffs; sudden weather changes.
BEST TIME: Spring to autumn.
ENQUIRIES: (067) 92 2788.
ADDRESS: NSWNPWS district office, Box 72, Narrabri 2390.

Scenic enjoyment ✓✓✓
Day activities ✓✓
Family camping ✓✓✓
Hard bushwalking ✓✓✓

Myall Lakes National Park
260 km N. Mid-North Coast weather district. Car access (unsealed) off Pacific Highway at Bulahdelah or via Tea Gardens-Hawks Nest.

DESCRIPTION: Page 334.
NOTES: Bookings required for Bombah Point camp. Lake water unsuitable for drinking.
WARNING: Dangerous tidal race in lower Myall River.
BEST TIME: Year-round.
ENQUIRIES: (049) 87 3108.
ADDRESS: As for Barrington Tops.

Scenic enjoyment ✓✓
Day activities ✓✓✓
Family camping ✓✓✓
Hard bushwalking ✓

Oxley Wild Rivers National Park
550-560 km N, 110 km E of Tamworth. Northern Tablelands weather district. Short unsealed access roads off Oxley Highway at 18 and 37 km E of Walcha. Track into Yarrowitch Gorge section requires 4WD.

The Apsley and Yarrowitch Gorges national parks have been brought together in this new park which encompasses the wild and spectacular gorge country of the Apsley and Macleay rivers. It has magnificent waterfalls – including Wollomombi Falls (at 470 m the highest in Australia) and Gara Falls, which can be reached from the Armidale-Dorrigo road at Wollomombi. The rivers and rapids are excellent for rafting and canoeing.

The area is rich in flora and fauna: there are 700 species of native plants, 170 species of native birds, many reptiles thrive among the rocks, and there are kangaroos, wallaroos and rock wallabies on the gorge slopes.

Above Apsley Falls the escarpment edge can be easily reached on foot and two lookout platforms are provided. In the Yarrowitch section an easy half-day walk leads along the upper edge of the gorge to Yarrowitch Falls. Longer walking in either area calls for peak fitness and ranger advice should be sought on suitable routes and possible hazards.

NOTE: Rainwater tank at campsite in Yarrowitch section but no other facilities. Apsley Gorge accessible to caravans.
BEST TIME: Spring to autumn.
ENQUIRIES: (067) 72 1733.
ADDRESS: NSWNPWS district office, Box 402, Armidale 2350.

Scenic enjoyment ✓✓✓
Day activities ✓✓
Family camping ✓
Hard bushwalking ✓✓

Royal National Park
40 km S. Metropolitan weather district. Car access off Princes Highway at Loftus and Waterfall. Vehicle entrance fee. Trains Sydney-Loftus, Engadine, Heathcote, Waterfall, Otford, or occasionally direct to Royal National Park station. Ferry Cronulla-Bundeena.

DESCRIPTION: Page 319.
NOTES: Permit required for camping. Wood fires prohibited. Walkers should carry water.
VISITOR CENTRE: Audley.
BEST TIME: Year-round.
ENQUIRIES: (02) 521 2230.
ADDRESS: As for Heathcote.

Scenic enjoyment ✓✓✓
Day activities ✓✓✓
Family camping ✓✓
Hard bushwalking ✓✓

Sydney Harbour National Park
Metropolitan weather district. Suburban car or bus access to most sections. Ferries to Manly (for North Head) and Taronga Zoo (for Ashton Park). Boat access to Clark Island, and to Shark and Rodd Islands by arrangement.

Port Jackson's massive sandstone headlands, returned to the public after generations of military use, are notable for the magnificent views they command rather than for their own natural qualities. But a covering of bush remains in many parts of the 350 ha park, and efforts are being made to regenerate as much more as possible.

Wind-stunted coastal scrubs and heaths at North Head are fairly characteristic of the original vegetation. Some gullies in Ashton Park and at Dobroyd Head include relic rainforest species. On Grotto Point, dwarfed eucalypts shelter an attractive heath community including flannel flowers, native fuchsia, Christmas bells, grevilleas and banksias. Possums are the only prominent mammals to survive so close to suburbia, but lizards and native birds are fairly abundant.

Harbour parks staff are in provisional charge of **Botany Bay National Park.** The 26 ha at Congwong Bay gazetted in 1984 has been increased to 73 ha – the first steps in a long-term plan of land acquisitions.

NOTES: Camping prohibited. Cooking appliances only. Bookings required for Shark or Rodd Island and Quarantine Station visits. Weekend vehicle entrance fee at Ashton Park.
BEST TIME: Year-round.
ENQUIRIES: (02) 337 5511.
ADDRESS: Sydney Harbour National Park, Greycliffe House, Vaucluse 2030.

Scenic enjoyment ✓✓✓
Day activities ✓✓✓
Family camping ×
Walking, climbing ✓

Thirlmere Lakes National Park
90 km S. South Coast and Illawarra weather district. Car access off Remembrance Driveway 2 km S of Picton. Train-bus connection Sydney-Couridjah.

Floating islands of peat drift with the wind in five narrow, interconnecting freshwater lakes. The deepest point is 7 metres and the average depth only 3 metres. Three lakes are overgrown with waterweed, and another is available for power boating. One quiet expanse remains for swimming and canoeing.

Forested hills surrounding the lakes are included in a reserve of more than 630 ha. It was dedicated mainly on scientific grounds: the lakes represent an ancient river course cut off from its drainage system, and they support biological communities that are unusual in the Sydney region. A rare purple waterlily is noticeable over the deeper sections.

BEST TIME: Year-round.
ENQUIRIES: (02) 521 2230.
ADDRESS: As for Heathcote.

Scenic enjoyment ✓
Day activities ✓✓✓
Family camping ✓
Hard bushwalking ✓

Tomaree National Park
225 km NE, adjoining Nelson and Anna Bays. Hunter weather district. Car access off Pacific Highway from Raymond Terrace to Nelson Bay.

Land initially available for this new park comprises 809 ha in a broken coastal strip south and west of the entrance to Port Stephens. Proposed additions are likely to increase the area to 2000 ha.

Sea cliffs up to 100 metres high, formed out of volcanic flows from the New England plateau, are the outstanding feature of the park. Vegetation ranges from coastal scrubs and heaths to sedges and eucalypt forests.

BEST TIME: Spring to autumn.
ENQUIRIES: (049) 87 3108.
ADDRESS: As for Barrington Tops.

Scenic enjoyment ✓✓
Day activities ✓✓
Family camping ×
Hard bushwalking ✓

Warrabah National Park
540 km N, 80 km N of Tamworth. Northwest Slopes and Plains weather district. Car access from northern outskirts of Manilla.

Walkers willing to do some rock-hopping can follow the Namoi River along 15 km of cascades, rapids and pools penned by waterworn granite outcrops. Small, sandy beaches make pleasant campsites near popular swimming and fishing spots. Canoeing or rafting are feasible, but require experience. Portages are frequent and the whole trip can take three days.

The Namoi descends 245 metres through the park, down a narrow gorge surmounted by huge granite tors. Surrounding woodlands in the 2635 ha reserve, which is 8 km at its widest point, are dominated by white cypress pine, red gum and ironbark. Tall stands of river oak casuarinas and some river red gums line the Namoi's banks. Grey kangaroos, wallaroos and possums are common, and skinks and geckoes abound on the rocky slopes. The bird population includes wedge-tailed eagles and rainbow birds.

NOTE: Boil river water before drinking.
BEST TIME: Year-round.
ENQUIRIES: (067) 72 1733.
ADDRESS: As for Oxley Wild Rivers.

Scenic enjoyment ✓✓
Day activities ✓✓
Family camping ✓
Walking, climbing ✓

Warrumbungle National Park
500 km NW, 35 km W of Coonabarabran. Central West Slopes and Plains weather district. Car access from Coonabarabran and Gilgandra via Tooraweenah, dry weather from Coonamble. Anti-freeze needed in winter. Vehicle entry fee.
DESCRIPTION: Page 337.
NOTES: Permits required for camping, rock climbing. Bookings required for cabins. Fire restrictions. Boil all water – tap or creek – before drinking.
BEST TIME: Spring, autumn.
VISITOR CENTRE: Canyon Camp.
ENQUIRIES: (068) 25 4364 or 42 1311.
ADDRESS: NSWNPWS district office, Box 39, Coonabarabran 2357.

Scenic enjoyment ✓✓✓
Day activities ✓✓
Family camping ✓✓✓
Hard bushwalking ✓✓✓

Werrikimbe National Park
540 km NE, 127 km W of Wauchope. Northern Tablelands weather district. Car access off Oxley Highway between Wauchope and Walcha. Roads are steep and narrow, and used by logging trucks.

Untouched rainforest grows in deep gorges cut into the eastern margin of the New England plateau by the Hastings River and its tributaries. Eucalypt woodland, heath and swamps dominate flatter parts of the plateau. Around the northern campsite, Mooraback, mobs of grey kangaroos, wallaroos and wallabies feed on natural grasslands and former grazing paddocks.

Platypuses, echidnas and bandicoots are sometimes seen, and greater gliders and dingoes are often heard at night. A strong torch trained upwards between tall trees may spotlight gliders, grey-headed flying foxes or some of the 10 species of bats recorded in the 34 753 ha park.

Short walks from the campsites take in Cobcroft's Bush, a big rainforest stand surrounded by tall eucalypts, and an area near Mooraback Creek where grass trees grow more than 3 metres tall. Longer walks suited to overnight camping trips strike out to the Hastings River gorges and the 66 metre drop of Upper Falls.
BEST TIME: Year-round.
ENQUIRIES: (067) 72 1733.
ADDRESS: As for Oxley Wild Rivers.

Scenic enjoyment ✓✓
Day activities ✓
Family camping ✓
Hard bushwalking ✓✓

Woko National Park
350 km N, 30 km NW of Gloucester. Mid-North Coast weather district. Car access off Gloucester-Walcha Road, turn off for Curricabark.

Mountainous terrain forming part of the watershed between the Little Manning and Barnard Rivers take up much of the 8274 ha park. Former farmland flanked by tall eucalypts with a dense understorey provides camping and picnic sites on the banks of the Little Manning. A short trail leading off from the camping area passes rock outcrops where orchids, staghorns and elkhorns grow profusely. Rainforests covering most of the park are important habitats for birds such as the brush turkey and native pigeon.
BEST TIME: Spring to autumn.
ENQUIRIES: (049) 87 3108.
ADDRESS: As for Barrington Tops.

Scenic enjoyment ✓✓
Day activities ✓
Family camping ✓
Hard bushwalking ✓✓

Wollemi National Park
150 km NW. Central Tablelands and Hunter weather districts. Car access to boundaries only, along Windsor-Singleton Road or off Lithgow-Rylstone Road to Glen Davis or Newnes.
DESCRIPTION: Page 330.
WARNINGS: Gorges flood suddenly. Avoid remote areas during periods of high fire danger.
BEST TIME: Spring to autumn.
ENQUIRIES: Northern section (065) 43 2274; southern section (047) 87 8877; Colo area (045) 75 1671.
ADDRESS: As for Blue Mountains.

Scenic enjoyment ✓✓✓
Day activities ✓
Family camping ×
Hard bushwalking ✓✓✓

WALKING IN THE WARRUMBUNGLES

The way to the Grand High Tops

Spires, domes and the sharp ridges of weather-worn volcanic plugs challenge rock climbers and hikers on day walks in Warrumbungle National Park. Overnight campsites link the short trails into extended bushwalks through heaths and eucalypt woodland between the rugged towers.

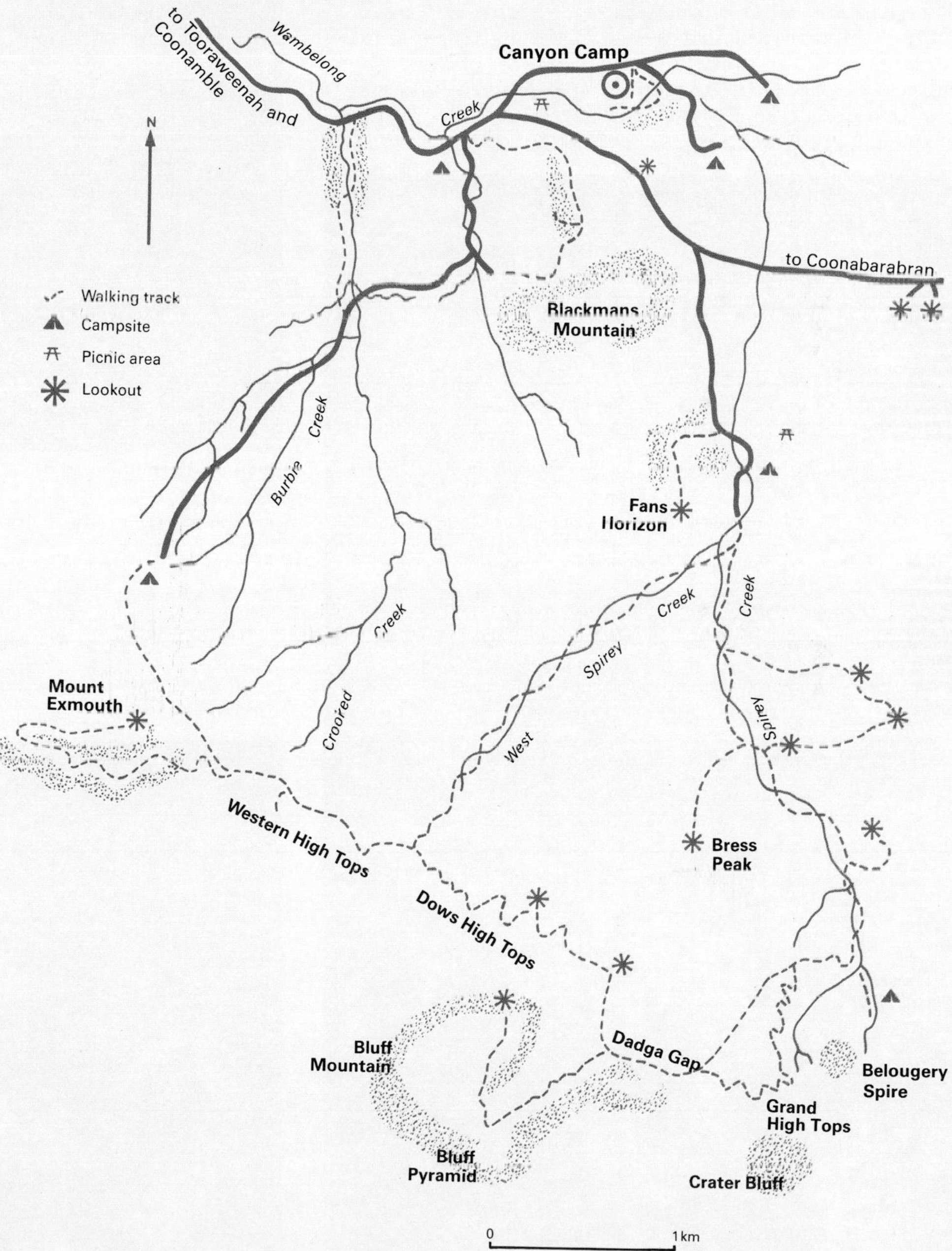

Birdlife in the eastern parks

One of the things Australians take for granted, but newcomers marvel at, is the abundance of birdlife: more than 700 native species, with habits and habitats almost as varied as their numbers. Some birds remain in one territory, which they defend fiercely against outsiders, while others range from the coast to the inland. There are birds which live and feed in the rainforest canopy, others that are ground or swamp dwellers. Their eating habits range from aerial feeding, like the swallows, through fruit, nectar, seeds, flowers, rodents, lizards, crustacea and other birds. Nests vary from earth mounds, built by the brush-turkey, through scrapes in the ground, elaborately woven nests, nests of mud, of moss or of grasses held together with cobweb, to rough platforms of sticks. Every national park holds some part of this dazzling diversity.

Above: Black-winged stilt with the first of its four eggs

Right: Pink cockatoo, often called the Major Mitchell, found in inland areas

Left: Musk lorikeet feeding on eucalyptus flowers

Below: The handsome regent bowerbird lives in coastal rainforest

Above left and right: Two birds of the great open inland – the wedge-tailed eagle, largest bird of prey in Australia, and the emu

Below: The red-browed race of double-eyed fig-parrot is rare in NSW but may be spotted high in northern region rainforest. Right: The crimson rosella lives along the edges of eucalypt woodland

LISMORE & GRAFTON REGIONS

Rainforest 'islands' gain international protection

A LONG CHAPTER of heated controversy closed in 1986 when rainforest parks and reserves in northern New South Wales were granted World Heritage status. By international treaty most of the state's last significant stands of 'big scrub', comprising about 100 000 ha, are forever spared from logging.

Passions had begun to stir over the fate of the dwindling rainforests in the early 1970s. Aware of the jobs and revenue at stake in the forest industry, the state Labor government when it took office in 1976 was in favour of logging. Conservationists' indignation came to a head in 1979 at Terania Creek, in what is now Nightcap National Park. Their demonstrations secured a suspension of logging – although a long judicial enquiry later favoured its resumption.

But by 1982 the government had been converted to the cause of conservation. That year it adopted a bold and controversial policy: general logging was to be phased out and several major rainforest areas were to be protected in national parks. Legislation declaring new parks and reserves and expanding existing ones was passed in 1984.

Meanwhile moves were being made at national level to develop an overall approach to the preservation of a dwindling resource. In 1984 the Commonwealth government set up a working group of representatives from the timber industry, conservation movement, unions and research organisations together with national and state forestry and conservation authorities. Its task was to advise on practical ways in which governments might resolve the conflicting demands of rainforest use and protection of a national resource. The result of its report was that in 1986 a federally funded national rainforest conservation programme was set up.

To emphasise the importance it placed on such matters, the New South Wales government recommended to the Commonwealth that seven major rainforest areas be nominated for World Heritage listing. Officials were far from confident that Unesco would consider the nomination of disjointed areas, scattered along the scarp edge of the Great Dividing Range and across the northern tablelands. But the ruling committee accepted the concept of a terrestrial chain of islands, comparable with the Galapagos Islands where Charles Darwin started to formulate his theory of the origin of species.

Indeed these forest 'islands', cut off from one another for eons, have an equivalent scientific value. Through what they share – notably the ancient antarctic beech – and what they do not share, much of the evolutionary history of plants and animals, and of the continent itself, can be traced.

The World Heritage national parks in this section are Mount Warning, Border Ranges, Nightcap, Gibraltar Range, New England, Dorrigo and Washpool. Two more, Barrington Tops and Werrikimbe, fall within the Sydney region.

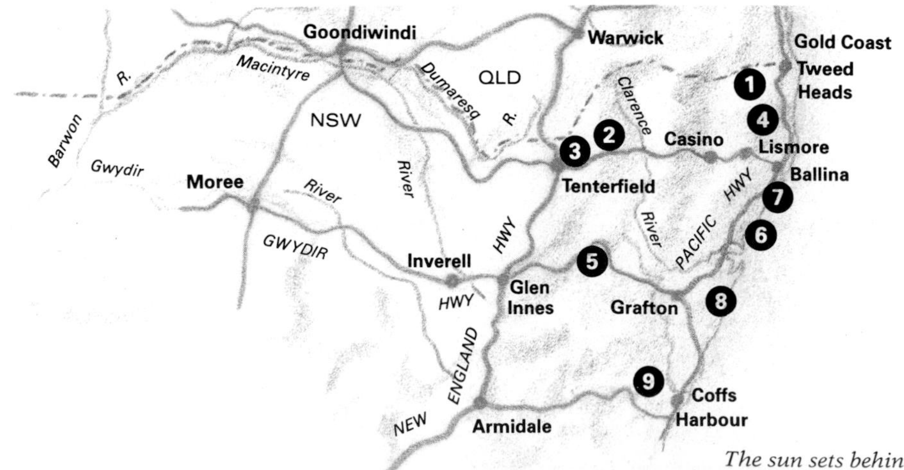

Featured parks **Pages**

(1) Mount Warning........... 350
(2) Boonoo Boonoo........... 351
(3) Bald Rock.................... 352-353
(4) Nightcap...................... 354
(5) Gibraltar Range.......... 355
(6) Bundjalung.................. 356
(7) Broadwater.................. 357
(8) Yuraygir....................... 358-359
(9) Dorrigo......................... 360-361

Your access and facilities guide to all national parks in this region starts on page 362

The sun sets behind Mt Warning. When it rises, this is the first point on mainland Australia to be struck by its rays

Bangalow palms – called piccabeens just over the border in Queensland – are prolific on the lower slopes

MOUNT WARNING NATIONAL PARK

Climbers emerging on to the bare heights of Mt Warning from its forested flanks come upon a panorama that stops them in their tracks. Ranged in the distance on three sides, forming the steep rim of a huge bowl, are the eroded flanks of the ancient Tweed volcano (map, page 15). Mt Warning itself, at 1157 metres perhaps only half its original height, was the plug of magma that set in the volcano's main vent after its final outpourings.

A zigzag climb to the summit from the park entrance at Breakfast Creek takes most people more than 2 hours and has an extremely steep last section. At low level the track penetrates a dense subtropical rainforest where giant stinging trees, figs and bangalow palms are prominent. As the altitude increases this merges into a temperate rainforest with a mossy floor and an understorey of ferns. Birds abound in the 2210 ha park.

Mt Warning's distinctive peak is visible from far out at sea. James Cook named it as a navigation marker for reefs off Point Danger, where HMS Endeavour *almost ran aground.*

BOONOO BOONOO NATIONAL PARK

Eucalypt forests cloak high ridges enclosing the winding valley of the Boonoo Boonoo River (locally called the Bunny B'noo). Banksias, paperbarks, tea-trees and cypress pine line the watercourse, often shading open expanses of smooth granite and enticing rock pools. Beyond a rest area and camping ground, an easy track leads to a viewing platform over the Boonoo Boonoo Falls, which cascade for 210 metres into a rainforested gorge. The poet A.B. (Banjo) Paterson did his courting here at the turn of the century: he married the daughter of the station owner who put through the first track to the falls. A further track leads steeply down into the gorge, where rock wallabies are sometimes seen. Grey kangaroos, wallaroos and wallabies range over the higher parts of the 2442 ha park.

Precipitous granite faces flank the abrupt edge of the Boono Boonoo Falls

Popular swimming holes are strung along the river

Wattles bloom earliest among a profusion of wildflowers

Littered with boulders and deeply scored by weathering, Bald Rock is not true granite but adamellite, with a slightly different mineral content. It formed underground about 220 million years ago.

Lomandra and flowering prickly whitebeard grow with surprising vigour in poor, sandy soils collecting in a crack

BALD ROCK NATIONAL PARK

An immense dome of granitic rock, 750 metres long and 500 metres wide, bulges 200 metres above a surrounding forest of tall eucalypts. The summit of Bald Rock stands 1341 metres above sea level, commanding broad views over rocky highlands and out to the peaks of the Scenic Rim and the Tweed coast. Run-off of rain from its weathered surface supports a zone of luxuriant tree growth around the base, but trees on more distant ridges are noticeably shorter and sparser. Parts of the rock itself have been colonised by heaths, and one deep layer of humus at the eastern end has a stand of cypress pine. Lower-lying gullies are swampy. About 100 bird species inhabit the 5450 ha park, along with grey kangaroos, wallaroos, wallabies, possums and marsupial 'cats'. Echidnas frequent the summit, which is reached by a walking track of 2 km, taking about an hour each way.

Cool creeks flow year-round in hundreds of forested gullies leading down from the Nightcap Range, which has the highest rainfall in NSW. Its peaks top 900 metres in the west of the park. Below: Extensive stands of bangalow palms take over from rainforest trees on some of the lower slopes

NIGHTCAP NATIONAL PARK

A decade of controversy over the logging of NSW's finest remaining rainforests ended in 1983 with the dedication of more than 4000 ha of former state forest land as a national park. It takes its name from the Nightcap Range, which forms the southern rim of the Tweed volcanic basin. The Nightcap Track, a pioneer packhorse trail linking Lismore and Murwillumbah, crosses the eastern extremity of the park. Another marked walking track branches from it and leads about 10 km west to Tuntable Falls or to Mt Matheson and Mt Nardi – the latter surmounted jarringly by two television towers and a radio repeater mast.

Less strenuously, subtropical rainforest can be seen at its best around Terania Creek, the focus of anti-logging demonstrations in the late 1970s. From picnic and camping grounds at the end of the approach road, a 500 metre walking track to Protesters Falls gives a good sampling. Even better examples are found to the north, along an old logging trail of about 2 km past Circle Pool to Terania Creek Basin. Newton Drive and Googarna Road give access to further walking routes in the central and western parts of the park.

Towering eucalypts surround Boundary Falls, on the western edge of the park

Water erosion carves holes in a band of sedimentary rock

Mists close in near Raspberry Lookout. The range receives some winter snowfalls, and visitors should be prepared for cold snaps at any time

GIBRALTAR RANGE NATIONAL PARK

Tors of granite stud a forested plateau standing nearly 1200 metres above sea level at the edge of the New England Tablelands. Deep gorges dissect a park of 17 273 ha, and lookouts along the Gwydir Highway command striking views of steep rock faces and tumbling waterfalls. Eucalypts dominate forests on granite-derived soils, interspersed with heaths and some alpine and swamp communities. But the park also has zones of volcanic soils supporting rainforests. This diversity of habitats attracts well over 200 bird species. Also here is a marsupial mouse found in no other park, and the rare rufous rat-kangaroo. Walking trails of 1-8 km have been developed and picnic grounds are widely provided.

Bundjalung National Park

On the beach reaching south to Woody Head, wave erosion of foredunes exposes coffee rock — a cemented mixture of sand grains and peaty organic material

Endangered animals have gained an important sanctuary by the preservation of Bundjalung. Behind nearly 40 km of beaches, surrounded by heavily used holiday areas, the 17 545 ha park embraces an unusual diversity of habitats. It has coastal heathlands, swamps, lagoons, eucalypt forests, rare coastal rainforests and the unspoilt Esk River flowing through its central wilderness zone. Red-crowned, topknot and wompoo pigeons nest in the forests and little terns and pied oyster-catchers by the shore. Ground parrots feed on the heaths. Mammals include kangaroos, wallabies, potoroos, pygmy possums and a rare tree rat. Sheltered bays for swimming and boating are found in the south near the major camping area at Woody Head. Inland waterways are suitable for canoeing. Away from the beach, bushwalkers find most scope in the central area, south of Jerusalem Creek.

Left: Tidal pools pit easily eroded coffee rock on Broadwater Beach. Intriguing cave formations are found close by

Heath pea

Guinea flower

Heath banksia

Tea-tree

BROADWATER NATIONAL PARK

Spring wildflowers bloom brilliantly on heathlands and swampy lowlands behind the 7 km reach of Broadwater and Evans Head Beaches. Well inland are wooded ridges – dunes formed about 60 000 years ago when the sea level was higher. A layer of black or dark brown organic coffee rock, running shallowly under the 3709 ha park and outcropping along the beach, may date from the same period.

Flowers and birdlife are best seen on the 3 km Salty Lagoon walk, starting just inside the southern boundary. Dry heathlands dominated by grass-trees and wallum banksia merge into wetter sections where scrubs are stunted and insect-eating sundews and parasitic plants are prolific. Towards the end of the track, sedges and rushes overgrow the swampy margins of Salty Creek. Herons, ibis and brolga breed in the area and jabiru have been seen. Honeyeaters flock on the heaths. Sea eagles and ospreys hunt over a shore thronged by smaller birds.

A fine example of restoration can be seen just inside the northern boundary. A disused rock-fill quarry was turned into a lake – immediately popular with birds and kangaroos – and disturbed dunes were replaced. Volunteers have planted thousands of trees and shrubs.

Sprengelia heath

PARKS OF THE LISMORE AND GRAFTON REGIONS

FACILITIES

Cabins

Caravan park

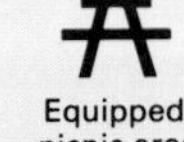
Equipped picnic area

Bush camping allowed

Lavatory building

Established campsite

Campsite but no car access

Note: Popular parks without campsites usually have public camping grounds nearby. If in doubt, call enquiries number.

PARK RATINGS No interest ✗ Some interest ✔ Major interest ✔✔ Outstanding ✔✔✔

186 km W of Lismore, 28 km N of Tenterfield. Northern Tablelands weather district. Car access off Mt Lindesay Highway N of Tenterfield.
DESCRIPTION: Page 353.
BEST TIME: Spring, autumn.
ENQUIRIES: (067) 32 1177.
ADDRESS: NSWNPWS district office, Box 281, Glen Innes 2370.

Scenic enjoyment ✔✔
Day activities ✔
Family camping ✔
Hard bushwalking ✔

Boonoo Boonoo

188 km W of Lismore, 30 km N of Tenterfield. Northern Tablelands weather district. Car access off Mt Lindesay Highway N of Tenterfield.
DESCRIPTION: Page 351.
BEST TIME: Spring.
ENQUIRIES: (067) 32 1177.
ADDRESS: As for Bald Rock.

Scenic enjoyment ✔✔✔
Day activities ✔✔
Family camping ✔
Hard bushwalking ✔✔

Border Ranges National Park

75 km NW of Lismore, 30 km N of Kyogle. Northern Rivers weather district. Car access from Tweed Range Scenic Drive, which crosses the park. It is signposted on the Murwillumbah-Kyogle road at Lillian Rock, or on the Kyogle-Woodenbong road at Wiangaree.

Enlargement of the Border Ranges National Park to 31 229 ha in 1983 made a major contribution to the Scenic Rim concept of a continuous chain of parks stretching along the McPherson Range from the Gold Coast hinterland to the eastern escarpment of the Darling Downs near Toowoomba. The park now incorporates the most important rainforest areas remaining on the NSW side of the border with Queensland.

Remnant stands of subtropical, warm-temperate, cool-temperate and dry rainforest are all sampled in the new park, though they have been confined by agricultural and forestry encroachment to steep and broken mountain slopes. A well-maintained forest drive makes the eastern part of the park with its walking trails, picnic grounds, waterfalls and lookouts easily accessible. Visitors are advised to start from Lillian Rock to avoid potentially dangerous descents of the steep escarpment at this end of the road. Hikers contemplating long walks to mountain peaks and river gorges need map-reading and compass experience to tackle the dense wilderness forests.
NOTE: Check road condition with park office before setting out, especially after heavy rains.
BEST TIME: Spring, autumn
ENQUIRIES: (066) 28 1177.
ADDRESS: NSWNPWS district office, Box 91, Alstonville 2477.

Scenic enjoyment ✔✔✔
Day activities ✔✔✔
Family camping ✔
Hard bushwalking ✔

Broadwater National Park

45 km SE of Lismore, 30 km S of Ballina. Northern Rivers weather district. Car access off Pacific Highway S of Ballina through Broadwater or 11 km N of Woodburn through Evans Head.
DESCRIPTION: Page 357.
NOTE: No water supply.
BEST TIME: Spring.
ENQUIRIES: (066) 28 1177.
ADDRESS: As for Border Ranges.

Scenic enjoyment ✔✔
Day activities ✔✔
Family camping ✗
Hard bushwalking ✔

Bundjalung National Park

60 km NE of Grafton, 50 km S of Ballina. Northern Rivers weather district. Car access off Pacific Highway – for northern section from Woodburn via Evans Head; for central section 5 km S of Woodburn; for southern section 38 km S of Woodburn via Iluka.
DESCRIPTION: Page 356.
NOTES: Drinking water available only at Woody Head. Fee charged for Woody Head camping – booking recommended (Box 15, Iluka 2460). No spearfishing in marine reserve around Woody Head.
WARNING: Walking prohibited in RAAF bombing range north of Jerusalem Creek.
BEST TIME: Spring, autumn.
ENQUIRIES: (066) 28 1177.
ADDRESS: As for Border Ranges.

Scenic enjoyment ✔✔
Day activities ✔✔✔
Family camping ✔✔✔
Hard bushwalking ✔

Cathedral Rock National Park

130 km SW of Grafton, 45 km NE of Armidale. Northern Tablelands weather district. Car access off Dorrigo-Armidale road 6 km and 12 km S of Ebor.

A heavy chain helps visitors pull themselves up the final leg of a steep climb on Cathedral Rock, one of the giant granite tors strewn over the northern slopes of Round Mountain. From the superb summit vantage point rainforests, eucalypt woodlands, banksia heath and swamps fall away to the north of the mountain peak in a park of 6529 ha. A small gallery of rare pygmy cypress pines grows in the woodlands alongside messmates, mountain gums and New England blackbutt. Parma wallabies, brush-tailed rock wallabies and wallaroos are among the mammals which inhabit the park's various habitats. Birds include wedge-tailed eagles, glossy and yellow-tailed black cockatoos and thornbills.

Formed walking trails strike out over rough country from the Barokee camping ground. The track to Native Dog Creek is about 11 km long and hikers should be prepared to camp out overnight to allow plenty of time to explore around the tors and tackle some of the climbs.
BEST TIME: Spring, autumn.
ENQUIRIES: (066) 57 2309.
ADDRESS: NSWNPWS district office, Box 170, Dorrigo 2453.

Scenic enjoyment ✔✔✔
Day activities ✔✔
Family camping ✔
Walking, climbing ✔✔

Dorrigo National Park

143 km S of Grafton, 60 km W of Coffs Harbour. Mid-North Coast weather district. Car access off Bellingen-Dorrigo road; turn off Pacific Highway at Raleigh, 25 km N of Nambucca Heads.
DESCRIPTION: Page 360.
VISITOR CENTRE: Park entrance.
BEST TIME: Spring, autumn.
ENQUIRIES: (066) 57 2309.
ADDRESS: As for Cathedral Rock.

Scenic enjoyment ✔✔✔
Day activities ✔✔
Family camping ✗
Hard bushwalking ✔✔

Gibraltar Range National Park

90 km W of Grafton, 70 km E of Glen Innes. Northern Tablelands weather district. Gwydir Highway crosses park.
DESCRIPTION: Page 355.
VISITOR CENTRE: Dandahra Creek entrance on Gwydir Highway.
BEST TIME: Spring to autumn.
ENQUIRIES: (067) 32 1177.
ADDRESS: As for Bald Rock.

Scenic enjoyment ✔✔✔
Day activities ✔✔✔
Family camping ✔✔✔
Hard bushwalking ✔✔

Guy Fawkes River National Park

110 km SW of Grafton, 80 km NE of Armidale. Northern Tablelands weather district. Car access along unsealed road off Armidale-Grafton road at Dundurrabin and Hernani.

Wilderness reaches of the Guy Fawkes River wind through deeply cut gorges and over waterfalls and rapids on a northward course through this 35 326 ha park. Heavy summer rains usually give sufficient depth of water for canoeing, and swollen rapids can be negotiated on inflated rubber mattresses.

Grassy flats shaded by rough-barked 'apple' (angophora) line stretches of riverbank and make excellent camping spots on overnight hikes. Rainforest grows in moister areas within the gorge. Eucalypt woodlands and scrub occupy drier areas and much of the high ground of the surrounding plateau.

Grey kangaroos, shaggy wallaroos and red-necked and swamp wallabies abound throughout the park. Timid rock wallabies keep to the higher, broken ground; potoroos, pademelons and parma wallabies find refuge in the patches of rainforest. Birdlife includes brilliant flame robins, yellow robins, thornbills, rosellas and whipbirds.

Walking trails include a 10 km track that strikes out west towards the river from camping and picnic grounds at Chaelundi Falls, on a tributary of the Guy Fawkes.
BEST TIME: Spring, autumn.
ENQUIRIES: (066) 57 2309.
ADDRESS: As for Cathedral Rock.

Scenic enjoyment ✔✔✔
Day activities ✔✔
Family camping ✔
Hard bushwalking ✔✔✔

Mount Warning National Park

107 km N of Lismore, 15 km SW of Murwillumbah. Northern Rivers weather district. Car access off Murwillumbah-Kyogle road at Dum Dum.
DESCRIPTION: Page 350.
NOTE: Strong cold winds frequent at summit – take warm, waterproof clothing.
BEST TIME: Spring, autumn.
ENQUIRIES: (066) 28 1177.
ADDRESS: As for Border Ranges.

Scenic enjoyment ✔✔✔
Day activities ✔✔
Family camping ✗
Hard bushwalking ✗

New England National Park

160 km SW of Grafton, 80 km E of Armidale. Northern Tablelands weather district. Car access off Armidale-Dorrigo road.

Eastern edges of the New England Plateau end abruptly in the park with steep cliffs and heavily forested ridges sloping to deep valleys of the Bellinger River system. Apart from camping and picnic grounds near the entrance, and short but strenuous walks to escarpment lookouts, the 29 881 ha park is a wilderness.

Along the circular track of the Eagle's Nest walk, sweeping views of the Bellinger Valley open up from crests of low sub-alpine forest. Permanent waterfalls tumbling over glistening rock faces at Rainbow Spray and Weeping Rock freeze in winter to form striking ice cascades. Longer walks, including the self-guiding Lyrebird nature trail, take up to 4 hours to complete. They pass through cool-temperate rainforest, gullies thick with tall tree-ferns, stunted heaths on exposed peaks and impressive stands of negrohead beech coloured by spring-flowering beech orchids.

The 7000 ha Black Scrub, formerly part of a state forest, is a recent addition to the park. It preserves an outstanding example of untouched blackbutt forest, a type extensively logged throughout NSW.

Fire trails are followed for extended bushwalks, linking with trails in the adjoining Bellinger River State Forest. With ranger advice wilderness hikers select routes from the escarpment along ridges and valley floors, but the going is rough and walkers should be experienced and well-equipped to cope with sudden severe weather, including snowfalls in winter.

NOTE: Bookings required for campsites and cabins during holidays.

VISITOR CENTRE: Near Point Lookout.

BEST TIME: Spring, autumn.

ENQUIRIES: (066) 57 2309.

ADDRESS: As for Cathedral Rock.

Scenic enjoyment ✔✔✔
Day activities ✔✔
Family camping ✔✔✔
Hard bushwalking ✔✔✔

Nightcap National Park

43 km N of Lismore, 30 km W of Brunswick Heads. Northern Rivers weather district. Car access to Mt Nardi from Lismore via Nimbin (sealed); to Terania Creek via The Channon (unsealed); to Nightcap Track via Dunoon (unsealed).

DESCRIPTION: Page 354.

NOTE: Camping only at Terania Creek, limited to 1 night.

WARNING: Campers should leave if heavy rains persist: causeways may flood.

BEST TIME: Spring, autumn.

ENQUIRIES: (066) 28 1177.

ADDRESS: As for Border Ranges.

Scenic enjoyment ✔✔✔
Day activities ✔✔
Family camping ×
Hard bushwalking ✔✔✔

Nymboida National Park

65 km W of Grafton, 60 km NE of Glen Innes. Northern Tablelands weather district. Vehicle access (4WD recommended) along unsealed track N from old Grafton-Glen Innes road 41 km SW of Grafton. Accessible by canoe from Buccarumbi, 50 km SW of Grafton.

Broad waters of the Nymboida River are a welcome relief to white-water canoeists in the short stretch flanked by this 1368 ha park. Farther upstream, on the course from Buccarumbi to Jackadgery on the Gwydir Highway, rapids challenge the most experienced paddlers and dangerous gorges and waterfalls demand portage of craft and supplies over rough, broken ground. Land-based visitors reach the park along service tracks through the vast buffer zone of Ramornie State Forest, which helps ensure an undisturbed wilderness habitat of eucalypt forest, with some rainforest in sheltered gullies.

BEST TIME: Spring, autumn.

ENQUIRIES: (066) 42 0613.

ADDRESS: NSWNPWS district office, Box 97, Grafton 2460.

Scenic enjoyment ✔✔✔
Day activities ×
Family camping ×
Hard bushwalking ✔

Washpool National Park

80 km W of Grafton, 75 km E of Glen Innes. Northern Tablelands weather district. Car access along unsealed road off Gwydir Highway between Grafton and Glen Innes.

A wilderness of warm-temperate rainforest, formerly under state forest management, was preserved from logging by the declaration of this 27 715 ha park in 1983. New, high-standard walking trails around the clear headwaters of Coombadjha Creek, just north of the popular Gibraltar Range National Park, lead among unspoilt coachwood-banksia and Sydney bluegum communities. Lower reaches of Coombadjha and Washpool Creeks, which eventually feed into the Clarence River, flow through trackless forests tackled by only the most experienced hikers.

BEST TIME: Spring, autumn.

ENQUIRIES: (067) 32 1177.

ADDRESS: As for Bald Rock.

Scenic enjoyment ✔✔
Day activities ✔✔
Family camping ✔✔
Hard bushwalking ✔✔✔

Yuraygir National Park

47-54 km E of Grafton. Northern Rivers weather district. Car access off Pacific Highway – to northern section via Brooms Head road; to central section via Wooli road from Ulmarra; to southern section via unsealed forestry road 39 km S of Grafton (give way to logging trucks).

DESCRIPTION: Page 358.

NOTE: No fresh water supplies.

BEST TIME: Spring, autumn.

ENQUIRIES: (066) 42 0613.

ADDRESS: As for Nymboida.

Scenic enjoyment ✔✔✔
Day activities ✔✔✔
Family camping ✔✔✔
Hard bushwalking ✔

1. Bald Rock NP
2. Boonoo Boonoo NP
3. Border Ranges NP
4. Broadwater NP
5. Bundjalung NP
6. Cathedral Rock NP
7. Dorrigo NP
8. Gibraltar Range NP
9. Guy Fawkes River NP
10. Mount Warning NP
11. New England NP
12. Nightcap NP
13. Nymboida NP
14. Washpool NP
15. Yuraygir NP

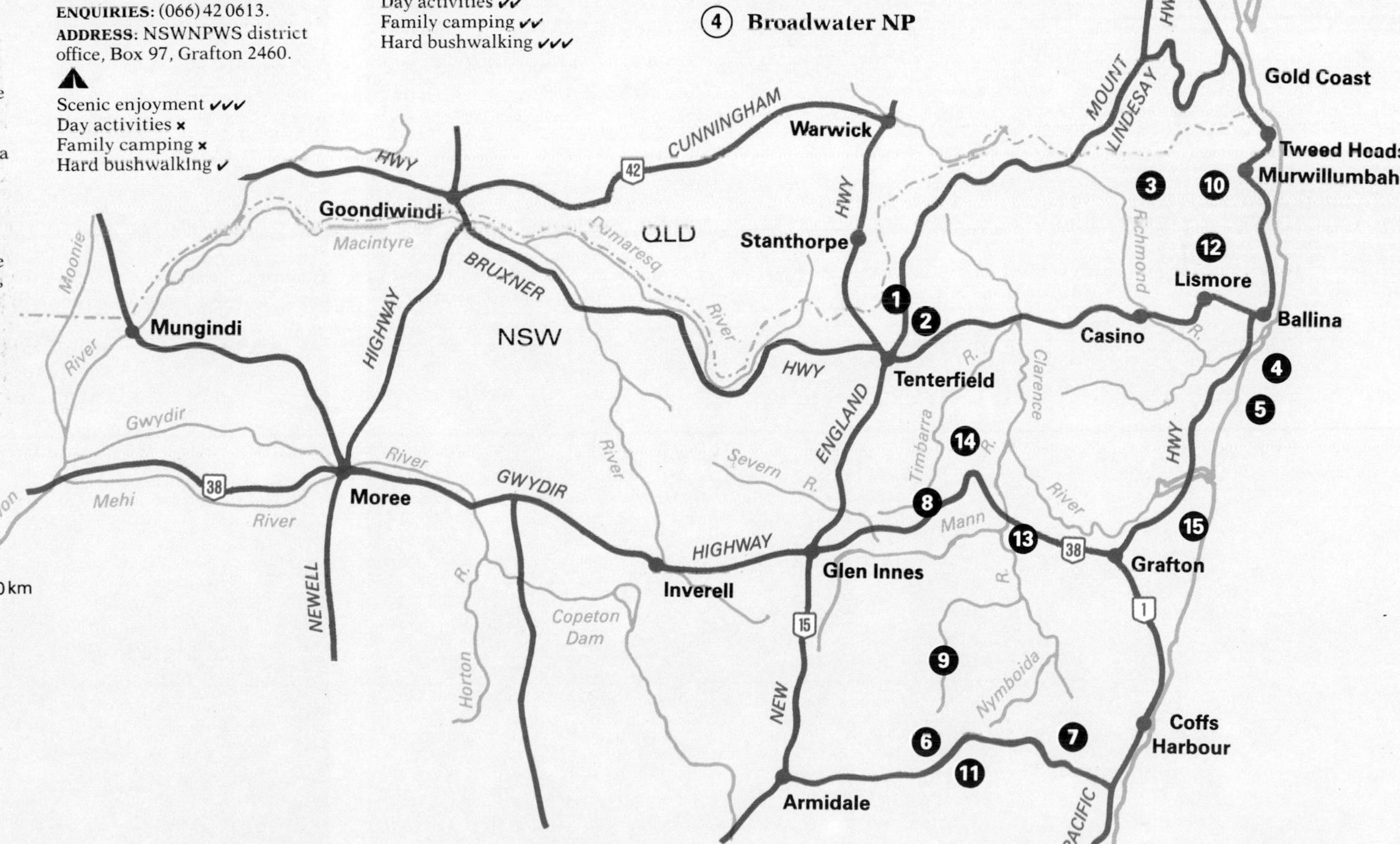

Eastern blue-tongued lizard – found from coastal heaths to mountain forests

Green tree frog – easily identified by its horizontal pupil

A red-fingered mangrove crab defends its territory

Male red kangaroos vary in colour from pale to brick red; females are usually blue-grey

Wildlife in the eastern parks

As our towns and cities expand, as more land is cleared and forest trees are felled, the pressure increases on available habitat for much of our wildlife. As well, introduced animals such as the feral cat and fox are in direct competition with native carnivores.

National parks provide a refuge for many species. One of the greatest pleasures of a park visit is to get away from campsite or car park, settle down comfortably and, above all, quietly and simply enjoy these creatures and the world of which they are a part.

Spotted-tailed quoll (left) – largest of the carnivorous marsupials

Mountain pygmy-possum – the only Australian mammal restricted to alpine and subalpine areas

Visitor activities in the national parks of New South Wales and the Australian Capital Territory

An ideal way to explore Royal National – by kayak, with time to stop off to fish

Cross-country skiers break Kosciusko's winter stillness

CAMPING

Bush camping — away from it all, no facilities other than those you create.
Camping — a pit toilet and a tap but no other facilities.
Family camping — established camping ground with showers, toilets, barbecue areas and where you can probably take a caravan, but check beforehand.

Abseiling (district ranger's approval required)
Bald Rock, Blue Mountains, Goulburn River, Kanangra-Boyd, Mootwingee, Mount Kaputar, Warrumbungles, Wollemi.

Bird watching
All national parks.

Bush camping
All national parks.

Bushwalking
All national parks.

Camping
All national parks **except** Royal, Sydney Harbour, Ku-ring-gai Chase.

Canoeing/boating
Bouddi, Kinchega, Myall Lakes, Sydney Harbour; lakes and estuaries of most coastal parks – e.g. Ben Boyd, Brisbane Waters, Bundjalung, Crowdy Bay, Hat Head, Ku-ring-gai Chase, Mimosa Rocks, Royal National, Yuraygir.

Canyoning
Blue Mountains, Gibraltar Range, Guy Fawkes River, Kanangra-Boyd, Werrikimbe, Wollemi.

Car touring
All national parks.

Caving (permits required)
Blue Mountains, Kanangra-Boyd, Kosciusko.

Cave tours
Yarrangobilly Caves (Kosciusko).

Cycling
Most national parks.

Fishing, beach/ocean
From the edges of all coastal national parks **except** Bouddi.

Fishing, freshwater (angler's licence required)
Gibraltar Range, Guy Fawkes River, Kinchega, Kosciusko.

Geological studies
Kosciusko, Mount Kaputar, Warrumbungle – and don't take the rocks.

Historical studies
Kosciusko, Namadgi, Royal, Sturt, Sydney Harbour, Willandra.

Horse riding
Kosciusko (through commercial operators), Ku-ring-gai Chase (extensive trails, permit needed), Namadgi (eastern section).

Rock climbers find testing faces for their expert and challenging sport in several NSW parks

Liloing
Blue Mountains, Gibraltar Range, Guy Fawkes River, Morton, Werrikimbe, Wollemi.

Photography
All national parks.

Picnicking
All national parks.

Power boating
Myall Lakes.

Orienteering (approval needed)
Most national parks.

Rafting, white water (organised or small groups; advise district ranger)
Nymboida, Oxley Wild Rivers; and Kanangra-Boyd, Morton, Wollemi after heavy rains.

Rock climbing
Blue Mountains, Goulburn River, Kanangra-Boyd, Wollemi.

Skiing, cross country/downhill (notify park office of trip details)
Kosciusko.

Scuba diving
Bouddi (but illegal to take the fish; viewing only).

Snorkelling
Bouddi, Myall Lakes.

Surfing
All north and south coastal parks.

Swimming
All north and south coastal parks, Myall Lakes.

Tobogganing
Kosciusko.

Walking along coastal tracks and beaches
All coastal parks.

Water skiing
Myall Lakes.

Wildflower studies
Kinchega (spring), Kosciusko (summer).

Windsurfing
Crowdy Bay, Hat Head, Myall Lakes, Yuraygir.

Yachting
Myall Lakes.

Wildlife observation
All national parks.

A typical national park camp site, well sheltered, with basic facilities such as toilet block and barbecues

Bushwalking in the spectacular and untouched gorge country of Oxley Wild Rivers

An alternative way to experience a national park – going with the flow, by air mattress

NOTE: The boundary of all coastal national parks is the high water mark.

Rock orchids (above) do no harm to host trees, but strangler figs with their twining prop roots (right) can kill. The figs grow from seeds lodged high in other trees – blown there or carried by birds

LAMINGTON NATIONAL PARK

Lord Lamington, governor of Queensland from 1896 to 1902, visited the plateau named in his honour only once – and marked the event by shooting a koala. 'Its cries were terrible,' he was reported as saying 40 years later. Some 100 km south of Brisbane, the state's most popular park, declared in 1915 and now covering more than 20 000 ha, occupies the north-western rim and rivers dissected outer slopes of the ancient Tweed volcano.

The main access roads reach privately run holiday lodges at Binna Burra and Green Mountains. Park picnic and camping grounds adjoin Green Mountain. Walking tracks, ranging in length from 2 km to 24 km, make up a network totalling more than 160 km. Binna Burra has a short 'senses trail' with a guiding rope and Braille descriptions. Sighted people are invited to try it blindfolded. Other walks lead through varied forests to lookouts, caves, river gorges and dozens of waterfalls.

Subtropical rainforests including tall red 'cedar' and hoop pine cover most of Lamington. But above 900 metres on the McPherson Range it has the northermost stands of antarctic beech, a temperate rainforest species. There are also areas of wet eucalypt forest, and even some dry heaths surrounded by mallee eucalypts. Bird species include the spine-tailed logrunner, Australian ground thrush, Albert lyrebird and rare rufous scrub bird.

Guinea flower

Flower-like fungi help to break down leaf litter (below)

Left: Coomera Falls, 5 km south of Binna Burra, drop 64 metres

Blechnum, a water fern

South-easterly currents push a constant procession of waves on to Main Beach, which makes a straight sweep of 35 km from Point Lookout. Heaths and swamps cover a lowland strip between eroding foredunes and wooded hind dunes

BLUE LAKE NATIONAL PARK

Tenders were called in 1984 for a traffic bridge between North Stradbroke Island and the mainland just south of Brisbane – so far linked only by vehicle ferries. A park of just 500 ha around Lake Kaboora, already damaged by heavy visiting, looked likely to come under disastrous pressure from a rapid increase in sightseers and island residents. Conservationists urged the Queensland government to declare a greatly enlarged park, revoking many of the sand mining leases that cover two-thirds of the island although only about 10 per cent has been mined.

In the present park, eucalypt woodlands surround the sandy margins of a freshwater 'window' lake, where the island's raised, lens-shaped water table emerges. Popular with swimmers, it is a 2.5 km walk from the park entrance and a similar distance from the surf at Main Beach.

Water ferns and other aquatic plants spread over and round Lake Kaboora. Its waters are fresh though the surrounding sands are saline

PARKS OF THE BRISBANE REGION

FACILITIES

Cabins

Caravan park

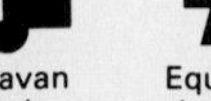
Equipped picnic area

Bush camping allowed

Lavatory building

Established campsite

Campsite but no car access

Note: Popular parks without campsites usually have public camping grounds nearby. If in doubt, call enquiries number.

PARK RATINGS No interest ✗ Some interest ✔ Major interest ✔✔ Outstanding ✔✔✔

Alton National Park

440 km W, 75 km E of St George. Darling Downs, Maranoa weather district. Moonie Highway skirts park boundary.

Smooth-barked apple, narrow-leafed ironbark and cypress pine dominate the hardy woodlands of this undeveloped 560 ha park. Sandplains rise gently to low ridges covered by heath and hummock grassland sparsely scattered with eucalypts and grass-trees. Winter and spring rains bring striking displays of wildflowers.

BEST TIME: Spring.

ENQUIRIES: (076) 35 0688.

ADDRESS: QNPWS regional office, Box 7054, Toowoomba 4352.

Scenic enjoyment ✔
Day activities ✗
Family camping ✗
Hard bushwalking ✗

Bendidee National Park

360 km SW, 45 km N of Goondiwindi. Darling Downs, Maranoa weather district. Car access off Cunningham Highway 59 km W of Inglewood. Follow signs for Bendidee State Forest.

Forest species prolific in the adjoining Bendidee State Forest intrude sparsely into the brigalow and belah scrublands of this undeveloped 930 ha park. Tea-tree, wilga and vines grow among the predominant acacias and casuarinas in an area of low rainfall. After a good soaking, however, flowering and fruiting plants attract a big bird population and their small retinue of keen birdwatchers.

BEST TIME: Spring, for wildflowers.

ENQUIRIES: (076) 61 3710.

ADDRESS: QNPWS district office, Hermitage Research Station, via Warwick 4370.

Scenic enjoyment ✔
Day activities ✗
Family camping ✗
Hard bushwalking ✗

Blackall Range National Parks

105-110 km N, 16-22 km W of Nambour. South Coast, Curtis and Moreton weather district. Car access to Mapleton Falls off Nambour-Kenilworth road 3 km W of Mapleton; to Kondalilla off Montville-Flaxton road, turning off Bruce Highway at Landsborough. Obi Obi Gorge reached on foot from Baroon Pocket road 12 km N of Maleny or from Western Ave. 1 km S of Montville.

Heavily timbered mountain parks in the Blackall Range, less than an hour's drive from Sunshine Coast beaches, preserve waterfalls and remnant rainforests in a region largely cleared for farming.

Falls on Skenes Creek in **Kondalilla National Park** (128 ha) drop 80 metres over a series of cascades into a misty valley of rainforest with piccabeen palms and distinct bunya pines. A formed 4.6 km walking trail loops around a deep pool at the base of Kondalilla Falls before climbing to lookout points with views over the creek and north to ranges around the headwaters of Mary River. The creek hosts a population of Queensland lungfish, an unusual animal sharing many of the characteristics of amphibians, including an air-breathing lung which supplements oxygen absorption by the gills in fouled or evaporating water. The lungfish is a completely protected species.

A 26 ha park surrounds the lesser cascades of **Mapleton Falls** on a tributary to the lower reaches of Obi Obi Creek. Walking trails from popular picnic grounds wander through eucalypt forest which intermingles with rainforest on sheltered, moister slopes.

A strenuous hike along a rocky creek course from Baroon Pocket leads to **Obi Obi Gorge National Park** (80 ha). Steep walls, topped with rainforest rich in epiphytic orchids and ferns, pinch the creek and quicken its flow at the Narrows.

NOTE: No facilities at Obi Obi Gorge.

WARNING: Obi Obi Creek dangerous after heavy rain.

BEST TIME: Spring, autumn.

ENQUIRIES: (071) 82 4189.

ADDRESS: QNPWS district office, Box 350, Gympie 4570.

Scenic enjoyment ✔✔✔
Day activities ✔✔✔
Family camping ✗
Hard bushwalking ✔

Blue Lake National Park

60 km E, 10 km E of Dunwich on North Stradbroke Island. South Coast, Curtis and Moreton weather district. Car access to park boundary from Dunwich. Car ferries to Dunwich from Redland Bay and Cleveland.

DESCRIPTION: Page 386.

BEST TIME: Spring, autumn.

ENQUIRIES: (07) 202 0200.

ADDRESS: QNPWS regional centre, Box 42, Kenmore 4069.

Scenic enjoyment ✔✔
Day activities ✔✔
Family camping ✗
Hard bushwalking ✗

Bunya Mountains National Park

240 km NW, 50 km S of Kingaroy. Darling Downs, Maranoa weather district. Car access off Warrego Highway at Jondaryan or Dalby.

The largest remaining natural stand of bunya pines, a species greatly depleted by early rainforest timber-getters, was preserved in this 12 000 ha park in 1908. It was Queensland's second national park and is one of the state's most popular, with easy access off a sealed through road, big picnic grounds, a kiosk and two camping areas. Walking trails form a network through the dense bunya pine and hoop pine rainforest, leading to waterfalls, gorges and lookouts over the Darling Downs.

Before European settlement of the area Aboriginal tribes gathered here to feast on the plentiful crop of nuts from the bunya pine. The nuts, about the size of a small hen's egg, grow in big cones in the tree's distinctively rounded crown. They take 2-3 years to mature and taste like chestnuts when roasted.

BEST TIME: Spring, autumn.

ENQUIRIES: (074) 68 3127.

ADDRESS: MS 501, via Dalby 4405.

Scenic enjoyment ✔✔✔
Day activities ✔✔✔
Family camping ✔✔✔
Hard bushwalking ✔✔

Burleigh Head National Park

90 km S, 15 km S of Southport. South Coast, Curtis and Moreton weather district. Car access off Pacific Highway at Burleigh Heads.

Basalt boulders line the shores below Big Burleigh, a steep headland at the entrance to Tallebudgera Creek hemmed in by intense residential and tourist development along the Gold Coast. Short nature trails loop through the 24 ha park, sampling vine forest, tall eucalypt forest, low woodland with pandanus and patches of tussock grassland.

BEST TIME: Spring, autumn.

ENQUIRIES: (075) 35 3183.

ADDRESS: 6 Peggs Road, Burleigh Heads 4220.

Scenic enjoyment ✔✔
Day activities ✔
Family camping ✗
Hard bushwalking ✗

Conondale National Park

140 km NW. South Coast, Curtis and Moreton weather district. Car access to both park sections off Conondale-Kenilworth road. Turn off Bruce Highway at Landsborough.

Tangled woody vines in tall rainforest with flooded gums, bunya pines and palms cover the mountainous slopes of this 2000 ha park. The area is an undeveloped wilderness reserve, without tracks or facilities of any kind. Visitors reach the edges of the park along rough backblock tracks, but rarely attempt the daunting trek into the dense forest undergrowth.

NOTE: Bush camping restricted in numbers and frequency.

BEST TIME: Spring.

ENQUIRIES: (071) 82 4189.

ADDRESS: Bruce Highway, Monkland, Gympie 4570.

Scenic enjoyment ✔✔
Day activities ✗
Family camping ✗
Hard bushwalking ✗

Cooloola National Park

230 km N, 65 km NE of Gympie. South Coast, Curtis and Moreton weather district. Northern section accessible from Gympie-Rainbow Beach road or from Noosa (by 4WD) via ferry and along beach. Southern section accessible by boat from Boreen Point, Elanda and Tewantin. Tours operate from Rainbow Beach as well as Noosa and Tewantin.

DESCRIPTION: Page 382. **Noosa River National Park** (469 ha) preserves an undeveloped area of forest and swamp communities on the river's southern banks downstream from Lake Cootharaba. **Mount Pinbarren National Park** (23 ha) covers a peak clothed in hoop pine rainforest in the uplands west of Cooloola, about 5 km north of Pomona. **Pipeclay National Park** (2 ha) preserves an Aboriginal ceremonial site off the Rainbow Beach road.

VISITOR CENTRE: Off Kinaba Island – boat access.

BEST TIME: Spring, autumn.

ENQUIRIES: (071) 49 7364 (southern Cooloola) or 85 3245 (Kinaba); (071) 86 3160 (northern Cooloola).

ADDRESS: QNPWS Box, Elanda, via Tewantin 4565 (s. Cooloola); QNPWS, Box 30, Rainbow Beach 4570.

Scenic enjoyment ✔✔✔
Day activities ✔✔✔
Family camping ✔✔✔
Walking, canoeing ✔

Crows Nest Falls National Park

180 km W, 50 km N of Toowoomba. Darling Downs, Maranoa weather district. Car access to northern section along unsealed road E from Crows Nest.

Perseverance Creek flows over a jumble of huge boulders on its course north from the man-made lake of Perseverance Dam. Eucalypt forest and heathland cover high ground and ridges above the creek and the glistening granite gorge of Crows Nest Falls. Tall rainforest thrives in the sheltered environment around deep pools enjoyed by swimmers. Short trails branch off a main walking track from popular picnic grounds. It takes about 2 hours to explore the northern section of this 949 ha park.

The park's undeveloped southern section, often referred to as **Perseverance National Park**, is southwest of the dam. Walkers find their own way into its forests.

BEST TIME: Autumn, spring.

ENQUIRIES: (076) 98 1296.

ADDRESS: Box 68, Crows Nest 4355.

Scenic enjoyment ✔✔
Day activities ✔✔
Family camping ✗
Hard bushwalking ✔

1. **Alton NP**
2. **Bendidee NP**
3. **Blackall Range NPs**
4. **Blue Lake NP**
5. **Bunya Mountains NP**
6. **Burleigh Head NP**
7. **Conondale NP**
8. **Cooloola NP**
9. **Crows Nest Falls NP**
10. **D'Aguilar Range NPs**
11. **Freshwater Creek NP**
12. **Girraween NP**
13. **Glass House Mountains NPs**
14. **Lake Moogerah Peaks NPs**
15. **Lamington NP**
16. **Main Range NP**
17. **Mooloolah River NP**
18. **Moreton Island NP**
19. **Mount Barney NP**
20. **Mount Mistake NP**
21. **Natural Arch NP**
22. **Noosa NP**
23. **North Coast Rail NPs**
24. **Queen Mary Falls NP**

D'Aguilar Range National Parks

30-45 km NW. South Coast, Curtis and Moreton weather district. Car access via The Gap (Mt Nebo Rd).

A steep, narrow road from Brisbane's outskirts climbs mountain slopes covered in eucalypt forest and rainforest to a string of national parks below the high peaks of D'Aguilar Range.

A walking trail through adjoining state forest links the two smallest parks, **Jolly's Lookout** (11 ha) and **Boombana** (38 ha), both popular for picnics and their sweeping views over the Samford Valley. A circuit track in Boombana passes some superb examples of red bloodwood and small-leaf fig.

Tall flooded gums dominate the rainforest of **Manorina National Park** (139 ha) on the trail to Mt Nebo Lookout.

A self-guiding nature walk in **Maiala National Park** (1140 ha) helps visitors identify trees and understand rainforest ecology. The easy circuit trail takes less than an hour and descriptive booklets are available at the start of the track. Longer walks lead along creek banks to Green's Falls, and through an impressive stand of brush cypress pines.

NOTE: Camping at Manorina.

BEST TIME: Spring, autumn.

ENQUIRIES: (07) 289 0200.

ADDRESS: C/- Post Office, Mt Nebo 4520.

Scenic enjoyment ✔✔
Day activities ✔✔✔
Family camping ✔✔
Hard bushwalking ✔

Freshwater Creek National Park

35 km N, 15 km NW of Redcliffe. South Coast, Curtis and Moreton weather district. Bruce Highway skirts the park.

An important remnant of wallum country with banksias, eucalypts and grass trees is preserved in this park of nearly 100 ha. The area is undeveloped and mainly of scientific interest as a representative sample of a vegetation type fast disappearing from southeast Queensland.

BEST TIME: Spring, autumn.

ENQUIRIES: (07) 202 0200.

ADDRESS: As for Blue Lake.

Scenic enjoyment ✔
Day activities ×
Family camping ×
Hard bushwalking ×

Girraween National Park

260 km SW, 34 km S of Stanthorpe. Darling Downs, Maranoa weather district. Car access off New England Highway 26 km S of Stanthorpe.

DESCRIPTION: Page 385.

VISITOR CENTRE: Park headquarters.

BEST TIME: Spring.

ENQUIRIES: (076) 84 5157.

ADDRESS: Wyberba, via Ballandean 4382.

Scenic enjoyment ✔✔✔
Day activities ✔✔
Family camping ✔✔✔
Hard bushwalking ✔✔✔

Glass House Mountains National Park

65 km N. South Coast, Curtis and Moreton weather district. Car access off Bruce Highway between Beerburrum and Glass House Mountains township.

Domed hills and lopsided peaks of the Glass House Mountains rise abruptly from low plains behind the Sunshine Coast. The nine tallest hills, as well as several lower prominences, mark the centres of separate volcanic eruptions around 25 million years ago. Eroded remnants of the volcanic plugs are preserved in four national parks. **Beerwah** (245 ha), **Coonowrin** (113 ha), **Ngungun** (49 ha) and **Tibrogargan** (291 ha).

Well-defined but rough and unmaintained tracks have been trodden through each of the parks and, with the exception of Mt

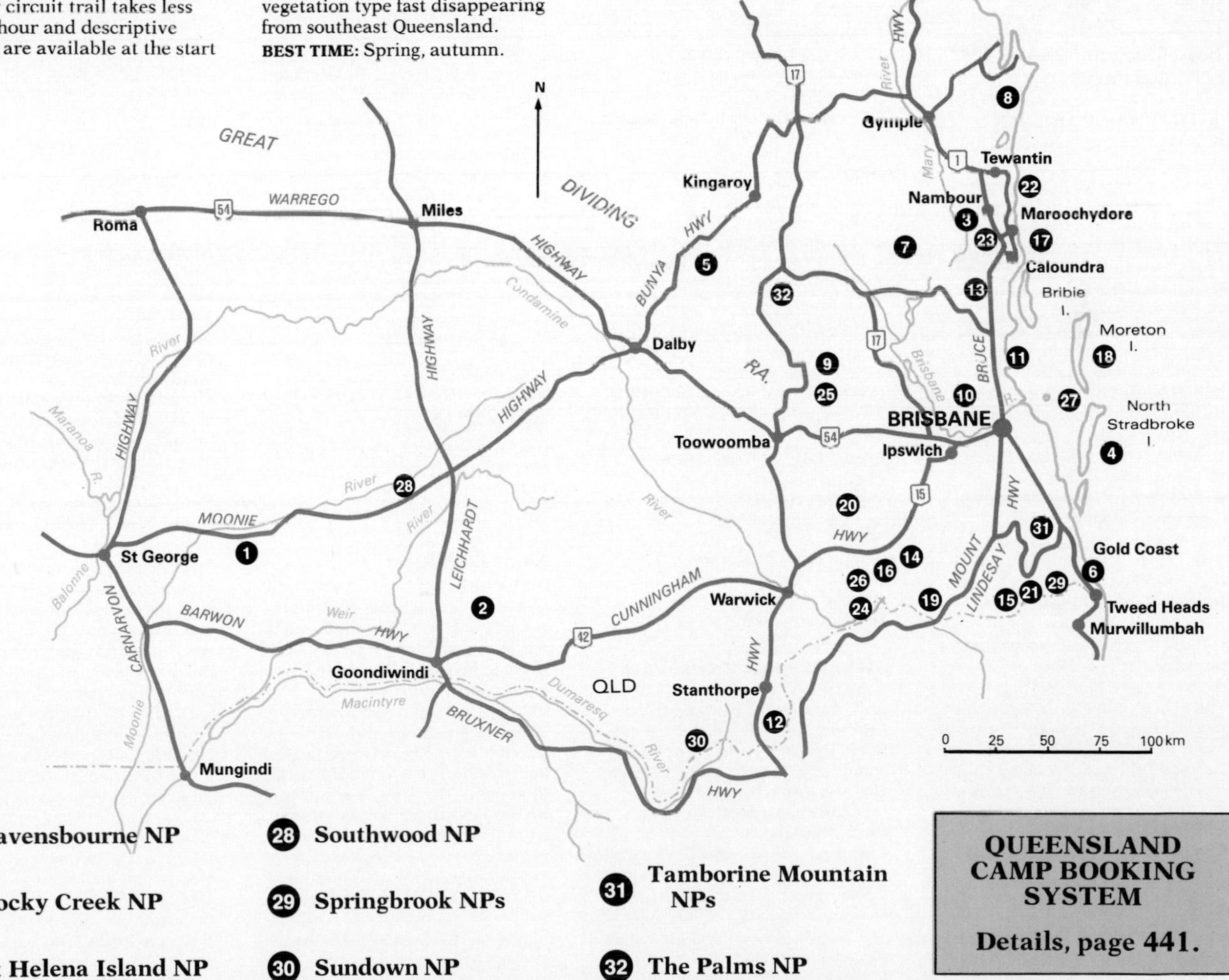

25. **Ravensbourne NP**
26. **Rocky Creek NP**
27. **St Helena Island NP**
28. **Southwood NP**
29. **Springbrook NPs**
30. **Sundown NP**
31. **Tamborine Mountain NPs**
32. **The Palms NP**

QUEENSLAND CAMP BOOKING SYSTEM

Details, page 441.

Coonowrin, the peaks can be climbed by energetic hikers prepared for some steep clambering over rocks. Mt Coonowrin (375 m) and the east face of Mt Tibrogargan (291 m) should only be attempted by experienced and well-equipped rock climbers.

Rainforest species occur in small pockets of closed forest, but eucalypt forest including ironbark, bloodwood, blackbutt and tallow wood dominates the lower slopes. Heath plants grow in areas of shallow soil on steep rocks. Ground orchids – particularly the small, white-flowered helmet orchid – are common.

NOTE: Picnic facilities at Beerwah and Tibrogargan.

BEST TIME: Spring, autumn.

ENQUIRIES: (071) 94 6630.

ADDRESS: Roy's Road, Beerwah 4519.

Scenic enjoyment ✔✔
Day activities ✔
Family Camping ×
Walking, climbing ✔✔

Lake Moogerah Peaks National Parks

110 km SW. South Coast, Curtis and Moreton weather district. Car access off Cunningham Highway via Boonah.

Rocky cliffs and peaks around Lake Moogerah dam tower over the broad expanse of Fassifern Valley and its patchwork of cultivated fields. Steep faces of sound rock fretted with narrow cracks have made the easily accessible northern peak of Mt French famous among rock climbers in Queensland. Over 150 ascent routes of varying degrees of difficulty have been established on cliffs familiarly known as Frog Buttress. On any fair weekend the climbers provide a gripping spectacle for visitors contented with easy walks through the surrounding eucalypt forest, or a drive to the lookout points in a separate section of 63 ha **Mount French National Park.**

Walking tracks have been formed and marked in two larger national parks around peaks south of Lake Moogerah. Piccabeen palms grow profusely in one of the three main gorges at **Mount Greville** (182 ha) on a spur running off the Main Range. Rocky outcrops on steep slopes break the forest cover and views from the peak reach south to the McPherson Range.

The double peaks of **Mount Moon** form a hilly mass running south from Mt Alford in the central section of Teviot Range. White mahogany, narrow-leafed ironbark, spotted gum and yellow box grow in forests covering gullies and ridges in a park of 119 ha.

The slopes of **Mount Edwards National Park** (364 ha) rise from the northern shores of Lake Moogerah. Reynolds Creek flows out of the reservoir through a wide gorge between two peaks, Mt Edwards and Little Mt Edwards, with sloping slabs of rock extending almost 1 km back from the water. To the east, bare cliff faces of this undeveloped park drop to cultivated fields lining Cunningham Highway.

NOTE: Picnic facilities at Mt French.

BEST TIME: Spring, autumn.

ENQUIRIES: (07) 202 0200.

ADDRESS: As for Blue Lake.

Scenic enjoyment ✔✔✔
Day activities ✔
Family camping ×
Climbing ✔✔✔

Lamington National Park

100 km S. South Coast, Curtis and Moreton weather district. Car access S of Pacific Highway from Beenleigh via Canungra, or from Nerang via Beechmont. Buses from Brisbane some days.

DESCRIPTION: Page 370. **Mount Chinghee National Park** (722 ha) to the west of Lamington covers undeveloped spurs, ridges and slopes of vine forest with hoop pine emerging above the high canopy. The park is reached on foot from the Lions Tourist Road south of Mt Lindesay Highway at Innisplain. **Sarabah National Park** preserves an almost pure stand of black bean trees covering 1 ha on the road from Canungra to Green Mountains.

NOTE: No bush camping within 4 km of Binna Burra or O'Reilly's lodges.

BEST TIME: Spring, autumn.

ENQUIRIES: (075) 33 3584.

ADDRESS: Via Nerang 4211.

Scenic enjoyment ✔✔✔
Day activities ✔✔✔
Family camping ✔✔✔
Hard bushwalking ✔✔✔

Main Range National Park

115 km SW. South Coast, Curtis and Moreton weather district. Cunningham Highway crosses park. Southern areas reached by rough dry-weather track between Boonah and Killarney.

Mt Mitchell and Mt Cordeaux form the steep ridges of Cunningham's Gap, a deep saddle in the Main Range which allows Cunningham Highway to run easily west towards Warwick. Walking tracks from camping and picnic grounds around the highway lead north and south to the mountain peaks through areas of rainforest, grassy eucalypt forest, heavy scrub along creek beds and rocky mountain slopes covered with grasses. A huge 'rock lily', related to the Gymea lily of NSW, grows in abundance on the most popular of the walks to Mt Cordeaux. Its branching flower spikes, up to 4 metres tall, are covered in vivid scarlet blooms in early summer. The Spicers Gap area, reached from the eastern side of the range, has a bush camp and picnic areas.

The 11 500 ha park has absorbed three formerly separate parks, **Cunningham's Gap, Jirramun** and **Mount Roberts,** in an unbroken band of mountainous terrain reaching for more than 35 km north from the NSW border.

Abundant birdlife in the park includes bellbirds, satin bowerbirds, crimson rosellas and red-tailed black cockatoos, which feed on the profuse stands of casuarinas. Tall forest around the picnic and camping grounds supports large numbers of greater gliders, which can be spotted with the help of a strong torch as they feed in the treetops at night. Brush-tailed possums also visit the camp after dusk – visitors are advised to keep food out of their reach.

Long grasses covering the steep, rocky heights of Mt Cordeaux provide cover and den sites for the brush-tailed rock wallaby – the only wallaby species in the park likely to be encountered by day. But this shy animal is rarely seen for long, preferring to retire swiftly and with great agility over seemingly impassable cliffs.

BEST TIME: Spring, autumn.

ENQUIRIES: (076) 66 1133.

ADDRESS: MS 394, Warwick 4370.

Scenic enjoyment ✔✔✔
Day activities ✔✔
Family camping ✔✔✔
Hard bushwalking ✔✔✔

Mooloolah River National Park

95 km N, 16 km SE of Nambour. South Coast, Curtis and Moreton weather district. Car access along unsealed road off Bruce Highway from Tanawha.

Muddy river shores backed by melaleuca swamps and marsh – the habitat of the rare ground parrot – flank eastern banks of the Mooloolah River in a park of 670 ha, less than 5 km upstream from the river's mouth at the resort town of Mooloolaba.

Low-lying sand flats inland from the fringing belts of melaleuca support a community of wallum banksias, low scrub and heath giving striking displays of wildflowers in spring. Light clay and sandstone ridges to the north are covered with grassy eucalypt forest. The undeveloped park preserves vegetation of a type fast disappearing from the coastal lowlands of south-eastern Queensland.

BEST TIME: Spring, for wildflowers.

ENQUIRIES: (071) 82 4189.

ADDRESS: As for Blackall Range.

Scenic enjoyment ✔
Day activities ✔
Family camping ×
Hard bushwalking ×

Moreton Island National Park

50 km NE. South Coast, Curtis and Moreton weather district. Vehicle ferries from Bulimba, Manly, Cleveland and Scarborough (roads suitable 4WD only). Passenger ferry from Hamilton or Redcliffe. Accessible by private boat.

DESCRIPTION: Page 379.

NOTE: Camping grounds outside present park boundaries.

BEST TIME: Spring, autumn.

ENQUIRIES: (075) 48 2710.

ADDRESS: C/o Tangalooma, Moreton Island 4004.

Scenic enjoyment ✔✔
Day activities ✔✔✔
Family camping ✔✔✔
Hard bushwalking ✔✔

Mount Barney National Park

130 km SW of Brisbane, 14 km NE of Woodenbong. South Coast, Curtis and Moreton weather district. Car access along unsealed road off Lindesay Highway 11 km S of Rathdowney, via Yellow Pinch camping reserve. Walking access to northern section (formerly **Mount Maroon-Mount May National Park**) off unsealed road from Maroon; turn off Lindesay Highway at Rathdowney. Permission needed to cross private property.

Bushwalkers gather at campsites around the Logan River in the foothills around Mt Barney before tackling strenuous climbs over steep sandstone ridges towards the many peaks of this 11 500 ha park. Creek courses – some strewn with huge boulders of coarse granite – are followed wherever possible, but in places rock walls tower over waterfalls and shallow rapids in gorges too narrow for safe passage.

Eucalypt forest of yellow stringybark, tallow wood, red bloodwood and narrow-leafed grey gum dominate the slopes of the mountainous block. Moist, sheltered gullies have luxuriant growth of shrubs and scramblers – including introduced lantana – and dense vine forest patches. Walking tracks, though not maintained, are well-defined by heavy use.

On the ridge crests eucalypts become more widely spaced above a sparse ground cover of grasses and herbs. Some high slopes are clothed in low scrub of banksia, acacia and leptospermum. Over 20 orchid species have been noted on drier slopes to the east of Mt Barney.

The park's southern section, formerly **Mount Lindesay National Park,** covers an isolated peak capped by a striking cliff line visible from Lindesay Highway.

NOTE: Camping facilities nearby at Yellow Pinch.

BEST TIME: Spring, autumn.

ENQUIRIES: (07) 202 0200.

ADDRESS: MS 161, Boonah 4310.

Scenic enjoyment ✔✔✔
Day activities ×
Family camping ×
Walking, climbing ✔✔✔

Mount Mistake National Park

120 km SW, 30 km S of Laidley. South Coast, Curtis and Moreton weather district. 4WD access along rough track from Allora, 26 km N of Warwick – dry weather only. Walkers' access from end of Laidley Valley Road S from Laidley or from Goomburra State Forest camping ground.

Good campsites are rare on the steep slopes of the Mt Mistake Range, a spur running off the Main Range north of Cunningham's Gap. Groups are forced to pitch tents closely together in limited space. Bushwalkers heading for the 5500 ha park's high peak take advantage of a former logging track past a dilapidated, century-old sawmill. The trail climbs through eucalypt forest before encountering the plundered rainforest patches, now thick with a tangle of nettles and lantana.

BEST TIME: Spring, autumn.

ENQUIRIES: (076) 66 1133.

ADDRESS: As for Main Range.

Scenic enjoyment ✔✔
Day activities ×
Family camping ×
Hard bushwalking ✔✔

Natural Arch National Park

110 km S, 38 km S of Nerang. South Coast, Curtis and Moreton weather district. Nerang-Murwillumbah road skirts park.

DESCRIPTION: Page 373.

NOTE: Take a torch for night walks.

VISITOR CENTRE: At park entrance.

ENQUIRIES: (075) 33 6156.

ADDRESS: Natural Arch, via Nerang 4211.

Scenic enjoyment ✔✔✔
Day activities ✔✔
Family camping ×
Hard bushwalking ×

Noosa National Park

155 km N. South Coast, Curtis and Moreton weather district. Car access off Bruce Highway to Noosa Heads.

DESCRIPTION: Page 383.

BEST TIME: Spring, autumn.

ENQUIRIES: (071) 47 3243.

ADDRESS: Park Road, Noosa Heads 4567.

Scenic enjoyment ✔✔
Day activities ✔✔
Family camping ×
Hard bushwalking ×

North Coast Rail National Parks

91-115 km N, 15 km S-5 km N of Nambour. South Coast, Curtis and Moreton weather district. Car access off Bruce Highway between Landsborough and Kulangoor.

Four parks, **Dularcha** (138 ha), **Eudlo Creek** (39 ha), **Tucker's Creek** (53 ha) and **Ferntree Creek** (20 ha) preserve bushland flanking stretches of the Brisbane-Cairns railway from Landsborough to just north of Nambour. At Dularcha the rails were torn up after the line was diverted; walkers can follow the old track to a disused tunnel burrowing through a scrub-covered hillside. Tall eucalypt forest dominates the smaller parks, which remain undeveloped – though Tucker's Creek seems destined to be surrounded by Nambour's growing suburban sprawl.

BEST TIME: Spring, autumn.

ENQUIRIES: (071) 82 4189.

ADDRESS: As for Blackall Range.

Scenic enjoyment ✔
Day activities ✔
Family camping ×
Hard bushwalking ×

Queen Mary Falls National Park

210 km SW, 10 km E of Killarney. Darling Downs, Maranoa weather district. Car access off Warwick-Legume road 4 km S of Killarney.

Headwaters of Spring Creek, a tributary of the Condamine River, churn white over a series of steep cascades before plunging vertically over the 40 metre drop of Queen Mary Falls. The sound of rushing water becomes a roar as visitors make their way along the falls pathway from roomy picnic grounds at the park entrance. Guard rails line the cliff edge walk for safe but unobstructed vantage points over the waterfall, gorge and a dense wall of rainforest thriving in the persistently moist atmosphere.

Higher though less impressive falls break the course of Blackfellow's Creek north of Queen Mary Falls. Drops of 45 and 60 metres are surrounded by vine forest with silky oak, brush box and hoop pine. This section of the national park's 340 ha is named after the distinct peak of **Blackfellow's Knob.**

BEST TIME: Spring, autumn.

ENQUIRIES: (076) 61 3710.

ADDRESS: As for Bendidee.

Scenic enjoyment ✔✔
Day activities ✔
Family camping ×
Hard bushwalking ×

Ravensbourne National Park

170 km W, 45 km NE of Toowoomba. South Coast, Curtis and Moreton weather district. Car access off Hampton-Esk road.

Tall red cedar, blackbean and rosewood, the grand prizes of early timber-getting, survive in this 100 ha park as superb examples of rainforest trees once common on the eastern Darling Downs. Walks ranging from a short self-guiding nature trail to half-day hikes wind through the rainforest, tall eucalypt forest on drier slopes and dense groves of piccabeen palms. Views of the Scenic Rim mountains sweep south from the higher of the park's two picnic grounds.

BEST TIME: Spring, autumn.

ENQUIRIES: (076) 98 1296.

ADDRESS: As for Crows Nest Falls.

Scenic enjoyment ✔✔
Day activities ✔✔
Family camping ×
Hard bushwalking ×

Rocky Creek National Park

190 km SW of Brisbane, 32 km E of Warwick. Darling Downs, Maranoa weather district. Access on foot from unsealed road east of Emu Vale; turn off Cunningham Highway for Emu Vale at Warwick. Permission needed to cross private property.

An undeveloped and infrequently visited scenic reserve of 64 ha on the narrow course of Rocky Creek preserves small patches of hoop pine rainforest in the steep gullies and gorge around a double-drop waterfall of 125 metres. Eucalypt forest tops a high plateau above the falls.

Determined hikers can continue on from Rocky Creek to **Merivale National Park,** a patch of untouched hill country covering 4 ha to the north. Scrub with silky oak and white cedar grows close to the park's small creek. Ridges to the south support forest with grey gums and acacias over a ground cover of kangaroo grass.

BEST TIME: Spring.

ENQUIRIES: (076) 61 3710.

ADDRESS: As for Bendidee.

Scenic enjoyment ✔✔
Day activities ×
Family camping ×
Hard bushwalking ×

Saint Helena Island National Park

8 km NE of Manly. South Coast, Curtis and Moreton weather district. Access restricted to organised tours from Manly wharf.

Ruins of a prison which operated from 1867 to 1932 are preserved in Queensland's first historic site national park, covering 75 ha of low, sandy St Helena Island. The prison achieved a high degree of self-sufficiency after extensive clearing for agriculture, quarrying and the construction of buildings – including a church and a morgue. Fringing mangroves and a thin belt of forest lining the eastern shores are all that remain of St Helena's natural vegetation.

BEST TIME: Spring, autumn.

ENQUIRIES: (07) 396 5113.

ADDRESS: Box 66, Manly 4179.

Scenic enjoyment ×
Day activities ✔
Family camping ×
Hard bushwalking ×

Southwood National Park

345 km W, 130 km SW of Dalby. Darling Downs, Maranoa weather district. Moonie Highway skirts park.

Fences completely surrounding this undeveloped 7100 ha park keep straying stock away from its important remnant of brigalow acacia scrubland. Wilga, belah, cypress pine, casuarinas and eucalypts are intermingled with the brigalow, and in spring wildflowers colour the low shrubs and trees. Areas of rough ground with a regular pattern of depressions up to 150 mm deep are characteristic of gilgai soil formations, attributed to clays swelling and cracking during alternate wet and dry periods.

BEST TIME: Spring for wildflowers.

ENQUIRIES: (076) 35 0688.

ADDRESS: As for Alton.

Scenic enjoyment ✔
Day activities ×
Family camping ×
Hard bushwalking ×

Springbrook National Parks

100 km S, 20 km SW of Mudgeeraba. South Coast, Curtis and Moreton weather district. Car access from Pacific Highway from Mudgeeraba.

Tallebudgera, Currumbin and Nerang Creeks, waterways which find their way out to sea along the Gold Coast, rise on the high Springbrook plateau just over 20 km inland. A chain of four national parks, **Mount Cougal** (811 ha), **Warrie** (600 ha), **Gwongorella** (534 ha) and **Wunburra** (140 ha), reaches north from the plateau's steep cliffline, supporting dense subtropical rainforest and tall eucalypt forest.

Headwaters of the streams rush through the parks, down rocky courses broken by rapids and impressive cascades including the 109 metre drop of Purling Brook Falls in Gwongorella. A deep rock pool 1 km downstream from the base of the falls is enjoyed by swimmers. Short tracks lead to lookouts over the falls and deep valleys and walks of 4-5 km strike out from picnic and camping grounds through rainforest festooned with vines and epiphytic orchids. Warrie has one walk of 17 km.

The undeveloped parks, Mt Cougal and Wunburra, provide a wilderness experience for seasoned hikers prepared for strenuous climbs through trackless bush.

NOTE: Camping facilities at Gwongorella – car park nearby.

BEST TIME: Spring, autumn.

ENQUIRIES: (075) 33 5147.

ADDRESS: Springbrook, via Mudgeeraba 4215.

Scenic enjoyment ✔✔✔
Day activities ✔✔✔
Family camping ✔✔
Hard bushwalking ✔

Sundown National Park

305 km SW, 85 km SW of Stanthorpe. Darling Downs, Maranoa weather district. Car access in dry conditions off Stanthorpe-Glenlyon road 15 km S of Texas turnoff. 4WD access into park's northern section W from New England Highway at Ballandean.

The Severn River deeply dissects this 6700 ha park on the western edge of Queensland's granite belt with a broad gorge stretching almost 10 km along its meandering course. Waters noted for their clarity are bordered by high cliffs on the outer course of river bends and densely vegetated overflow flats on the short inner curve. Reeds grow profusely in scattered patches along quieter reaches. Forests of cypress pine and eucalypts and wide rocky outcrops cover steep gorge slopes.

Moderate rainfall and rocky soils support woodlands with dense understoreys in most of the park, though patches of vine scrub grow in deeper gorges. Small populations of superb lyrebirds and scrub turkeys occur.

Hikers find their own way along the Severn's banks for extended walks over easy terrain, with many deeper spots in the river suitable for swimming.

BEST TIME: Spring, autumn.

ENQUIRIES: (067) 37 5235.

ADDRESS: Via Stanthorpe 4380.

Scenic enjoyment ✔✔✔
Day activities ✔
Family camping ✔
Hard bushwalking ✔✔

Tamborine Mountain National Parks

75 km S. South Coast, Curtis and Moreton weather district. Car access S of Beenleigh off Tamborine Village-Oxenford road.

DESCRIPTION: Page 374. The Tamborine parks cover plots of less than 20 ha at **Panorama Point, Macrozamia Grove** and **MacDonald Park. Joalah** is a 40 ha park, **The Knoll** 85 ha, **Palm Grove** 118 ha, **Witches Falls** 130 ha, and the largest of the group embraces 230 ha at **Cedar Creek.**

NOTE: No picnic facilities at Joalah or Macrozamia Grove.

BEST TIME: Spring for wildflowers, autumn.

ENQUIRIES: (075) 45 1171.

ADDRESS: C/o P.O., Tamborine North 4272.

Scenic enjoyment ✔✔✔
Day activities ✔✔
Family camping ×
Hard bushwalking ×

The Palms National Park

230 km NW, 8 km NE of Cooyar. Darling Downs, Maranoa weather district. Car access off New England Highway from Cooyar.

A dense grove of tall, slim-trunked piccabeen palms encloses a 500 metre nature trail through this 12 ha park. Tree ferns are intermingled with the palms, and towards outer edges of the grove more complex rainforest develops.

BEST TIME: Spring, autumn.

ENQUIRIES: (076) 98 1296.

ADDRESS: As for Crows Nest Falls.

Scenic enjoyment ✔
Day activities ✔
Family camping ×
Hard bushwalking ×

Swirling tidal action erodes a wave-cut volcanic shelf at One Tree Rocks – one of only four outcrops in a huge island of sand. Right: Waterlilies deck a brackish lagoon

FRASER ISLAND

Sediments eroded from the Great Dividing Range, then pulled by longshore currents from beaches as far south as Sydney, have accumulated in the world's biggest sand island, 120 km long and up to 22 km wide. Fraser Island's only anchors of rock are three tiny volcanic outcrops at Orchid Point, in the northeast, and one on the west coast. All the rest is sand, piling to more than 200 metres above sea level and reaching down 60 metres to the continental shelf. Nutrient salts in sea spray have fostered the germination of windborne spores and seeds carried from the mainland by birds, giving many valleys between the island's high dune ridges a deep covering of humus that supports tall rainforests. Rain soaking into the sand is held above sea level in a water table that appears at the sides of the island in gushing streams or fluctuating 'window' lakes. There are also perched lakes – rain traps with cemented beds – high among the inland dunes.

The natural balance of Fraser Island's fragile sand environment is easily disturbed; without careful management its attractions could be destroyed. It was to protect these that Fraser was declared a Recreation Area, with a board to co-ordinate policies for management and recreation. QNPWS and the Department of Forestry look after day-to-day management.

Wedding bush

Fine sands border Lake McKenzie, north of Central Station in a state forest area. Fraser Island has the world's greatest concentration of perched lakes – rain traps formed well above sea level when vegetable matter and minerals combine to cement depressions among the high dunes

Plants compete in a rainforest pocket at the junction of Hell Hole and Violet Gorges

A kookaburra spies out for reptile prey above Carnarvon Creek, lined with cabbage-tree palms and casuarinas

Left: Beyond the eroding sandstone cliffs of the main gorge, seen from Boolimba Bluff lookout, a capping of basalt soils supports forests. Trees flowering in the foreground are cassinias

CARNARVON NATIONAL PARK

Carnarvon Creek cuts a 30 km gorge through outcropping sandstone, between eroded white walls that sometimes rise more than 200 metres. Tributaries feed in from narrow side chasms, dark and choked with ferns and mosses. Tall eucalypts, casuarinas, wattles, palms and cycads flourish in the main gorge, beside a waterway that has never been known to dry. The Carnarvon Range is part of Queensland's central belt of uptilted sandstone, through which rainwater seeps into the Great Artesian Basin.

A network of walking tracks, covering about 20 km, takes visitors from a downstream camping ground to all points of scenic interest – the gorge is crossed no fewer than 18 times, and a full-length return trip takes a day. Highlights such as the Moss Gardens, the Amphitheatre, Ward's Canyon and the Art Gallery take half a day. The Art Gallery is the most accessible of many caves with fine examples of Aboriginal rock painting and stencilling. Many parts of the creek are suitable for swimming.

Carnarvon Gorge is the most popular section of the 223 000 ha park and has facilities for visitors. The Mt Moffatt, Salvator Rosa and Ka Ka Mundi sections are rugged and isolated, and call for bushwalking experience.

Native hibiscus

Galeola on spotted gum

PARKS OF THE ROCKHAMPTON REGION

FACILITIES

Cabins

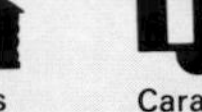
Caravan park

Equipped picnic area

Bush camping allowed

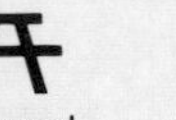
Lavatory building

Established campsite

Campsite but no car access

Note: Popular parks without campsites usually have public camping grounds nearby. If in doubt, call enquiries number.

PARK RATINGS No interest ✘ Some interest ✔ Major interest ✔✔ Outstanding ✔✔✔

Auburn River National Park

385 km S, 42 km SW of Mundubbera. South Coast, Curtis and Moreton weather district. Car access off Burnett Highway at Mundubbera via Durong and Hawkwood roads (part unsealed, some creeks flood).

Woodlands of a 400 ha park are bisected by the Auburn River, flowing over pink granite boulders in a series of cascades and rock pools. Two short walking trails in the area of the falls lead to a lookout and to the riverbank. Care should be taken when walking in the rocky creek bed.

NOTE: Take drinking water.
BEST TIME: All year.
ENQUIRIES: (071) 22 2455.
ADDRESS: QNPWS district office, Box 101, Maryborough 4650.

Scenic enjoyment ✔
Day activities ✔
Family camping ✔
Hard bushwalking ✘

Blackdown Tableland National Park

160 km W, 55 km SE of Blackwater. Central Highlands and Central West weather district. Car access from Capricorn Highway 11 km W of Dingo (forestry road – gravel, unsuitable for caravans). Permit needed from QNPWS in Rockhampton or at Blackdown Tableland. Access may be restricted in wet weather or in high fire risk periods.

A two-part park of nearly 24 000 ha occupies an undulating sandstone plateau 800-950 metres above sea level – generally 15°C cooler than the surrounding plains. Tall, dense forest covers the plateau, cut by Mimosa Creek and its many tributaries into rugged gorges. Waterfalls drop into pools fringed with cabbage-tree palms, tree-ferns and many other ferns. Lilly-pillies grow along some creeks, and the cliffs and sandstone outcrops support elkhorns and orchids. Isolated by cliffs up to 600 metres high, the tableland has many species of animals and plants that are found nowhere else. They include a trapdoor spider, a Christmas beetle, a lizard, a macrozamia cycad, a callistemon tree, a wattle and a stringbark.

Walking tracks cover about 20 km. Climbing is not advised – the cliff edges can crumble. Several streams run throughout the year, providing pools in which walkers can cool off.

NOTES: Campers need containers to carry water from creek. Boil water for drinking.
WARNING: Area subject to fog in wet weather, heavy frosts in winter.
BEST TIME: Spring, autumn.
ENQUIRIES: (079) 27 6511.
ADDRESS: Via Dingo 4702.

Scenic enjoyment ✔✔✔
Day activities ✔✔
Family camping ✔✔✔
Hard bushwalking ✔✔✔

Cania Gorge National Park

250 km S, 100 km SE of Biloela. South Coast, Curtis and Moreton weather district. Car access off Burnett Highway 13 km NW of Monto, then 13 km along Moonford Road.

DESCRIPTION: Page 406.
NOTE: Take water – tank in gorge picnic area may be empty.
BEST TIME: Spring and autumn.
ENQUIRIES: (071) 22 2455.
ADDRESS: As for Auburn River.

Scenic enjoyment ✔✔
Day activities ✔✔
Family camping ✘
Hard bushwalking ✔

Cape Palmerston National Park

275 km N. Central Coast, Burdekin and Isaacs weather district. 4WD access from Bruce Highway at Ilbilbie, 45 km SE of Sarina.

Diverse landforms and vegetation in this 7000 ha park include Ince Bay on the northern side of the cape, with mangroves and salt pans, a range of hills with patches of vine forest and groves of palms, and a long, sandy beach facing Temple Island.

Between Cape Palmerston and Mt Funnel, a distinctively shaped volcanic plug, are expanses of gilgai ground, difficult to drive or even walk over. High rainfall and alternate wetting and drying of the soil causes areas of ground a metre or so across to rise up some 15 cm.

Freshwater lagoons, attracting many birds, are within easy walking distance of 4WD tracks. Burdekin duck – unusual this far south – may be seen. They are identified by white head and neck and a chestnut band around the breast.

BEST TIME: Winter (access difficult at other times).
ENQUIRIES: (079) 57 6292.
ADDRESS: QNWPS district office, Box 623, Mackay 4740.

Scenic enjoyment ✔✔
Day activities ✘
Family camping ✘
Hard bushwalking ✔✔

Carnarvon National Park

460 km SW. Central Highlands weather district. Car access to Carnarvon Gorge section off Carnarvon Developmental Road via Consuelo road 20 km S of Rolleston (unsealed – may be impassable after heavy rains). 4WD access to Mt Moffat section from Injune via Womblebank station; to Salvator Rosa section from Dawson Developmental Road through Cungelella station (inform station owners); to Ka Ka Mundi section from Dawson Developmental Road via Yandaburra station (unformed road).

DESCRIPTION: Page 401.
NOTES: Gas cooking only at gorge camp. Carry water on longer walks.
WARNING: Salvator Rosa and Mt Moffatt subject to heavy frosts in winter.
BEST TIME: Carnarvon Gorge and Ka Ka Mundi, April to October; Salvator Rosa and Mt Moffatt, April-May or September.
ENQUIRIES: (079) 82 2246.
ADDRESS: Carnarvon Gorge via Rolleston 4702; Mt Moffatt via Mitchell 4465; Salvator Rosa and Ka Ka Mundi sections c/o P.O., Springsure 4722.

Scenic enjoyment ✔✔✔
Day activities ✔✔
Family camping ✔✔✔
Hard bushwalking ✔✔✔

Castletower National Park

155 km SE. South Coast, Curtis and Moreton weather district. Car access from Bruce Highway at Iveragh siding, 30 km S of Gladstone (dirt road).

A steep granite outcrop juts from hilly woodlands of ironbark and bloodwood, cut by the headwaters of four creeks. Difficulty of access has meant the park of nearly 5000 ha is undeveloped, but it offers a challenge to experienced bushwalkers and those with a good enough head for heights to make their way up the 550 m peak.

NOTES: Campers should take water. Walkers should wear sturdy shoes and long trousers because of speargrass.
BEST TIME: Autumn to spring.
ENQUIRIES: (079) 76 1621.
ADDRESS: QNPWS district office, Roseberry Street, Box 315, Gladstone 4680.

Scenic enjoyment ✔✔
Day activities ✘
Family camping ✘
Walking, climbing ✔

Coalstoun Lakes National Park

360 km S, 45 km E of Gayndah. South Coast, Curtis and Moreton weather district. 4WD or foot access (3 km) from Isis Highway at Coalstoun Lakes township.

Mt LeBrun, a volcanic cone standing 200 metres above surrounding farmlands, contains two connecting craters that hold water after rain. The lakes and their margins of vine forest are protected in a park of 26 ha.

The volcano was active until about 50 000 years ago. Pumice is found at the lake edges, along with basalt fragments and volcanic 'bombs' – solidified lumps of ejected lava.

BEST TIME: Year-round.
ENQUIRIES: (071) 22 2455.
ADDRESS: As for Auburn River.

Scenic enjoyment ✔
Day activities ✘
Family camping ✘
Hard bushwalking ✘

Dipperu National Park

330 km NW. Central Coast, Burdekin and Isaacs weather district. Car access by good gravel road from Peak Downs Highway, 106 km SW of Mackay.

Numerous permanent lagoons attract a great variety of birds, making the 11 000 ha park of special interest to naturalists. Among larger waterfowl, royal spoonbills, strawnecked ibis, jabirus and brolgas may be seen. Plains covered with brigalow and belah scrubs are home to grey kangaroos, swamp and black-striped wallabies, northern native 'cats' and rufous rat-kangaroos. Walking cross-country is easy, and the lagoons provide water for bush campers. But after the summer rains the main watercourse, Bee Creek, spreads to as much as 16 km wide.

BEST TIME: Spring.
ENQUIRIES: (079) 57 6292.
ADDRESS: As for Cape Palmerston.

Scenic enjoyment ✔
Day activities ✘
Family camping ✘
Hard bushwalking ✘

Epping Forest National Park

520 km NW, 150 km NW of Clermont. Central Highlands and Central West weather district.

NO PUBLIC ACCESS

Only scientists with official permission may visit this area of more than 2600 ha reserved to protect the sole colony of the Queensland hairy-nosed wombat. Grassy woodlands have well-drained sandy soils – ideal for the wombats' complex burrow systems.

ENQUIRIES: (079) 27 6511.
ADDRESS: As for Fitzroy Caves.

Eurimbula National Park

220 km SE. South Coast, Curtis and Moreton weather district. 4WD access off Miriam Vale-Seventeen Seventy road – permit needed from QNPWS in Gladstone. Impassable after heavy rain. Boat access from Seventeen Seventy.

Beaches, creeks, swamps, estuaries and sand dunes support an array of tropical and subtropical vegetation. Coastal forests of eucalypts and melaleucas give way to wallum heaths dominated by banksias. Moreton Bay ash is prominent in tall inland forests with understoreys of cabbage-tree palms. Vine thickets and patches of hoop pine rainforest occur on sandy soils, with piccabeen palms in the wetter tracts of rainforest. The 7830 ha park rises no more than a few metres above sea level.

James Cook made his second Australian landing to the south at Bustard Bay and climbed Round Hill Head, on which the town of Seventeen Seventy now stands. Nearby is **Round Hill National Park,** an area of some 300 ha with similar hoop pine rainforest. 4WD vehicle needed.

NOTES: Take water – creeks are tidal.
BEST TIME: Autumn to spring.
ENQUIRIES: (079) 76 1621.

ADDRESS: As for Castletower.

Scenic enjoyment ✔✔
Day activities ✖
Family camping ✖
Hard bushwalking ✖

Fitzroy Caves National Park
22 km N. Central Coast, Burdekin and Isaacs weather district. Car or foot access by 2 km of dirt road from The Caves township on Bruce Highway.
DESCRIPTION: Page 407.
BEST TIME: Autumn to spring.
ENQUIRIES: (079) 27 6511.
ADDRESS: QNPWS regional centre, Box 1395, Rockhampton 4700.

Scenic enjoyment ✔
Day activities ✔
Family camping ✖
Hard bushwalking ✖

Great Sandy National Park
410 km SE, 70 km NE of Maryborough. South Coast, Curtis and Moreton weather district. Vehicular barge services from Urangan and River Heads to Urang Creek, Moon Point and Woralie Road, from River Heads to Woongoolbuer Road and Balarragan; from Inskip Point to Hook Point in S of island. Island tracks 4WD only – often impassable.
DESCRIPTION: Page 399. Between Fraser Island and the mainland off Urangan, **Woody and Little Woody Islands** (660 ha) form another national park. Accessible by boat, these rocky islands are covered in eucalypt forest with some mangrove flats. Bush camping allowed on Woody Island (no facilities – take water) but not on Little Woody Island.
NOTE: Camping and vehicle access permits required. Fees apply. Take gas stove.
BEST TIME: May to October.
ENQUIRIES: (071) 86 3160 (Fraser Island); (071) 22 2455 (Woody and Little Woody Islands).
ADDRESS: QNPWS, Box 30, Rainbow Beach 4570 (for Fraser Island); as for Auburn River (Woody and Little Woody Islands).

Scenic enjoyment ✔✔✔
Day activities ✔✔
Family camping ✔✔✔
Hard bushwalking ✔✔

1 **Auburn River NP**
2 **Blackdown Tableland NP**
3 **Cania Gorge NP**
4 **Cape Palmerston NP**
5 **Carnarvon NP**
6 **Castletower NP**
7 **Coalstoun Lakes NP**
8 **Dipperu NP**
9 **Epping Forest NP**
10 **Eurimbula NP**
11 **Fitzroy Caves NP**
12 **Great Sandy NP**
13 **Heron Island NP**
14 **Isla Gorge NP**
15 **Keppel Islands NPs**
16 **Kroombit Tops NP**
17 **Litabella NP**
18 **Lonesome NP**
19 **Mazeppa NP**
20 **Mount Bauple NP**
21 **Mount Colosseum NP**
22 **Mount Jim Crow NP**
23 **Mount Walsh NP**
24 **Northumberland Islands NPs**
25 **Peak Range NP**
26 **Robinson Gorge NP**
27 **Simpson Desert NP**
28 **Snake Range NP**
29 **West Hill NP**
30 **Woodgate NP**
31 **Yeppoon NPs**

QUEENSLAND CAMP BOOKING SYSTEM

Details, page 441.

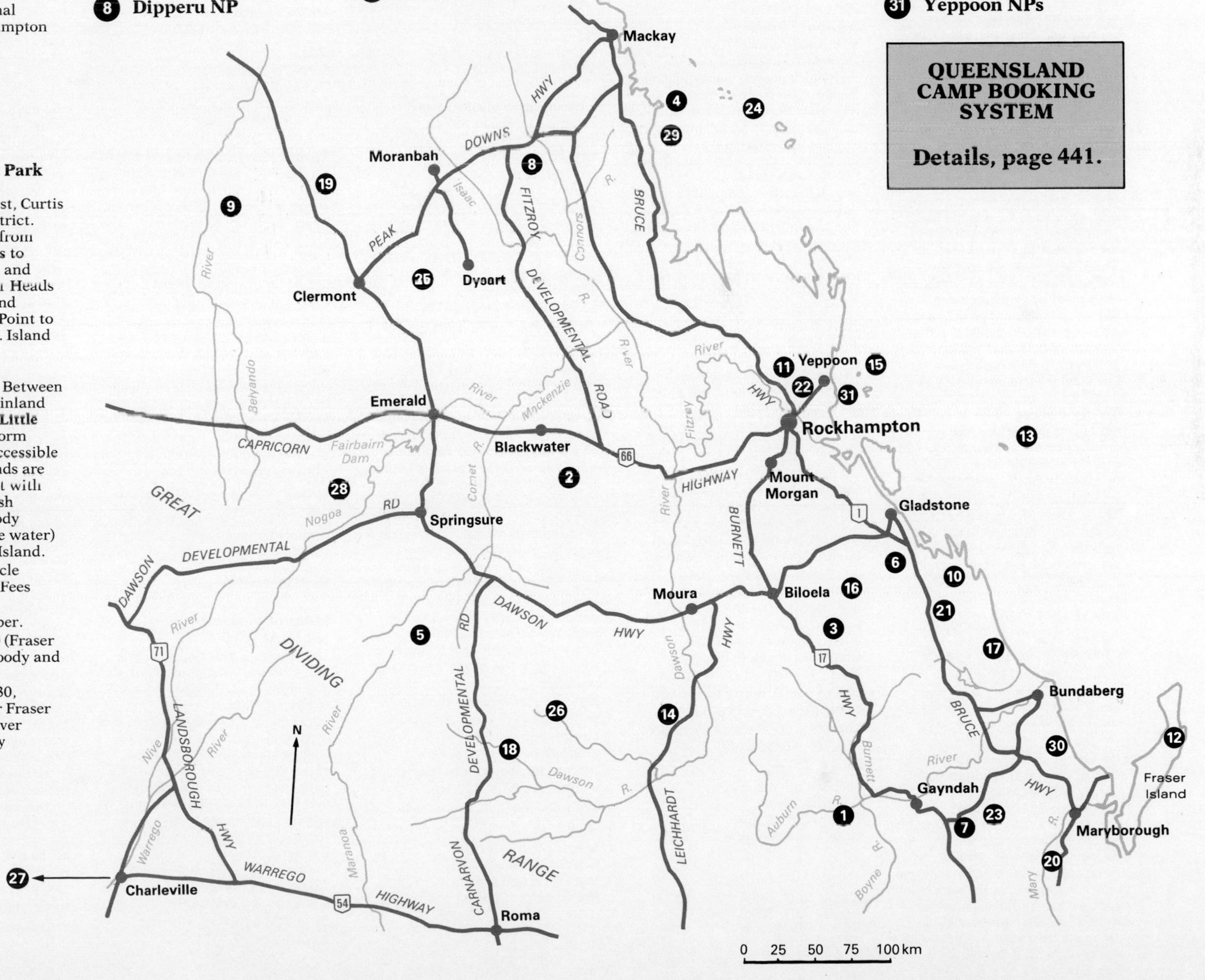

0 25 50 75 100 km

PARKS OF THE ROCKHAMPTON REGION

Heron Island National Park
140 km E, 70 km NE of Gladstone. Central Coast, Burdekin and Isaacs weather district. Helicopter flights from Gladstone daily; launch service six days a week.

A cay of coral debris, 17 ha in area, perches on part of an extensive reef. The national park preserves two-thirds of the cay, sharing it with a tourist resort and marine research station. Casuarina, pandanus and tournefortia trees flourish although the annual rainfall averages only about 500 mm. Inland are dense thickets of pisonia – sometimes called the bird-killing tree. It produces sticky seeds from which nesting noddy terns often cannot free themselves. Three turtle species, the greenback, hawksbill and loggerhead, migrate to lay their eggs in the beach sands.

Most recent of the islands of the Capricorn group to become a national park is **Wilson Island,** a sand and shingle cay of 2 ha some 15 km north of Heron Island. It is a breeding ground for roseate and black-naped terns. Other nearby park islands are **Erskine** (2 ha), **North West** and **Wreck** (111 ha) and **Tyron** (6 ha).

Three islands of the Bunker group, **Hoskyn** (8 ha), **Fairfax** (16 ha) and **Lady Musgrave** (20 ha), are national parks with special scientific status. During the nesting season of the brown gannet, from September to February, these islands may not be visited. At other times they are ideal for reef diving and snorkelling. Lady Musgrave Island's lagoon, within a horseshoe reef, offers a particularly safe anchorage.

NOTES: Camping is permitted only on Lady Musgrave Island (except September-February; no facilities), North West Island (minimal facilities) and Tryon Island (no facilities; limit 30 campers).
BEST TIME: Autumn to spring.
ENQUIRIES: (079) 27 6511.
ADDRESS: As for Fitzroy caves.
Scenic enjoyment ✔✔✔
Day activities ✔✔
Family camping ✖
Hard bushwalking ✖

Isla Gorge National Park
285 km S. Central Highlands and Central West weather district. Foot access off Leichhardt Highway 30 km S of Theodore.

Steep cliffs dropping to Isla Creek can be viewed from a lookout 1.5km from the main road along a rough track. Below are caves, arches and overhangs of sandstone, rewarding walkers who make the descent with a rich variety of forms and colours. Elsewhere the 7800 ha park is sparsely vegetated with eucalypt forest, some brigalow and bottle trees.

NOTES: Campers in park should take water.
WARNING: Cliff edges may crumble.
BEST TIME: Spring and autumn.
ENQUIRIES: (079) 27 6511.
ADDRESS: QNPWS district office, Box 175, Taroom 4420.
Scenic enjoyment ✔
Day activities ✔✔
Family camping ✖
Hard bushwalking ✔

Keppel Islands National Parks
60 km NE. Central Coast, Burdekin and Isaacs weather district. Launches servicing Great Keppel Island resort from Rosslyn Bay, near Yeppoon, leave campers on other islands by arrangement.

Eighteen continental islands – the peaks of coastal ranges when the sea level was lower – are grouped within 20 km of the two largest, Great and North Keppel. The bay in which they lie offers safe anchorages and calm waters over white sand, making them ideal for swimming or snorkelling. Pandanus and casuarinas behind the beaches yield to open woodland with poplar gums, bloodwoods, ironbarks and scented gums.

Rising to 130 metres, **North Keppel Island,** a national park of 580 ha, is the largest and highest of the 11 island-parks, the others being **Corroboree Island** (20 ha), **Sloping Island** (8 ha), **Miall Island** (40 ha), **Barren Island** (81 ha), **Middle Island** (65 ha), **Halfway Island** (8 ha), **Humpy Island** (65 ha), **Pelican Island** (8 ha), **Divided Island** (8 ha), and **Peak Island** (28 ha). Middle Island has an underwater observatory.

NOTES: North Keppel picnic area has water but campers should take their own. No water on all other islands except Humpy, which has developed campsite. Take gas stove when camping.
BEST TIME: Autumn to spring.
ENQUIRIES: (079) 27 6511.
ADDRESS: QNPWS district office, Box 770, Yeppoon 4703.
Scenic enjoyment ✔✔
Day activities ✔
Family camping ✔✔
Hard bushwalking ✖

Kroombit Tops National Park
170 km S, 60 km SW of Calliope. South Coast, Curtis and Moreton weather district. Difficult foot access from forestry road off Calliope-Monto road at Diglum Creek (obtain permit from Forestry Department at Monto).

Cliffs of the Calliope Range, up to 100 metres high, overlook a park of 450 ha. It preserves a remnant of hoop pine rainforest on rough terrain, with small waterfalls fringed by ferns and palms.

BEST TIME: Spring, winter.
ENQUIRIES: (079) 76 1621.
ADDRESS: As for Castletower.
Scenic enjoyment ✔
Day activities ✖
Family camping ✖
Walking, climbing ✔

Littabella National Park
230 km SE, 40 km NW of Bundaberg. South Coast, Curtis and Moreton weather district.
NO PUBLIC ACCESS.

Private property surrounds 2400 ha of flat heathlands bordered by a freshwater lagoon and close to a state forest. It is an important refuge for wildlife – particularly birds – and managed as a scientific area.

ENQUIRIES: (071) 22 2455.
ADDRESS: As for Auburn River.

Lonesome National Park
440 km SW via Duaringa, 510 km via Biloela. Central Highlands weather district. Car access off Carnarvon Developmental Road 85 km S of Rolleston. Arcadia Valley Road (gravel) crosses park. Rock outcrops – unsuitable for caravans. Creek crossings may flood.

Behind broken cliffs 200 metres high, looming over the Dawson River, sandstone plateaux and ridges are wooded with eucalypts and brigalow. A lookout gives panoramic views of the 3370 ha park and the Arcadia Valley. Aptly named, the park is home to many species of kangaroos and wallabies.

NOTE: No water at picnic area.
WARNING: Cliff faces unstable – climbing should not be attempted.
BEST TIME: Autumn to spring.
ENQUIRIES: (079) 82 2246.
ADDRESS: As for Carnarvon Gorge.
Scenic enjoyment ✔✔
Day activities ✔
Family camping ✖
Hard bushwalking ✖

Mazeppa National Park
445 km NW, 75 km N of Clermont. Central Highlands and Central West weather district. Gregory Developmental Road passes boundary.

A flat 4000 ha expanse of undeveloped scrubland, set aside for scientific study, slopes gently westward to Mazeppa Creek. The scrub contains brigalow, wilga and sandalwood, but it is dominated by gidgee – a low, weeping acacia also known as stinking wattle because of the unpleasant odour it gives off at the approach of rain.

BEST TIME: Autumn, spring.
ENQUIRIES: (079) 82 2246.
ADDRESS: QNPWS district office, Box 906, Emerald 4720.
Scenic enjoyment ✔
Day activities ✖
Family camping ✖
Hard bushwalking ✖

Mount Bauple National Park
420 km S, 35 km S of Maryborough. South Coast, Curtis and Moreton weather district. Car access from Bruce Highway 32 km S of Maryborough via 2 km of rough road.

Early confusion over placenames has left the present Mt Bauple some 2 km away. It is Mt Guyra (138 metres) that dominates a park of 540 ha, its slopes covered with eucalypts, vine thickets and some hoop pine rainforest. Rugged sections pose a challenge to rock scramblers but the dense forest on steep slopes makes walking difficult.

BEST TIME: Year-round.
ENQUIRIES: (071) 22 2455.
ADDRESS: As for Auburn River.
Scenic enjoyment ✔
Day activities ✖
Family camping ✖
Hard bushwalking ✔

Mount Colosseum National Park
180 km SE. South Coast, Curtis and Moreton weather district. Car access off Bruce Highway 8 km S of Miriam Vale.

Curving spurs on the eastern face of Mt Colosseum (489 metres) suggest the walls of a Roman arena. Steep slopes in the 840 ha park are forested with eucalypts and vine thickets. The summit, reached with some rock scrambling, gives views out to the Barrier Reef islands of the Capricorn and Bunker groups.

NOTE: Campers should take water – streams are seasonal.
BEST TIME: Spring, autumn.
ENQUIRIES: (079) 74 5238.
ADDRESS: As for Castletower.

Scenic enjoyment ✔✔
Day activities ✖
Family camping ✖
Hard bushwalking ✖

Mount Jim Crow National Park
30 km NE. Central Coast, Burdekin and Isaacs weather district. Rockhampton-Yeppoon road passes park.

Rising 218 metres above the surrounding countryside, the volcanic plug of Jim Crow forms a conspicuous landmark. The higher slopes and the crest have few trees except for some hoop pines. Farther down, Moreton Bay figs are found among vine scrub. The flat to rolling ground of the rest of the 144 ha park supports mixed eucalypts. In the southwest the park is bordered by a creek which forms pools covered with waterlilies.

A track of sorts climbs to the summit, but the scrambling ascent calls for skill and fitness.

BEST TIME: Year-round.
ENQUIRIES: (079) 27 6511.
ADDRESS: As for Keppel Islands.
Scenic enjoyment ✔
Day activities ✖
Family camping ✖
Hard bushwalking ✖

Mount Walsh National Park
350 km S. South Coast, Curtis and Moreton weather district. Access on foot through private property for 1 km from the end of Rifle Range Road, off Biggenden-Maryborough road 7 km S of Biggenden (enquire before crossing range).

Eucalypt forest covers most of a hill park of 3000 ha, with vine scrub and hoop pine on the lower eastern slopes. Mountain heaths and mallee eucalypts grow near the 645 metre summit.

The peak is best suited to rock climbing, but with determination an experienced bushwalker can find a route among tumbled boulders and up gullies to the summit. About 6 hours are needed for the return trip. A creek on the west side of the mountain forms a deep swimming pool.

Fairlies Knob National Park preserves 40 ha of low rainforest on difficult terrain in the Sea View Range NE of Mount Walsh. Access is on foot up a steep track off an unsealed road from Aramara.

NOTE: Take water when camping.
BEST TIME: Year-round.
ENQUIRIES: (071) 22 2245.

ADDRESS: As for Auburn River.

Scenic enjoyment ✔
Day activities ×
Family camping ×
Walking, climbing ✔

Northumberland Islands National Parks

150-250 km N. Central Coast, Burdekin and Isaacs weather district. Island waters accessible by boat from Mackay, but not all parks have safe landing sites.

Rocky national parks in the Northumberland chain lie undisturbed except for the infrequent visits of holidaying boat owners. Some offer safe harbour off sheltered, beach-lined bays, but many present an inaccessible cliff face, or have only the poorest of anchorage.

Slopes rise steeply from predominantly rocky shores to a height of 327 metres on **Prudhoe Island** (518 ha), largest in the chain and closest to Mackay. Soils are stony with vegetation limited to tussock grassland and poorly developed vine scrub, though some hoop pines stand out. A reef-bound beach and camping ground line the island's western coast.

Flat, stony kangaroo grassland stretches between beaches on the northeastern and western shores of **Digby Island** (154 ha), largest in the Beverley group, south of Prudhoe. Boats have fair shelter here as long as seas are not too rough. Anchorage and landing sites are poor or non-existing on the group's smaller islands: **Renou** (16 ha), **Minster** (105 ha), **Beverlac** (26 ha), **Hull** (26 ha), **Still** (8 ha), **Henderson** (53 ha), **Noel** (129 ha), **Keelan** (26 ha) and **Penn** (5 ha). Grasslands, scrub thickets, stunted eucalypts and patches of rainforest sparsely vegetate these rocky outcrops.

Bloodwoods, Moreton Bay ash and tea-tree cover **Curlew Island,** largest in the Guardfish cluster of six national park islands with a total area of 708 ha. The rocky outcrops of **Hirst, Treble, Bluff, Wallace** and **Dinner Islands** make up the rest of the group.

Two national park islands in the Percy group provide a safe haven for boats towards their sheltered northwestern shores. Stunted eucalypts dominate the sparse vegetation on **North East Island** (308 ha). Eucalypt forest and some hoop pine grow on **South Island** (1619 ha), where a lagoon surrounded by swampland provides breeding habitats for waterbirds.

Wild Duck Island National Park (207 ha), in the North Point Isles group southwest of the Northumberlands, is one of the two known flatback turtle rookeries in eastern Australia.

BEST TIME: Spring, autumn.
ENQUIRIES: (079) 57 6292.
ADDRESS: As for Cape Palmerston.

Scenic enjoyment ✔✔
Day activities ×
Family camping ×
Hard bushwalking ×

Peak Range National Park

400 km NW. Central Highlands and Central West weather district. Car access to Gemini Mountains and Wolfang Peak sections beside Peak Downs Highway about 40 km NE of Clermont; unsealed roads towards Eastern Peak section from 10 km S of Clermont.

Volcanic plugs in what the explorer Ludwig Leichhardt called the Peak Range – part of the Denham Range – are reserved in a fragmented new park covering a total area of nearly 1750 ha. It includes the Gemini Mountains, Castor and Pollux, rising to 678 metres on the western side of the Peak Downs Highway, Wolfang Peak about 10 km south on the other side of the highway, and Eastern Peak, well to the southeast and difficult to reach. The roadside peaks jut abruptly from sparsely wooded grasslands. Climbing involves some rock scrambling – sturdy footwear is needed.

BEST TIME: Autumn.
ENQUIRIES: (079) 27 6511.
ADDRESS: As for Mazeppa.

Scenic enjoyment ✔
Day activities ×
Family camping ×
Walking, climbing ✔

Robinson Gorge National Park

445 km SW. Central Highlands and Central West weather district. 4WD access off Leichhardt Highway 9 km N of Taroom (89 km from park). Creek crossings for last 18 km. Conventional vehicles can reach north end of park but foot descent to gorge is difficult.

Damp and cool, Robinson Gorge winds for over 12 km between cliffs up to 90 m high. With its side gorges – some mere fissures in the sandstone, others wind-torn into contorted shapes – it can take days to explore. In some narrow parts visitors have to swim, or float through on inflatable mattresses. The keen-eyed find examples of Aboriginal art. Warm hues of rock belie the coolness of the narrowest sections, which the sun seldom touches.

Bottlebrushes, cabbage-tree palms, wattles and boronia flourish, and the fern gardens and moss-covered cliff bases hold special delight in their contrast to the dusty and often very hot plateau above. The park extends over 8900 ha, most of it covered in eucalypt forest. Emus, grey kangaroos and whiptail wallabies can be seen, and dingoes occasionally venture near a camp.

From the road's end, it is a short walk to the rim of the gorge and a scramble to the bottom. The whole park is best suited to experienced and well-equipped bushwalkers.

NOTE: Take water – creeks are seasonal and waterholes become foul.
WARNING: Area subject to intensely cold weather in winter.
BEST TIME: Spring and autumn.
ENQUIRIES: (079) 27 6511.
ADDRESS: As for Isla Gorge.

Scenic enjoyment ✔✔✔
Day activities ×
Family camping ✔
Hard bushwalking ✔✔

Simpson Desert National Park

100 km W of Birdsville. Western weather district. 4WD access from Birdsville.

Quartz sands coated with red iron oxides glow deeply at dawn and dusk in a sea of dunes running in parallel waves up to 300 km long over much of the Simpson Desert. The ridges occur every 200 to 600 metres and rise to 30 metres, making travel difficult and tedious, even in 4WD vehicles. Claypans and stony plains occasionally interrupt the pattern of dunes and dry salt lakes occurring in Queensland's southwestern corner and across the border in South Australia, where this 550 000 ha park is joined by an even bigger conservation park. In total the Simpson Desert is a forbidding wilderness more than twice the size of Tasmania.

Desert canegrass grows sparsely on the unstable crests and upper slopes of the dunes, with stunted mulga woodland, scrub and hummock grass on the lower slopes and flats. Daisies, desert peas, yellowtops and many other flowering annuals have brief growing periods after rain, but their seeds lie dormant in the sand for most of the year.

NOTES: Entry permit required. Intending visitors should inform QNPWS and Birdsville police of proposed itinerary.
WARNING: Visitors must be fully equipped for outback survival. Carry all water and fuel supplies, spare parts and radio transceiver.
BEST TIME: Spring.
ENQUIRIES: (079) 27 6511.
ADDRESS: QNPWS regional centre, Box 1395, Rockhampton 4700.

Scenic enjoyment ✔✔
Day activities ×
Family camping ×
Hard bushwalking ×

Snake Range National Park

400 km W, 70 km W of Springsure. Central Highlands weather district. **NO PUBLIC ACCESS.**

In an area already remote, a natural amphitheatre is further isolated by its fringe of 60m cliffs. With a single narrow entrance through which several watercourses pass, the basin is an undisturbed area of ecualypt forest and woodland of brigalow, sandalwood and ironbark. The unusual yapunyah grows here; its leaves are eaten by koalas. Caves and overhangs of the sandstone shelter Aboriginal paintings. The 1210 ha park was created mainly to preserve the environment for scientific study.

ENQUIRIES: (079) 82 2246.
ADDRESS: As for Mazeppa.

West Hill National Park

250 km N. Central Coast, Burdekin and Isaacs weather district. Accessible by boat only.

Low vine scrub tucked into a broad hollow behind the 680 ha park's sandy foredunes develops into patches of rainforest, with Moreton Bay figs and white cedar competing for canopy space at around 30 metres. Coast banksia and Moreton Bay ash grow in a grassy forest to the west, beyond a broad corridor of grassland sparsely dotted with shrubs. Mangroves line inlets on the park's northern boundary.

The pyramidal peak of **West Hill Island National Park** (398 ha) rises to the north less than 1 km offshore. Rainforest slopes fall steeply to the island's rocky southern shores. To the north and west fine beaches fringe lower-lying scrubland and a narrow spit points towards the mainland. A connecting sandbank is exposed at low tide.

BEST TIME: Spring, autumn.
ENQUIRIES: (079) 57 6292.
ADDRESS: As for Cape Palmerston.

Scenic enjoyment ✔
Day activities ×
Family camping ×
Hard bushwalking ×

Woodgate National Park

330 km SE. South Coast, Curtis and Moreton weather district. Car access of Bruce Highway 1 km E of Childers. 4WD needed for park tracks and to reach one of two camping areas.

Close to the point where the Burrum River flows into Hervey Bay, a park of 5500 ha affords safe swimming and excellent opportunities for fishing in rivers or from the 6 km stretch of beach. Sand dunes, small swamps, mangrove flats, heaths and eucalypt forests provide a variety of habitats. Birds are prolific: more than 200 species have been recorded. Bird watchers can use a hide along a 6 km walking track. Another track of similar distance has a 200 metre boardwalk above a swamp.

On the opposite, southern side of the Burrum River is **Burrum River National Park,** with similar terrain and vegetation. The 1620 ha park is undeveloped. It is reached by the Burrum Heads road from the Bruce Highway. Sand tracks into the park are usable by conventional vehicles when rain has firmed the sand – otherwise 4WD is needed.

BEST TIME: Year-round (spring for wildflowers).
ENQUIRIES: (071) 22 2455.
ADDRESS: As for Auburn River.

Scenic enjoyment ✔✔
Day activities ✔✔
Family camping ✔✔
Hard bushwalking ×

Yeppoon National Parks

50 km NE. Central Coast, Burdekin and Isaacs weather district. Car access by coast road between Yeppoon and Emu Park. Buses daily to Yeppoon and Mulambin.

Headlands in a three-part park – officially called **Double Head, Rosslyn Head, Bluff Point, Mulambin National Park** – make splendid vantage points for vistas over the pretty islands in Keppel Bay. They shelter wide beaches where swimming is safe except in summer, when box jellyfish may be present.

Double Head and Rosslyn Head at the north end of one beach, Bluff Point at the other, and tiny Mulambin in the south make up the 107 ha park. On elevated parts, the wind has stunted the eucalypts; there are also heaths and mangrove flats. Walkers along tracks on Double Head and Bluff Point may spy nests of green tree ants, stitched together with leaves. Bluff Point, 121 metres high, has a picnic area.

BEST TIME: Autumn, spring.
ENQUIRIES: (079) 27 6511.
ADDRESS: As for Keppel Islands.

Scenic enjoyment ✔✔
Day activities ✔✔
Family camping ×
Hard bushwalking ×

Plants and wildlife in Queensland parks

With 15 different natural regions within its boundaries Queensland has a greater variety of landforms, vegetation types and wildlife species than any other state. Physically it ranges from desert to reef – taking in mulga, Mitchell grass downs, brigalow, rainforest, swamp and mangrove on the way. The state has about 67 per cent of the total number of native mammal species, 80 per cent of the birds and about 56 per cent of the species of reptiles and amphibians.

Although the state is large, as more land is cleared and forest trees are felled and swamps drained, so wildlife habitat comes under threat. The 314 national parks provide a home or refuge to the whole range of Queensland wildlife. Each one also has some part of the state's wonderful diversity of plants and trees for the visitor to enjoy.

Above: The rufous bettong feeds at night on grasses and tubers which it digs up with its strongly clawed front legs

It is a lucky visitor who manages to see the rare Albert's lyrebird, here returning to feed its chick

The nation's only carnivorous bat, the ghost bat Macroderma gigas, takes supper to a feeding site

Incubation period for the eggs of the emerald ground-dove is 14-16 days; it is shared by the male and female

A park inhabitant and regular visitor to Queensland gardens, a yellow-bellied sunbird feeds on grevillea. Banksia serrata, above, is a favourite food of honeyeaters

Plants and wildlife in Queensland parks

Brahminy kite – often seen along mangrove-fringed bays and inlets

The loggerhead turtle's main egg-laying season is from October to May. The loggerhead can be distinguished from other sea-turtles by the five shields on either side of its shell

As its habitat decreases with the development of the state's coastal heathlands the ground parrot is becoming increasingly rare

The delicate agile wallaby is the most common member of the kangaroo family in tropical coastal areas

Queensland's own – bottle trees make their unique mark on the landscape

Brolgas wander widely for food: although usually seen on coastal swamplands they sometimes disperse as far as the Simpson Desert

Gould's goanna is an adaptable species – its habitats range from coastal sclerophyll forest to the deserts

TOWNSVILLE REGION

A mighty river creates new land

YEAR BY YEAR, Bowling Green Bay National Park is growing. Just east of Townsville, it occupies part of Australia's most important river delta. Sedimentary deposits of the powerful Burdekin River form a huge triangle with the sugar town of Ayr at the centre of its 60 km base. Its apex is the long, gently curving sandspit of Cape Bowling Green. Water-saturated gravel beds underlie the triangle. South of the cape, where the surface channels of the Burdekin discharge into the Coral Sea, islands are engulfed by silt and beaches are advancing. To the west, sand flats and mangroves are claiming the bay.

Boosted by phenomenal summer rains in its main catchments – 500 km apart, near Ingham and Mackay – the Burdekin's annual outflow is the greatest of any river on the east coast. It meets a languid sea, shielded by reef ramparts that form an almost continuous barrier here. There are no strong ocean waves or currents to sweep away the river's burden of erosion debris. Sediments settle in a spreading fan. Southeasterly 'Trade Winds', blowing steadily from autumn to spring, ease sands and silts up the cape and round into the bay.

The Great Dividing Range has no influence – it retreats 200 km inland. Coastal ranges govern local climates. On each side of the Burdekin delta these ranges are set far back, and aligned southeast-to-northwest. Moisture-laden winds slip by and drop their rains towards Cairns. So although Townsville and Bowen are not spared the equatorial drenchings of summer, they share the most strongly pronounced dry season south of Cape York Peninsula. Winter and spring days are reliably sunny; nights under clear skies are surprisingly cool.

Isolated granite outcrops bring scenic relief on Townsville's lowland plain. Half an hour's drive east, the Mt Elliot massif in the inland section of the Bowling Green Bay park has rainforest of true tropical complexity – the southernmost in Australia. Others are preserved within easy reach to the north, at Mt Spec (often referred to as Crystal Creek National Park) and Jourama.

Magnetic Island, part suburban, offers a fine sampling of drier rainforest, dominated by hoop pines and vines, among its steep eucalypt woodlands. With varied walks, sheltered swimming bays and coral formations, the island rivals many others in the region that are better publicised in the south, but far more difficult and expensive to reach.

Featured parks	Pages
1 Magnetic Island	418-419
2 Jourama	420
3 Bowling Green Bay	421-423
4 Mount Spec	424-425
5 Wallaman Falls	426-427
6 Conway	428-429
7 Cape Hillsborough	430-431
8 Eungella	432-435
9 Hinchinbrook Island	436-438
10 Edmund Kennedy	439
11 Porcupine Gorge	440

Your access and facilities guide to all parks in this region starts on page 441

Rainforest trees crowd Finch Hatton Creek, in Eungella National Park

Coral fragments lighten the granite sands of Radical Bay. The island has many fringing reefs and some offshore structures

Bell flower favours moist sites

MAGNETIC ISLAND NATIONAL PARK

Cool creek gullies lead up towards Mt Cook from a dozen quiet bays in the shelter of granite headlands. Pockets of rainforest merge into slopes of hoop pine and eucalypt woodlands studded with boulders and steep rock outcrops. More than half of the island is taken up by a national park of 2720 ha. The remainder forms part of the urban area of Townsville. Park entry points are reached along easy walking or cycling routes from ferry wharves at Picnic Bay and Arcadia.

More than 20 km of marked trails link sandy bays on the northern and eastern sides of the island with lookouts on higher ridges. Balding, Radical, Florence and Arthur Bays enjoy good reputations for swimming. Small fringing reefs of coral are common. Mt Cook (550 metres) can be climbed from north of Nelly Bay but no trail is marked; the park ranger at Picnic Bay should be consulted. Wildlife on the island includes rock wallabies, many birds, and koalas – seen most often near the Forts, above Florence Bay. The fort complex was built during World War II to protect Townsville.

Hoop pine exploits soil trapped behind a natural sea wall of boulders. These trees, related to the Norfolk Island pine and similarly salt-tolerant, grow mostly on headlands

Right: Wattles, flowering in early spring, dress the slopes above Gowrie Bay

Grassy sedges cloak a damp slope above Jourama Falls

Jourama National Park

Waterview Creek tumbles over slabs of pinkish granite to a boulder-strewn bed containing many fine swimming holes. Beyond a luxuriant fringe of river plants, and some rainforest trees and shrubs in moist gullies, the granite hills of the 1100 ha park support eucalypt forests with a scattering of cycads in the understorey. A track from the end of the approach road winds 1 km to the base of the main falls and zigzags for a similar distance to the lookout above. It is not a difficult walk, but shoes should be worn – not thongs. Keen bushwalkers can make a harder climb towards the source of the creek. Rock scaling is not recommended: boulders are loose in many of the faces.

Buttressed roots of many trees beside Waterview Creek show that they are rainforest species, though the canopy formed by their foliage is not dense here. Waterholes among a jumble of granite boulders offer easy opportunities for relief from the usual heat and humidity of the district

Bands of resistant porphyry create rapids when Alligator Creek is in flood

Bowling Green Bay National Park

The unadorned rock wallaby blends in with its habitat

A steep horseshoe range, rising to 1234 metres at Mt Elliot, and two isolated coastal outliers surround Alligator Creek – the only part of a 55 000 ha wilderness accessible year-round by car. Lowland areas reach north to another granite massif at Cape Cleveland, and east across mangrove flats and salt pans to Cape Bowling Green. The highland section – formerly Mt Elliot National Park – is mostly covered by grassy eucalypt woodlands. But although the district has a generally low rainfall, the range's height and alignment enable it to catch enough moisture to support Australia's southernmost tropical rainforest. Swimming is popular at Alligator Creek; a walk to falls upstream takes 2½ hours each way.

Native rosella

MOUNT SPEC NATIONAL PARK

Rainforests cloak the summits and much of the escarpment of the Paluma Range, above eucalypt forests with understoreys of grasses and acacias. Heights towards Mt Spec (960 metres) command fine views of the lowlands reaching to Halifax Bay, with the Palm Islands rising to the northeast. At McCleland's Lookout, near Big Crystal Creek, a track of about 1 km links picnic grounds with a series of lookouts. Longer tracks leading north and west through the range were the pack trails of tin miners in the 1920s. Little Crystal Creek, much nearer the Bruce Highway, has waterfalls, cascades and inviting swimming holes in a rainforested valley.

Green ringtail and striped possums reach the southern limit of their range here. Pademelons are likely to be seen on the Paluma Dam road, early or late in the day, and platypuses are sometimes sighted in quiet pools. Among many interesting birds are the northern log runner, the Victorian riflebird and bowerbirds.

Umbrella fern

Rainforest trees shade a little waterfall and rock pool typical of Crystal Creek. This structure may soon collapse – the rocks are cracking and seedlings are starting to widen the gaps

Fallen logs readily decompose in the high humidity of a rainforest, yielding their nutrients to support other plants. Most fertility in such forests is held above ground rather than in the soil – which is why fires can spell their doom

Youthful misfortune tied this liane in a knot. Some violent force – probably a blow from a falling branch – bent its growing tip towards the ground. Recovering, the plant turned upwards again but its shoot grew through a loop

Left: Buttress roots are characteristic of nearly all the taller trees in tropical and subtropical rainforests

Wallaman Falls' sheer drop of 279 metres is the largest permanent clear drop fall in Australia. In a process that has gone on for thousands of years, since the final uplift of the Great Dividing Range, water action is cutting back the gorge of Stony Creek deeper and deeper into the rock escarpment

Wallaman Falls National Park

The usual rule of tropical travel – avoid the summer 'Wet' – is worth breaking at Wallaman Falls. Discomforts are forgotten at the sight of Stony Creek in full flow, spilling into a precipitous canyon on its way to join the Herbert River. The total height of the falls is not the greatest in Australia – two in northern NSW exceed it – but a single sheer drop of 279 metres is unsurpassed. Other sections above the main drop, crowded by luxuriant rainforest, are impressive in their own right.

A lookout with road access commands superb views of the falls and gorge, centrepieces of a hilly park of 600 ha where forests of eucalypts and casuarinas dominate the more open slopes. A track of 4 km zigzags to the foot of the falls, past a second lookout; the walk takes about 1½ hours. A short track along Stony Creek, near the camp, reaches many good swimming holes. Birdlife is prolific and wallabies, possums and platypuses may be seen.

Plants colonise stream-washed boulders wherever some silt collects

Right: Tree deaths in a misty rainforest above the gorge have opened the leaf canopy and allowed in more light, encouraging the vigorous growth of palm thickets

Fungi colonise a charred trunk

Volcanic rocks of the Beak, east of Shute Harbour, break down to make a shingle beach

Fruits of Guettarda speciosa

A blossom of beach hibiscus, just opening

Mangrove seedlings of two different species spring up among older plants at Shute Bay. A dozen species may be found in the one tropical mangrove community

Bent trunks of pandanus palm show the direction of prevailing south-easterlies

CONWAY NATIONAL PARK

Coastal ranges reaching 560 metres, but plunging abruptly into the waters of Whitsunday Passage, dominate a largely undeveloped park of 23 800 ha. Bushwalkers on the connecting Mt Rooper and Swamp Bay tracks (7 km) gain striking views of the Whitsunday Islands. An easy circuit walk of 1 km can be taken from the camping ground near Shute Harbour, at the northern end of the park. Tall eucalypt forests on the slopes merge into lowland rainforests, with hoop pine emerging on some headlands. Possums, gliders and bandicoots are common in the bush, along with brush turkeys, scrubfowl and honeyeaters. Wading birds throng quiet bays, some of which are important as dugong and turtle breeding grounds.

Golden orb weaver – really three times this size

Hoop pine rainforest backs the Division Rocks, which break the main beach in two

Boggy ground suits a lily

Left: A fig tree's buttress roots support an immense mass in relatively shallow soils

Cape Hillsborough National Park

A steep-walled rock mass, rising to almost 300 metres, dominates the main headland of Cape Hillsborough. To the east, the spit-linked peninsulas of Andrews Point and Wedge Island form a deep curve giving shelter to narrow beaches studded with boulders. At low tide the beaches make a walking route to complement the 800 ha park's 8 km of tracks. These wander through dunes, coastal scrub, lowland hoop pine rainforest and up into grassy eucalypt forests, taking in eight lookout points. Hidden Valley has a self-guiding circuit of 2 km on which characteristic plants and animals are identified. Big brush turkeys frequent a picnic ground, and brush-tailed rock wallabies and sugar gliders may be glimpsed at night. An unformed but marked trail, taking about 6 hours and requiring fitness, leads west to Smalleys Beach. Swimming is popular in the sheltered bays except in summer, when marine stingers may be about. Then campers strike inland to a freshwater swimming hole at well-shaded Cascade Creek, which usually flows at a good level in the early months of the year.

Wedge Island, linked to Andrews Point by a shingle causeway, can be reached at low tide. In the background is Brampton Island, also a national park

EUNGELLA NATIONAL PARK

Rainforest raiders made red 'cedar' their first target. By the 1820s its timber was Australia's leading export. Later it went as furniture into grand colonial mansions and even railway carriages. Today *Toona australis* is rare, but fine examples survive on the Clarke Range at Eungella. Many are seen on the rainforest discovery walk, near Broken River camping ground, or along the Valley View track above Eungella township (pronounced Young-la).

Development in a park of nearly 50 000 ha is limited to the Eungella-Broken River-Crediton Creek area, in the southwestern corner, and Finch Hatton Gorge to the east. Together they offer a variety of forest walks of no great difficulty, 2-8 km in length, linking lookout points and good swimming spots. The rest of the park is a high and rugged wilderness where not even the most experienced bushwalkers should venture without consulting rangers.

Rough-scaled cyathea tree ferns spring up where openings in the rainforest canopy allow some direct sunlight, or filtered light all day. Right: Fruits of a rainforest solanum species – related to potatoes, eggplants and nightshades

Right: Climbers claim support from a towering tree

Casuarinas take over at the rainforest edge. About a third of the park, on drier country in the inaccessible northwest, has eucalypt forests. And Eungella has two types of rainforest. Some species high in the range, such as tulip oak, silver quandong and white beech, are not of tropical origin – they have affinities with trees now found far to the south

Cyatheas favour creekside sites at high altitude. They need mist and rain as well as some sun

Finch Hatton Creek tumbles over the Araluen Falls, following an eons-old path cut in tough igneous rock. The creek is the only known home of an amazing frog *(see page 38)*

EUNGELLA NATIONAL PARK

Maidenhair ferns and umbrella ferns (below) need damp sites

Small herbs and ferns take advantage of extra light beside a creek near Mt Dalrymple, the highest point in the park at 1280 metres. Platypuses are frequently seen in quiet pools

Bruguiera mangrove in flower

Left: Buttress roots of a rainforest tree, slender but strong, wander far and wide to ensure it a firm anchorage

Above: The twisting root of a strangler fig descends from a host tree that may be doomed

Forests reach to the tide limit at Orchid Beach, tucked behind Cape Richards at the island's northern extremity. Boats are easily landed here and at many other spots along the sandy east coast. But stormy seas may force a long wait to get off. Cautious campers take extra supplies

HINCHINBROOK ISLAND NATIONAL PARK

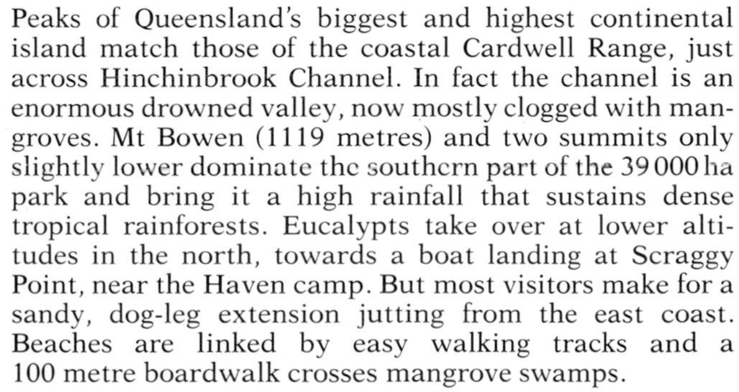

Navigable channels cut the mangrove swamps of Missionary Bay. Clear beaches lie just northeast, past the forested Kirkville Hills

Peaks of Queensland's biggest and highest continental island match those of the coastal Cardwell Range, just across Hinchinbrook Channel. In fact the channel is an enormous drowned valley, now mostly clogged with mangroves. Mt Bowen (1119 metres) and two summits only slightly lower dominate the southern part of the 39 000 ha park and bring it a high rainfall that sustains dense tropical rainforests. Eucalypts take over at lower altitudes in the north, towards a boat landing at Scraggy Point, near the Haven camp. But most visitors make for a sandy, dog-leg extension jutting from the east coast. Beaches are linked by easy walking tracks and a 100 metre boardwalk crosses mangrove swamps.

Hinchinbrook Island National Park

Hinchinbrook is the biggest whole-island national park in the world. The channel separating it from the mainland is up to 6 km wide but heavily silted and colonised by tall mangroves, especially at the southern end. James Cook charted 'Mt Hinchinbrook' as the summit of a ridge that he presumed to be part of the mainland. The channel was not discovered for a further 73 years

EDMUND KENNEDY NATIONAL PARK

Among the swamps behind Rockingham Bay it is easy to imagine the despair of the explorer Edmund Kennedy. Put ashore in 1848 with 12 men, horses and a sheep flock, he had to reach Cape York. But in a maze of creeks and mangroves the party had to search for more than 30 km to the south to discover an inland route. Exhaustion, illness and depletion of supplies doomed the mission before any positive progress was made. Nine men were left to die along the way. Kennedy survived almost to the Cape but was speared to death by Aborigines.

Two bayside camping grounds, fairly popular in the dry season but reliant on seasonal creeks for water, are accessible in the 6200 ha park. A boardwalk is built over mangroves to the beach and a loop walking track of 2 km gives a sampling of rainforest and swampy communities of tea-tree, paperbark, fan palms and sedges. The area is an important breeding ground for waterfowl.

Woodlands of melaleuca and leptospermum surround sedge-bordered swamps of sword grass. Creek-fed, the swamps shrink in the dry season, but damp mud protects the tree roots. Other swamps are tidal and overgrown by mangroves

Serene in its sandstone canyon, Porcupine Creek creates a surprising oasis in country where good rains are unreliable

PORCUPINE GORGE NATIONAL PARK

Flat woodlands of eucalypts and acacias give no hint of the existence of Porcupine Gorge until travellers are within about 200 metres. Suddenly a gaping canyon reveals itself – relatively shallow at first in the south, but deepening and narrowing to a point at which the fissure is only 500 metres wide, but the walls are up to 150 metres high. Farther north the gorge opens out again at the Pyramids, in the area favoured by bush campers.

Porcupine Creek, flowing year-round, has penetrated a lava-flow plain of basalt and cut into underlying beds of softer sedimentary rocks. These give a rich variety of colours to the walls that tower over the watercourse with its fringing casuarinas and callistemons. Parrots abound and duck and bittern frequent the creek. Pools are suitable for swimming in autumn. The 2938 ha park has no formed tracks, but nimble visitors can enter the gorge from the southern lookout.

PARKS OF THE TOWNSVILLE REGION

FACILITIES

 Cabins

 Caravan park

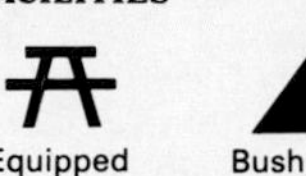 Equipped picnic area

 Bush camping allowed

Lavatory building

Established campsite

Campsite but no car access

Note: Popular parks without campsites usually have public camping grounds nearby. If in doubt, call enquiries number.

PARK RATINGS No interest ✖ Some interest ✔ Major interest ✔✔ Outstanding ✔✔✔

Bladensburg National Park

630 km SW, 25 km S of Winton. Western weather district. Access by unformed property tracks.

An area of 33 700 ha next to Bladensburg station was set aside in 1984 to preserve low, flat-topped ridges of woodland, gidgee scrub and hummock grasslands, broken occasionally by denser vegetation around semi-permanent waterholes. The park is undeveloped.

BEST TIME: Winter, spring.

ENQUIRIES: (079) 27 6511.

ADDRESS: QNPWS regional centre, Box 1362, Rockhampton 4700.

Scenic enjoyment ✔
Day activities ✖
Family camping ✖
Hard bushwalking ✖

Bowling Green Bay National Park

30 km SE. North Coast, Tableland and Peninsula weather district. Car access to Mt Elliot area off Bruce Highway 24 km S of Townsville; tracks to Cape Cleveland area, off Bruce Highway 34 km S, require 4WD in wet conditions.

DESCRIPTION: Page 421.

BEST TIME: Autumn to spring.

ENQUIRIES: (077) 74 1411.

ADDRESS: QNPWS regional centre, Box 5391, Townsville 4810.

Scenic enjoyment ✔✔
Day activities ✔✔
Family camping ✔✔
Hard bushwalking ✔✔

Brampton Island National Park

300 km SE, 40 km NE of Mackay. Central Coast, Burdekin and Isaacs weather district. Accessible by boat. Flights and launch daily from Mackay.

Brampton's 464 ha national park shares its continental island with a tourist resort which opened in 1933 as a holiday farm. Livestock bared some slopes, but most remain heavily forested with eucalypts. Walking tracks over hill terrain link sheltered bays with shallow, shelving beaches popular for swimming and snorkelling. Panoramic views from Brampton Peak (213 m) look out over seas studded with scores of islands and reefs.

At very low tide visitors can wade 500 metres across coral reefs and sandbanks to **Carlisle Island,** a 520 ha undeveloped national park. Casuarinas on sandy soils along the shoreline fringe thorn bush and dense vine scrub behind. Mangroves crowd muddy lowland areas and substantial patches of rainforest grow on sheltered slopes among tall eucalypt forests. In the absence of developed trails walkers and bush campers follow seasonal creekbeds, but some sections require clambering over boulders and around steep cliff faces. Ferns grow thickly towards the island's highest points, giving way to grasses on the gentle ridge line.

National parks preserve eight other islands around the same latitude as Brampton and Carlisle, ranging 90 km east to the coral cay of **Bushy Island** (2 ha). Private or chartered boats provide the only access to Bushy and the undeveloped parks of **Penrith Island** (162 ha), **Aspatria Island** (105 ha), **Scawfell Island** (1090 ha), **Calder Island** (150 ha), **Wigton Island** (259 ha), **Cockermouth Island** (259 ha) and **Allonby Island** (36 ha). Campers must carry plenty of water and be fully equipped for emergencies – they are likely to be alone with no means of communication.

BEST TIME: Autumn, winter, spring.

ENQUIRIES: (079) 57 6292.

ADDRESS: QNPWS district office, Box 623, Mackay 4740.

Scenic enjoyment ✔✔✔
Day activities ✔✔
Family camping ✖
Hard bushwalking ✔

Cape Hillsborough and Wedge Island National Park

370 km SE, 45 km NE of Mackay. Central Coast, Burdekin and Isaacs weather district. Car access off Bruce Highway from turn-offs at Mt Ossa and Yakapari.

DESCRIPTION: Page 431.

BEST TIME: Autumn, spring.

ENQUIRIES: (079) 59 0410.

ADDRESS: As for Brampton.

Scenic enjoyment ✔✔✔
Day activities ✔✔✔
Family camping ✔✔
Hard bushwalking ✔

Cape Upstart National Park

170 km SE, 80 km SE of Ayr. Central Coast, Burdekin and Isaacs weather district. Car access to park boundary off Bruce Highway from Guthalungra. Approached by sea, the massive weathered granite block of Cape Upstart appears as an island. The low swampy neck joining it to the mainland is invisible from a distance. Along the cape's northern and eastern shores unbroken ramparts or rock rise steeply from the sea with acacia thickets clinging to shallow patches of soil. Low vine scrub grows in some gullies with hoop pine surviving in moister spots between huge boulders.

Less forbidding shores line the cape's western face on Upstart Bay. Narrow, rocky headlands enclose sandy beaches with inshore waters deep enough for beaching a boat. Scrub of Burdekin plum, eucalypt and pandanus grows in a narrow belt behind the beaches.

BEST TIME: Autumn to spring.

ENQUIRIES: (077) 74 1411.

ADDRESS: As for Bowling Green Bay.

Scenic enjoyment ✔✔
Day activities ✖
Family camping ✖
Hard bushwalking ✖

Conway National Park

310 km SE, 8 km E of Airlie Beach. Central Coast, Burdekin and Isaacs weather district. Car access off Bruce Highway from Proserpine. Buses Proserpine-Shute Harbour.

DESCRIPTION: Page 429.

NOTE: Limit of 4 days on camping.

BEST TIME: Spring.

ENQUIRIES: (079) 46 9430.

ADDRESS: QNPWS district office, Box 332, Airlie Beach 4741.

Scenic enjoyment ✔✔
Day activities ✔✔
Family camping ✔
Hard bushwalking ✔✔

Edmund Kennedy National Park

175 km NW, 12 km N of Cardwell. North Coast, Tableland and Peninsula weather district. Car access off Bruce Highway 4 km N of Cardwell along unsealed track – impassable after heavy rains.

DESCRIPTION: Page 439.

NOTES: Limit of 7 days on camping. No fresh water in park.

BEST TIME: Autumn, spring.

ENQUIRIES: (070) 66 8601.

ADDRESS: QNPWS district office, Box 74, Cardwell 4816.

Scenic enjoyment ✔
Day activities ✔
Family camping ✔✔
Hard bushwalking ✖

Eungella National Park

430 km SE, 85 km W of Mackay. Central Coast, Burdekin and Isaacs weather district. Car access off Bruce Highway from Mackay or from Mount Ossa, 46 km N of Mackay. Bus tours from Mackay.

DESCRIPTION: Page 432.

BEST TIME: Autumn to spring.

ENQUIRIES: (079) 58 4552.

ADDRESS: C/o P.O., Dalrymple Heights 4741.

Scenic enjoyment ✔✔✔
Day activities ✔✔✔
Family camping ✔✔✔
Hard bushwalking ✔✔

BOOKING A CAMPSITE

A convenient site booking system operates for all national park camping in Queensland.

Apply to the park address at least 6 weeks before your visit. Give the name of any club or group involved, the leader's name, address and vehicle registration number, number of vehicles and group members, dates of visit, number and type of camping structures, and acceptability of alternative dates or areas. Enclose a stamped self-addressed envelope for the reply.

If the park is unstaffed a camping permit will be issued with the site allocation. At staffed parks a permit must be obtained from the ranger.

No fees are charged for bookings or permits. For Great Sandy NP, however, there is an island access fee and a camping fee.

Gloucester and Middle Islands National Park

190-220 km SE, 20 km E-50 km SE of Bowen. Central Coast, Burdekin and Isaacs weather district. Accessible by boat from Bowen, Dingo Beach and Airlie Beach.

Islands of the Gloucester and Middle Islands park are strung in a chain from the mouth of Edgecumbe Bay, just south of lighthouse-capped **Holbourne Island National Park** (34 ha), towards the northern entrance of Whitsunday Passage. Short, steep spurs and valleys clothed in eucalypt woodland and tussock grassland descend from the hilly backbone of 2460 ha Gloucester Island, the biggest in the chain. A ridge about 400 metres high overlooks sheltered anchorage at Northwest Beach where boats from Bowen are pulled ashore for picnics, swimming and camping holidays.

To the south a conical peak features prominently on the skyline of Saddleback Island. The peak is joined to a flat-topped rise at the island's northern end by a low saddle bare of vegetation. Fringing reefs of coral form an inner rubble area with patches of living coral exposed at low tide. Towards the seaward edge, where the coral is constantly below water, the patches are much denser and make for rewarding snorkelling.

Thick, stunted scrub of narrow-leafed ironbark, poplar gum and bloodwood covers high, hilly Armit Island, closest to the Whitsundays. Kangaroo and spear grasses grow on an area of level, open land near good beach landing spots on the island's southern shores.

Gloucester, Saddleback and Armit have established camping grounds, but visitors must take sufficient water for the length of their stay. Bush camping is permitted on the park's undeveloped islands, Gumbrell, Double Cone and Middle Islands.

BEST TIME: Autumn, spring.

ENQUIRIES: (079) 46 9430.

ADDRESS: As for Conway.

Scenic enjoyment ✔✔
Day activities ✔
Family camping ✔✔
Hard bushwalking ✖

Great Basalt Wall National Park

180 km SW, 100 km W of Charters Towers. Northern Tablelands weather district. Reached by road and track off Flinders Highway.

A 30 500 ha park announced in 1987, the Great Basalt Wall is

evidence of the last major volcanic activity in northern Australia – it is part of a 120 km lava flow. Basalt boulders and dense vegetation form a natural wall for much of the park's boundary. It is a rough area with a confusing landscape and is suitable for experienced and adventurous bushwalkers.
NOTE: No facilities but there is a camping reserve adjacent to the southern boundary.
BEST TIME: Autumn, winter.
ENQUIRIES: (077) 74 1411.
ADDRESS: QNPWS regional centre, Box 5391, Townsville 4810.

1. **Bladensburg NP**
2. **Bowling Green Bay NP**
3. **Brampton Island NP**
4. **Cape Hillsborough NP**
5. **Cape Upstart NP**
6. **Conway NP**
7. **Edmund Kennedy NP**
8. **Eungella NP**
9. **Gloucester Island NP**
10. **Great Basalt Wall NP**
11. **Hinchinbrook Island NP**
12. **Jourama NP**
13. **Lawn Hill NP**
14. **Magnetic Island NP**
15. **Mount Aberdeen NP**
16. **Mount Beatrice NP**
17. **Mount Blackwood NP**
18. **Mount Fox NP**
19. **Mount Spec NP**
20. **Orpheus Island NP**
21. **Porcupine Gorge NP**
22. **Reliance Creek NP**
23. **Wallaman Falls NP**
24. **Whitsunday Islands NPs**

Hinchinbrook Island National Park

100 km NW, 6 km E of Cardwell. North Coast, Tableland and Peninsula weather district. Accessible by boat from Cardwell.
DESCRIPTION: Page 437.
Hinchinbrook Channel National Park preserves 5600 ha of the southern mainland shores facing Hinchinbrook Island. Swamplands and melaleuca and pandanus woodland give way to dunes covered in dense casuarina and melaleuca scrub towards the high tide line. A wide belt of mangroves and low mangrove islands clog nearshore waters. A narrow passage to the main channel winds through the mangroves from a car park and launching ramp at Fishers Creek, 28 km S of Cardwell.

At the channel's southern entrance **Nypa Palms National Park** (340 ha) protects the most southerly know occurrence of nypa or mangrove palms. They grow in isolated clumps within a mixed mangrove community in the Herbert River delta.

Off the northern end of Hinchinbrook Island the national parks of **Tween Brook Island** (6 ha) and **Middle Brook Island** (16 ha) are off limits to the public to protect colonies of breeding seabirds. Daily tours are run from Cardwell to **North Brook Island** (65 ha). To the east seasonal streams rising on a steep granite ridge flow through the poorly developed rainforest of **Goold Island National Park** (830 ha).
BEST TIME: Winter, spring.
ENQUIRIES: (07) 66 8601.
ADDRESS: As for Edmund Kennedy.

Scenic enjoyment ✓✓✓
Day activities ✓✓
Family camping ✓✓✓
Hard bushwalking ✓✓

Jourama National Park

90 km NW. North Coast, Tableland and Peninsula weather district. Car access along unsealed road off Bruce Highway between Townsville and Ingham.
DESCRIPTION: Page 420.
BEST TIME: Autumn, spring.
ENQUIRIES: (077) 74 1411.
ADDRESS: As for Bowling Green Bay.

Scenic enjoyment ✓✓
Day activities ✓✓
Family camping ✓
Hard bushwalking ✓

Lawn Hill National Park

1100 km W, 410 km N of Mt Isa. Carpentaria, Gulf Rivers weather district. Car access south from Lawn Hill station, off Burketown-Camooweal road at Gregory Downs, 117 km S of Burketown. Roads impassable after rain.

Galleries of Aboriginal rock art grace the bare gorge walls of Lawn Creek in a park of 12 000 ha. Archeological excavations indicate continuous occupation of the area for more than 30 000 years.

Fan palms grow prolifically along the banks of Lawn Creek in an oasis surrounded by stony plains of hummock grasses. Permanent water and good shelter attract kangaroos, emus, wallaroos and an abundant bird population including the rare hooded parrot. Creek banks near the camping ground fall sharply to deep clear water inhabited by tortoises and harmless freshwater crocodiles.
BEST TIME: Winter, spring.
ENQUIRIES: (070) 51 9811.
ADDRESS: QNPWS regional centre, Box 2066, Cairns 4870.

Scenic enjoyment ✓✓
Day activities ✓
Family camping ✓
Hard bushwalking ✓

Magnetic Island National Park

10 km N, 1 km N of Picnic Bay. North Coast, Tableland and Peninsula weather district. Daily launches and vehicle ferry from Townsville.
DESCRIPTION: Page 419.
BEST TIME: Autumn, spring.
ENQUIRIES: (077) 74 1411.
ADDRESS: As for Bowling Green Bay.

Scenic enjoyment ✓✓✓
Day activities ✓✓✓
Family camping ×
Hard bushwalking ✓✓

Mount Aberdeen National Park

250 km SE, 40 km SW of Bowen. Central Coast, Burdekin and Isaacs weather district. Car access off Bowen Developmental Road.

Huge granite boulders strewn over steep slopes at the northern end of the Clarke Range make clambering to the summit of Mt Aberdeen (990 m) a rough and strenuous climb. Forest red gum grows profusely in eucalypt woodland over much of the 2900 ha park, split into two sections

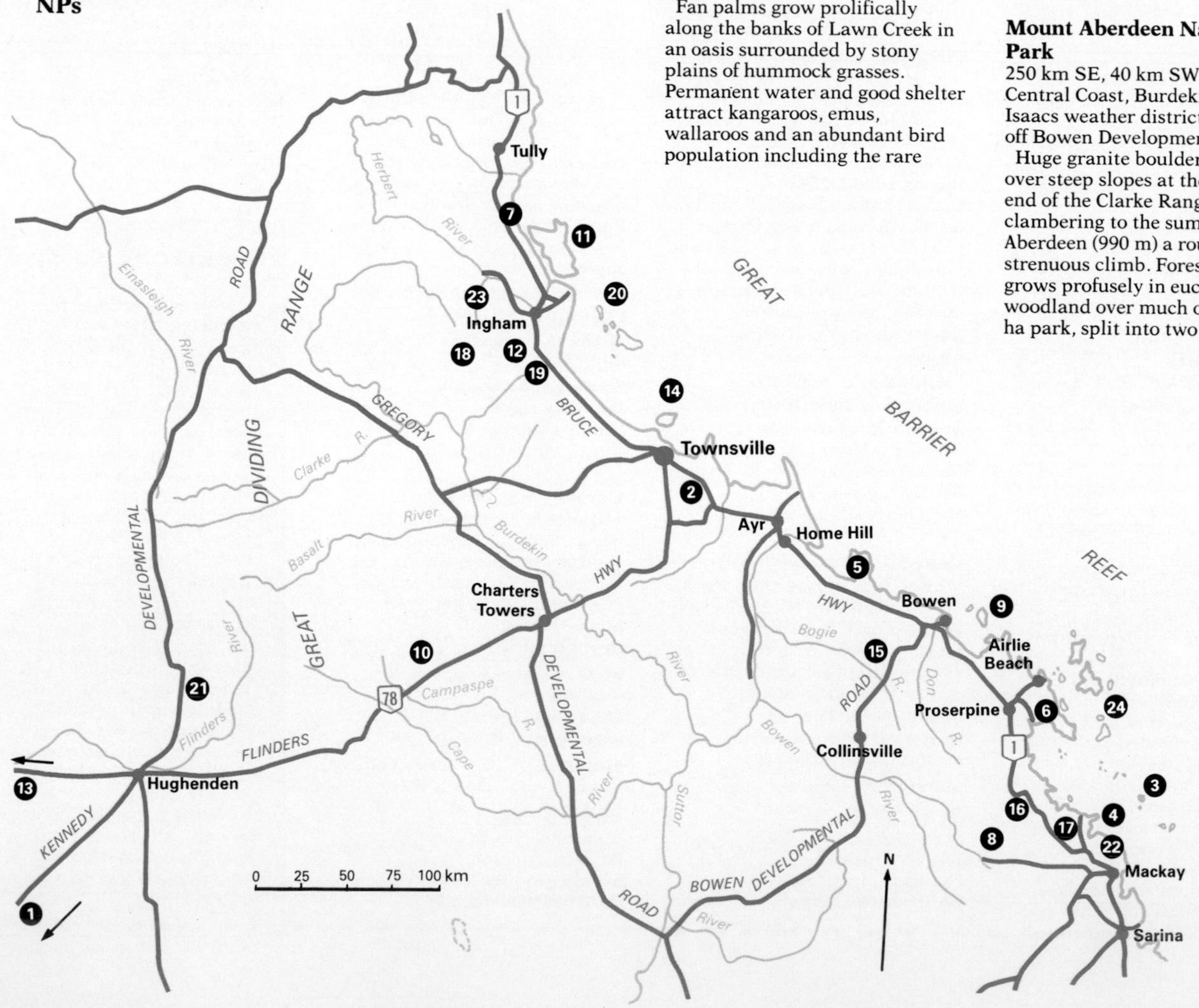

around the Elliot River valley. Moist, sheltered gullies support patches of low vine forest containing hoop pine.

BEST TIME: Autumn, spring.
ENQUIRIES: (079) 46 9430.
ADDRESS: As for Conway.

Scenic enjoyment ✔✔
Day activities ✖
Family camping ✖
Hard bushwalking ✔

Mount Beatrice National Park

330 km SE, 55 km S of Proserpine. Central Coast, Burkedin and Isaacs weather district. Access on foot from Bruce Highway at Yalboroo.

Eucalypt forest and patches of hoop pine rainforest clothe steep slopes rising to the peaks of Mt Beatrice (525 m), Mt Zillah (502 m) and Mt Catherine (476 m) in the distinct mountainous block of this 1140 ha park. Seasonal streams flow through deep gullies to lower-lying scrubland before joining Alligator Creek.

BEST TIME: Autumn, spring.
ENQUIRIES: (079) 57 6292.
ADDRESS: As for Brampton.

Scenic enjoyment ✔
Day activities ✖
Family camping ✖
Hard bushwalking ✖

Mount Blackwood National Park

370 km SE, 30 km NW of Mackay. Central Coast, Burdekin and Isaacs weather district. Foot access from Seaforth road off Bruce Highway at Kuttabul. Permission to cross private property must be arranged.

A television tower atop Mt Blackwood (590 m) stands out above a sea of low-lying sugarcane fields. Patches of hoop pine rainforest grow among eucalypt forest over a 1000 ha park preserved from development by precipitous slopes unsuited to agriculture.

Two smaller parks preserve similar mountainous outcrops on the coastal fringe north of Mackay. Double-peaked **Mt Jukes** (547 m), just north of Mt Blackwood, carries only a sparse cover of vegetation over its 600 ha. Bare rock faces give little opportunity for plant life to develop, though some eucalypt forest and rainforest have grown on soils collected in sheltered gullies.

Mt Mandurana, also known as The Leap, rises 316 metres above a small settlement on the Bruce Highway. A spur rising from the roadside provides the easiest access to a rocky peak through grassy patches, eucalypt forest and vine scrub in a park of 100 ha.

BEST TIME: Autumn, spring.
ENQUIRIES: (079) 57 6292.
ADDRESS: As for Brampton.

Scenic enjoyment ✔
Day activities ✖
Family camping ✖
Hard bushwalking ✖

Mount Fox National Park

180 km NW, 65 km SW of Ingham. North Coast, Tableland and Peninsula weather district. Car access along unsealed road S of Trebonne, 8 km W of Ingham.

The rocky volcanic cone of Mt Fox rises to 811 metres around a long-extinct crater. A thick growth of grasses masks big rocks scattered over the crater floor and makes walking difficult because of unsure footing. To the south erosion has breached the crater rim and grasses, mainly kangaroo grass, spill out over gentle slopes. Patches of low rainforest grow in moister, sheltered areas of the 200 ha park.

BEST TIME: Winter, spring.
ENQUIRIES: (077) 74 1411.
ADDRESS: As for Bowling Green Bay.

Scenic enjoyment ✔✔
Day activities ✖
Family camping ✖
Hard bushwalking ✖

Mount Spec National Park

70 km NW. North Coast, Tableland and Peninsula weather district. Car access to Little Crystal Creek and Paluma Dam off Bruce Highway 67 km N of Townsville; to Big Crystal Creek along unsealed road 69 km N.

DESCRIPTION: Page 424.
BEST TIME: Autumn, spring.
ENQUIRIES: (077) 74 1411.
ADDRESS: As for Bowling Green Bay.

Scenic enjoyment ✔✔✔
Day activities ✔✔✔
Family camping ✔✔
Hard bushwalking ✔

Orpheus Island National Park

75 km NW, 20 km SE of Lucinda. North Coast, Tableland and Peninsula weather district. Accessible by boat from Lucinda. Resort launch from Lucinda.

Cabins of a small tourist resort on Hazard Bay are backed by the low forests and grassland of this 1400 ha park. The island is 11 km long but less than 2 km at its widest, with hilly outcrops rising to round 120 metres linked by narrow saddles. Eucalypts cover most of the island, interspersed with patches of tussock and rainforest in sheltered gullies. Coral reefs fringe rocky shores and strips of sandy beach popular for swimming and snorkelling.

BEST TIME: Autumn, spring.
ENQUIRIES: (070) 66 8601.
ADDRESS: As for Edmund Kennedy.

Scenic enjoyment ✔✔
Day activities ✔✔
Family camping ✖
Hard bushwalking ✖

Porcupine Gorge National Park

430 km W, 50 km N of Hughenden. Carpentaria, Gulf Rivers weather district. Car access N from Hughenden along Kennedy Developmental Road (mostly unsealed). Road impassable after heavy rains.

DESCRIPTION: Page 440.
BEST TIME: Autumn, spring.
ENQUIRIES: (077) 74 1411.
ADDRESS: As for Bowling Green Bay.

Scenic enjoyment ✔✔✔
Day activities ✔
Family camping ✖
Hard bushwalking ✔✔

Reliance Creek National Park

400 Km SE, 10 km NW of Mackay. Central Coast, Burdekin and Isaacs weather district, Car access from Mackay along Habana road.

Rising on the slopes of mountainous outcrops close to the coast, Reliance Creek's short course flows through a patchwork of sugarcane fields towards a mangrove-clogged sea outlet. On its lower reaches the creek waters a 14 ha park around the depression of Palm Swamp. Well-developed palm-vine forest has been preserved here from the clearing and swamp drainage which has accompanied the expansion of the sugar industry. The park has not been developed, but provides an excellent environment for ecological study of a forest type fast disappearing from the tropical coast south of Ingham.

BEST TIME: Autumn, spring.
ENQUIRIES: (079) 57 6292.
ADDRESS: As for Brampton.

Scenic enjoyment ✔
Day activities ✖
Family camping ✖
Hard bushwalking ✖

Wallaman Falls National Park

160 km NW, 50 km W of Ingham. North Coast, Tableland and Peninsula weather district. Car access along unsealed road W of Trebonne, 8 km W of Ingham.

DESCRIPTION: Page 427.

Wilderness parks of eucalypt forest and rainforest surround lesser falls on the Herbert River and its tributaries north of Wallaman. Only seasoned bushwalkers prepared for rockhopping along creek banks and steep climbs through dense undergrowth attempt the treks to **Herbert River Falls** (2400 ha), **Yamanie Falls** (9700 ha), **Herkes Creek Falls** (500 ha), **Sword Creek Falls** (500 ha), **Garrawalt Falls** (500 ha), and **Broadwater Creek Falls** (500 ha).

BEST TIME: Late summer for falls viewing, spring or autumn for camping.
ENQUIRIES: (077) 76 1700.
ADDRESS: 2 Herbert Street, Box 1293, Ingham 4850.

Scenic enjoyment ✔✔✔
Day activities ✔✔
Family camping ✔✔
Hard bushwalking ✔

Whitsunday Islands National Parks

230-300 km Se, 50-120 km N of Mackay. Central Coast, Burdekin and Isaacs weather district. Accessible by boat from Shute Harbour, Airlie Beach, Seaforth and Mackay. Launches and charter boats from Shute Harbour and Airlie Beach; flights from Mackay and Proserpine.

Islands around Whitsunday Passage are the peaks of a mountain range that was joined to the mainland across a deep valley until it was flooded by rising sea levels about 8000 years ago. Rough, hilly terrain with precipitous cliffs and craggy peaks are striking features of the island landscapes. Drowned valleys around the big mountainous islands, Hook and Whitsunday, form fjord-like inlets capable of sheltering ocean liners. Many smaller islands have shallower bays which offer good anchorage for yachts and launches off shores lined with sandy beaches and fringing reefs of coral.

Eucalypt forests dominate the island's vegetation cover. Dense vine scrub crowds moist gullies and belts of casuarina fringe the high water line. Hoop pine rainforest grows untouched on well-watered and sheltered slopes. Tussock grassland dotted with grass-trees and cycads occurs on slopes exposed to strong prevailing winds.

A few of the islands are owned freehold, but most are national parks. Even the popular tourist resorts have carved out only small leases on the islands they occupy. Cruises from Mackay and Shute Harbour bring the resort island parks within easy reach for day-visit walks along extensive formed trails to quiet beaches away from the tourist facilities. Many trips include the underwater coral reef observatory on Hook Island.

Water taxis and chartered boats provide dependable access to many of the uninhabited islands. Established camping sites have been developed at the parks of **Whitsunday Island** (10 930 ha), **Thomas Island** (405 ha), **Henning Island** (40 ha), **North Molle Island** (259 ha), **Outer Newry Island** (58 ha), **Rabbit Island** (348 ha), and **Shute Island** (13 ha).

Popular camping grounds without facilities, but with good boat access and pleasant beachfront sites, are found on **Hook Island** (5180 ha), **Border Island** (388 ha), **Cid Island** (388 ha), **Shaw Island** (1659 ha), **Haslewood Island** (800 ha) and **Tancred Island** (6 ha). Some islands are little more than rocky outcrops of no attraction to holiday makers. Parks of less than 20 ha are on **Seaforth, Dungurra, Arkhurst, Langford, Bird, Black, Repair, Mid Molle, Planton, Denman, Nunga, Gungwiya, Yerumbinna, Wirrainbcia, Ireby, Sillago, Buddi Buddi, Pincer, Blackcombe, Acacia, Mausoleum, North Repulse, Yiundalla, Anchorsmith, Anvil, Locksmith, Bellows** and **Goat Islands,** and **Surprise Rock.**

Much better chances of shelter and a safe landing site can be expected on larger national park islands of around 20-50 ha on **Volskow, Triangle, Comston, Baynham, Gaibirra, Little Lindeman, Perseverance, Deloraine, Dumbell, Esk, Nicolson, Workington, Harold, Edward, Silversmith, Hammer, Ingot, Tinsmith, South Repulse** and **East Repulse Islands.** Largest of the undeveloped islands are **Mansell, Keyser, Maher, Pentecost, Pine, Teague, Lupton, Ladysmith** and **Blacksmith Islands** at around 100 ha, **Linne Island** (405 ha) and **Goldsmith Island** (648 ha).

NOTE: No camping in resort island parks of **Lindeman Island** (700 ha) **Newry Island** (53 ha) and **South Molle** (400 ha). There is a private camping area at **Long Island** (1030 ha). Check with ranger about availability of water at campsites; supplies must be carried to most islands.

BEST TIME: Autumn to spring.
ENQUIRIES: (079) 46 9430.
ADDRESS: As for Conway.

Scenic enjoyment ✔✔✔
Day activities ✔✔✔
Family camping ✔✔✔
Hard bushwalking ✔

THE KILLER OF CORAL

MANY kinds of starfish eat living corals. Few of them do much damage – except for the voracious crown-of-thorns (pictured). Adults grow as big as dustbin lids, and each can bare a square metre of reef surface in a week. Local infestations hurt the tourist trade, but scientists no longer regard them with much alarm. Crown-of-thorns plagues seem to be part of a natural, recurring pattern – and damaged reefs regenerate in a few years.

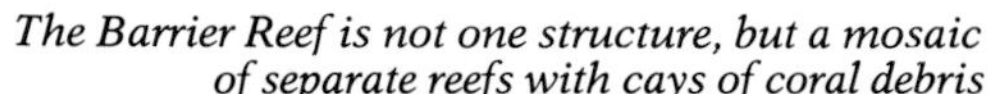

The Barrier Reef is not one structure, but a mosaic of separate reefs with cays of coral debris

An Australian Institute of Marine Science diver surveys a section of reef. Towed by a boat, he uses an aquafoil to control depth and angle of approach

Guarding an

ALL BUT 1.5 per cent of the Great Barrier Reef region is managed as a marine park. Embracing nearly 350 000 square kilometres of the waters, coral reefs and seabed off the Queensland coast between Cape York and Fraser Island, it is the biggest area of planned conservation in the world. The only exclusions are islands – many of them protected as national parks – and some inshore waters that are governed by port authorities.

Oil drilling and other mining are prohibited throughout the marine park. What else may be permitted depends on a system of zoning prescriptions. Tourist operations and commercial fishing are allowed in many zones. But where reefs are regarded as especially delicate and vulnerable, such activities are banned. Control is exercised mainly through the issue of permits specifying who can do what in a given zone, and what conditions must be met.

The Great Barrier Reef Marine Park Authority was set up by federal legislation in 1975, and the park was de-

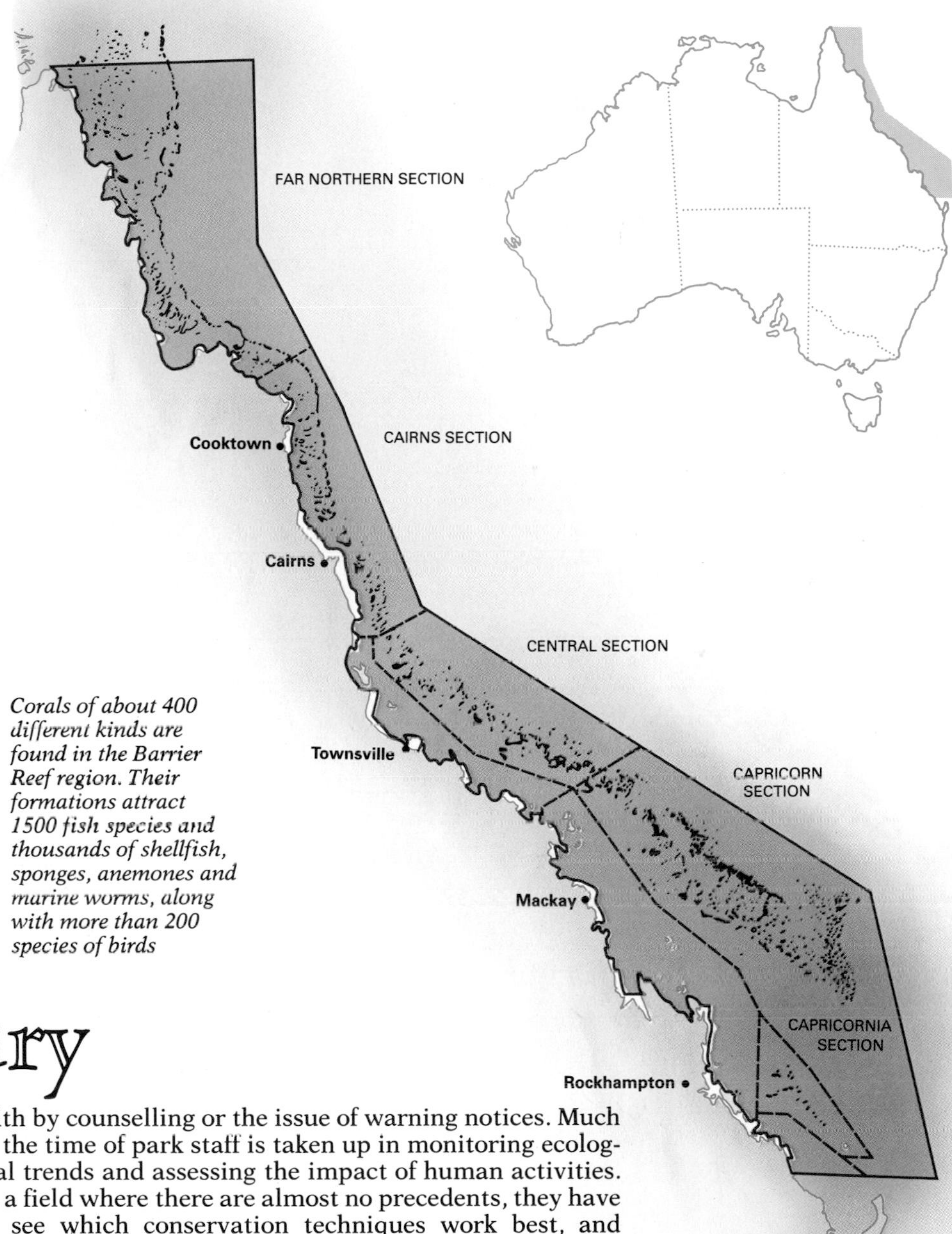

Corals of about 400 different kinds are found in the Barrier Reef region. Their formations attract 1500 fish species and thousands of shellfish, sponges, anemones and marine worms, along with more than 200 species of birds

When fully operational, the Great Barrier Reef Marine Park will be the world's biggest zone of systematic conservation

underwater treasury

clared in sectional stages between then and 1983. Planning was slow and careful because management of a marine environment is much more complicated than running a park on land. Rather than preserving tangible things that stay more or less in the same place, it is a matter of preserving processes. Some of these – fish migrations, for example – have no set geographical boundaries. Many, such as the periodic infestations by the crown-of-thorns starfish, are poorly understood.

Day-to-day management is delegated to the Queensland National Parks and Wildlife Service. Its operations have been reorganised so that the marine park and the island national parks are looked after jointly, along with some state marine parks. Compliance with zoning rules is aided by surface and aerial patrols. Air crews engaged in general coastal surveillance also send in observations.

In the park's early years, inspectors have concentrated on an educational role. Infringements are usually dealt with by counselling or the issue of warning notices. Much of the time of park staff is taken up in monitoring ecological trends and assessing the impact of human activities. In a field where there are almost no precedents, they have to see which conservation techniques work best, and whether management programmes are achieving their objectives. Among the tasks has been the tagging of thousands of reef fish to discover their movements.

Major assistance in research is provided by the federally funded Australian Institute of Marine Science, based near Townsville. Its key programmes are aimed at a better understanding of the nature of reef systems and their ecological processes. Other scientific research is conducted from four island stations spread through the reef region. Studies at Heron Island, Orpheus Island and One Tree Island are supported by the Queensland, James Cook and Sydney Universities respectively. The Australian Museum maintains a station on Lizard Island.

Mountain waters bubble over the Boulders on the approach to Bellenden Ker National Park

CAIRNS REGION

Rainforest relics of a vanquished kingdom

IF TREES had their own paradise, it could have been the Atherton Tableland. Two million years or more of volcanic upheavals coated it with lava to produce mineral-rich basaltic soils. Temperatures encourage year-round growth. And the cloud-shrouded peaks of the Bellenden Ker Range, beside the coast just east of the tableland, mark the region of Australia's most lavish rains.

Such perfection made it too obvious a target. Even before timber-getters could pick over the fine softwoods of the rainforests, farmers trekked up the gorges from Cairns and Innisfail to clear arable land. Gold-rush money made a ready market for their produce – and when the gold ran out the miners, too, took up farming or horticulture. Before long the forests of the coastal lowlands also disappeared, giving way to West Indian sugarcane.

What remains on the plateau, among dairy pastures, cornfields and tobacco plantations, is a scattering of patches that were too hard to lay bare. All these forest remnants are associated with bolder landforms – volcanic peaks and craters, or broken ridges and steep gorges with rushing rivers and waterfalls. So in spite of their smallness they hold exceptional scenic interest.

Most are protected now as national parks. And some are so easily reached from Cairns that half a dozen can be toured in a day – though that is too short a time to see the wildlife they harbour, let alone to take in the complexities of plant interdependence in tropical rainforests.

Not far south, in Bellenden Ker National Park, bigger forests rule on steamy mountain slopes that sap the energy of any climber. To the north towards Cooktown, they have strongholds in Daintree, Dagmar Range, Cape Tribulation and Cedar Bay National Parks. Access is unlikely in the summer wet season and limited at the best of times – boding well for their future as rare biological reservoirs.

Cairns flourishes as a big-game fishing base, but it has little to offer in offshore scenery. Within economical distance there is only the tiny coral cay of Green Island, its forest pathways and beaches and reef trampled and littered by 200 000 visitors a year. But the submarine world is undisturbed – and visible from a glass-walled gallery built 6 metres below the coral shelf.

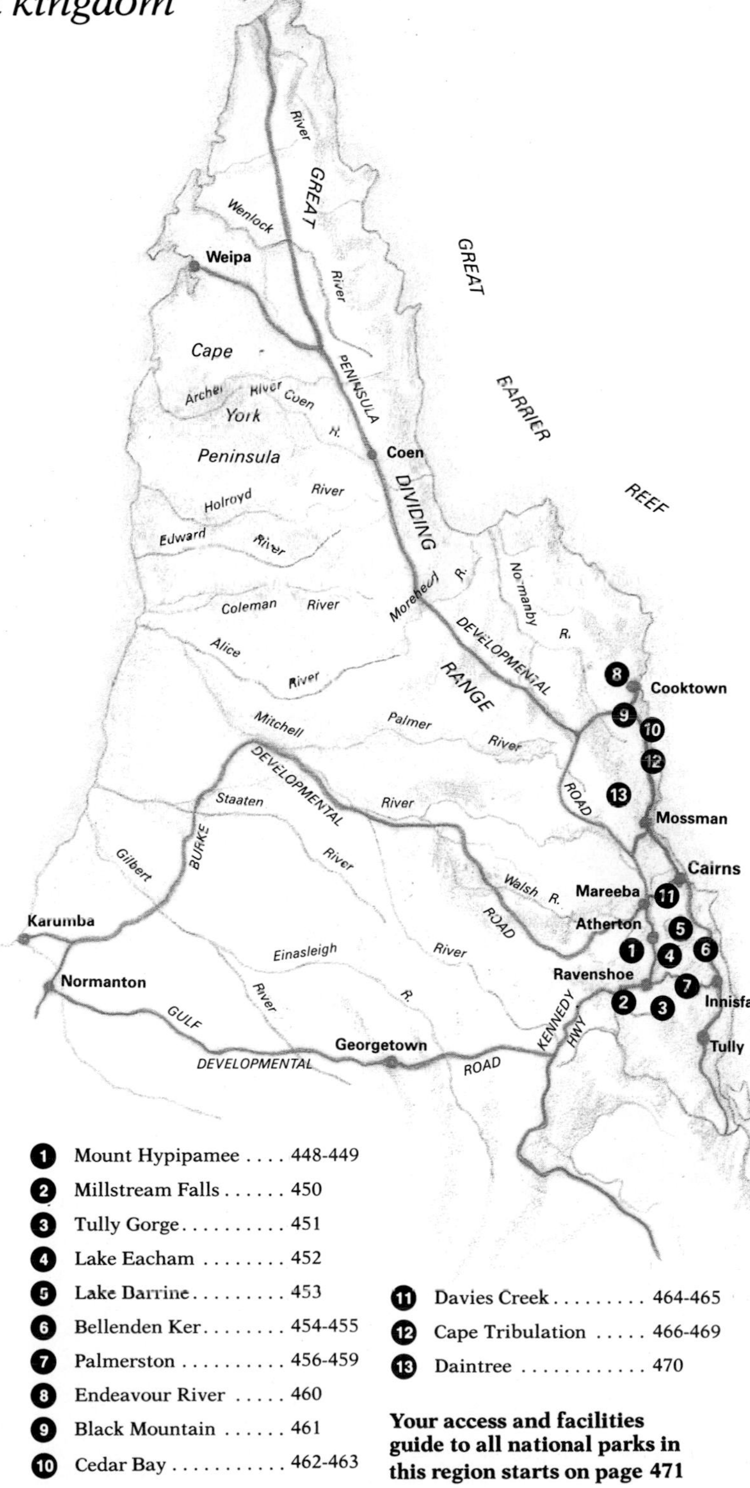

1 Mount Hypipamee 448-449
2 Millstream Falls 450
3 Tully Gorge 451
4 Lake Eacham 452
5 Lake Barrine 453
6 Bellenden Ker 454-455
7 Palmerston 456-459
8 Endeavour River 460
9 Black Mountain 461
10 Cedar Bay 462-463
11 Davies Creek 464-465
12 Cape Tribulation 466-469
13 Daintree 470

Your access and facilities guide to all national parks in this region starts on page 471

Mount Hypipamee National Park

A hole big enough to swallow a tower office block, with sheer walls plunging to a murky lake, gapes unnervingly among the rainforest of the Atherton Tableland. This cavity is a volcanic freak, with faces of granite instead of the usual basalt. Molten magma below could find no point of weakness through which to well up and build a cone. Instead its gases blasted a way out, and the rock material vanished in vapour and ash.

Towering kauri and black pine are dominant in a dense growth of rainforest trees and some eucalypts in the 360 ha park surrounding the crater. An easy track leads from picnic grounds to the crater rim. The route back passes the Barron River at Dinner Falls, where swimming is possible. Some 300 bird species frequent the area.

Staghorns are epiphytes that attach themselves to trees but live off dropped plant matter and moisture in the air

Right: Swimmers find cool refreshment at Dinner Falls, where a tributary creek spills into the Barron River

Left: Lake Hypipamee, its surface coated with algae, lies 60 metres below the crater rim. Rainforest trees (right) cloak the granite walls of the vast cavity. Fungi (above) encrusting their trunks grow profusely in warm, humid air

MILLSTREAM FALLS NATIONAL PARK

Queensland's widest waterfall – 65 metres across in full flow, and dropping 20 metres over a glistening shelf of dark basalt – makes a magnificent sight in autumn, as soon as possible after the North Queensland 'Wet' has ended. The flow continues year-round, however, even though the surrounding hills on the western slopes of the Atherton Tableland are dry and support only an open forest of eucalypts. Bottlebrush thickets border the Millstream – an important tributary of the Herbert River – on its course through the 370 ha park. Short walks are possible around the falls and the picnic ground above, and swimming is popular. Platypuses are commonly seen in placid pools above the falls, most often early or late in the day.

Lush, spray-fed plant growth protects soils above the falls from erosion by the torrential rains of the wet season

The Tully's bed is bone-dry here – but the river's former power can be seen in the cavernous cut it has made in a rainforested plateau

Tully Gorge National Park

References in outdated maps and tourist guides to a Tully 'Falls' national park leads many a traveller to disappointment. Unless the gorge is seen towards the end of a heavy summer wet season, when conditions are bound to be uncomfortable, there are no waterfalls worthy of the name. At most times the flow of the Tully River is harnessed upstream by the Koombooloomba Dam, for power generation. But the 500 ha park remains impressive for its views of the steep, rainforested gorge. There is usually some river water, and a creek flows by the picnic ground. A 1.5 km track leads to a fine lookout.

LAKE EACHAM NATIONAL PARK

Lake Eacham and nearby Lake Barrine are maars – volcanic craters without cores and with little accumulation of ejected material around them. They were formed about 10 000 years ago when water trapped underground was superheated by rising magma and exploded. Eacham, 65 metres deep, covers nearly a tenth of the 490 ha rainforest park. It has no visible outflow but the level drops about 4 metres during the dry season, presumably by seepage through the crater's lower wall.

Among about 80 species of large-leafed trees surrounding the lake are several types of stinging trees; it is wise to be able to identify and so avoid these as contact with them causes a painful irritation. Marsupials are fairly active by day in the gloom under the rainforest canopy. They include the musky rat-kangaroo – smallest of the macropods and the only one with a hind-foot first toe to aid climbing. The area is a stronghold of saw-shelled tortoises, and parrots and other birds abound. But the most beautiful sight to greet visitors is likely to be that of the 10 cm Ulysses or mountain blue butterfly. A 6.5 km track encircles the lake and other paths lead to seasonal waterfalls. The lake is ideal for swimming.

Slender trees and climbers, including native monstera, crowd the crater rim

Ipomoea, a vigorous tropical climber

Left: Deep volcanic soils beside Lake Barrine support a jungle of rainforest species, with lawyer vine Calamus sp *prominent in front*

Kauri pines, which evolved tens of millions of years before flowering trees, tower near the main lake track. They are closely related to species in New Zealand and New Caledonia. Each of this pair measures more than 6 metres around its straight bole

LAKE BARRINE NATIONAL PARK

Cassowaries are sometimes seen on the tracks that surround the 100 ha crater of Lake Barrine. Visitors should give them a wide berth – bigger and stronger than emus, they can inflict serious injury with their feet. Other birds of the 490 ha park include tooth-billed and satin bowerbirds, scrub fowl, brush turkeys, whipbirds, riflebirds, honeyeaters and many parrots. They have returned with the prohibition of water-skiing, which used to shatter the peace of the lake. A launch still makes scenic cruises, starting mid-morning and mid-afternoon. Swimming is popular. Walkers see most types of big rainforest trees, and in better light beside the lake there is a good chance of spotting pythons draped on the overhanging branches. They are harmless to humans.

Cycads, which recover from burning, are prominent in fire-prone foothill areas on the fringes of the rainforest. Right: Mist shrouds South Peak in the Bellenden Ker Range. Summit plants draw more moisture from mist and cloud than they do from rain

BELLENDEN KER NATIONAL PARK

Peaks ranked along the Bellenden Ker Range are almost constantly swathed in mist or cloud. In 31 000 ha this park has an extraordinary span of altitude, from 80 metres above sea level by the Bruce Highway to 1622 on the domed summit of Bartle Frere, Queensland's highest mountain. Experienced bushwalkers making the 15 km ascent on the new ungraded track to the summit see a transformation of forest types. Trees become shorter, their leaves smaller; the number of species and canopy layers diminishes. But ferns and orchids remain common. Above 1500 metres there is cloudforest – dense-canopied but only of scrub height. Australia's only native rhododendron grows here, flowering in the wet season when cloud cover is continuous. The park is largely undeveloped. Access for visitors not equipped for climbing is restricted to picnic areas near low-level waterfalls, where there are short walks and swimming is popular.

Palms and ferns overhang a shallow backwater of Josephine Creek. Cycad fronds (below) resemble those of palms, but the trees bear cones instead of flowers

Tough igneous boulders in Little Babinda Creek are wave-cut by a turbulent current flowing from the slopes of South Peak

Dense forest hems the fast-flowing Beatrice River, a tributary of the North Johnstone crossing the western end of the park

Below the soaking mists that cloak the Francis Range, the forest canopy seems to be impenetrable. But where there has been cyclone damage (below) more light comes in and vines compete with replacement trees

PALMERSTON NATIONAL PARK

Rainforest trees, although cut back when parts of the road were straightened, still wall the narrow, winding Palmerston Highway. A park of 14 200 ha straddles the road for 16 km, culminating at the eastern end in a pass overlooking the deep gorge of the North Johnstone River. Tracks lead down to the gorge, tributary creeks and waterfalls. There is swimming near a picnic area on Goolagan Creek and at the Henrietta Creek camping ground. Forest walks take from 30 minutes to a day.

This area receives an average annual rainfall of about 3500 mm – among the highest in Australia – concentrated between December and March. On deep, basalt-derived soils, tropical rainforest reaches the peak of its development. The park has more than 500 tree species, nearly all buttressed and vine-covered and hard to tell apart. Birdsnest and basket ferns flourish. Emerald doves and king parrots are prominent among a big population of birds.

Crawford's Lookout commands a striking view of the North Johnstone River, surging through a sharply cut gorge. A new 500 m track leads down to the gorge

A fig tree bristles with epiphyte ferns – birdsnests, basket ferns and other species. They draw most of their moisture from the air

PALMERSTON NATIONAL PARK

Rhaphidophora (top left) is a hardy climber with roots that creep upwards in the grooves of tree bark. Swamp water fern (left) and club moss (above) grow closest to the edges of rivers and creeks

Across tidal mudflats, the dunes of the park are backed by a rainforested coastal range

ENDEAVOUR RIVER NATIONAL PARK

A reserve of 1840 ha extending over mudflats and sand dunes north of the Endeavour River is chiefly of historical and scientific interest. On the opposite bank in 1770 Lieut. James Cook careened his reef-holed ship for repairs, giving the botanists Joseph Banks and Daniel Solander weeks ashore for the study of Australian plants. Part of the dune area supports a tall scrub community found nowhere else. Across the river, **MT COOK NATIONAL PARK** covers nearly 500 ha on the outskirts of Cooktown. Its forested peak, rising steeply to 432 metres, dominated a watercolour by Cook's draughtsman, Sydney Parkinson – the first known Australian landscape painting.

Mangroves colonise and help to stabilise river silts in the west of the park. Their expansion is perhaps the only change since James Cook sent parties to explore the area

Rainforest shrubs invade wherever they find fertility

Black Mountain National Park

Dark lichen coats boulders of granite – some as big as houses – carried down the slopes of Black Mountain (475 metres). A park of 780 ha embraces a section of the Black Trevethan Range. The rocky summits are bare but lower slopes support shorter rainforest plants and some scattered vine thickets that are leafless in the dry season. The area was reserved principally as a habitat of Queensland rock wallabies. Just outside the park, sidetracks from the main road lead to waterfalls on the Annan River and Mumgumby Creek – best seen in autumn as soon as the Cooktown road is open.

DAVIES CREEK NATIONAL PARK

An enormous flat granite boulder makes a perfect platform for viewing the 100 metre drop of the Davies Creek Falls. (There is a short walking track above the falls.) The stream, originating on Mt Tip Tree (1241 metres) in the Lamb Range, has a strong year-round flow through the park of 480 ha perches on the dry northwestern edge of the Atherton Tableland. Grassy eucalypt forests and woodlands, studded with grass-trees and big termite mounds, occupy broken slopes on each side of the creek. In contrast to the tree-crowded waterways of nearby rainforest parks, Davies Creek downstream of the falls has many open spots on its banks. There are good swimming holes near picnic areas. Walkers use a forestry trail, taking about 3 hours, to see more of the park.

Shelves of granite and lightly wooded slopes beside Davies Creek, below its falls, leave open areas where picnickers and swimmers enjoy winter sunshine

Right: Spray-loving shrubs and ferns overhang the foaming waters of Davies Creek Falls

Huge mounds built by colonies of grass-eating termites are common in the open woodlands

Papilio – widespread in Queensland

Rainforest reaching to the waterline at Bailey Point can be seen from Thornton Beach, a popular stop for tourist buses from Cairns

CAPE TRIBULATION NATIONAL PARK

Mt Sorrow presents a forbidding wall behind Cape Tribulation

Rainforest wilderness reaches from the heights of the Thornton Range to the Coral Sea, between the Daintree and Bloomfield Rivers. But its integrity is compromised by the exclusion of many coastal sections. When a national park of 17 000 ha was proclaimed in 1981 some enclaves of settlement or other development were necessarily left out. But a long and lonely northern strip from Cape Tribulation to Bloomfield was also excised. This became the focus of heated controversy when bulldozers moved in at the end of 1983 to clear the way for a 32 km road. A conservationist protest, with some actions reminiscent of the Gordon River blockade, soon turned into a political wrangle.

The park itself is entirely undeveloped. It includes the former Thornton Peak National Park, climbing to 1375 metres. Seasoned walkers can explore forests that are exceptional in their diversity of plants and wildlife. Seaside activities are concentrated outside the park.

Tangled mangroves flank Cape Tribulation Beach

Boulders of igneous rock make a platform north of Thornton Beach. The material has an exceptionally high density: when pebbles of it are thrown down they rebound back and forth. An accumulation of such pebbles on a nearby foreshore is known as the Bouncing Rocks

Cape Tribulation National Park

Tall piccabeen palms fringe Cooper Creek, which flows out at Thornton Beach. The denser rainforest of the national park closes in behind

Right: Palms, rainforest shrubs and twining lianes compete for light in a moist gully

Among a jumble of lowland rainforest species, even the clefts of broken rocks in midstream make a seeding ground for new plants

Towards the end of the dry season, when water levels are low, the boulder-strewn bed of the Mossman River makes a path for adventurous visitors to climb the forest-hemmed gorge. There is also a short nature walk from the park's popular picnic area and swimming hole

DAINTREE NATIONAL PARK

Upland tropical rainforests and woodlands cover the steep eastern scarps of the Windsor Tableland in a wilderness park of 56 000 ha. Waterfalls spill into fast-flowing streams that feed the Daintree River. The forests are a stronghold of tree frogs, tree kangaroos, ringtail possums and the golden bowerbird, which although the smallest of its kind may build a bower 10 metres high. Only the most seasoned and self-sufficient bushwalkers penetrate much of the park. There is a 3 km walking track from the car park at the Mossman River picnic area.

PARKS OF THE CAIRNS REGION

FACILITIES

Cabins

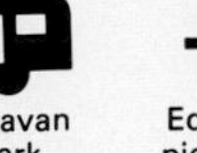
Caravan park

Equipped picnic area

Bush camping allowed

Lavatory building

Established campsite

Campsite but no car access

Note: Popular parks without campsites usually have public camping grounds nearby. If in doubt, call enquiries number.

PARK RATINGS No interest ✘ Some interest ✔ Major interest ✔✔ Outstanding ✔✔✔

Archer Bend National Park

750 km NW, 180 km NW of Coen. North Coast, Tableland and Peninsula weather district. 4WD only off Peninsula Developmental Road 107 km N of Coen via Merluna station (permission to cross station property must be pre-arranged). Roads impassable after heavy rains.

Seasonal floodwaters of the Archer River spread over an alluvial plain up to 8 km wide and sweep down to the Gulf of Carpentaria with such force that patches of grassy ground are stripped of vegetation. The river and its swamps and lagoons contain water even at the height of the dry season, supporting a diverse population of waterfowl and big numbers of freshwater crocodiles.

Rainforest crowds the riverbanks, giving way to thorn scrubs and melaleuca woodland towards the outer edges of the flood plain. Patches of grassy woodland occupy much of the northern section of this 166 000 ha park. Low sandstone ridges in the southwest support forests of eucalypt.

NOTE: Visitors must be fully equipped for outback survival.
BEST TIME: Winter.
ENQUIRIES: (070) 51 9811.
ADDRESS: QNPWS regional centre, Box 2066, Cairns 4870.

Scenic enjoyment ✔
Day activities ✘
Family camping ✘
Hard bushwalking ✘

Barron Gorge National Park

30 km NW. North Coast, Tableland and Peninsula weather district. Car access off Kennedy Highway at Kuranda. Train Cairns-Barron Falls.

A railway winds through rainforest and patches of eucalypt woodland in this 2800 ha park on its steep climb from Cairns to Kuranda on the Atherton Tableland. The trip is a popular tourist excursion and offers superb views of the gorge. Tinaroo Dam holds back the Barron's waters for irrigation and much of the flow at the falls is diverted for hydro-electric power generation. However, the falls are turned on for the tourist train and passengers are treated to the spectacle of water crashing down the 260 m drop.

BEST TIME: Winter.
ENQUIRIES: (070) 51 9811.
ADDRESS: As for Archer Bend.

Scenic enjoyment ✔✔✔
Day activities ✔
Family camping ✘
Hard bushwalking ✘

Bellenden Ker National Park

60 km S. North Coast, Tableland and Peninsula weather district. Car access off Bruce Highway from turnoffs at Babinda, Pawngilly and 5 km S of Gordonvale.

DESCRIPTION: Page 454.
NOTES: Hikers should lodge their itinerary with park ranger at Josephine Falls. Carry drinking water in winter and extra clothing to guard against sudden rainstorms and temperature drops at night.
WARNING: Cloud can cover the mountain peaks at short notice; care is needed to avoid getting lost.
BEST TIME: Winter.
ENQUIRIES: (070) 67 6304.
ADDRESS: QNPWS, Box 93, Miriwinni 4871.

Scenic enjoyment ✔✔✔
Day activities ✔✔
Family camping ✘
Hard bushwalking ✔✔✔

Black Mountain National Park

305 km N, 30 km S of Cooktown. North Coast, Tableland and Peninsula weather district. Cairns-Cooktown road skirts western boundary.

DESCRIPTION: Page 461.
BEST TIME: Winter.
ENQUIRIES: (070) 53 4533.
ADDRESS: As for Archer Bend.

Scenic enjoyment ✔✔
Day activities ✘
Family camping ✘
Hard bushwalking ✘

Cape Melville National Park

510 km NW, 200 km N of Cooktown. North Coast, Tableland and Peninsula weather district. Vehicle access by 4WD only from Cooktown north via Starcke station (permission to cross private property must be pre-arranged). Roads impassable after heavy rains. Accessible by boat from Cooktown.

Jumbled granite boulders, some covered by black lichen, cap the Melville Range above a coast of rocky headlands and white sandy beaches lining Bathurst Bay. Vine scrub grows in hollows between the boulders and vine forest has developed on a small area of tableland.

Swamps scattered at the base of the range support palms, tea-tree and heath communities. In the south of the 36 000 ha park, slopes drop abruptly to a broad plain of eucalypt and paperbark forest interspersed with extensive areas of heath and grevillea scrubland.

Islands of the **Flinders Group National Park** (3000 ha) lie off the western end of Bathurst Bay. Sheer cliffs drop to the sea around Stanley and Flinders Islands, the two largest of the group, separated by a narrow channel and clothed in eucalypt forest. Mangroves completely cover three smaller islands. There is a QNPWS base on Flinders.

BEST TIME: Winter.
ENQUIRIES: (070) 51 9811.
ADDRESS: As for Archer Bend.

Scenic enjoyment ✔✔
Day activities ✘
Family camping ✘
Hard bushwalking ✘

Cape Tribulation National Park

140 km N, 64 km N of Mossman. North Coast, Tableland and Peninsula weather district. Car access north from Mossman; 4WD recommended year-round, and essential December-March. Vehicle ferry crosses Daintree River.

DESCRIPTION: Page 467.
BEST TIME: Winter.
ENQUIRIES: (070) 51 9811.
ADDRESS: As for Archer Bend.

Scenic enjoyment ✔✔✔
Day activities ✔✔
Family camping ✘
Hard bushwalking ✔✔

Cedar Bay National Park

320 km N, 50 km S of Cooktown. North Coast, Tableland and Peninsula weather district. Rough track south from Cooktown via Bloomfield cuts through park. Cedar Bay itself accessible only by water. Cairns-Bloomfield about 200 km by Cape Tribulation road (4WD from Daintree ferry); often closed after rain.

DESCRIPTION: Page 462.
BEST TIME: Winter.
ENQUIRIES: (070) 51 9811.
ADDRESS: As for Archer Bend.

Scenic enjoyment ✔✔✔
Day activities ✘
Family camping ✘
Hard bushwalking ✔✔

Chillagoe-Mungana Caves National Parks

220 km W. North Coast, Tableland and Peninsula weather district. Car access off Burke Developmental Road at Chillagoe, road difficult in wet conditions. Train Cairns-Chillagoe weekly. Bus tours Cairns-Chillagoe twice weekly.

Caves around the small township of Chillagoe contain fossils of coral and other marine organisms trapped about 400 million years ago when sediments covered coral reefs in a shallow sea. Earth movements lifted and tilted the limestone bed, and fault line cracks allowed fluctuating ground water levels to carve out vast chambers. Lime-bearing water constantly dripping into the caverns has created impressive formations including stalactites and stalagmites, flowstones resembling a frozen waterfall, and helictites.

Nine individual national parks preserve the formations: **Royal Arch Cave** (1500 ha), **Tower of London and Donna Caves** (178 ha), **Jubilee and Piano Caves** (126 ha), **Cathedral Cave** (20 ha), **Geck and Spring Caves** (35 ha), **Eclipse Cave** (1 ha), **Ryan Imperial Cave** (1 ha), **Markham Cave** (1 ha) and **Royal Archway Cave** (1 ha).

Daily tours guided by park rangers follow tracks through mazes of chambers and galleries at Royal Arch Cave and Donna Cave. Donna and Trezkinn Caves are electrically lit. Visitors to Royal Arch, Pompeii, Bohemia and several others should carry battery torches. Smaller cave systems can be visited without a guide, but a strong torch is need to supplement low filtered daylight for exploring side passages and darker recesses.

NOTE: Camping and picnic facilities are at Royal Arch Cave.
BEST TIME: Winter.
ENQUIRIES: (070) 94 7163.
ADDRESS: QNPWS district office, Box 38, Chillagoe 4871.

Scenic enjoyment ✔✔✔
Day activities ✔✔✔
Family camping ✔✔
Hard bushwalking ✘

Dagmar Range National Park

100 km NW. North Coast, Tableland and Peninsula weather district. Mossman-Daintree road skirts eastern boundaries of park's two sections.

Rainforest thick with tangled vines creates a virtually impenetrable barrier on the lower slopes and in the interconnecting gullies of Dagmar Range. The forest canopy opens with the growth of tall eucalypts on higher slopes which rise to 298 metres at Kilkeary Hill, above canefields and mangrove flats at the mouth of the Daintree River. Drier, flatter areas support grassy eucalypt woodlands. Intermingling of forest types on diverse landforms creates a great variety of plant cover.

A close network of ridges and streams covers the 2500 ha park, broken into two sections at the northern and southern ends of the range.

NOTE: Permission for walking access over private property must be pre-arranged.
BEST TIME: Winter.
ENQUIRIES: (070) 51 9811.
ADDRESS: As for Archer Bend.

Scenic enjoyment ✔✔
Day activities ✘
Family camping ✘
Hard bushwalking ✔

Daintree National Park

80 km N, 5 km W of Mossman. North Coast, Tableland and Peninsula weather district. Car access to Mossman Gorge from Mossman. Unsealed road into undeveloped southwest of park off Peninsula Developmental Road 32 km north of Mount Molloy.

DESCRIPTION: Page 470.
BEST TIME: Winter.
ENQUIRIES: (070) 51 9811.
ADDRESS: As for Archer Bend.

Scenic enjoyment ✔✔
Day activities ✔✔
Family camping ✘
Hard bushwalking ✔✔

PARKS OF THE CAIRNS REGION

Davies Creek National Park

60 km W, 30 km S of Kuranda. North Coast, Tableland and Peninsula weather district. Car access off Kennedy Highway between Kuranda and Mareeba.

DESCRIPTION: Page 464.
BEST TIME: Winter.
ENQUIRIES: (070) 51 9811.
ADDRESS: As for Archer Bend.

Scenic enjoyment ✔✔
Day activities ✔✔✔
Family camping ×
Hard bushwalking ×

Dunk Island National Park

120 km S, 8 km SE of Clump Point. North Coast, Tableland and Peninsula weather district. Launch from Clump Point; flights from Cairns.

A forest-clad ridge forms the backbone of Dunk Island and separates the 730 ha national park from low-lying and mostly cleared ground in the western part of the island, where a busy resort complex overlooks Brammo Bay. Rainforest grows close to the water's edge, fringing a number of narrow beaches – some only accessible by boat. Walking tracks reach Mt Kootaloo (271 m) and the beach at Coconut Bay, which is as impressive as any near the resort. Walkers have a good chance of seeing the striking bright blue Ulysses butterfly.

A string of smaller islands are preserved as national parks along the coast between Mourilyan and Cardwell. They are largely undeveloped apart from some picnic areas, but many have pleasant beaches where small boats can be landed for day trips or extended camping holidays.

Kumboola Island (12 ha) and **Mung-um Nackum Island** (2 ha) are connected to Dunk by a reef, almost uncovered at low tide, and **Purtaboi Island** (6 ha) with its razorback ridges and sand flats sits off Brammo Bay to the north.

Stephens Island (24 ha), **Sisters Island** (5 ha), **Hutchinsons Island** (19 ha), and **Jessie Island** (6 ha) in the Barnard Group 30 km north of Dunk are continental islands covered with rainforest, melaleuca and mangrove forests. **Wheeler Island** (31 ha), **Coombe Island** (49 ha), **Smith Island** (10 ha), **Bowden Island** (10 ha) and **Hudson Island** (20 ha) in the Family Group 15 km south of Dunk are dominated by a mixture of mesophyll species with low patches of eucalypt and casuarina.

BEST TIME: Winter.
ENQUIRIES: (070) 66 8601.
ADDRESS: QNPWS district office, Box 74, Cardwell 4816.

Scenic enjoyment ✔✔✔
Day activities ✔✔
Family camping ✔
Hard bushwalking ✔

Ella Bay and Moresby Range National Parks

Both parks 100 km S; Ella Bay 10 km NE of Innisfail, Moresby Range 10 km SE. North Coast, Tableland and Peninsula weather district. Car access to Ella Bay off Bruce Highway from Innisfail via Flying Fish Point; to Etty Bay, just outside Moresby Range park boundary, off Bruce Highway at Mourilyan.

Parts of the broken wall of low mountain ranges lining the rainforest coast east of Innisfail are preserved as national parks north and south of the Johnstone River mouth. Only determined bushwalkers make it into the forest's dense, mosquito-infested undergrowth of sharp lawyer vines and pandanus leaves.

Faint tracks attributed to the constant passage of cassowaries have been followed to the ridge top of Moresby Range where open forest clear of undergrowth allows patchy views across lowland canefields to the west. To the east the slopes of this 240 ha park fall steeply to rocky outcrops on the shoreline.

Mt Maria, at the southern end of 3400 ha Ella Bay National Park, overlooks swampland and scattered scrub at the base of the Seymour Range.

BEST TIME: Winter.
ENQUIRIES: (070) 67 6304.
ADDRESS: As for Bellenden Ker.

Scenic enjoyment ✔
Day activities ×
Family camping ×
Hard bushwalking ✔

Endeavour River and Mount Cook National Parks

Endeavour River 340 km NW, 5 km W of Cooktown; Mount Cook 2 km SE of Cooktown. North Coast, Tableland and Peninsula weather district. Car access to both parks from Cooktown. Endeavour River accessible by boat.

DESCRIPTION: Page 460.
BEST TIME: Winter.
ENQUIRIES: (070) 51 9811.
ADDRESS: As for Archer Bend.

Scenic enjoyment ✔
Day activities ×
Family camping ×
Hard bushwalking ✔

Eubenangee Swamp National Park

80 km S, 16 km NW of Innisfail. North Coast, Tableland and Peninsula weather district. Car access off Bruce Highway from Miriwinni.

A boardwalk across pools of standing water strikes into the heart of melaleuca swampland fringing Eubenangee's open lagoons and lily ponds. The 1500 ha park is an important refuge for birdlife, particularly the waterfowl which flock to it during inland dry periods. Freshwater crocodiles inhabit the swamp throughout the year.

The track to the boardwalk climbs a grassy hill which offers a lookout over the swamp and a convenient spot for bird watching.

Basket ferns and orchids are among the epiphytic plants that cling to the branches of paperbarks. Rainforest, strewn with fallen logs and rocks covered in mosses, liverworts and lichen, grows in patches along creeks feeding the swamp, but a tangle of vines makes hard going even on the shortest of walks.

BEST TIME: Winter.
ENQUIRIES: (070) 51 9811.
ADDRESS: As for Archer Bend.

Scenic enjoyment ✔✔
Day activities ✔
Family camping ×
Hard bushwalking ×

Forty Mile Scrub National Park

240 km SW, 60 km SW of Mount Garnet. North Coast, Tableland and Peninsula weather district. Kennedy Highway passes through the park.

White cedar, coffee senna and poison peach, growing along the road margins of this 4600 ha park are among the species which have been quickest to reclaim land cleared during construction of the Kennedy Highway. Behind them, low dry scrub of Burdekin plum, kurrajong and bottle tree is distinguished by an understorey of turkey bush, and thickets of hard, corky-barked vines which shed leaves during the winter dry season. Red-legged pademelons and black-striped wallabies use the thickets as shelter from the fierce daytime heat. Grassy eucalypt woodland, containing bloodwoods and ghost gum, and some ironbark forest surround the scrubland.

BEST TIME: Winter.
ENQUIRIES: (070) 95 3768.
ADDRESS: As for Lake Eacham.

Scenic enjoyment ✔
Day activities ×
Family camping ×
Hard bushwalking ×

Frankland Islands National Parks

45 km SE, 20 km NE of Bramston Beach. North Coast, Tableland and Peninsula weather district. Boat access.

White sandy beaches and shady eucalypt forests make the national park islands in the Frankland group popular destinations for picnic trips from the small resort of Bramston Beach. **Normanby Island** (6 ha), **High Island** (69 ha), **Mabel Island** (2 ha), and **Round Island** (1 ha), all undeveloped, are easily reached by boat and have fringing reefs of coral which delight snorkellers.

BEST TIME: Winter.
ENQUIRIES: (070) 51 9811.
ADDRESS: As for Archer Bend.

Scenic enjoyment ✔✔
Day activities ✔✔
Family camping ×
Hard bushwalking ×

Graham Range National Park

70 km SE, 19 km NE of Miriwinni. North Coast, Tableland and Peninsula weather district. 4WD only along rough track from Bramston Beach, 12 km off Bruce Highway at Miriwinni.

Beach ridges and swales support forests of casuarinas, melaleucas and acacias at the base of steep slopes rising to around 700 metres near Mt Josey in the northern block of the Graham Range. Paperbarks and pandanus grow thickly in swampland behind the coastal ridges, protecting an isolated occurrence of pitcher plants, normally found on swamp margins north of Coen on Cape York Peninsula, over 500 km away. North of the swamp a small area of grassland is hemmed in by the 2900 ha park's predominant rainforest vegetation. Vines, particularly species of calmus, grow vigorously throughout the forest and acacias occur increasingly towards the summit of the range.

River and estuary areas flanking the park to the west and north are preserved as national parks in **Russell River** (350 ha) and **Mutchero Inlet** (450 ha). Palm vine forests, mangroves and low melaleuca forest dominate wetlands best reached by canoe or dinghy.

BEST TIME: Winter.
ENQUIRIES: (070) 67 6304.
ADDRESS: As for Bellenden Ker.

Scenic enjoyment ✔✔
Day activities ×
Family camping ×
Hard bushwalking ×

Green Island National Park

30 km NE. North Coast, Tableland and Peninsula weather district. Daily boat services from Cairns.

Coral cay development at Green Island is seen at a highly advanced stage. Casuarinas, pandanus and tournefortias fringe the 12 ha island, enclosing vegetation similar to mainland rainforest but lacking its diversity – there are only 40-odd species. Fine sands of reef debris ring the island with superb beaches. On the windward southeast corner they are cemented to form exposed masses of beach rock.

Walking tracks wind through the 7 ha national park forest, but most interest on the island is generated by the displays of a small resort, and the 500 ha marine park reef around the cay. An observatory 6 m below sea level allows comfortable viewing of underwater reef life. Walks over the reef can be taken at low tide, and glass-bottom boats make frequent trips each day.

Tree cover is not yet established on the two cays of **Michaelmas and Upolu Cays National Park** (3 ha), northeast of Green Island. The cays are at an early stage of development with only a thin covering of coarse grasses and hardy creepers nourished by the droppings of thousands of seabirds, predominantly sooty terns and crested terns, breeding in dense colonies.

BEST TIME: Winter.
ENQUIRIES: (070) 51 9811.
ADDRESS: As for Archer Bend.

Scenic enjoyment ✔✔✔
Day activities ✔✔✔
Family camping ×
Hard bushwalking ×

Grey Peaks National Park

30 km S. North Coast, Tableland and Peninsula weather district. No vehicle access. Park approached on foot from Yarrabah road off Bruce Highway at Kamma.

Trackless rainforest with fan palms and emergent eucalypts clothes the Grey Peaks ridge, rising to 250 metres at the northern end of the Malbon Thompson Range. Bushwalkers find their own way into the 900 ha park through open areas scattered with trees and patches of forest.

BEST TIME: Winter.
ENQUIRIES: (070) 51 9811.
ADDRESS: As for Archer Bend.

Scenic enjoyment ✔
Day activities ×
Family camping ×
Hard bushwalking ✔

1. Archer Bend NP
2. Barron Gorge NP
3. Bellenden Ker NP
4. Black Mountain NP
5. Cape Melville NP
6. Cape Tribulation NP
7. Cedar Bay NP
8. Chillagoe-Mungana Caves NPs
9. Dagmar Range NP
10. Daintree NP
11. Davies Creek NP
12. Dunk Island NP
13. Ella Bay and Moresby Range NPs
14. Endeavour River and Mount Cook NPs
15. Eubenangee Swamp NP
16. Forty Mile Scrub NP
17. Frankland Islands NPs
18. Graham Range NP
19. Green Island NP
20. Grey Peaks NP
21. Hasties Swamp NP
22. Hull River NP
23. Iron Range NP
24. Jardine River NP
25. Kurrimine NP
26. Lake Barrine NP
27. Lake Eacham NP
28. Lakefield NP
29. Lizard Island NP
30. Maria Creek and Clump Mountain NPs
31. Millstream Falls NP
32. Mitchell and Alice Rivers NP
33. Mount Hypipamee NP
34. Mount Major NP
35. Palmerston NP
36. Possession Island NP
37. Rokeby NP
38. Staaten River NP
39. Starcke NP
40. Topaz Road NP
41. Tully Gorge NP

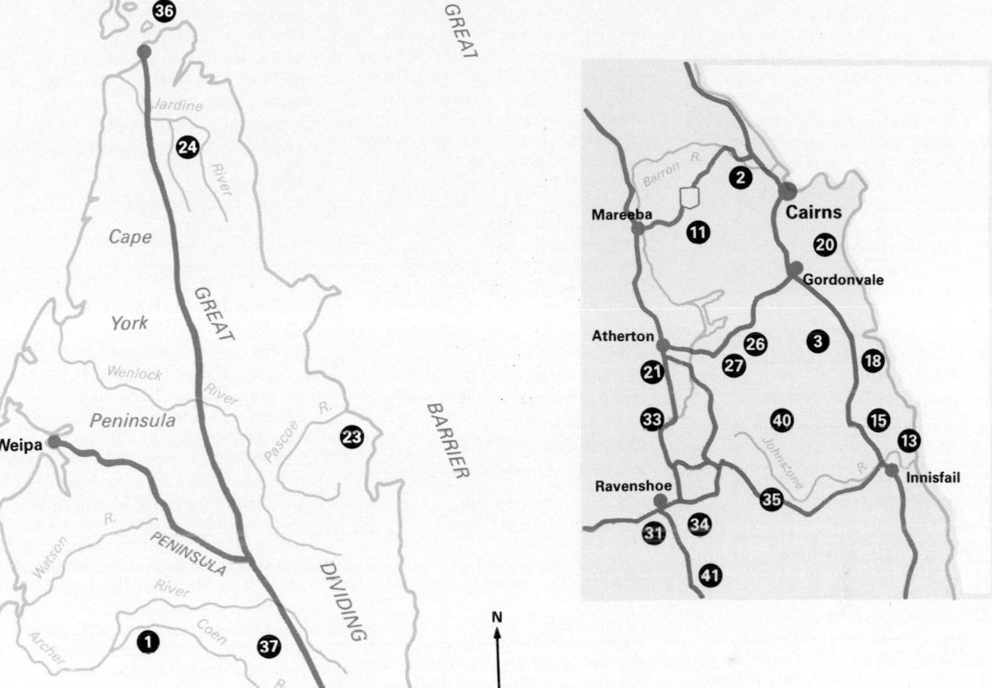

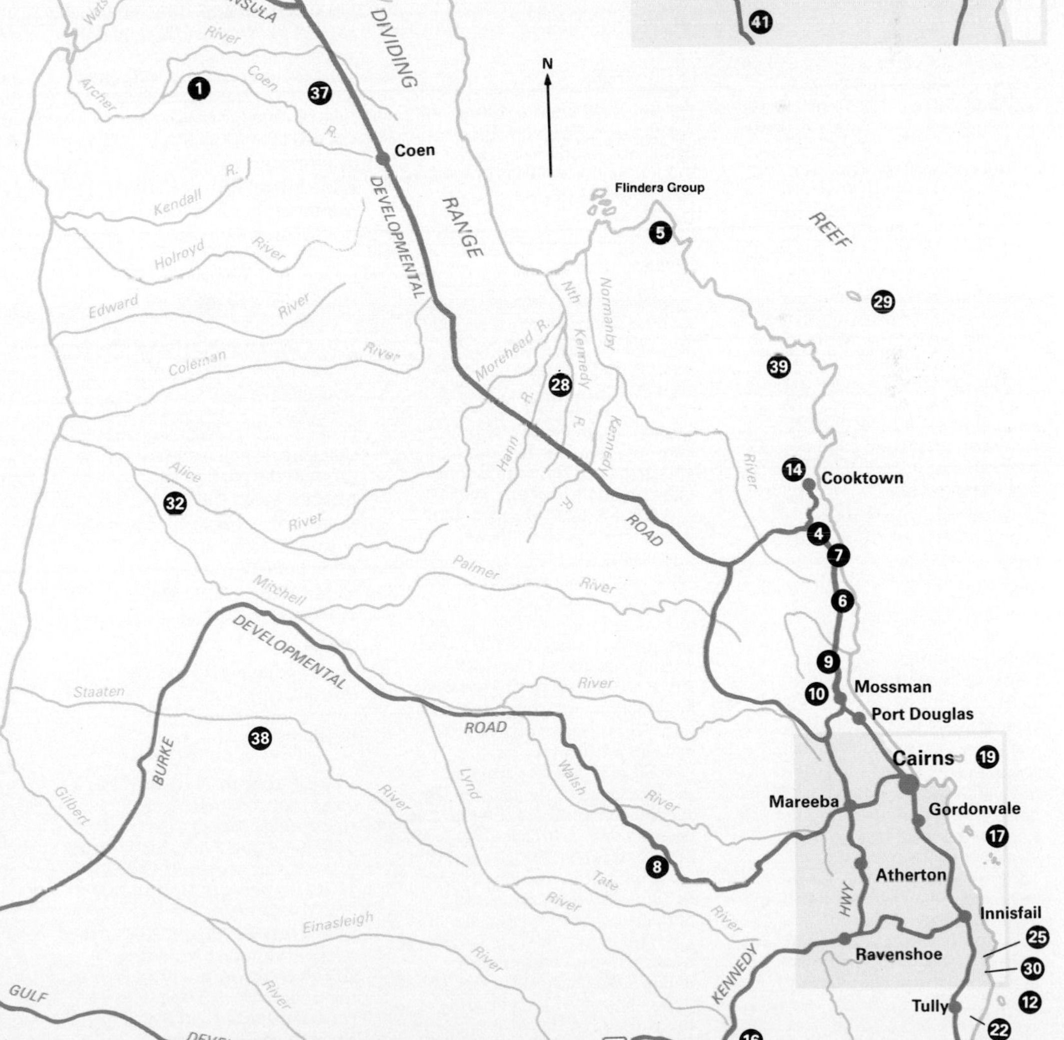

Hasties Swamp National Park
85 km SW, 4 km S of Atherton. North Coast, Tableland and Peninsula weather district. Car access off Herberton road from Atherton.

Preservation of this 60 ha swamp has secured an important habitat and breeding ground for a great diversity of waterfowl species. The area was once a camping and water reserve, but activities have been limited with the declaration of the national park to minimise disturbance to the birds. A hide on the swamp margin gives visitors a vantage point for birdwatching.

BEST TIME: Winter.
ENQUIRIES: (070) 95 3768.
ADDRESS: As for Lake Eacham.

Scenic enjoyment ✓
Day activities ✓
Family camping ×
Hard bushwalking ×

Hull River National Park
155 km S, 15 km E of Tully. North Coast, Tableland and Peninsula weather district. Car access along tracks from Lower Tully off Bruce Highway 5 km S of Tully.

Slopes around Mt Tam O'Shanter fall gently from high foothills covered with vine forest through tall grassy eucalypt woodland to paperback woodland on low-lying and poorly drained coastal soils. Waterfowl breed in sedge-lined swamps around the base of the hills. Creeks rising around Mt Tam O'Shanter and Mt Mackay wind through the 1100 ha park's mangrove flats to join the Hull and North Hull Rivers on their courses to Kennedy Bay.

BEST TIME: Winter.
ENQUIRIES: (070) 68 7183.
ADDRESS: Box 89, Mission Beach 4854.

Scenic enjoyment ✓
Day activities ×
Family camping ×
Hard bushwalking ×

Iron Range National Park
800 km N, 230 km N of Coen. North Coast, Tableland and Peninsula weather district. 4WD only off Peninsula Developmental Road 94 km N of Coen; track impassable after heavy rains.

Animals found in New Guinea but recorded no farther south in Australia, such as the palm cockatoo, eclectus parrot and grey cuscus, have an important refuge in the undisturbed lowland rainforests of Iron Range. Semi-deciduous vines grow profusely throughout the forest and in thickets, shedding leaves during the dry winters. Northern and western areas of this 35 000 ha wilderness reserve support eucalypts, turkey bush scrub on rocky slopes and stunted heath on the crests of the Janet and Tozer Ranges. Mangrove communities around the lower reaches of the Pascoe River include the unusual nypa or mangrove palm.

Little Roundback Hill, overlooking the beaches of Weymouth Bay on the park's northeastern boundary, was a depot for Edmund Kennedy's ill-fated expedition in 1848. Of eight men left here while Kennedy pushed on for Cape York, only two survived.

NOTE: Visitor must be fully equipped for outback survival.
BEST TIME: Winter.
ENQUIRIES: (070) 51 9811.
ADDRESS: As for Archer Bend.

Scenic enjoyment ✓✓✓
Day activities ×
Family camping ×
Hard bushwalking ×

Jardine River National Park
930 km N, 30 km S of Bamaga. North Coast, Tableland and Peninsula weather district. Vehicle access by 4WD only along rough track off Peninsula Developmental Road 120 km N of Coen; track impassable after heavy rains.

Eighteenth-century explorers named this vast wilderness in the Jardine River's catchment the 'wet desert'. The Jardine has Queensland's greatest year-round volume and water is abundant throughout the park. Vine scrubs, rainforest, sparse heathlands, swamps, overflow lagoons and grassless bogs full of poisonous plants made travel and even survival for early expeditions difficult and in some cases impossible.

The 235 000 ha national park remains virtually untouched and almost as forbidding to the best-equipped of modern 4WD safaris. A camping spot at the Jardine River crossing is one of the best known along the rough track to Cape York, but few travellers venture far from it.

Broad plateaux occupy much of the land around the head of the Jardine. Rainforest grows on the deepest soils, with eucalypt forest, heaths, scrub and bog vegetation elsewhere. Narrow depressions up to 30 metres deep dissect the plateaux; many are swampy and give rise to fast-flowing streams. Swamp forest containing paperbarks, palms and vine forest plants has developed in some of the valleys. To the west scores of freshwater streams cross the park's low sandy coastline, flowing through vegetated dunes from a low escarpment at the northern end of the Great Dividing Range.

NOTE: Visitors must be fully equipped for outback survival.
BEST TIME: Winter.
ENQUIRIES: (070) 51 9811.
ADDRESS: As for Archer Bend.

Scenic enjoyment ✓✓
Day activities ×
Family camping ×
Hard bushwalking ×

Kurrimine National Park
125 km S, 10 km E of Silkwood. North Coast, Tableland and Peninsula weather district. Car access off Bruce Highway at Silkwood via Kurrimine Beach.

A low-lying strip of dense rainforest interspersed with scrub backs Cowley Beach just north of the resort township at Kurrimine Beach. Swampy wetlands with tea-tree, palms and grasses lie in a shallow depression behind the coastal forest fringe, hemmed in to the west by sandy soils supporting tea-tree, acacias and grass-trees. A short walking track loops through the southern part of the 900 ha park.

BEST TIME: Winter.
ENQUIRIES: (070) 67 6304.
ADDRESS: As for Bellenden Ker.

Scenic enjoyment ✓✓
Day activities ✓
Family camping ×
Hard bushwalking ×

Lake Barrine National Park
60 km SW, 35 km SW of Gordonvale. North Coast, Tableland and Peninsula weather district. Gillies Highway between Gordonvale and Atherton passes through the park.

DESCRIPTION: Page 453.
NOTE: Lake cruises 1015 and 1515 daily April-January.
BEST TIME: Winter.
ENQUIRIES: (070) 95 3768.
ADDRESS: As for Lake Eacham.

Scenic enjoyment ✓✓✓
Day activities ✓✓✓
Family camping ×
Hard bushwalking ×

Lake Eacham National Park
70 km SW, 45 km SW of Gordonvale. North Coast, Tableland and Peninsula weather district. Car access off Gillies Highway between Gordonvale and Yungaburra.

DESCRIPTION: Page 452. A further 5 ha of rainforest straddling Gillies Highway are preserved in the undeveloped **Yungaburra National Park,** 2 km SW of Yungaburra township.

BEST TIME: Winter.
ENQUIRIES: (070) 95 3768.
ADDRESS: QNPWS district office, Box 21, Yungaburra 4872.

Scenic enjoyment ✓✓✓
Day activities ✓✓
Family camping ×
Hard bushwalking ×

Lakefield National Park
320 km N, 146 km NW of Cooktown. North Coast, Tableland and Peninsula weather district. Car access off Peninsula Developmental Road from Laura; 4WD access from Cooktown via Battlecamp. Roads impassable after heavy rains.

A vast river system comprising main streams and tributaries of the Bizant, Normanby, Hann, Morehead and North Kennedy Rivers drains this 528,000 ha park. During the wet season floodwaters break the rivers' banks and join to form immense bodies of open water before emptying into Princess Charlotte Bay. The waters attract a huge population of birds, and even in the dry season swamps, creeks and lily-covered lagoons are home to countless brolgas, magpie geese, Burdekin ducks, cormorants, egrets and jabirus. Both freshwater and saltwater crocodiles abound.

Many minor streams dry completely in winter, leaving bare sandy beds. Beyond the watercourses grasslands and woodlands dominated by bloodwood, Darwin stringybark, Molloy red box and Moreton Bay ash spread out over the floodplains. Rainforest grows on rich soils along the river banks and mangroves line mudflats along the coast and estuary shores.

Lakefield is the most accessible of the parks north of Cooktown. Rangers based at two former grazing station homesteads are well acquainted with its seasonal changes and visitors should take advantage of their advice on best spots for camping and canoeing.

NOTE: Visitors must be fully equipped for outback survival.
BEST TIME: Winter.
ENQUIRIES: (070) 60 2162.
ADDRESS: PMB29, Cairns Mail Centre 4870.

Scenic enjoyment ✓✓
Day activities ×
Family camping ×
Walking, canoeing ✓✓

Lizard Island National Park
270 km N. North Coast, Tableland and Peninsula weather district. Flights Cairns-Lizard Island. Accessible by boat.

Resort guests and campers stand in the footsteps of Lt James Cook at the lookout point on Lizard Island's highest peak. Cook climbed to what is now known as Cook's Look in 1770 to search the Coral Sea for a passage through the Great Barrier Reef's outer ramparts, just 20 km to the east.

Patches of coral reef virtually surround the continental island in a fringe which loops around a superb lagoon, popular for swimming and skin diving to view the reef's underwater life.

Grassland covering most of the 1010 ha national park makes for easy walking to Cook's Look, between patches of open forest, heath and rainforest. Swamps form in shallow depressions fed by seasonal streams and mangroves line parts of the island's coast.

Seabird rookeries on coral cays and rocky outcrops south of Lizard Island are also protected as national parks. Mangroves dominate most of the six cays of the **Turtle Group** (91 ha), **Nymph Island** (65 ha) and **Two Islands** (15 ha). **Three Islands** (41 ha) supports a dense cover of grasses with low shrubs and casuarinas, and mangroves along the edge of a sheltered lagoon. Only the largest of the three rocky outcrops of **Rocky Islets** (32 ha) has substantial vegetation of woodland, scrub and grasses.

BEST TIME: Winter.
ENQUIRIES: (070) 51 9811.
ADDRESS: As for Archer Bend.

Scenic enjoyment ✓✓✓
Day activities ×
Family camping ✓
Hard bushwalking ×

Maria Creek and Clump Mountain National Parks
Maria Creek 120 km S, 5 km SE of Silkwood. Access on foot from Murdering Point road off Bruce Highway at Silkwood. Clump Mountain 140 km S, 2 km S of Bingil Bay. Bingil Bay-Mission Beach road skirts park. North Coast, Tableland and Peninsula weather district.

Low palm swamps with scattered tea-trees and patches of vine forest on deeper soils spread over a 670 ha park hemmed in by the winding arms of Maria and South Maria Creeks. Grassland is patchily distributed and eucalypts grow on some low ridges. Mangroves line the creek mouths as they join to empty out to sea just south of Kurrimine township.

On a clear day breaks in the tree cover of Bicton Hill in Clump Mountain National Park (300 ha) give views over Maria Creek to Mourilyan in the north and as far as Hinchinbrook Island to the south. A well-maintained walking track from the Bingil Bay beachfront road climbs gentle slopes clothed in rainforest to the hilltop lookout. Two smaller patches of coastal rainforest occupy parks of 26 ha and 4 ha around Bingil Bay township.

NOTE: Picnic facilities at Clump Mountain.

BEST TIME: Winter.

ENQUIRIES: (070) 68 7183.

ADDRESS: As for Hull River.

Scenic enjoyment ✔✔
Day activities ✔✔
Family camping ✖
Hard bushwalking ✖

Millstream Falls National Park

140 km SW, 7 km W of Ravenshoe. North Coast, Tableland and Peninsula weather district. Car access off Kennedy Highway 5 km W of Ravenshoe.

DESCRIPTION: Page 450.

NOTE: 3 night limit on camping.

BEST TIME: Late autumn.

ENQUIRIES: (070) 95 3768.

ADDRESS: As for Lake Eacham.

Scenic enjoyment ✔✔✔
Day activities ✔✔
Family camping ✔
Hard bushwalking ✖

Mitchell and Alice Rivers National Park

670 km NW. North Coast, Tableland and Peninsula weather district. 4WD only via Kowanyama off Burke Developmental Road at Dunbar station. Roads impassable after heavy rains.

Sparse woodlands and grasslands occupy 37 000 ha of alluvial plains in the fork of the Mitchell and Alice Rivers. Galleries of dense forest grow along the rivers, which flow year-round.

NOTES: Visitors must be fully equipped for outback survival. Permission for transit must be pre-arranged with Kowanyama Aboriginal Community.

BEST TIME: Winter.

ENQUIRIES: (070) 51 9811.

ADDRESS: As for Archer Bend.

Scenic enjoyment ✔
Day activities ✖
Family camping ✖
Hard bushwalking ✖

Mount Hypipamee National Park

105 km SW, 24 km S of Atherton. North Coast, Tableland and Peninsula weather district. Car access off Kennedy Highway.

DESCRIPTION: Page 448.

NOTE: 1 night limit on camping.

BEST TIME: Winter.

ENQUIRIES: (070) 95 3768.

ADDRESS: As for Lake Eacham.

Scenic enjoyment ✔✔
Day activities ✔✔
Family camping ✖
Hard bushwalking ✖

Mount Major National Park

140 km SW, 7 km SE of Ravenshoe. North Coast, Tableland and Peninsula weather district. Access on foot off Ravenshoe-Vine Creek road.

The massive rhyolite bluff of Mt Major (1174 m) towers above steep slopes of vine jungle. Timbers sought for commercial uses, such as ash, silkwood, calophyllum, yellow walnut and quandong, have been protected from logging by the rough, broken ground and are now permanently preserved in the 750 ha park. Walkers who make the arduous trek to the mountain's peak along Vine Creek pass the 30 metre drop of a forest-shrouded waterfall. At the summit they gain views over the Atherton Tableland, **Dirran National Park** (4 ha) on the slopes of Mt Fisher to the north, and out to the coast. Though hot and steamy at its base, the mountain's peak can be buffeted by strong, cold winds even in summer.

BEST TIME: Winter.

ENQUIRIES: (070) 95 3768.

ADDRESS: As for Lake Eacham.

Scenic enjoyment ✔✔
Day activities ✖
Family camping ✖
Hard bushwalking ✔

Palmerston National Park

125 km S, 35 km W of Innisfail. North Coast, Tableland and Peninsula weather district. Palmerston Highway crosses the park.

DESCRIPTION: Page 457. A smaller patch of national park rainforest at **Palmerston Rocks** (11 ha) straddles the Palmerston Highway 15 km W of Innisfail. Similar forests are more difficult to reach at **McNamee Creek**, an area of 1150 ha about 15 km from South Johnstone now incorporated in the park. Forestry tracks crossing the park are rough, but generally passable in dry conditions. The creek's course can be followed on foot to small waterfalls, sandy beaches and a number of spots suitable for swimming.

BEST TIME: Winter.

ENQUIRIES: (070) 64 5115.

ADDRESS: Box 800, Innisfail 4860.

Scenic enjoyment ✔✔✔
Day activities ✔✔✔
Family camping ✔✔✔
Hard bushwalking ✖

Possession Island National Park

980 km N, 20 km N of Bamaga. North Coast, Tableland and Peninsula weather district. Accessible by boat from Bamaga and Thursday Island.

James Cook landed here in August 1770 to complete his Australian exploration and formally claim the east coast down to 38°S in the name of King George III. The 500 ha island of sandy beaches, mangrove swamps and mudflats below a low, scrub-covered ridge was declared a national park for historical reasons. An obelisk commemorates Cook's visit.

BEST TIME: Winter.

ENQUIRIES: (070) 51 9811.

ADDRESS: As for Archer Bend.

Scenic enjoyment ✔
Day activities ✖
Family camping ✖
Hard bushwalking ✖

Rokeby National Park

600 km N, 26 km N of Coen. North Coast, Tableland and Peninsula weather district. Peninsula Developmental Road crosses park; 4WD recommended – road impassable after heavy rains.

Rivers rising in the McIlwraith Range within 25 km of the Coral Sea take a long and winding course across wide floodplains before emptying into the Gulf of Carpentaria 350 km to the west. The Archer and Coen Rivers form much of the boundary of the 290 000 ha park, enclosing a variety of vegetation types, a great number of bird species and a big population of freshwater crocodiles.

NOTE: Visitors must be fully equipped for outback survival.

BEST TIME: Winter.

ENQUIRIES: (070) 51 9811.

ADDRESS: As for Archer Bend.

Scenic enjoyment ✔
Day activities ✖
Family camping ✖
Hard bushwalking ✖

Staaten River National Park

450 km W. North Coast, Tableland and Peninsula weather district. 4WD only off Burke Developmental Road from Highbury station. Permission to cross station property must be arranged. Tracks impassable after heavy rains.

Termite mounds 2-3 metres high dot the vast open plains of this 467 000 ha park. Broad-leafed tea-tree grows extensively and galleries of rainforest crowd close to the permanent waters of the Staaten River and its major tributaries, Emu, Pandanus, Back and Cockburn Creeks. Monsoonal rains each summer force the rivers to break their banks and spread over sparsely wooded floodplains. Inundation restricts the growth of understorey vegetation. Instead, grasses appear as the waters subside.

NOTE: Visitors must be fully equipped for outback survival.

BEST TIME: Winter.

ENQUIRIES: (070) 51 9811.

ADDRESS: As for Archer Bend.

Scenic enjoyment ✔
Day activities ✖
Family camping ✖
Hard bushwalking ✖

Starcke National Park

420 km N, 80 km N of Cooktown. North Coast, and Peninsula weather district. 4WD only north from Cooktown via Starcke station. Road impassable after heavy rains.

Limestone-capped ridges and plateaux around the headwaters of the Starcke and Jack Rivers are as rugged as any on Cape York Peninsula. Weathering has produced steep escarpments with bare cliff faces rising from sea level to over 400 metres along the eastern edge of this 8000 ha park. Heaths and scrubs grow on the exposed higher levels, with heavier vegetation on deeply dissected lower slopes and narrow valley floors. Eucalypt communities and well-developed rainforest are widespread. Grasslands are patchily distributed on areas of heavy basaltic soils.

To the south of Starcke station homestead **Mount Webb National Park** preserves a 220 ha remnant of tall semi-deciduous vine forest on a gently sloping hill rising to 400 metres.

NOTE: Visitors must be fully equipped for outback survival.

BEST TIME: Winter.

ENQUIRIES: (070) 51 9811.

ADDRESS: As for Archer Bend.

Scenic enjoyment ✔
Day activities ✖
Family camping ✖
Hard bushwalking ✖

Topaz Road National Park

95 km S, 24 km SE of Malanda. North Coast, Tableland and Peninsula weather district. Car access via Lamins Hill off Lake Eacham-Malanda road (part unsealed).

Remnant rainforests of the Atherton Tablelands lie undisturbed along the narrow gravel stretch of Topaz Road among agricultural backblocks on the slopes of Francis Range. The park covers a trackless patch of 37 ha in rugged country at the head of steep gullies with creeks eventually feeding into upper reaches of the Johnstone River.

BEST TIME: Winter.

ENQUIRIES: (070) 95 3768.

ADDRESS: As for Lake Eacham.

Scenic enjoyment ✔
Day activities ✖
Family camping ✖
Hard bushwalking ✖

Tully Gorge National Park

160 km S, 24 km S of Ravenshoe. North Coast, Tableland and Peninsula weather district. Car access from Ravenshoe.

DESCRIPTION: Page 451. Waterfalls in national parks at **Elizabeth Grant Falls** (480 ha) and **Cannabullen Falls** (350 ha) provide a more reliable spectacle than the depleted flow through Tully Gorge. But visitors need good maps and detailed directions from rangers to locate them in steep gullies feeding into Tully River from the east.

BEST TIME: Winter.

ENQUIRIES: (070) 95 3768.

ADDRESS: As for Lake Eacham.

Scenic enjoyment ✔✔
Day activities ✔✔
Family camping ✖
Hard bushwalking ✖

QUEENSLAND CAMP BOOKING SYSTEM

Details, page 441.

Birds, butterflies and wildlife in northern parks

In the north wildlife comes with all the exotic colour, abundance and size expected of the tropics. Everything is brighter and bigger. There are butterflies the size of birds – the Ulysses butterfly has a wingspan of about 100 millimetres. In the misty rainforests there are birds as bright as butterflies. There are, too, varieties of possum and glider not seen elsewhere, including oddities like the spotted cuscus, often mistaken for a monkey and creating alarming tales of illegal importation. Every park in the region has some part of this brilliant and fascinating selection of wildlife.

The green spotted triangle butterfly can be seen from Mackay to Cape York from January to May. It seems never to be still; even when feeding its wings are in constant motion

The Ulysses, or mountain blue, butterfly, one of the largest and most beautiful, is found only in rainforest where the corkwood tree grows

Buff-breasted paradise-kingfishers arrive from New Guinea early in November to establish breeding territory. By the end of April parents and young have gone

The purple-crowned superb fruit dove lives along the edge of northern rainforest

The first indication a cassowary is near may be the rumbling sound the bird makes when it becomes aware of intruders

A dainty green tree frog displays its disced fingers and toes

The mixture of yellow, grey, white and black in the green ringtail possum's coat creates the lime-green shade to the fur

Smallest member of the family, the golden bowerbird builds the biggest bower for its displays – two towers up to 3 metres high

Visitor activities in the national parks of Queensland

Abseiling
Girraween, Lamington, Mount French, Springbrook parks.

Bird watching
Bellenden Ker, Bunya Mountains, Cape Hillsborough, Cape York Peninsula parks, Carnarvon (Gorge), Eungella, Heron Island (Capricorn-Bunker cays), Kondalilla, Lakefield, Lamington, Maiala, Michaelmas Cay, Mount Spec, Noosa, Springbrook parks.

Bush camping
Auburn River, Brampton Island (Cumberland Island), Cape Palmerston, Carnarvon (Salvator Rosa, Mount Moffat), Cooloola, Eurimbula, Heron Island (Capricorn-Bunker cays), Lamington, Lizard Island, Robinson and Isla Gorges, Sundown, Whitsundays.

Burleigh Head is hemmed in by Gold Coast developments, but out on its headland it is possible to be away from it all

Reef walking in the clear waters off North West Island, moving slowly so as not to disturb the myriad marine life

Bush walking
Bellenden Ker, Blackdown Tableland, Cape Tribulation, Cooloola, Eungella, Hinchinbrook Island, Lamington, Moreton Island, Mount Barney, Main Range and other scenic rim parks, Sundown.

Camping
QNPWS campgrounds on more than 40 popular mainland and island national parks.

Canoeing/boating
Barron Gorge, Cooloola, Lakes Barrine and Eacham, Lawn Hill, Sundown and adjacent to many coastal and island national parks.

Caving
Chillagoe-Mungana Caves, Fitzroy Caves.

Cave tours
Chillagoe-Mungana Caves.

Fishing, ocean
Adjacent to Brampton Island (Cumberland Island), Burleigh Head, Cooloola, Great Sandy, Eurimbula, Heron Island (Capricorn-Bunker cays), Lizard Island, Moreton Island, Noosa and other coastal parks, Whitsundays.

4-W driving
Cape Palmerston, Cape Tribulation, Carnarvon (Mount Moffat), Cooloola, Eurimbula, Great Sandy, Iron Range, Jardine River, Lakefield, Moreton Island, Rokeby, Simpson Desert.

Geological studies
Black Mountain, Blackdown, Carnarvon, Chillagoe-Mungana Caves, Girraween, Glass House Mountains, Lawn Hill, Mount Barney, Mount Hypipamee, Simpson Desert and most national parks.

Historical studies
Cooloola, Edmund Kennedy, Endeavour River, Main Range, St Helena Island.

Liloing
Cooloola, Obi Obi Gorge and many swimming areas.

Photography
All national parks, ranging from the Simpson Desert to Great Barrier Reef cays.

Picnicking
More than 60 picnic grounds in the most popular and easily accessible parks relatively close to the coast and Dunk, Green and Hinchinbrook Islands and the Whitsundays.

Orienteering
Mount Barney.

Rafting, white water
Barron Gorge, Palmerston.

Rock climbing
Glass House Mountains, Mount Barney, Mount French.

Scuba diving/snorkelling
Adjacent to many coastal and island national parks, particularly Green and Lizard Islands, Heron Island (Capricorn-Bunker group), Whitsundays.

Human visitors may camp on the shores of Lady Musgrave Island and dive off its reef from March to August. But for the rest of the year it is reserved as a nesting place for the brown gannets

An excellent way to explore the forested hills, heathlands and swamps in Cooloola National Park is to travel by canoe to the headwaters of the Noosa River

Surfing
Adjacent to Burleigh Head, Cooloola, Great Sandy, Moreton Island, Noosa.

Swimming
In most national parks including Blue Lake, Bowling Green Bay, Brampton Island (Cumberland), Cape Hillsborough, Carnarvon, Cedar Creek, Davies Creek, Eungella, Girraween, Great Sandy, Jourama Falls, Lakes Eacham and Barrine, Lamington, Magnetic Island, Moreton Island, Natural Arch, Whitsundays, Woodgate.

Walking in forest to waterfalls/lookouts
Graded walking tracks in more than 50 popular parks including Bellenden Ker, Blackdown, Bunya Mountains, Carnarvon, Daintree, Eungella, Girraween, Lakes Eacham and Barrine, Lamington, Natural Arch, Palmerston, Queen Mary Falls, Springbrook and Tamborine parks.

Walking along coastal tracks and beaches
Blue Lake, Burleigh Head, Cape Hillsborough, Cape Tribulation, Cooloola, Dunk Island, Great Sandy, Hinchinbrook Island, Moreton Island, Noosa, Woodgate.

Wildflower studies
Blackdown Tableland, Burrum River, Cape York Peninsula parks, Cooloola, Girraween, Simpson Desert, Springbrook parks.

Wildlife observation
Most parks at night but especially Bunya Mountains, Cape York Pensinsula parks, Carnarvon (Gorge), Eungella, North Queensland rainforest parks.

Windsurfing
Adjacent to Burleigh Head, Cooloola, Magnetic, Moreton and Whitsunday islands.

Yachting
Adjacent to many coastal and island national parks but particularly Brampton Island (Cumberland Islands), Hinchinbrook Island, Lizard Island, Magnetic Island, Whitsundays.

NOTE: The boundary of all coastal national parks is the high water mark.

Young people strike off the track and use a creek as a path to make their own discoveries in Carnarvon National Park

A photographer attempts to capture the changing moods, shapes and colours of the Simpson Desert

CAMPING

Bush camping — away from it all, no facilities other than those you create.
Camping — a pit toilet and a tap but no other facilities.
Family camping — established camping ground with showers, toilets, barbecue areas and where you can probably take a caravan, but check beforehand.

INDEX

Bold numerals indicate major illustrated entries; *italic* numerals indicate other illustrations.

A

Aboriginal sites 43, 48, *56-7*, 66, 68, 74, *79*, 88, *92*, 96, 102, 121, 186, 227, *229*, 251, 256, *302*, 308, 312, 314, 322, 399, 401
Acacia aneura 26-7
Acacia Island NP (*see* Whitsunday Islands)
Acacias 21, 24-7, *74*, *127*, *351*
Acetosa *59*
Adelaide, SA 168
Admiral's Arch, SA *197*
Agile wallaby *414-5*
Albany, WA 27, 142
Albert's lyrebird *412*
Alexander Morrison National Park 137, 167
Alfred National Park 23, 232, 240, 241
Alice Springs, NT 12, 48
Alligator Creek, Qld *421*
Alligator Creek, SA 178, *179*
Alligator Rivers, NT 74
Allonby Island NP (*see* Brampton Island)
Alma River, Tas *260*
Alpine ash *300*
Alpine daisy *283*
Alpine strawflower *222*
Alton National Park 388
Amphibolorus vitticeps 192
Anakie Gorge, Vic. *201*
Anchorsmith Island NP (*see* Whitsunday Islands)
Andrews Point, Qld 431
Angourie NP (absorbed – *see* Yuraygir)
Angular pigface *184*
Annan River, Qld 461
Antarctic beech 370
Ants, harvester 27, 310
Anvil Island NP (*see* Whitsunday Islands)
Aotus *359*
Apsley Gorge NP (absorbed – *see* Oxley Wild Rivers)
Araluen Falls, Qld *434*
Aranda tribe 48, 56, 66
Arcadia, Qld 419
Archer Bend National Park 471
Archer fish 99
Arkhurst Island NP (*see* Whitsunday Islands)
Arnhem Land, NT 10, 26, 82, 88
 Escarpment 72, *74*, *77*, *83*
Artesian water 16
Arthur Bay, Qld 419
Arthur Range, Tas. *264*
Arthur River, Tas. 253
Asbestos Range National Park 254, 278, 279
Ash, mountain 24, 266, *267*
Aspatria Island NP (*see* Brampton Island)
Assassin bug *86*
Atherton Tablelands, Qld 16, 447, 448, 450, 464
Athrotaxis 266
Atmospheric pressure 12
Atrax robustus 34
Auburn River National Park 408, 478
Audley, NSW 31, 319
Australian Heritage Commission 256
Australian king parrot *238*
Australian pelican *239*
Australian sea lion *141*
Australian shelduck *237*
Avon Valley National Park 137, 166
Ayers Rock, NT 10, 42, 48, *50*, *52-3*
Ayr, Qld 417

Australian shelduck *237*
Avon Valley National Park 137, 166
Ayers Rock, NT 10, 42, 48, *50*, *52-3*
Ayr, Qld 417

B

Badgingarra National Park 137, 167
Bailey Point, Qld *466*
Balancing Rock, Qld *385*
Balconies, Vic. *229*
Balding Bay, Qld 419
Bald Island, WA *161*
Bald Rock National Park 348, **352-3**, 362, 366
Bales Beach, SA 177
Bandicoot, eastern barred *276*
Bangalow (*see* Piccabeen palms)
Banks, Joseph 460
Banksias 24, 27, *104*, *155*, *160*, *175*, *251*, *290*, *327*, *338*, *357*, *358*, *413*
Banksia serrata 413
Banteng cattle 88
Baobab *21*
Barn Bluff, Tas. *249*
Barren Island NP (*see* Keppel Islands)
Barren Ranges, WA 152
Barrengarry Creek, NSW *290*
Barrington Tops National Park 316, **335**, 342, 348
Barron Falls, Qld 16
Barron Gorge National Park 23, 471, 478
Barron River, Qld *448*
Barwon River, NSW 17
Basalt 10, *15*
Bass, George 319
Bass Strait 12, 14, 199, *202*, *207*, 219, *250*, 251
Bats *39*, 102, 407, *413*
Baw Baw National Park 232, *240*, 241
Baynham Island NP (*see* Whitsunday Islands)
Beach formation 18-19
Beach hibiscus *428*
Bearded dragon *70*, *192*
Bearded orchid *307*
Beatrice River, Qld *456*
Beech 20-1, 22-3, *214*, 245, *260*, *265*, 370
Beedelup Falls, WA *126*
Beedelup NP (*see* Pemberton)
Beedelup River, WA 126
Beerwah NP (*see* Glass House Mountains)
Beetle, leaf-eating 25
Bega River, NSW 292
Belah, 314
Belair National Park 189, 196
Belinup Hill, WA 162
Bell flower *419*
Bell-fruited mallee *155*
Bell, mountain *150*
Bellenden Ker National Park 23, *446*, 447, **454-5**, 471, 478, 479
Bellenden Ker Range, Qld 14, 447, *454*
Bellendena montana 275
Bellinger River, NSW 360
Bellows Island NP (*see* Whitsunday Islands)
Belmore Falls, NSW 290
Belougery Spire, NSW *336*
Ben Boyd National Park 281, **298-9**, 303, 366
Bendidee National Park 388
Ben Lomond National Park 242, **244-5**, 254, 278
Bennett's wallaby *277*
Bettong, rufous *412*
Beverlac Island NP (*see* Northumberland Islands)
Bibbulmun Track, WA 116
Big Crystal Creek, Qld 424
Big Hole, NSW 296
Billy Range, ACT *300*
Bimberi Range, ACT 300
Binna Burra, Qld 370, 371
Biosphere reserve 155
Bird Island NP (*see* Whitsunday Islands)
Birdsnest fern *361*, *458*
Bites and stings 34, 393
Black box *311*
Black Gin Gully, NSW *319*
Black Hill and Morialta Conservation Parks 168, **172-3**, 189, 196
Black Island NP (*see* Whitsunday Islands)
Black Mountain National Park 447, **461**, 471, 478
Black Point, WA 129
Black sands 18
Black Trevethan Range, Qld 461
Black-eyed Susan *177*
Black-footed rock-wallaby *140*
Blackall Range National Park 39, 388
Blackcombe Island NP (*see* Whitsunday Islands)
Blackdown Tableland National Park 408, 478, 479
Blackfellow's Knob NP (*see* Queen Mary Falls)
Blackheath, NSW 324
Blacksmith Island NP (*see* Whitsunday Islands)
Black-winted stilt *346*
Bladensburg National Park 441
Blechnum 371
Bloodwood Caves, Qld *406*
Bloodwood flower, *105*
Bloomfield River, Qld 463, 467
Blowhole, Tas. 270
Blue Lagoon, Qld *379*
Blue Lake National Park 368, **386-7**, 388, 479
Blue Mountains, NSW 14, 18, 330
Blue Mountains National Park *15*, 316, *317*, **324-7**, 342-3, 366, 367
Blue-winged parrot *277*
Bluff Island NP (*see* Northumberland Islands)
Bluff Knoll, WA 148
Bogong High Plains, Vic. *40*
Bogong National Park 199, **222-3**, 232, 240, 241
Bogong Plateau, Vic. *222*
Boiling Pot, Qld *383*
Bombah Point, NSW 334
Bond Gap, NT 61
Boolambayte Lake, NSW *334*
Boolimba Bluff, Qld *400*
Boombana NP (*see* D'Aguilar Range)
Boonoo Boonoo Falls, NSW *351*
Boonoo Boonoo National Park 348, **351**, 362
Boorabbin National Park 164
Border Island NP (*see* Whitsunday Islands)
Border Ranges National Park 23, 348, 362, 368
Boronia *306*, *325*, *358*
Boronia pinnata 306
Botany Bay NP (*see* Sydney Harbour)
Bottlebrush *105*, *118*
Bottle tree *415*
Bouddi National Park 316, **332-3**, 343, 366, 367
Bouddi Peninsula, NSW 332
Boundary Falls, NSW *355*
Bourke, NSW 12
Bowden Island NP (*see* Dunk Island)
Bowen, Qld 417
Bowerbirds *346*, *477*
Bowling Green Bay National Park 417, **421-3**, 441, 479
Box, black *311*
Box jellyfish *393*
Boy Martin Point, NSW *320*
Boyd, Benjamin 299
Brahminy kite *414*
Brampton Island National Park *431*, 441, 478, 479
Breakfast Creek, NSW 330, 350
Bremer Bay, WA 152
Brigalow 25
Brindabella Range, NSW 300
Brisbane, Qld 368
Brisbane Ranges National Park 199, **200-1**, 232, 240, 241
Brisbane Water National Park 343, 366
Broadleaf hopbush *312*
Broad-lip leek orchid *275*
Broadwater Beach, NSW *357*
Broadwater Creek Falls NP (*see* Wallaman Falls)
Broadwater National Park 348, **357**, 362
Brockman Forest NP (*see* Pemberton)
Broke Inlet, WA *129*
Broken Bay, NSW *322*, *332*
Broken Falls, Vic. *231*
Broken Hill, NSW 308, 312
Broken River, Qld 432
Brolga *415*
Brooks, John 106
Broome, WA 12
Bruguiera mangrove *436*
Bruny Island, Tas. 259
Brush-tailed rock wallaby *237*
Budawang National Park 303
Budderoo National Park 316, **331**, 343
Buddi Buddi Island NP (*see* Whitsunday Islands)
Buffalo Plateau, Vic. 221
Buffalo, water 41, 72, 88
Buff-breasted paradise-kingfisher *476*
Bug, assassin *86*
Bulga NP (*see* Tarra-Bulga)
Bundeena, NSW 319
Bundjalung National Park 348, **356**, 362, 366
Bunga Head, NSW 292
Bungarra lizard *141*
Bungle Bungle National Park 103, 166, *167*
Bungle Bungle Ranges, WA *8-9*
Bunya Mountains National Park 23, 388, 478, 479
Bunyeroo Valley, SA *182*
Burdekin River, Qld 417
Burleigh Head National Park 23, 388, *478*, 479
Burrawang *295*
Burrendong Dam, NSW 17
Burrowa-Pine Mountain National Park 232
Burrum River NP (*see* Woodgate)
Bush pea *201*
Bushfire 34-5, 219, 259
Bushy Island NP (*see* Brampton Island)
Butterflies *465*, *476*
Butterfly iris *171*
Button daisy *284*
Buttongrass 27, *262*
Bynguano Range, NSW *312*

C

Cabbage-tree palm *83*, *319*, *401*, *402*
Cairns, Qld 12, 417, 447
Caladenia *340*
Calamus *453*
Calder Island NP (*see* Brampton Island)
Calder River, Vic. 202
Callitris 337
Calochilus Robertsonii 307
Calothamnus 105, *118*
Calytrix 86
Camels *27*
Cameron Falls, Qld *375*

Canberra, ACT 12, 281
Candle heath *306*
Cania Gorge National Park 393, **406**, 408
Cannabullen Falls NP (*see* Tully Gorge)
Canunda National Park 168, **186-7**, 189, 196
Cape Arid National Park 142, **162-3**, 164, 166, 167
Cape Banks, SA 186
Cape Barren geese 175
Cape Boullanger, Tas. 268
Cape Bowling Green, Qld 417, 421
Cape Buffon, SA 186
Cape Cleveland NP (absorbed – *see* Bowling Green Bay)
Cape Cleveland, Qld 421
Cape du Couedic, SA *174*
Cape Ferguson, Qld *422*
Cape Forestier, Tas. *247*
Cape Hauy, Tas. 270
Cape Hillsborough and Wedge Island National Park 417, **430-1**, 441, 478, 479
Cape Le Grand National Park 141, 142, **156-7**, 164, 166, 167
Cape Leeuwin, WA 129, 142
Cape Leeuwin NP (absorbed – *see* Leeuwin-Naturaliste)
Cape Maurouard, Tas. *268*
Cape Melville National Park 471
Cape Moreton, Qld 379
Cape Naturaliste NP (absorbed – *see* Leeuwin-Naturaliste)
Cape Otway, Vic. 202
Cape Palmerston National Park 23, 408, 478
Cape Pillar, Tas. 270
Cape Range National Park 106, **108-9**, 115, 140, 166, 167
Cape Raoul, Tas. *258*, 259, 270
Cape Richards, Qld *437*
Cape Sandy, Qld *398*
Cape Schanck Coastal Park 199, **207**, 232, 240, 241
Cape Tribulation National Park 23, 447, 463, **466-9**, 471, 478, 479
Cape Upstart National Park 441
Cape Vancouver, WA 158
Cape York Peninsula, Qld 12, 14, 23, 417, 439, 478, 479
Capertee River, NSW 330
Captain James Cook NP (absorbed – *see* Croajingolong)
Cardwell Range, Qld 437
Carlisle Island NP (*see* Brampton Island)
Carnarvon, WA 11, 106
Carnarvon Creek, Qld *401*, *405*, 406
Carnarvon Gorge, Qld 401
Carnarvon National Park 393, **400-5**, 408, 478, *479*
Carnarvon Range, Qld 401
Cascade Creek, Qld 431
Cassia Hill, NT 61
Cassia, silver-leaf *59*
Cassinia 251, *400*
Cassowaries 453, *477*
Castletower National Park 408
Casuarinas 24-5, 27, *50*, *212*, *296*, 314, *334*, *358*, *401*, *433*
Catamaran, Tas. 259
Cathedral Cave NP (*see* Chillagoe-Mungana Caves)
Cathedral Rock National Park 362
Cathedrals, Qld *399*
Cats, feral *41*
Cave Creek, Qld *372*, 373
Cave formations *124-5*, 226, 268, 283, *407*
Cedar *146*, 432
Cedar Bay National Park 447, **462-3**, 471
Cedar Creek NP (*see* Tamborine Mountain)
Cedar Creek Falls, Qld *369*, *376*
Ceduna, WA 142
Celery-top pine *263*
Central Australia 12, 48, 99, 181
Central Station, Qld 395, 397
Central netted dragon *71*
Centralian blue-tongued lizard *71*
Cervantes, WA 130
Chalka Creek, Vic. 217
Channel Country, Qld. 16
Charlotte Pass, NSW 284, 287
Chewings Range, NT *61*
Chichester Range, WA *114*
Chichester Range NP (absorbed – *see* Millstream-Chichester)
Chillagoe-Mungana Caves National Park 471, 478
Christmas Island National Park 115
Chunda Bay, Qld *422*
Churchill National Park 232, 240, 241
Cid Island NP (*see* Whitsunday Islands)
Cinnamon fungus 116
Circle Pool, NSW 354
Circular Pool, WA *111*
Clarke Range, Qld 432
Cleland Conservation Park *35*, 168, **170-1**, 189, 196, *197*
Clematis *123*, *127*
Climate 10, 12, 16, 20-1
Cloudforest 454
Club moss *459*
Clump Mountain NP (*see* Maria Creek)
Coalstoun Lakes National Park 23, 408
Coast tea-tree *251*
Coasts 18-19
Cobberas-Tingaringy National Park 233, 240, 241
Cobourg Peninsula Aboriginal Land and Sanctuary (Gurig NP) 72, **88**, 89, 92, 93
Cockatoos *105*, *195*, *346*
Cockermouth Island NP (*see* Brampton Island)
Cocoparra National Park 303
Coffee rock *356*, *357*
Coffin Bay National Park 168, **184**, 189, 196
Coffs Harbour, NSW 393
Collier Range National Park 115
Colo River, NSW 330
Common brushtail possum *277*
Common heath 27, *239*, *251*
Common wombat *236*
Comston Island NP (*see* Whitsunday Islands)
Coneflower *151*
Conglomerate rock *329*
Conifers 20
see also Cycads, Pines
Conimbla National Park 303
Conondale National Park 23, 388
Conondale Range, Qld 39
Conway National Park 23, 417, **428-9**, 441
Cooinda, NT 77
Cook, James 218, 350, 438, 460
Cooks Beach, Tas. 246
Cooktown, Qld 447, 460
Cooloola National Park 368, **382**, 388, 478, *479*
Coombe Island NP (*see* Dunk Island)
Coomera Falls, Qld *371*
Coonowrin NP (*see* Glass House Mountains)
Cooper Creek, East Qld *468*
Cooper Creek, West Qld 16
Coorong National Park 168, 186, **188**, 189, 196, *197*
Coral 10, *18*, *95*, *108*, 418, *444-5*
Coral fern *212*
Coral Sea 417, 467
Cormorant, little pied *85*
Corner Inlet, Vic. 209
Correa reflexa 275
Corroboree Island NP (*see* Keppel Islands)
Cotter River, ACT 300
Cottonhead, grey *119*
Cowan Water, NSW 322
Crab, red-fingered mangrove *365*
Cradle Mountain *243*, 253
Cradle Mountain-Lake St Clair National Park 23, *34*, 42, 242, **248-9**, 254, 255, 259, 261, 278, 279
Crawford's Lookout, Qld *457*
Crediton Creek, Qld 432
Crimson rosella *347*
Crinum 383
Croajingolong National Park 23, 199, **218-9**, 233, 240, *241*
Crocodiles 35, *80-1*, *100*, 393
Crocodylus johnstoni 80, *100*
C. porosus 80-1
Crowdy Bay National Park 343, 366, 367
Crown-of-thorns starfish *444*
Crows Nest Falls National Park 388
Crystal Brook, Vic. *220*
Crystal Creek, NT 82
Crystal Creek, Qld *424*
Crystal Creek NP (absorbed – *see* Mount Spec)
Crystal Shower Falls, NSW *360*
Cumberland Basin, NSW 324
Cunningham's Gap NP (absorbed – *see* Main Range)
Curlew Island NP (*see* Northumberland Islands)
Curracurrang 320-1
Curry flower *160*
Curtis Falls, Qld *377*
Cyanophytes 20
Cyathea Falls, Vic. 214, *216*
Cyathea tree fern *432-3*
Cycads 20, *21*, 56, *59*, *295*, 374, *454-5*
Cyclones 12
Cyclorama Point, NSW 325
Cypress pine 183, *336*, 337

D

D'Aguilar Range National Park 23, 389
D'Entrecasteaux Coast, WA **128-9**
D'Entrecasteaux National Park 116, *128*, 129, 138, 166, 167
Dacrydium 263, *272*
Dagmar Range National Park 447, 471
Daintree National Park 23, 447, **470**, 471, 479
Daintree River, Qld 467, 470
Daisies *26*, *66*, *204*, *221*, *222*, *251*, *283*, *284*
Daisy bush *262*
Dales Gorge, WA *107*, *111*
Daly River, NT *16*
Damage to parks 31, 32, 36, 40-1
Dampier, William 106
Dandenong Ranges, Vic. 25
Darling Range (*see* Darling Scarp)
Darling River, NSW 16, 17, 308, 310
Darling Scarp, WA 11, 116, 118, *119*, 121, 136
Darlington Range, Qld 377
Darter *99*
Darwin, NT 12, 25, 72, 94
Darwin, Charles 348
Davies Creek Falls, Qld 464, *465*
Davies Creek National Park 447, **464-5**, 472, 479
Deception Range, Tas. *260*
Deep Creek Conservation Park 168, 189, 196
Deep River, WA 144, *145*, *146*
Deer 31, 88
Deloraine Island NP (*see* Whitsunday Islands)
Denison River, Tas. 272
Denman Island NP (*see* Whitsunday Islands)
Depot Beach, NSW *294*
Derby, WA 94
Derwent River, Tas. 16, 249, 259
Desert daisy *66*
Desert death adder *70*
Desert oak *50*
Deua National Park 281, **296-7**, 303
Deua River, NSW *296-7*
Devil's Kitchen, Tas. 270
Devil's Marbles Conservation Reserve 10, 48, **64-5**, 69, 92, *93*
Devonport, Tas. 242
Dharug National Park 316, 343
Diamantina River, Qld 16
Dicksonia tree fern *266*
Dicksons Falls, Vic. 221
Dieback 25, 116
Digby Island NP (*see* Northumberland Islands)
Diggers Camp, NSW 359
Dinner Falls, Qld *448*
Dinner Island NP (*see* Northumberland Islands)
Diplarrena moraea 275
Diplolaena 133
Dipperu National Park 408
Dirran NP (*see* Mount Major)
Distress signals 34
Diuris orchid *340*
Divided Island NP (*see* Keppel Islands)
Division Rocks, Qld *430-1*
Dock, flowering *311*
Dolerite 11, 15, *248*, *258*, 259
Don Dorrigo Scrub, NSW *360*
Donkey orchid *340*
Donnelly River, WA 129
Dorrigo National Park 23, 348, **360-1**, 362
Double-eyed fig-parrot *347*
Double Head, Rosslyn Head, Bluff Point, Mulambin NP (*see* Yeppoon)
Double Island Point, Qld 382
Double-tails orchid *204*
Downy stackhousia *157*
Dragonfly *403*
Dragons *70*, *71*, *192*
Drought 23, 26, 72
Drovers Cave National Park 138
Dryandra 27, 38, 140, *151*
Drysdale River National Park 103
Du Cane Range, Tas. 249
Dularcha NP (*see* North Coast Rail)
Dumbell Island NP (*see* Whitsunday Islands)
Dundubara, Qld 399
Dungurra Island NP (*see* Whitsunday Islands)
Dunk Island National Park 23, 472, 478, 479
Dunnart, fat-tailed *192*

E

Eagle, wedge-tailed *193*, *347*
Eaglehawk Neck, Tas. 270, *271*
East Alligator River, NT 74
East Repulse Island NP (*see* Whitsunday Islands)
Eastern barred bandicoot *276*
Eastern blue-tongued lizard *364*
Eastern Highlands 11, 14-15, 16, 18, 20
Echidnas *192*, 353
Eclipse Cave NP (*see* Chillagoe-Mungana Caves)
Eden, NSW 299
Edith Falls, NT 82
Edith River, NT 82
Edmund Kennedy National Park 417, **439**, 441, 478
Edward Island NP (*see* Whitsunday Islands)
Elanda, Qld. 382
Elkhorn 23, *406*
Elizabeth Grant Falls NP (*see* Tully Gorge)
Ella Bay National Park 23, 472
Elliott Range, Tas. *261*
Elliott River, Vic. 202
Emerald ground-dove *413*

Emily and Jessie Gaps Nature Park 48, **66-7**, 69, 92-3
Emu *347*
Enamel orchid *156*
Endeavour River National Park 447, **460**, 472, 478
Epacrids 27
Epacris heath *359*
Ephemeral plants 26, *201*, *310-1*
Epiphytes 22-3, *397*, *448*
Epping Forest National Park 38, 408
Era, NSW *31*
Eriostemon 358
Erosion 10-11, 14-15, 18-19
Erskine Island NP (*see* Heron Island)
Esk Island NP (*see* Whitsunday Islands)
Esk River, NSW 356
Esperance, WA 142
Esperance Bay, WA 142, 156
Eubenangee Swamp National Park 472
Eucalypts 21, 24-5, 27, *96*, 116, *147*, *170*, *172*, *204*, *215*, *230*, 266, *267*, *290*, *355*
Eucalyptus diversicolor 24
E. marginata 116
E. regnans 24, 266, *267*
Eucla National Park 164
Eudlo Creek NP (*see* North Coast Rail)
Eungella National Park 23, 39, *416*, 417, **432-5**, 441, 478, 479
Eurimbula National Park 408-9, 478
Eurobin Falls, Vic. 220, 221
Evans Head Beach, NSW 357
Evaporation 12
Everlasting pea *171*
Evolution of plants 20-1, 24-5
Exmouth, WA 106, 109
Exmouth Gulf, WA 109
Eyre Peninsula, SA 16, 184, 185

F

Fairfax Island NP (*see* Heron Island)
Fairlies Knob NP (*see* Mount Walsh)
Falcon, peregrine *194*
Falls Creek, Vic. 222
Fantail, grey *276*
Fat-tailed dunnart *192*
Feral animal damage 40-1, 181
Fern Gully, Vic. 214
Fern Tree Gully National Park *30*, 233, 240, 241
Ferns *85*, 203, *212*, *214*, *253*, *267*, *361*, *424*, *435*, *458*, *459*
see also Tree ferns
Ferntree Creek NP (*see* North Coast Rail)
Fig-parrot, double-eyed *347*
Fig Tree Point, Qld 382
Figs 20, *23*, *84*, *96*, *370*, *374*, *430*, *436*, *458*
Filmy fern *214*, *267*
Finch Hatton Creek, Qld *416*, *434*
Finch Hatton Gorge, Qld 39, 432
Finger flower *178*
Finke Gorge National Park 48, **56-9**, 69, 92, 93
Finke River, NT 56
Finlayson Range, Qld *462*
Fire 12, 21, 24-5, 34-5
Fishbone fern *253*
Fitzgerald Beach, WA *153*
Fitzgerald Inlet, WA *153*
Fitzgerald River National Park 142, **152-5**, 164, 166, 167
Fitzroy Basin, Qld 393
Fitzroy Caves National Park 39, 393, **407**, 409, 478
Fitzroy Crossing, WA 94
Fitzroy Falls, NSW 290, 291
Fitzroy River, WA 98, *101*
Five-fingered fern *85*
Flagpole Hill, Tas. 251
Flame robin *239*, *327*
Flat Rock Shelter, Vic. *229*
Fleurieu Peninsula, SA 168
Flinders Bay, WA 129
Flinders Blow, Qld *398*
Flinders Chase National Park 168, **174-5**, 189, 196, *197*
Flinders Group NP (*see* Cape Melville)
Flinders, Matthew 319
Flinders Ranges, SA 15, 16, 168, 178
Flinders Ranges National Park 168, *169*, **180-3**, 189, 196
Floodplains *16*
Florence Bay, Qld 419
Flowering dock *311*
Forestier Peninsula, Tas. 259
Forests 20-5
Fortescue Bay, Tas. *270*
Fortescue Falls, WA 111
Fortescue River, WA *114*
Forty Mile Scrub National Park 472
Fourth Creek, SA 172
Francis Range, Qld *457*
Frank Hann National Park 164
Frankland Islands National Park 472
Frankland Range, Tas. 264
Frankland River, WA 144, *147*
Franklin Gorge, Tas. *260*
Franklin River, Tas. 42, 256-7, 260-1, *263*
Fraser Island, Qld 18, 43, 382, 393, **394-9**
Fraser, Malcolm 257
Fraser National Park 234, 240, 241
French Island, Vic. 200
Frenchman Peak, WA *157*
Frenchman's Cap, Tas. *260*, *262*
Frenchman's Cap NP (absorbed – *see* Wild Rivers)
Fresh water 16-17
Freshwater Creek, Qld 382
Freshwater Creek National Park 389
Freycinet National Park 242, **246-7**, 254, 278, 279
Freycinet Peninsula, Tas. 259
Fringed lily *383*
Frogs, *38*, 39, *364*, *477*
Frost 12-13
Fuchsia, native *275*
Fungus 116, *371*, *427*, *449*
Funnel-web spider 34

G

Gaibirra Island NP (*see* Whitsunday Islands)
Galeola *401*
Gammon Ranges, SA *15*
Gammon Ranges National Park 189, 196
Gap Creek, Qld 462, *463*
Gardner Lake, WA 158
Garie, NSW 319
Garrawalt Falls NP (*see* Wallaman Falls)
Gastric-brooding frog *38*, 39
Geck and Spring Caves NP (*see* Chillagoe-Mungana Caves)
Geese, Cape Barren 175
Geikie Gorge National Park 94, *95*, **98-101**, 103, 166, 167
Gentian, mountain *220*
Gentianella *267*
Geology 10-11, 14-15
George Gill Range, NT 68
Ghost bat *39*, 407
Ghost gum *49*, *54*, *63*, *67*
Giants' Stairway, NSW 324
Gibb River, WA 94
Gibraltar Range National Park 23, 348, **355**, 362, 366, 367
Gibson Desert, WA 30
Gibson Steps, Vic. 225
Girraween National Park *13*, 368, **384-5**, 389, 478, 479
Glacial action *14*, 15, 242, *249*, *270*
Glass House Mountains National Park *381*, 389-90, 478
Gleichenia (coral) fern *212*
Glenaladale NP (absorbed – *see* Mitchell River)
Glenbrook, NSW 324
Glenelg River, Vic. *226*
Glennie Islands, Vic. *210*
Gloucester and Middle Islands National Park 441
Gloucester Tops, NSW 335
Glow-worm 274
Gneiss 10
Goannas 175, *415*
Goat Island NP (*see* Whitsunday Islands)
Goats, feral *41*
Golden bowerbird *477*
Golden Island, SA *184*
Golden orb weaver *429*
Golden-shouldered parrot *39*
Goldsmith Island NP (*see* Whitsunday Islands)
Gondwanaland 10-11, 20, 22-3
Goodenia ovata 204
Goolagan Creek, Qld 457
Goold Island NP (*see* Hinchinbrook Island)
Goongarrie National Park 165
Gooseberry Hill National Park 138
Gordon River, Tas. 10, 256, *257*, 260-1, 272
Gordon Valley, Tas. 256
Goulburn River National Park 343, 366, 367
Gould's goanna *415*
Govetts Leap, NSW 324
Gowrie Bay, Qld *419*
Grafton, NSW 348
Graham Range National Park 23, 472
Grampians, Vic. 226
Grampians National Park *198*, 199, **228-31**, 234, 239, 240, 241
Grampians *thryptomene 239*
Grand Canyon, Vic. *229*
Grand High Tops, NSW *337*, *345*
Granite 10-11, *11*, *147*, *156*, *159*, *208*, *213*, 385
Granite Arch, Qld *385*
Grass-trees 27, *119*, *136*, *143*, *151*, *170*, *171*, *172*, *201*, *382*
Grass trigger plant *260*
Grasshopper, Leichhardt's *38*
Grasslands 21, 26
see also Hummock grasses, Tussock grasses
Gray, Robin 256
Great Artesian Basin 11, 16, 341, 401
Great Australian Bight 12, *18-19*, 26, 142, 184
Great Barrier Reef 19, 42, *43*, **444-5**
Great Basalt Wall National Park 441-2
Great Dividing Range 12, *14*, 16, 18, 27, 199, 203, 228, 281, 337, 348, 368, 394, 417
Great Lakes, Tas. 259
Great Ocean Road, Vic. 202, 225
Great Oyster Bay, Tas. 247
Great Sandy Desert, WA 12, 30
Great Sandy National Park *392*, **398-9**, 409, 478, 479
Great Sandy Strait 396
Green Island National Park 19, 23, 447, 472, 478
Green Mountains, Qld 370
Greenmount National Park 138
Green ringtail possum *477*
Green spotted triangle butterly *476*
Green tree frog *364*
Gregory National Park 89, 92, 93
Grevillea 27, *105*, *133*, *200*, 201, *413*
Grey cottonhead *119*
Grey fantail *276*
Grey kangaroo *294*
Grey Peaks National Park 23, 472
Grose Valley, NSW *324*
Ground-dove, emerald *413*
Ground parrot *414*
Gudgenby Nature Reserve, ACT 300
Guettarda speciosa 428
Guinea flower *133*, *177*, *357*, *370*, *383*
Gulf of Carpentaria, NT 26
Gull, silver *188*
Gungwiya Island NP (*see* Whitsunday Islands)
Gums *25*, *26*, *37*, *49*, *54*, *63*, *67*, *86*, *120*, *181*, *217*, *220*, *283*, *284*, *286*, *288*, 295
Gurig National Park 72, **88**, 89, 92, 93
Guringai tribe 322
Guy Fawkes River National Park 362, 366, 367
Gwongorella NP (*see* Springbrook)

H

Hacking River, NSW 31, 319
Hairy cutleaf daisy *222*
Hairy leek orchid *275*
Hakea 27, *154*, *323*
Halfway Island NP (*see* Keppel Islands)
Halifax Bay, Qld 424
Halls Creek, WA 94
Halls Gap, Vic. 228
Hamelin Pool, WA *20*
Hamersley Inlet, WA *152*
Hamersley Range, WA 10, 15, *26*
Hamersley Range National Park 106, *107*, **110-13**, 115, 166
Hamersley River, WA 152
Hammer Island NP (*see* Whitsunday Islands)
Hancock Gorge, WA 111
Hardenbergia 123, *127*
Harold Island NP (*see* Whitsunday Islands)
Hartog, Dirk 106
Hartz Mountains National Park 273, 278
Harvester ants 27, 310
Haslewood Island NP (*see* Whitsunday Islands)
Hassell Beach, WA *158*
Hassell National Park 165
Hasties Swamp National Park 474
Hastings River, NSW 38
Hastings River mouse 38, *39*
Hat Head Beach, NSW *338*
Hat Head National Park 316, **338-9**, 343, 366, 367
Hattah-Kulkyne National Park 36, 39, 199, **217**, 234
Hawke, Bob 257
Hawk's Head, WA *133*
Haycock Point, NSW *299*
Haystack Rock, NSW *299*
Hazards, Tas. *246*
Heath banksia *357*
Heathcote National Park 343
Heathlands 27, *155*, *382*
Heath-leafed banksia *290*
Heath pea *357*
Heaths 27, *144*, *150*, *153*, *222*, *239*, *251*, *266*, *274*, *306*, *319*, *325*, *326*, *357*, *359*, 393
Heat waves 12
Heavitree Gap, NT 48
Hell Fire Bay, WA 156
Hell Hole Gorge, Qld *400*
Hellyer Gorge State Reserve 242, **252-3**, 254, 278
Hellyer, Henry 253

Hellyer River, Tas. *252*, 253
Henderson Island NP (*see* Northumberland Islands)
Henning Island NP (*see* Whitsunday Islands)
Henrietta Creek, Qld 457
Herbert River, Qld 427, 450
Herbert River Falls NP (*see* Wallaman Falls)
Heritage Commission (Aust.) 17, 43, 256
Herkes Creek Falls NP (*see* Wallaman Falls)
Heron Island National Park 410, 445, 478
Heysen, Hans 168
Hibbertia 133, 177, 357, 370, 383
Hibiscus *153, 382, 401, 428*
Hidden Valley, Qld 431
Hidden Valley National Park 103, 166
High Island NP (*see* Frankland Islands)
Hinchinbrook Channel, Qld 437
Hinchinbrook Channel NP (*see* Hinchinbrook Island)
Hinchinbrook Island National Park 23, 417, **436-8**, 442, 478, 479
Hirst Island NP (*see* Northumberland Islands)
Hobart, Tas. 259
Holbourne Island NP (*see* Gloucester and Middle Islands)
Holgate, Harry 256
Honeyeater, New Holland *105*
Honey-possum *104*
Honeysuckle banksia *338*
Hook Island NP (*see* Whitsunday Islands)
Hoop pine *419, 430-1*
Hop *26*
Hopbush, broadleaf *312*
Hopetoun, WA 152
Horizontal scrub *274*
Hoskyn Island NP (*see* Heron Island)
Houtman Albrolhos Islands, WA *18*
Hovea *151, 337*
Hudson Island NP (*see* Dunk Island)
Hull Island NP (*see* Northumberland Islands)
Hull River National Park 474
Hummock grasses *26, 111*
Humpy Island NP (*see* Keppel Islands)
Hunter River, NSW 335
Huon pine *263, 272*
Hutchinsons Island NP (*see* Dunk Island)
Hybanthus calycinus 123
Hydro Electric Commission, Tas. 256

I

Ibis, straw-necked *195*
Igneous rocks 10
Illawarra Escarpment, NSW *331*
Indian Ocean 123
Ingham, Qld 417
Ingot Island NP (*see* Whitsunday Islands)
Initiation Rock, NT *56-7*
Innes National Park 189, 196, *197*
Innisfail, Qld 447
Insect, sap-sucking 25
Ipomoea *452*
Ireby Island NP (*see* Whitsunday Islands)
Iris *171, 275*
Iron Range National Park 23, 39, 474, 478
Ironbark *340*
Ironstone *175*
Isla Gorge National Park 410
Island Arch, Vic. *224*
Islands 18 19

J

Jabiru Lake, Qld 378, *379*
Jacana plant *77*
Jacanas 77
Jackson's Creek, Vic. 206
Jamieson Valley, NSW 324
Jane Brook, WA 118
Jardine River National Park 474, 478
Jarrah 25, 116, *127*
Jellyfish, box *393*
Jerusalem Creek, NSW 356
Jessie Island NP (*see* Dunk Island)
Jim Jim Falls, NT 80
Jirramun NP (absorbed – *see* Main Range)
Joalah NP (*see* Tamborine Mountain)
Joffre Gorge, WA 111
Johannsen's Cave, Qld 407
John Forrest National Park 116, **118-9**, 138, 166
John Hayes Rock Hole, NT *62*
Jolly's Lookout NP (*see* D'Aguilar Range)
Josephine Creek, Qld *455*
Jourama Falls, Qld *420*
Jourama National Park 23, 417, **420**, 442, 479
Jubilee and Piano Caves NP (*see* Chillagoe-Mungana Caves)
Jussieu Peninsula, SA 185

K

Ka Ka Mundi NP (absorbed – *see* Carnarvon)
Kakadu National Park 16, *33*, 38, 42, 43, 72, *73*, **74-81**, 89, 92, 93
Kalamina Gorge, WA 111
Kalamunda National Park 116, **136**, 138
Kalbarri National Park 16, 19, 116, *117*, **132-5**, 138, 166, *167*
Kanangra-Boyd National Park 316, **328-9**, 343, 366, 367
Kanangra Falls, NSW *328*
Kanangra Plateau, NSW 328
Kanangra Walls, NSW *329*
Kangaroo fern *214*
Kangaroo Island, SA 168, 174-7, *197*
Kangaroo paw *104*
Kangaroos *140, 193, 294*, 308, *365*
Kapok bush flower *96*
Karri 24, *105, 127*, 144, *145, 147*
Katatjuta *51, 54, 55*
Katherine Gorge National Park 72, **82-7**, 89, *92*, 93
Katherine River, NT 82, *85, 87, 92*
Katoomba, NSW 324
Kauri pine *453*
Kedumba Creek, NSW *326*
Keelan Island NP (*see* Northumberland Islands)
Keep River National Park 89, *92*, 93
Keilor Plains, Vic. *206*
Kennedia 338
Kennedy, Edmund 439
Kentbruck Heath, Vic. 226
Keppel Islands National Park 410
Keyser Island NP (*see* Whitsunday Islands)
Kimberleys, WA 10, 12, 15, 16-17, 19, 25, 94, 99, 102, 140
Kinchega National Park *41*, 308, *309*, **310-1**, 315, 366, 367
King Billy pine *263*, 266
King George Sound, WA 142
King Merrimen Island, NSW *302*
Kingia grass-tree *151*
Kinglake National Park 199, **203-5**, 234, 240, 241
King's Canyon National Park *10*, 48, **68**, 69, 92, 93
King's Creek, NT 68
Kirkville Hills, Qld *437*
Kite, brahminy *414*
Koala *197, 200*
Kondalilla NP (*see* Blackall Range)
Koombooloomba Dam, Qld 451
Kosciusko National Park *13*, 281, **282-9**, 300, 303, 305, 306, *366*, 367
Kroombit Tops National Park 23, 410
Kumboola Island NP (*see* Dunk Island)
Kununurra, WA 94
Ku-ring-gai Chase National Park 316, **322-3**, 332, 343, 366
Kurrimine National Park 474

L

Lace monitor *406*
Lachlan River, NSW 17, 308
Lady Musgrave Island NP (*see* Heron Island)
Ladysmith Island NP (*see* Whitsunday Islands)
Lagarostrobus franklinii 150
Laguna Lookout, Qld 383
Lake Albert, SA 188
Lake Alexandrina, SA 188
Lake Argyle, WA 16, 94
Lake Baker, Tas. *245*
Lake Barrine National Park 23, 447, 452, **453**, 474, 478, 479
Lake Bonney, SA 186
Lake Catani, Vic. 221
Lake Cawndilla, NSW *310*
Lake Cootharaba, Qld *382*
Lake Dobson, Tas. 266, *267*
Lake Dove, Tas. *248*
Lake Eacham National Park 23, 447, **452**, 474, 478, 479
Lake Eyre, SA 16
Lake Eyre National Park 191, 196
Lake Hypipamee, Qld *448*
Lake Kaboora, Qld 386, 387
Lake McKenzie, Qld *395*
Lake Menindee, NSW 310
Lake Moogerah Peaks National Park 390
Lake Mungo, NSW 308, 314
Lake Pedder, Tas. 256, 259, 264, 272
Lake St Clair, Tas. 16, *249*, 259
Lake Surprise, Vic. *227*
Lake Youl, Tas. *245*
Lakefield National Park 474, 478
Lakes 16, *17*
perched 394, *395*
window *387*, 394
Lakes Walk, NSW 283
Lambertia *154*
Lamb Range, Qld 464
Lamb's poison *128*
Lamington, Lord 370
Lamington National Park 23, 368, **370-1**, 390, 478, 479
Land Conservation Council (Vic.) 199
Landforms 10-11
Langford Island NP (*see* Whitsunday Islands)
Launceston, Tas. 242
Lawn Hill National Park 442, 478
Lawyer vine *453*
Le Grand Beach, WA 156
Leaching *299*
Leaf-eating beetle 25
Learmonth, WA 109
Leatherwood *262*
Leeches 35, 290
Leeuwin-Naturaliste National Park 116, **122-5**, 138, 166, *167*
Legges Tor, Tas. 245
Leichhardt's grasshopper *38*
Lemon Bight, Tas. *247*
Lennard River, WA 96, *97*
Leschenaultia *160*
Lesmurdie Falls National Park 138
Liane *425*
Lignotubers 24, 26
Lilies 27, *383, 430*
Limestone 10, *109, 128*, 130, *184, 224*, 225, 226, 268
Lincoln National Park 168, **185**, 191, 196
Lind National Park 234, 240, 241
Lindeman Island NP (*see* Whitsunday Islands)
Linne Island NP (*see* Whitsunday Islands)
Lion Island, NSW *322, 332*
Lismore, NSW 348, 354
Littabella National Park 410
Little Babinda Creek, Qld *455*
Little Beach, NSW 332
Little corella *195*
Little Crystal Creek, Qld 424
Little Desert National Park *16-17*, 39, 199, 234, 240, 241
Little Garie Beach, NSW 319
Little Hell, Tas. 245
Little Lindeman Island NP (*see* Whitsunday Islands)
Little penguin *194, 237*, 322
Little pied cormorant *85*
Livistona alfredii 114
L. mariae 58
Lizard Island National Park 23, 445, 474, 478, 479
Lizards *71, 141, 310, 364, 406*
Loch Ard Gorge, Vic. *224-5*
Locksmith Island NP (*see* Whitsunday Islands)
Loggerhead turtle *414*
Lomandra 126, 353
Lomatia *262*
London Bridge, Vic. *225*
Lonesome National Park 410
Long Island NP (*see* Whitsunday Islands)
Long-nosed potoroo *276*
Long Point, WA *144*
Long Pool, WA 121
Lord Howe Island, NSW *42*
Lorikeet, musk *346*
Lowe, Douglas 256
Lower Glenelg National Park 199, **226**, 234, 240, 241
Lupton Island NP (*see* Whitsunday Islands)
Lyrebirds *238, 412*

M

Mabel Island NP (*see* Frankland Islands)
MacDonald Park NP (*see* Tamborine Mountain)
MacDonnell Ranges, NT 10, 15, 48, *49*, 61, 66
Mackay, Qld 417
Macquarie Harbour, Tas. 261
Macquarie Marshes, NSW *17*
Macquarie Pass National Park 344
Macquarie River, NSW 17
Macroderma gigas 39, 407, *413*

Macrozamia (*see* Cycads)
Macrozamia Grove NP (*see* Tamborine Mountain)
Magnetic Island National Park 417, **418-9**, 442
Magnolias 20
Maher Island NP (*see* Whitsunday Islands)
Maiala NP (*see* D'Aguilar Range)
Maidenhair fern *435*
Main Beach, Qld *386*
Main Range National Park 23, 368, 390, 478
Maitland Bay, NSW *332-3*
Maits Rest, Vic. 202
Major Mitchell cockatoo *346*
Mallacoota Inlet, Vic. *219*
Mallacoota NP (absorbed – *see* Croajingolong)
Mallee 26, *27*, *155*, *183*
Mallee Cliffs National Park 39, 315
Malleefowl *38*, 39, 199, *237*
Mambray Creek, SA *178*
Mandalay Beach, WA *144*
Mandu Mandu Beach, WA *108*
Mangrove Creek, WA 109
Mangroves *18*, *99*, *109*, 116, 209, *422*, *429*, *436*, *460*
Manjimup, WA 116
Manning River, NSW 335
Manorina NP (*see* D'Aguilar Range)
Mansell Island NP (*see* Whitsunday Islands)
Mapleton Falls NP (*see* Blackall Range)
Margaret River, WA 123
Maria Creek National Park 23, 474-5
Maria Island, Tas. 259
Maria Island National Park 259, **268-9**, 273, 278, 279
Marine parks 444-5
Markham Cave NP (*see* Chillagoe-Mungana Caves)
Marley, NSW 319
Marramarra National Park 316, 344
Marri *25*, *120*, *127*
Marron 126
Mausoleum Island NP (*see* Whitsunday Islands)
Mayfly orchid *239*
Mazeppa National Park 410
McCarrs Creek, NSW *323*
McCleland's Lookout 424
McKenzie River, Vic. *231*
McNamee Creek NP (*see* Palmerston)
McPherson Range, Qld 15, 368, 370
McRaes Isthmus, Tas. *268*
Megalong Valley, NSW 324
Melaleucas (*see* Paperbarks)
Melastoma *382*
Melbourne, Vic. 36, 199
Memory Bay, SA *185*
Mercury Passage, Tas. 269
Merivale NP (*see* Rocky Creek)
Metamorphic rock 10
Miall Island NP (*see* Keppel Islands)
Michaelmas and Upolu Cays NP (*see* Green Island)
Mickey Creek, Qld 403
Mid Molle Island NP (*see* Whitsunday Islands)
Mid Mt Barren, WA 152
Middle Brook Island NP (*see* Hinchinbrook Island)
Middle Island NP (*see* Keppel Islands)
Middle Lagoon, NSW 292
Mildura, Vic. 217, 308
Millstream-Chichester National Park 106, **114**, 115, 166
Millstream Falls National Park 447, **450**, 475
Millstream palm *20-1*
Millstream River, Qld 450
Mimosa Rocks National Park 281, **292-3**, 303, 366
Mining 106
Minnamurra River, NSW 331
Minnie Water, NSW 358
Minster Island NP (*see* Northumberland Islands)
Miriwung tribe 92
Misery Bluff, Tas. 245
Missionary Bay, Qld *437*
Mitchell and Alice Rivers National Park 475
Mitchell grass 26
Mitchell River National Park 23, 234, 240, 241
Mitchell, Thomas 341
Moates Lake, WA 158
Moleside Creek, Vic. *226*
Moloch horridus 71
Monitor, lace *406*
Monsoon 12, 23, 72
Monstera, native *452*
Mooloolah River National Park 390
Moore River National Park 138
Mootwingee National Park 308, **312-3**, 315, 366
Moresby Range NP (*see* Ella Bay)
Moreton Island National Park 368, **378-81**, 382, 390, 478, 479
Morialta Creek, SA 172
Mornington Peninsula, Vic. 207
Morton National Park *14*, 281, **290-1**, 303, 367
Morwell National Park 234, 240, 241
Moss Gardens, Qld 401, *404*
Mosses 20
Mossman River, Qld *470*
Mount Aberdeen National Park 442-3
Mount Barney National Park 368, 390, 478
Mount Bauple National Park 23, 410
Mount Beatrice National Park 443
Mount Blackwood National Park 23, 443
Mount Buffalo National Park 199, **220-1**, 234-5, 240, 241
Mount Burrumbush NP (absorbed – *see* Bowling Green Bay)
Mount Chinghee NP (*see* Lamington)
Mount Colosseum National Park 410
Mount Cook NP (*see* Endeavour River)
Mount Cougal NP (*see* Springbrook)
Mount Eccles National Park 199, **227**, 235, 240, 241
Mount Edwards NP (*see* Lake Moogerah Peaks)
Mount Elliot NP (absorbed – *see* Bowling Green Bay)
Mount Field National Park 23, 259, **266-7**, 273, *278*, 279
Mount Fox National Park 443
Mount French NP (*see* Lake Moogerah Peaks)
Mount Greville NP (*see* Lake Moogerah Peaks)
Mount Hypipamee National Park 23, 447, **448-9**, 475, 478
Mount Imlay National Park 303
Mount Jim Crow National Park 410
Mount Jukes NP (*see* Mount Blackwood)
Mount Kaputar National Park 316, **340-1**, 344, 366
Mount Lindesay NP (absorbed – *see* Mount Barney)
Mount Major National Park 475
Mount Mandurana NP (*see* Mount Blackwood)
Mount Manypeaks Nature Reserve 142, **158-61**, 165
Mount Maroon-Mount May NP (absorbed – *see* Mount Barney)
Mount Mistake National Park 390
Mount Moffatt NP (absorbed – *see* Carnarvon)
Mount Moon NP (*see* Lake Moogerah Peaks)
Mount Pinbarren NP (*see* Cooloola)
Mount Remarkable National Park 168, **178-9**, 191, 196
Mount Richmond National Park 235, 240, 241
Mount Roberts NP (absorbed – *see* Main Range)
Mount Spec National Park 23, 417, **424-5**, 443, 478
Mount Tempest NP (absorbed – *see* Moreton Island)
Mount Walsh National Park 23, 410-1
Mount Warning National Park 23, 348, *349*, **350**, 362, 368
Mount Webb NP (*see* Starcke)
Mount William National Park 255, *278*, *279*
Mountain ash 24, 266, *267*
Mountain bell *150*
Mountain blue butterfly *476*
Mountain gentian *220*
Mountain gum *220*
Mountain heath *266*
Mountain pea *151*
Mountain pygmy-possum *236*, 285, *365*
Mountain rocket *275*
Mountains 10-15
Mouse, Hastings River 38, *39*
Mt Arid, WA 162
Mt Bartle Frere, Qld 454
Mt Bimberi, ACT 300
Mt Bishop, Vic. *208*
Mt Bogong, Vic. 222
Mt Boulder, Vic. *213*
Mt Bowen, Qld 437
Mt Bruce, WA 111
Mt Conner, NT 10
Mt Cook (Cooktown), Qld 460
Mt Cook (Magnetic I.), Qld 419
Mt Coryah, NSW *340*
Mt Dalrymple, Qld 435
Mt Dove, Tas. *246*
Mt Elliot, Qld 417, 421
Mt Etna, Qld 39
Mt Field, Tas. 259
Mt Field West, Tas. 266
Mt Finnigan, Qld 462
Mt Freycinet, Tas. 246
Mt Giles, NT 60
Mt Gudgenby, ACT *301*
Mt Hotham, Vic. 222
Mt Kaputar, NSW 341
Mt Kosciusko, NSW 10, 15, *280*
Mt Le Grand, WA 156
Mt Lidgbird, NSW *42*
Mt Lofty Ranges, SA *35*, 168, 170
Mt Manypeaks, WA *143*, 158
Mt Maria, Tas. 269
Mt Matheson, NSW 354
Mt Mistake, Qld 368
Mt Moffatt, Qld 401
Mt Mullen, Qld 382
Mt Nardi, NSW 354
Mt Narryer, WA 11
Mt Norman, Qld 385
Mt Olga, NT 50
Mt Ossa, Tas. 249
Mt Ragged, WA *162*
Mt Remarkable, SA 178
Mt Rooper, Qld 429
Mt Sorrow, Qld *467*
Mt Tamborine, Qld 374
Mt Tempest, Qld *379*
Mt Tip Tree, Qld 464
Mt Warning, Qld/NSW *15*, *350*, 373
Mt Wellington, Tas. 259
Mt William, Vic. 228
Mt Wilson, NSW *15*, *327*
Mulga 26-7
Mumgumby Creek, Qld 461
Mungo Brush, NSW 334
Mungo National Park *12*, 16, 308, **314**, 315
Mung-um Nackum Island NP (*see* Dunk Island)
Murchison Gorge, WA *117*, *132*
Murchison Highway, Tas. 253
Murchison River, WA 132, *133*, *167*
Murramarang National Park 281, **294-5**, 303
Murramarang Range, NSW 294
Murray River, Vic./SA 16, 17, 25, 188, *217*
Murray Valley, Vic. *13*
Murrumbidgee River, NSW 16
Murwillumbah, NSW 354
Musgrave Range, NT 10
Musk daisy *204*
Musk lorikeet *346*
Mutchero Inlet NP (*see* Graham Range)
Muttonbird Island, Vic. 225
Myall Lakes National Park 16, 316, **334**, 344, 366, 367
Myrtle beech *22*, *214*, *260*, *265*

N

Naas River, ACT *300*
Nalbaugh National Park 304
Namadgi National Park 281, **300-1**, 304, 366
Nambung National Park 116, **130-1**, 138, 166
Nambung River, WA 130
Nandewar Range, NSW 14, *341*
Nangar National Park 304
Napier Range, WA 96, 99
Naracoorte Caves Conservation Park 168, 191, 196
National Estate 43, 256
National Park management 30-3, 35
National Parks and Primitive Areas Council 316
Native fuchsia *275*
Native hibiscus *382*, *401*
Native monstera *452*
Native rosella *421*
Native violet *123*, *325*
Natural Arch National Park 23, 368, **372-3**, 390-1, 479
Nature's Window, WA 132
Negrohead beech 22, *23*
Neerabup National Park 138
Nelly Bay, Qld 419
Nelson Lagoon, NSW 292
Nerang River, Qld 372, 373
New England National Park 23, 348, 362-3
New England Tablelands, NSW 25, 355, 385
New Holland honeyeater *105*
Newry Island NP (*see* Whitsunday Islands)
Ngungun NP (*see* Glass House Mountains)
Nicolson Island NP (*see* Whitsunday Islands)
Nightcap National Park 23, 348, **354**, 363, 368
Nightcap Range, NSW 15, 354
Nightcap Track, NSW 354
Ninety Mile Beach, Vic. *17*
Ningadhun, NSW *341*
Ningaloo, WA 166
Nobby Island, SA *176*
Noel Island NP (*see* Northumberland Islands)
Noisy scrub bird 158
Noosa Head, Qld 383
Noosa Hill, Qld 383
Noosa National Park 368, **383**, 391, 478, 479
Noosa Plain, Qld 382
Noosa River, Qld 382
Noosa River NP (*see* Cooloola)
Norman Bay, Vic. 212
Normanby Island NP (*see* Frankland Islands)
Normans Beach, WA 158
Nornalup Inlet, WA 142, 144, *145*
North Brook Island NP (*see* Hinchinbrook Island)
North Coast Rail National Park 391
North East Island NP (*see* Northumberland Islands)
North Johnstone River, Qld 456, *457*
North Keppel Island NP (*see* Keppel Islands)
North Molle Island NP (*see* Whitsunday Islands)

North Repulse Island NP (*see* Whitsunday Islands)
North Stradbroke Island, Qld *40*, 386
North West Cape, WA 12, 106, 109
North West Island NP (*see* Heron Island)
Northumberland Islands National Park 23, 411
Nourlangie Rock, NT 74, *75*, *76*, 92
Nowra, NSW 290
Nullarbor National Park *27*, 191, 196
Nullarbor Plain, WA 19, 26, 142
Numbat *38*, *141*
Numinbah Valley, Qld 372
Nunga Island NP (*see* Whitsunday Islands)
Nungatta National Park 304
Nutambulla Creek, NSW *312*
Nuyts, Pieter 142, 144
Nuyts Wilderness, WA 144, 166
Nymboida National Park 363, 367
Nymphaea 77, *394*
Nymph Island NP (*see* Lizard Island)
Nypa Palms NP (*see* Hinchinbrook Island)

O

O'Hara Island, NSW *294*
Oaks *50*, *267*
Obi Obi Gorge NP (*see* Blackall Range)
Obiri Rock, NT (*see* Ubirr)
Ocean Lake, Qld *399*
Oceans 18-19
Odonata dragonfly *403*
Oil drilling 106
Olga River, Tas. 256
Olgas, NT 10, 48, 50, *54-5*
Olive python *141*
One Tree Island, Qld 445
One Tree Rocks, Qld 394
Open forests 24-5
Orb weaver, golden *429*
Orchid Beach, Qld *437*
Orchid Point, Qld *394*
Orchids 23, 27, *156*, *157*, *204*, *239*, *252*, *275*, *307*, *323*, *340*, *370*
Ord River, WA 16, 94
Organ Pipes National Park 15, *41*, 199, **206**, 235, 240, 241
Ormiston Creek, NT 60
Ormiston Gorge and Pound National Park 48, **60**, 69, 92, *93*
Orpheus Island National Park 23, 443, 445
Orroral Peak, ACT 300
Oscar Range, WA 99, 102
Osprey *195*
Otway National Park 19, 23, 199, **202**, 235, 240, 241
Otway Range, Vic. *202*
Outer Newry Island NP (*see* Whitsunday Islands)
Ovens Valley, Vic. 221
Overland Track, Tas. 249, 255
Oxley Wild Rivers National Park 344, *367*
Oxylobium 159

P

Pademelons *277*, 424
Palm Creek, NT 56, *59*
Palm Grove NP (*see* Tamborine Mountain)
Palm Islands, Qld 424
Palm Valley, NT 56, *58*
Palmerston National Park 23, 447, **456-9**, 475, 478, 479
Palmerston Rocks NP (*see* Palmerston)
Palms *20-1*, 23, *58*, *76*, *83*, *319*, *350*, *374*, *383*, *397*, *402*, *429*, *468*
Paluma Range, Qld 424
Pambula, NSW 299
Pandani 266
Pandanus palm *76*, *383*, *429*
Panorama Point NP (*see* Tamborine Mountain)
Paper daisy *221*, *251*
Paper-heath *150*
Paperbarks 25, 27, *76*, *88*, *118*, *129*, *175*, *188*, *251*, *334*, *359*
Papilio butterfly *465*
Paradise-kingfisher, buff-breasted *476*
Pardalote, striated *277*
Parker River, Vic. 202
Parkinson, Sydney 460
Parrots *39*, 63, *194*, *238*, *414*
Paterson, A.B. (Banjo) 351
Paterson's curse *171*
Peak Charles National Park 165
Peak Island NP (*see* Keppel Islands)
Peak Range National Park 411
Pearce, Tom 224
Pearl bluebush *27*
Peas *128*, *151*, *160*, *170*, *171*, *201*, *357*
Pelican Island NP (*see* Keppel Islands)
Pelicans *188*, *239*, *334*
Pelsaert, Francis 135
Pemberton National Parks 116, **126-7**, 138, 166
Pencil pine *20*, 266
Penguins *194*, *237*, 322
Penn Island NP (*see* Northumberland Islands)
Penrith Island NP (*see* Brampton Island)
Pentecost Island NP (*see* Whitsunday Islands)
Peregrine falcon *194*
Perentie *70*
Perseverance Island NP (*see* Whitsunday Islands)
Perseverance NP (*see* Crows Nest Falls)
Perth, WA 11, 116
Pets in parks 37
Phebalium *336*
Phillip Island, Vic. 200
Phyllodes 26
Phytophthera cinnamoni 116
Piccabeen (bangalow) palm *350*, *354*, *374*, *397*, *468*
Picnic Bay, Qld 419
Picnic Point, Vic. *210*
Piesse Brook, WA 136
Pigeon (Aboriginal outlaw) 96
Pigface, angular *184*
Pigs, feral *41*
Pilbara, WA 114
Pile Valley, Qld 397
Pimelea *136*, *185*
Pimpernel *313*
Pincer Island NP (*see* Whitsunday Islands)
Pine Island NP (*see* Whitsunday Islands)
Pines *20*, *263*, 266, *272*, *336*, 337, *419*, *430-1*, *453*
Pink cockatoo *195*, *346*
Pink robin *275*
Pinnacles Desert, WA 130-1
Pipeclay NP (*see* Cooloola)
Pitt Water, NSW 322
Plains of Heaven, Tas. 245
Planning a visit 37
Plant evolution 20-1, 24-5
Planton Island NP (*see* Whitsunday Islands)
Platycerium grande 372
Platypus *236*, 435, 450
Poached-egg daisy *26*
Point Avoid, SA 184
Point Danger, NSW/Qld 350
Point d'Entrecasteaux, WA *128*, 129
Point Gardner, WA 158
Point Hicks, Vic. *218*, 219
Point Lookout, Qld 386
Pondalowie Bay, SA *197*
Porcupine Creek, Qld *440*
Porcupine Gorge National Park 417, **440**, 443
Porcupine grass (*see* Hummock grasses)
Porongurup National Park 165, 166, 167
Porongurup Range, WA 142
Port Arthur, Tas. 170
Port Campbell National Park *6*, 19, 199, 202, **224-5**, 235, 240, 241
Port Davey, Tas. 259, 264
Port Douglas, SA 184
Port Essington, NT 88
Port Hacking, NSW 319
Port Hedland, WA 12, 19, 106
Port Jackson, NSW 316
Port Lincoln, SA 185
Port Phillip basin, Vic. 201
Portsea, Vic. 207
Possession Island National Park 475
Possums *39*, *140*, *277*, 285, *477*
Potoroo, long-nosed *276*
Powers of rangers 33
Precipitous Bluff, Tas. *265*
Pretty Beach, NSW *294*
Prickly bitter pea *160*
Prickly solanum *313*
Prickly whitebeard *353*
Prince Regent River, WA *17*
Princess Margaret Rose Caves, Vic. 226
Protesters Falls, NSW 354
Providential Cove, NSW 319
Prudhoe Island NP (*see* Northumberland Islands)
Psyllids 25
Public participation 36
Pultenaea 178
Purple-crowned superb fruit dove *476*
Purpose of national parks 30-1
Purtaboi Island NP (*see* Dunk Island)
Putty Beach, NSW 332, *333*
Pygmy-possum, mountain *236*, *365*
Pyramidal Rock, Tas. *268*
Pyramids (Girraween), Qld *384-5*
Pyramids (Porcupine Gorge), Qld 440
Python Pool, WA 114

Q

Quarry Bay, WA 123
Quartzite 10, *15*, 67
Queen Mary Falls National Park 391, 479
Quokka *140*, 161
Quoll, spotted-tailed *364*
Quoraburagun Pinnacles, NSW *299*

R

Rabbit Island NP (*see* Whitsunday Islands)
Radical Bay, Qld *418*, 419
Raffles Bay, NT 88
Rainbow Beach, Qld 382
Rainfall 12-13, 146
Rainforests 15, 22-3, *290*, *374*, *376*, *396*, 406, *425*, *449*, *468*, *469*
Rangers 32-3
Raspberry Lookout, NSW 355
Ravensbourne National Park 391
Recherche Archipelago, WA 156, 162, *163*
Redback spider 34
Red cedar 432
Red-fingered mangrove crab *365*
Red Gorge, WA *110*, 111
Red kangaroo *365*
Red Rock NP (absorbed – *see* Yuraygir)
Red-rumped parrot *194*
Red-tailed black cockatoo *105*
Red-tailed tropic bird 122
Red tingle *147*
Refuge Cove, Vic. 36
Regeneration 24-5
Regent bowerbird *346*
Reliance Creek National Park 443
Remarkable Rocks *174*
Renou Island NP (*see* Northumberland Islands)
Repair Island NP (*see* Whitsunday Islands)
Restoration of parks 40-1, 357
Rhaphidophora 459
Rhyolite 10, 15
Ribbon gum *283*
Richea pandanifolia 274
Richmond Beach, NSW 295
River red gum *25*, *37*, *63*, *120*, *181*, *217*
Rivers 16, *17*
Robins *275*, *327*
Robinson Gorge National Park 411, 478
Rock art *43*, 66, 68, 74, *79*, *92*, 96, 102, *229*, 312, 401
Rock orchid *323*, *370*
Rock parrot *194*
Rock types 10, 14-15
Rocket, mountain *275*
Rockhampton, Qld 393
Rockingham Bay, Qld 439
Rocky Cape National Park 242, **250-1**, 255, 278, 279
Rocky Creek National Park 391
Rocky Islets NP (*see* Lizard Island)
Rocky Pool, WA 136
Rocky River, SA 175
Roe Creek, NT 61
Rokeby National Park 475, 478
Rosellas *347*, *421*
Rosenberg's goanna 175
Rosette Rock, Vic. 206
Rosewood Creek, NSW 360
Rossiter Bay, WA 156
Rottnest Islands, WA 140, 161
Rough Range, WA 106
Round Hill NP (*see* Eurimbula)
Round Island NP (*see* Frankland Islands)
Rowsley Fault, Vic. 201
Royal Arch Cave NP (*see* Chillagoe-Mungana Caves)
Royal Archway Cave NP (*see* Chillagoe-Mungana Caves)
Royal bluebell *307*
Royal hakea *154*
Royal National Park 19, 31, 316, **318-21**, 344, *366*
Rudall River National Park *30*, 115
Rufous bettong *412*
Rufous tree-creeper *126*
Ruined Castle, Vic. *223*
Russell Falls, Tas. *266*
Russell Gully, Qld *406*
Russell Range, WA 162
Russell River NP (*see* Graham Range)
Ryan Imperial Cave NP (*see* Chillagoe-Mungana Caves)

S

Safety and survival 34-5
Safety Cove, Tas. *19*
Saint Helena Island National Park 391, 478
Salmon gum *86*
Salt Creek, SA 188
Salt production 106
Saltbush 26, *27*, *306*, *314*
Salty Creek, NSW 357
Salty Lagoon, NSW 357
Salvator Rosa NP (absorbed – *see* Carnarvon)
Sand
  dunes *144*, *153*, 186, *187*, *379*
  islands 386, 394
  lunettes *314*
  mining 40, 379, 386, 399
  movement 18-19, 186, *187*, *398*
  types 18
Sandplains *12*, 27, *27*, 132
Sandstone 10, *117*, *134*, *173*, *202*, *293*
Sap-sucking insect 25
Sarabah NP (*see* Lamington)
Savannah *86*
Sawfish 99
Scaevola 130
Scaly-tailed possum *140*
Scarlet banksia *160*
Scawfell Island NP (*see* Brampton Island)
Scenic Rim, Qld 353, 368
Scented paperbark *251*
Schouten Island, Tas. *246*
Scott National Park 139, 166
Scraggy Point, Qld 437
Scrub bird, noisy 158
Scrublands 26, *27*
Sea-eagle, white-bellied *177*
Seaforth Island NP (*see* Whitsunday Islands)
Sea lions *141*, *177*
Seal Bay Conservation Park 168, **176-7**, 191, 196
Sedimentary rocks 10
Serpentine National Park 139, 166
Serra Range, Vic. 228
Seven Mile Beach National Park 304-5
Seventeen Mile Creek, NT 82
Shale 10, *107*
Shannon Forest Park, WA 116, 139
Shark Bay, WA 19, 20
Shaw Island NP (*see* Whitsunday Islands)
Shelduck *237*
Sherbrooke River, Vic. 225
Shingleback lizard *141*, *310*
Shiny tea-tree *260*
Shoal Bay, Tas. *268*
Shoalhaven River, NSW *14*, 296
Shores 18-19
Short-beaked echidna *192*
Shothole Canyon, WA 106
Shrubby velvet bush *239*
Shute Bay, Qld *429*
Shute Harbour, Qld 429
Shute Island NP (*see* Whitsunday Islands)
Signalling for help 34
Sillago Island NP (*see* Whitsunday Islands)
Silver banksia *251*
Silver gull *188*
Silver-leaf cassia *59*
Silver tails *313*
Silver tea-tree *157*
Silversmith Island NP (*see* Whitsunday Islands)
Simpson Desert, Qld 41, 415
Simpson Desert National Park 168, 411, 478, *479*
Simpson's Gap National Park 48, **61**, 69, 92, 93
Sir James Mitchell National Park 139
Sisters Hills, Tas. 251
Sisters Island NP (*see* Dunk Island)
Slate 10
Slaty helmet orchid *239*
Sloping Island NP (*see* Keppel Islands)
Smalleys Beach, Qld 431
Small helmet orchid *239*
Smith Island NP (*see* Dunk Island)
Smokebush *150*
Smoky Cape, NSW 338
Snake Creek, WA 114
Snake Range National Park 411
Snakebite 34
Snakes *70*, *141*
Snappy gum *26*
Snow daisy *284*
Snow gum *284*, *286*, *288*
Snowy Mountains, NSW 11, 14
Snowy River, NSW 16
Snowy River National Park *36*, 199, 235, 240, 241
Soft tree fern *214-5*
Soil types 15, 26-7
Solander, Daniel 460
Solanum *182*, *313*, *432*
Somerset, Tas. 253
South Alligator River, NT 74, 77
South Island NP (*see* Northumberland Islands)
South Molle Island NP (*see* Whitsunday Islands)
South Peak, Qld *454*, 455
South Repulse Island NP (*see* Whitsunday Islands)
Southern cross *160*
Southern Ocean 12, 129, 142, 144, 152, *156*, 186, 202, 225
Southern plains banksia *155*
Southport, SA 186
Southwest National Park 23, *35*, 42, 259, 261, **264-5**, 273, 278, *279*
Southwood National Park 391
Spencer Gulf, SA 178
Spider bites 34
Spider orchid *157*, *340*
Spiders 34, *429*
Spinifex, coastal 26, *218*
Spinifex, inland (*see* Hummock grasses)
Spitfire Creek, Qld *378*
Sponge fruit *313*
Spotted gum *295*
Spotted-tailed quoll *364*
Sprengelia heath *357*
Springbrook National Park 23, 391, 478, 479
Springbrook Plateau, Qld 372
St Mary Peak, SA *181*
Staaten River National Park 475
Stackhousia, downy *157*
Stacks Bluff, Tas. *244-5*
Staghorn 23, *372*, *397*, *448*
Starcke National Park 475
Starfish, crown-of-thorns *444*
Steiglitz grevillea *200*, 201
Stephens Island NP (*see* Dunk Island)
Still Island NP (*see* Northumberland Islands)
Stilt, black-winted *346*
Stingray 99
Stings and bites 34, 393
Stirling Range, WA 140, 142
Stirling Range National Park 142, **148-51**, 165, 166, 167
Stirling Range smokebush *150*
Stokes National Park 165, 166
Stony Creek, Qld *426*, 427
Stony Creek, Vic. 201
Storm Bay, Tas. 259
Storm Boy 188
Stradbroke Islands, Qld 382
Strahan, Tas. 261
Strangler fig *23*, *370*, *436*
Strawflower, alpine *222*
Straw-necked ibis *195*
Striated pardalote *277*
Striped possum *39*
Strzelecki National Park 255, 278, 279
Strzelecki Ranges, Vic. 214
Sturt National Park 315, 366
Sturt's desert rose *109*
Sugar glider *276*
Sugarloaf Rock, WA *122*
Sunbird, yellow-bellied *413*
Sundew *325*
Sundown National Park 391, 478
Sunshine 12
Sunshine Beach, Qld 383
Superb fruit dove, purple-crowned *476*
Superb lyrebird *238*
Surprise Rock NP (*see* Whitsunday Islands)
Survival and safety 34-5
Swamp Bay, Qld 429
Swamp lily *383*
Swamp water fern *459*
Swampgrass 27
Swan River, WA *121*
Sword Creek Falls NP (*see* Wallaman Falls)
Sydenham Inlet, Vic. 219
Sydney, NSW 12, 316, 319, 322
Sydney flannel flower *307*
Sydney Harbour National Park 40, 344, 366

T

Taillefer Rock, Tas. *246*
Tallow Beach, NSW 332
Tamborine Mountain National Parks 23, 368, *369*, **374-7**, 391, 479
Tammar wallaby *192*
Tancred Island NP (*see* Whitsunday Islands)
Tan wattle *127*
Tangalooma, Qld 379
Tanglefoot beech 245
Tarlo River National Park 305
Tarra-Bulga National Park 23, 199, **214-6**, 235, 240, 241
Tarra Valley 214
Tarra Valley NP (*see* Tarra-Bulga)
Tasman, Abel 142
Tasmanian oak *267*
Tasmanian pademelon *277*
Tasmanian tiger 39, 266
Tasman Peninsula, Tas. 259
Tasman Peninsula State Reserves 259, **270-1**, 273
Tasman Sea 259, 299, 334
Tasman's Arch, Tas. 270
Tathra National Park 139
Taylors Landing, SA 185
Tea Tree Bay, Qld *383*
Tea-trees 27, *154*, *157*, *251*, *260*, *357*
Teague Island NP (*see* Whitsunday Islands)
Teewah Creek, Qld 382
Temperature 12, 14
Templetonia retusa 185
Terania Creek, NSW 348, 354
Termite mounds *109*, *113*, *465*
Tessellated Pavement, Vic. 206
Tessellated Pavements, Tas. 270, *271*
The Amphitheatre, NT 56
The Amphitheatre, Qld 401, *402*
The Art Gallery, Qld 401
The Beak, Qld *428*
The Drum and Drumsticks, NSW *19*
The Gorge, Vic. 221
The Horn, Vic. 221
The Knoll NP (*see* Tamborine Mountain)
The Lakes National Park 16, *17*, 235, 240, 241
The Leap NP (*see* Mount Blackwood)
The Loop, WA *132*
The Palms National Park 23, 391
Thirlmere Lakes National Park 344
Thistle Cove, WA *156*
Thistle Island, SA *185*
Thomas Island NP (*see* Whitsunday Islands)
Thomas River, WA 162
Thornton Beach, Qld *466*, 467, 468
Thornton Peak NP (absorbed *see* Cape Tribulation)
Thornton Range, Qld 467
Thorny devil *71*
Thouin Bay, Tas. *246*
Thredbo, NSW 285
Three Islands NP (*see* Lizard Island)
Three Moon Creek, Qld 406
Three Sisters, NSW *327*
Thurra River, Vic. *218*
Thylacine (Tasmanian tiger) 39, 266
Tibrogargan NP (*see* Glass House Mountains)
Tick bites 34
Tidal River, Vic. *209*, *212*
Tidbinbilla Nature Reserve, ACT 300
Tides 18-19, 94
Timor Sea 72
Tinaroo Dam, Qld 16
Tin Can Bay, Qld 393
Tingle, red *147*
Tinsmith Island NP (*see* Whitsunday Islands)
Todd River, NT 48, 63
Tomaree National Park 344
Toolbrunup Peak, WA *149*
Toona australis 432
Topaz Road National Park 23, 475
Torndirrup National Park 165, 166
Tower Hill Range, Tas. *245*
Tower of London and Donna Caves NP (*see* Chillagoe-Mungana Caves)
Townsville, Qld 417
Trachyte 10, 15,
Trade winds 12, 417
Traveller Range, Tas. 249
Treble Island NP (*see* Northumberland Islands)
Tree-creeper, rufous *126*
Tree evolution 20-1, 24-5
Tree ferns *25*, *203*, *214-5*, *230*, *253*, *266*, *432-3*
Tree frog *477*
Trephina Gorge Nature Park 48, **62-3**, 69, 92, 93
Triangle Island NP (*see* Whitsunday Islands)
Triodia (*see* Hummock grasses)
Tropic bird, red-tailed *122*
Tropic of Capricorn 393
Truchanas Nature Reserve 259, **272**, 273
Truchanas, Olegas 272
Tryon Island NP (*see* Heron Island)
Tucker's Creek NP (*see* North Coast Rail)
Tully Gorge National Park 23, 447, **451**, 475
Tully River, Qld *451*
Tunnel Creek National Park 94, **102**, 103, 166
Tuntable Falls, NSW 354
Turtle Group NP (*see* Lizard Island)
Turtles *33*, *414*
Tussock grasses 26-7, *97*, *182*, *284*
Tweed Range, NSW 15
Tweed volcano, NSW/Qld *15*, 350, 354, 368, 370, 373
Tween Brook Island NP (*see* Hinchinbrook Island)
Twelve Apostles, Vic. *225*
Twofold Bay, NSW 299
Two Islands NP (*see* Lizard Island)
Two Peoples Bay, WA *143*
Two Peoples Bay Nature Reserve 142, **158-61**, 165

U

Ubirr *43*, *78-9*, 92
Uluru National Park 15, 42, 48, **50-5**, 69, 92, 93
Ulysses butterfly *476*
Umbrella fern *424*, *435*
Unadorned rock wallaby *421*

V

Valley of the Winds, NT *54*
Van Diemen Gulf 74, 88
Varanus gouldii 141
Vegetation 20-7
Victorian Alps, Vic. 11, 14, 32, 199
View Point, Vic. 221
Violet Gorge, Qld *400*, *404*
Violet, native *123*, *325*
Vivonne Bay, SA *176*
Volcanoes 10-11, 14-15, 227, *336*, 337, 341, 452-3
Volskow Island NP (*see* Whitsunday Islands)
Voluntary park work 36

W

Wadbilliga National Park 305
Waddy Point, Qld 399
Wajurda Head, NSW 292
Wallabies *140*, *192*, *193*, *237*, *277*, 294, *414-5*, *421*
Wallace Island NP (*see* Northumberland Islands)
Wallaga Lake National Park 281, **302**, 305
Wallaman Falls National Park 23, 417, **426-7**, 443
Warrangarra whitegum 385
Wallaroo *236*
Walls of China, NSW *314*
Walls of Jerusalem National Park 23, 255, 278
Wallum heathlands 393
Walpole, WA 144
Walpole-Nornalup National Park *24*, 142, **144-7**, 165, 166, 167
Walpole River, WA 144
Walyunga National Park *28-9*, 116, **120-1**, 139, 166
Walyunga Pool, WA 121
Wandoo 25, *119*
Wapenga Lake, NSW 292
Waratah 27, *307*
Ward's Canyon, Qld 401, *403*
Warrabah National Park 344
Warren Beach, WA 129
Warren cedar *146*
Warren NP (*see* Pemberton)
Warren River, WA 126
Warrie NP (*see* Springbrook)
Warrumbungle National Park 316, **336-7**, 345, 366
Warrumbungle Range, NSW 14
Washpool National Park 23, 348, 363
Water buffalo 41, 72, 88
Water fern *371*, *459*
Waterfall Bay, Tas. 270
Waterfall Gully, SA 170
Waterfalls *173*, *216*
Waterlily *77*, *394*
Waterloo Bay, Vic. *209*, *211*, 212
Waterview Creek, Qld *420*
Watheroo National Park 139
Wathumba Creek, Qld 399
Watsonia *136*
Wattamolla, NSW *319*, *320*
Wattles *126*, *307*, *351*, *384*, *419*
see also Acacia
Wave action 18-19
Waychinicup River, WA *158*
Weano Gorge, WA 111, *112*
Weather patterns 12, *13*
Wedding bush *394*
Weddin Mountains National Park 305
Wedge Island, Qld *431*
Wedge Island NP (absorbed – *see* Cape Hillsborough)
Wedge-tailed eagle *193*, *347*
Weeds *36*, *171*, 206, *330*
Wentworth Falls, NSW 326
Werrikimbe National Park 38, 345, 348, 366, 367
West Cape Howe National Park 165, 167
West Head, NSW 322
West Hill Island NP (*see* West Hill)
West Hill National Park 411
Western grey kangaroo *140*, *193*
Western Port Bay, Vic. 200
Wetlands 17, 72
Wheeler Island NP (*see* Dunk Island)
Whisky Bay, Vic. *210*
Whitebeard, prickly *353*
White-bellied sea-eagle *177*
White Cliffs, NSW 12, 312
Whitsunday Islands National Park 23, 443, 478, 479
Whitsunday Passage, Qld 429
Wigton Island NP (*see* Brampton Island)
Wilcannia, NSW 12
Wild Duck Island NP (*see* Northumberland Islands)
Wild Rivers National Park, 23, *42*, 256-7, 259, **260-3**, 273, 278
Wilderness Society, Tas. 36, 256-7
Wildlife conservation 38-9
Willandra Lakes, NSW 16, 26, 42, *43*, 308, 314
Willandra National Park 281, 305, 366
William Bay National Park 165, 167
Wilpena Pound, SA 178, *180-1*
Wilson Island NP (*see* Heron Island)
Wilson Range, Vic. *212*
Wilsons Promontory National Park *22*, 23, 36, 199, **208-13**, 235, *240*, 241
Wimmera River, Vic. *16*
Windjana Gorge National Park 94, **96-7**, 103,166
Winds 14
Windsor Tableland, Qld 470
Windy Harbour, WA 129
Wineglass Bay, Tas. 246, *247*
Wingan Inlet NP (absorbed – *see* Croajingolong)
Wirrainbeia Island NP (*see* Whitsunday Islands)
Witches Falls NP (*see* Tamborine Mountain)
Witjira National Park 191, 196
Woko National Park 345
Wolfe Creek Crater National Park 103, 166
Wolgan River, NSW 330
Wollemi National Park 316, **330**, 345, 366, 367
Wollemi River, NSW 330
Wombats 38, *236*
Wombelano Falls, Vic. *204*
Wonga wonga *340*
Wonnangatta-Moroka National Park 235, 240, 241
Woodgate National Park 411, 479
Woodlands 21, 24-5, *119*, 130, 170
Woods Well, SA *188*
Woody and Little Woody Islands NP (*see* Great Sandy)
Woody Head, NSW 356
Wooloroo Brook, WA 121
Woongoolbver Creek, Qld *396*
Workington Island NP (*see* Whitsunday Islands)
World Heritage List 42-3, 256-7, 308, 314, 348, 368
Wreck Island NP (*see* Heron Island)
Wunburra NP (*see* Springbrook)
Wyndham, WA 94
Wyperfeld National Park *27*, 39, 235, *240*

Y

Yakka *170*, *171*
Yalgorup National Park 139, 166
Yallingup Cave, WA *124-5*
Yamanic Falls NP (*see* Wallaman Falls)
Yampire Gorge 111
Yanchep National Park 139, *166*, 167
Yarangobilly Caves, NSW 283
Yardie Creek, WA *109*
Yarra River, Vic. 203
Yarrowitch Gorge NP (absorbed – *see* Oxley Wild Rivers)
Yarrunga Valley, NSW *291*
Yellow-bellied sunbird *413*
Yellow-footed rock wallaby *193*
Yellow Water, NT *77*
Yeppoon National Park 411
Yerumbinna Island NP (*see* Whitsunday Islands)
Yiundalla Island NP (*see* Whitsunday Islands)
Yokinup Bay, WA 162
Younghusband Peninsula, SA 188
Yungaburra NP (*see* Lake Eacham)
Yuraygir National Park 348, **358-9**, 363, 366, 367

Z

Zamia (*macrozamia*) (*see* Cycads)
Zamia Grove NP (*see* Tamborine Mountain)
Zieria *177*
Zircon, oldest *11*

Rules that protect our parks and wildlife

NATIONAL PARKS are at the mercy of their visitors. Careless actions can do irreparable harm. Rules aimed at preventing damage are plain and simple:

- Use only the fireplaces provided, or your own portable cooker if there are none. Observe all fire ban notices or broadcasts.
- Never take a cat or dog into a park.
- Leave firearms and any other hunting weapons or equipment at home.
- Never leave litter. Take out anything you have brought in, or use the rubbish bins that are provided.
- Avoid disturbing plants, rocks and animals — and on no account remove any of them.
- Obey 'No Entry' signs. As well as protecting fragile areas, they may be for your own safety.
- Keep your vehicle to formed roads and marked parking zones.

Addresses

Park services

Australian National Parks and Wildlife Service
Box 636, Canberra City 2601. (062) 46 6211
Conservation Commission of the Northern Territory
Box 1046, Alice Springs 5750. (089) 50 8211
New South Wales National Parks and Wildlife Service
Box N189, Grosvenor Street P.O., Sydney 2000. (02) 237 6500.
Queensland National Parks and Wildlife Service
Box 190, North Quay 4000. (07) 224 0414.
Great Barrier Reef Marine Park Authority
Box 1379, Townsville 4810. (077) 71 2191
South Australian National Parks and Wildlife Service
GPO Box 1782, Adelaide 5001. (08) 216 7777
Tasmanian National Parks and Wildlife Service
Box 210, Sandy Bay 7005. (002) 30 8033
Victorian National Parks Service
240 Victoria Parade, East Melbourne 3002. (03) 651 4011
National Parks Authority of Western Australia
Hackett Drive, Nedlands 6009. (09) 386 8811

Park associations

National Parks Association of the Australian Capital Territory
Box 457, Canberra City 2601. (062) 49 4554
National Parks Association of New South Wales
275c Pitt Street, Sydney 2000. (02) 264 7994
National Parks Association of Queensland
GPO Box 1752, Brisbane 4001
Nature Conservation Society of South Australia
310 Angas Street, Adelaide 5000. (08) 223 5155
Tasmanian Conservation Trust
GPO Box 684, Hobart 7001. (002) 34 3552
Victorian National Parks Assocation
285-287 Little Lonsdale Street, Melbourne 3000. (03) 602 4877
Conservation Council of Western Australia
537 Wellington Street, Perth 6000. (09) 321 4507

Park foundations

New South Wales National Parks and Wildlife Foundation
GPO Box 2666, Sydney 2001. (02) 27 7971
National Parks Foundation of South Australia
19 Wilsden Street, Walkerville 5081
Australian Conservation Foundation
672b Glenferrie Road, Hawthorn 3122. (03) 819 2888

Australian Trust for Conservation Volunteers

NSW: Box 2397, Queen Victoria Building P.O., Sydney 2000. (02) 451 4026
Vic.: Box 412, Ballarat 3350. (053) 32 7490
WA: Box 160 Mundaring 6073

Environment centres

ACT: Childers Street Building, Kingsley Street, Canberra 2600. (062) 48 0885
NT: Box 2120, Darwin 5794
NSW: 399 Pitt Street, Sydney 2000. (02) 267 7722
18 Argyle Street, Sydney 2000. (02) 27 4714
Qld: 147 Ann Street, Brisbane 4000. (07) 221 0188
SA: 240 Rundle Street, Adelaide 5000. (08) 223 5393
Tas.: 102 Bathurst Street, Hobart 7000. (002) 34 5566
Vic.: 419 Lonsdale Street, Melbourne 3000. (03) 602 4877
WA: 794 Hay Street, Perth 6000. (09) 321 5942

Wilderness Society

ACT: Box 188, Civic Square, Canberra 2608. (062) 49 8011
NSW: 362 Pitt Street, Sydney 2000. (02) 267 7929
SA: 291a Rundle Street, Adelaide 5000. (08) 223 6917
Tas.: 130 Davey Street, Hobart 7000. (002) 349 3666
Vic.: 8/399 Lonsdale Street, Melbourne 3000. (03) 67 5884
WA: 794 Hay Street, Perth 6000. (09) 321 2269

Bushwalking federations

NT: Box 1938, Darwin 5794
NSW: 399 Pitt Street, Sydney 2000. (02) 267 7722
Qld: GPO Box 1573, Brisbane 4001
SA: Box 178, Unley 5061
Tas.: Box 190, Launceston 7250
Vic.: GPO Box 815f, Melbourne 3001
WA: 2 Pearl Parade, Scarborough 6019

Youth Hostels associations

NT: Box 39900, Winnellie 5789. (089) 83 3902
NSW: 355 Kent Street, Sydney 2000. (02) 29 5068
Qld: 462 Queen Street, Brisbane 4000. (07) 221 2022
SA: 72 South Terrace, Adelaide 5000. (08) 51 5583
Tas.: 133a Elizabeth Street, Hobart 7000. (002) 34 9617
Vic.: 122 Flinders Street, Melbourne 3000. (03) 63 5421
WA: 257 Adelaide Terrace, Perth 6000. (09) 325 5844

Acknowledgments

The publishers and editors are deeply indebted to administrators, interpretation officers and rangers of the various national parks services. Countless people spent long hours supplying or verifying information; in particular, Sandra Bardwell, John Dengate, Kevin Goss, Leonie Heard, Tim Kahn, Don Marshall, Chris Mobbs, Rodney Musch, Ann Prescott, Greg Siepen, Sweton Stewart, Andrew Tatnell, Shona Whitfield and Cliff Winfield. Others assisted in planning the touring photographer's itineraries, or gave him considerable help in the field.

Thanks are also due to the staff of the National Herbarium, Royal Botanic Gardens, Sydney, for their assistance in plant identification, and to botanist A. R. Rodd.

Reference sources: The publishers acknowledge their indebtedness for information gained from the following books: *Atlas of Australian Resources* (Division of National Mapping); *Australia, a Timeless Grandeur,* Helen Grasswill (Landsdowne Press); *Australian Vegetation,* R. H. Groves, ed. (Cambridge University Press); *Australia's Endangered Species,* Derrick Ovington (Cassell); *Australia's 100 Years of National Parks* (NSW National Parks and Wildlife Service); *Complete Book of Australian Mammals,* Ronald Strahan, ed. (Angus and Robertson); *Discover Australia's National Parks,* Robert Raymond (Ure Smith); *Discover Australia's National Parks and Naturelands,* Michael and Irene Morcombe (Landsdowne Press); *Life on Earth,* David Attenborough (Reader's Digest-Collins-BBC); *National Parks of New South Wales,* Alan Fairley (Rigby); *National Parks of New South Wales* (Gregory's); *National Parks of Queensland,* Tony Groom (Cassell); *National Parks of Victoria,* Alan Fairley (Rigby); *National Parks of Victoria* (Gregory's); *National Parks of Western Australia,* C. F. H. Jenkins (National Parks Authority of WA); *Regional Landscapes of Australia,* Nancy and Andrew Learmonth (Angus and Robertson); *The Face of Australia,* C. F. Laseron, revised by J. N. Jennings (Angus and Robertson); *The Franklin Blockade,* Robin Tindale and Pam Waud, eds (Wilderness Society); *The Heritage of Australia* (Macmillan, Australian Heritage Commission); *The Value of National Parks* (Australian Conservation Foundation).

Photographs
Most photographs were taken by Robin Morrison, except for: (t = top, c = centre, b = bottom, l = left, r = right) 6-7: Jean-Paul Ferrero, Auscape. 11: t, Richard Woldendorp; b, Research School of Earth Sciences, ANU. 20: b, Photo Index. 28-9: Richard Woldendorp. 30: b, Dept of Conservation Forests & Lands, Vic. 31: l, cb, Sutherland Shire Library. 32: tl, bl, br, Dept of Conservation Forests & Lands, Vic. 33: tl, Ian Morris, Australian NPWS; br, Queensland NPWS. 34: Tasmanian NPWS. 35: cl, Tasmanian NPWS; tr, Bob Mossel; br, Jeffery Cutting. 36: t, Queensland NPWS; b, Dept of Conservation Forests & Lands, Vic. 37: Conservation Commission of the NT. 38: tl, bl, Hans & Judy Beste; tr, Stephen Donellan; br, R. C. Lewis, CSIRO Division of Entomology. 39: tl, R. & A. Williams, National Photographic Index (NPI); tc, tr, Hans & Judy Beste; br, Ralph & Daphne Keller. 40: r, and 41: tl, br, Dept of Conservation Forests & Lands, Vic. 41: bc, Graham Robertson; tr, New South Wales NPWS. 42: t, C. Veitch. 52: Michael Jensen/Auscape. 53: Jean-Paul Ferrero/Auscape. 70: Jean-Paul Ferrero/Auscape. 71: tl, Jean-Paul Ferrero/Auscape; tr, M. W. Gillam/Auscape; b, Jiri Lochman/Auscape. 90: tl, tr, Hans & Judy Beste/Auscape; cl, bl, Jean-Paul Ferrero/Auscape; br, Graeme Chapman/Auscape. 91: t, Hans & Judy Beste/Auscape; bl, B. Thomson/NPI; br, R. Jenkins/NPI. 92: tl, Cliff Winfield. 92-3: NT Conservation Commission. 104: tl, tr, bl, Cliff Winfield; br, Jean-Paul Ferrero/Auscape. 105: tl, cl, bl, Cliff Winfield; tr, James Rule/ANT; br, Graeme Chapman/Auscape. 118-21, 136: Richard Woldendorp. 140: tl, CLiff Winfield; bl, Esther Beaton/Auscape; tr, br, Jean-Paul Ferrero/Auscape. 141: tl Jiri Lochman/Auscape; tr, Esther Beaton/Auscape; cl, bl, br, Cliff Winfield. 166: tr, br, WA Dept of Conservation & Land Management; bl, Cliff Winfield. 167: tr, cl, WA Dept of Conservation & Land Management; bl, Cliff Winfield. 170-3: Bob Mossel. 192: l, Gunther Deichmann/Auscape; tr, Jean-Paul Ferrero/Auscape; cr, Hans & Judy Beste/Auscape; br, C. A. Henley/Auscape; 193: l, Jean-Paul Ferrero/Auscape; tr, C. A. Henley/Auscape; br, Graham Robertson/Auscape. 194: tl, Jack & Lindsay Cupper/Auscape; bl, L. Robinson/NPI; tr, Jean-Paul Ferrero/Auscape; br, Hans & Judy Beste/Auscape. 195: l, tc, Graeme Chapman/Auscape; tr, M. P. Kahl/Auscape; br, Lindsay Cupper/Auscape. 196-7: South Australian NPWS. 200-1, 203-5: Bill Bachman. 236: tl, Hans & Judy Beste/Auscape; others, Jean-Paul Ferrero/Auscape. 237: tl, Hans & Judy Beste/Auscape; others, Jean-Paul Ferrero/Auscape. 238: tl, Jean-Paul Ferrero/Auscape; bl, Hans & Judy Beste/Auscape; tr, Graeme Chapman/Auscape. 239: bc, G. Cheers/ANT; others, Hans & Judy Beste/Auscape. 240-1: Dept of Conservation Forests & Lands, Vic. 256: tl, Michael Patterson. 257: Michael Patterson. 274: l, C. A. Henley/Auscape; br, J. Burt/ANT. 275: tl, tc, Esther Beaton/Auscape; cl, Graeme Chapman/Auscape; bl, Michael Seyfort/ANT; br, Otto Rogge/ANT. 276: tl, Jean-Paul Ferrero/Auscape; bl, tr, C. A. Henley/Auscape; br, Geoff Moon/Auscape. 277: tl, cr, Jean-Paul Ferrero/Auscape; bl, L. Robinson/NPI; tr, Esther Beaton/Auscape; br, R. H. Green/NPI. 278-9: Rodney Musch. 300-1: ACT Parks & Conservation Service. 306: tl, Bob Mossel; tr, b, Jean-Paul Ferrero/Auscape. 307: tl, bl, Jean-Paul Ferrero/Auscape; tr, G. Cheers/ANT; bc, Esther Beaton/Auscape; br, Hans & Judy Beste/Auscape. 346: l, Jean-Paul Ferrero/Auscape; tc, M. P. Kahl/Auscape; tr, b, Hans & Judy Beste/Auscape. 347: tl, Graham Robertson/Auscape; tr, bl, Jean-Paul Ferrero/Auscape; br, C. A. Henley/Auscape. 364: t, Hans & Judy Beste/Auscape; b, H. Rowney; c, G. B. Baker/ NPI. 365: tl, David P. Maitland/Auscape; tr, b, Jean-Paul Ferrero/Auscape. 366-7 New South Wales NPWS. 393: R. V. Southcott. 412: t, Jean-Paul Ferrero/Auscape; b, Glen Threlfo/Auscape. 413: tl, G. B. Baker/NPI; tr, bl, br, Hans & Judy Beste/Auscape. 414: tl, F. Woerle/Auscape; tr, Jean-Paul Ferrero/Auscape; bl, Graeme Chapman/Auscape. 415: tl, Jean-Paul Ferrero/Auscape; tr, Graeme Chapman; br, F. Woerle/Auscape. 444: tl, The Photo Library; bl, Australian Institute of Marine Science. 445: The Photo Library. 476-7: Hans & Judy Beste/Auscape. 478-9: Queensland NPWS.

Typesetting by Smithys, Sydney

Colour separation by Toppan Printing Co. Ltd., Hong Kong

Printed and bound by Dai Nippon Printing Co. Ltd, Hong Kong